Lionel J. Trotter, J. Trotter Lionel

History Of India Under Queen Victoria

Vol. II

HISTORY OF INDIA

UNDER QUEEN VICTORIA

FROM 1836 TO 1880.

BY

CAPTAIN LIONEL J. TROTTER

AUTHOR OF "WARREN HASTINGS," "STUDIES IN BIOGRAPHY," ETC.

VOL. II.

LONDON:

W. H. ALLEN & CO., 13, WATERLOO PLACE,
PALL MALL, S.W.

—

1886.

LONDON:

PRINTED BY WOODFALL AND KINDER,

MILFORD LANE, STRAND, W.C.

CONTENTS.

BOOK IV.

BOOK V.

CHAPTER I.

BOOK VI.

BOOK VII.

Contents.

BOOK IV.

LORD CANNING.

1857-58.

INDIA UNDER QUEEN VICTORIA.

—:o:——

CHAPTER I.

THE SECOND RELIEF OF LUCKNOW.

WITH the fall of Delhi closes the great turning act of the drama which opened with the second year of Lord Canning's rule. The neck of the rebellion was fairly broken on the day when Wilson ordered dinner to be laid for his staff beneath the vaulted roof of the Dewán-i-Khás. Other fights have yet to be recorded; fresh efforts will yet be made to check the victorious march of British arms. All Oudh and Rohilkhand still teem with open insurrection; anarchy still runs riot through the North-Western Provinces. In Gwáliár a mutinous soldiery are treating their noble young sovereign, Jayaji Sindhia, with a sullen deference that may at any moment blaze into headlong revolt. All through Central India, from the Ganges to the borders of Sind, from the marble cliffs of the Narbadda up to the plains of the Lower Satlaj, rebellion still breaks out in fitful flashes, or smoulders on beneath the utmost pressure of British watchfulness and British pluck. The Dánápur mutineers and other followers of Kúnwar Singh become a daily terror to the ill-guarded dwellers in the province of Bahár, now placed under the temporary rule of Canning's able deputy, John Peter Grant. In Lower Bengal, mutineers are plundering, fighting, and fleeing by turns, according as circumstances favour or frown upon them. Assam itself has barely escaped the hazards of an outbreak planned between a local chief and the Sepoys of a local regiment, but forestalled by the timely intervention of a hundred sailors from the Indian Navy with two guns. In short, from the Himalayas down to the neighbourhood of Calcutta, there is yet but little safety for the lives of stray Christians or the goods of peaceful natives outside the chief stations that cover the main lines of road.

Nevertheless, the end is visibly drawing near; the tide of rebellion is steadily running down. With the collapse of the Gogaira outbreak, quiet once more reigns throughout the Panjáb as securely as if that province were an English shire. Its neighbour, Sind, threatened now and again with stirrings of a Sepoy mutiny, owes its freedom from outward disorder partly to the sounder discipline, the more mixed composition of its native garrison, partly also to the wise control of statesmen like Bartle Frere and officers like General John Jacob. In Western India the plots of Sepoys at Kolúpur and Belgaum, of Mohammadan priests at Puna, of Marátha princes and their friends at Satúra, have been crushed or baffled by the timely action of Lord Elphinstone's Government; and a small but efficient army is already mustering for a march through Central India in aid of Sir Colin Campbell.

Among the numerous princes and nobles of Rájputúna, Colonel George Lawrence and a few worthy helpmates, such as Eden at Jaipur, Charles Showers at Udaipur, and Monck-Mason at Jodhpur, the three chief Rajput capitals, still upheld through all discouragements the honour and the influence of the British name. When Colvin ordered Lawrence to fall back with all available troops and treasure upon Agra, Lawrence quietly refused to abandon a great province to untold disaster; and the unwise order was not enforced. Dixon himself, whose best years had been spent in civilizing the wild highlanders of Mairwára, lay dying, in June, at Beúwar; but the memory of his good deeds kept the Mairs faithful to the Government which had "raised them from the dust;" and the Mairwára Battalion did admirable service against the rebels who crossed their path. The leading princes of Rájásthán—the land of Rajahs—cheerfully cast in their lot with the Power whose protection they and their fathers had enjoyed for half a century.* Their troops, if not always trustworthy, helped at least to succour Christian fugitives from Nimach, and to stay the march of rebellion in their own land.†

At Indór, the young Mahárája Holkar had remained staunch to the British cause in spite of the strongest temptations to betray it in its darkest need. At the age of twenty-one, he saw mutiny and rebellion spreading around him in seemingly resistless flood. But he had not sat in vain at the feet of such counsellors as Sir

---

* Rájásthán is another name for Rájputúna, "the Rajput Land."
† Kaye; Trotter.

Robert Hamilton, the British Resident, and his own Chief Minister, Rao Rámchandar Rao. During Sir Robert's absence on sick leave, his place was filled by Colonel Henry Durand, who had once helped to burst open the gates of Ghazni, had afterwards served as private secretary to Lord Ellenborough, and had since held with credit important posts in the civil and political service. Down to the end of June, Durand had seen no reason for distrusting Holkar, however weak his faith in the loyalty of any native prince. At Mhau, a British station thirteen miles from Indór, the Sepoys had not yet followed the example of their comrades at Nimach and Nasirábád.

On the morning of the 1st of July the storm, which had been quietly brewing for some time past, broke suddenly over the English at Indór. Holkar's soldiery had risen at last. The guns he had sent to protect the Residency were turned against our countrymen, and the work of slaughter, pillage, and destruction went on apace. Only a few troopers of the Bhopál Contingent followed their bold leader, Colonel Travers, in his desperate, if fruitless charge upon the guns. Within the Palace all was confusion, perplexity, dismay ; and Holkar himself knew not where to turn for help against his own troops, who urged him even with threats to come forth and show himself worthy of his famous forefather Jaswant Rao. After a cannonade of two hours, to which our two guns could return but feeble answer, Durand, too easily convinced of Holkar's treachery, and despairing of timely help from Mhau, resolved to withdraw his party from their post of peril and to make his way eastward to the outlying station of Sihór. While Holkar was yet thinking what to do, and Hungerford was getting his guns ready for a hurried march from Mhau to Indór, twenty-seven white people of both sexes, the women and children mounted on gun-waggons, the whole escorted by a small body of native horse and foot, passed out of the Indór Residency under a sharp but well-nigh harmless fire of grape and round-shot from the enemy's guns. A few other Christian fugitives who had escaped the slaughter in the civil lines made their way to the Palace, where Holkar took them under his special care.*

Durand's strong belief in Holkar's treachery had not only hastened his flight from Indór, but decided him against taking the short road to apparent safety at Mhau. When Hungerford's battery had gone half way to Indór, the news of Durand's departure sent it speeding back to its own station. That same evening the

* Kaye ; Malleson.

Sepoys at Mhau broke into mutiny, slew three of their officers, and were only deterred from further mischief by the fire from Hungerford's guns. Having sent the rebels flying from their lines towards Indór, the brave captain of artillery took command of the fort and station of Mhau, proclaimed martial law throughout the neighbourhood, and even ventured, in Durand's absence, to act as political agent at Holkar's Court.[*]

After a few days spent in riot and plunder, Holkar's soldiery settled down into a kind of sullen obedience to the commands of their royal master, of whose steadfast loyalty to our cause neither Hungerford nor Lord Elphinstone could cherish a doubt in the face of evidence which ought, one thinks, to have satisfied Durand himself. A few weeks later that officer returned to his former post, escorted by a body of troops from Bombay strong enough to keep the peace of Holkar's kingdom until Delhi should be won. Rebellion still ruffled the face of Bundalkhand, and the country around Ságar was far from quiet. But south of the Narbadda things looked nearly as peaceful as in ordinary years. The important province of Nágpur, albeit nearly bare of troops, made no serious effort to shake off the just rule of Commissioner Plowden. Berár also kept quiet. In Madras the misconduct of one regiment, the 8th Cavalry, brought into clearer relief the un-shaken loyalty of all the rest. The Nizam's dominions, so long a hotbed of anarchy and armed strife, now offered a cheering example of the sway which one or two master minds could wield at such a crisis over a turbulent soldiery and a discontented people. Thanks to the wise and vigorous statesmanship of the Nizam's Chief Minister, Sálar Jang, and to the steadfast courage of the British Resident, Colonel Davidson, nothing worse than a passing mutiny in July at Aurangabad, and a fierce but futile attack of armed Rohillas on the Residency, marred the general peacefulness of a realm whose active enmity would have raised all Southern India against our rule.[†]

In this month of September new actors were coming on the stage. As Blücher's Prussians followed up the victory which British stubbornness had won at Waterloo, so fresh troops from England are at last beginning to strengthen the hands of their long battling comrades. It is no longer a struggle between a handful of hard-pressed heroes and a host of irrepressible foes. Troops from England, so long expected, so slow in coming, were now landing almost daily in Calcutta, and frequently in Bombay.

[*] Kaye ; Malleson.   [†] Trotter ; Kaye.

Batches of soldiers, fresh from their long voyage round the Cape, and eager to smite down their quotas of accursed Pandies, were streaming up the Ganges and the great Trunk Road, to the delight of their countrymen everywhere, to the amazement, glad or sorrowful, of the many natives who had begun to lose all hope or fear of their ever coming. The unceasing, if sometimes scanty flow of white faces from Calcutta towards Cawnpore convinced alike the loyal and the disaffected how firmly England was bent on restoring her olden sway. Heaven itself seemed fighting against the rebels. Popular superstition, under the spell of a great fear, went so far as to mistake the sturdy forms of these new-comers for the avenging ghosts of white men and women slain by the mutineers.

Great, too, was the awe that fell on every neighbourhood through which Captain William Peel of the *Shannon* passed with his bold seamen and marines and their heavy howitzers on their upward journey to Cawnpore. Other troops, chiefly native, from Nipál, Madras, and Bombay, were already engaged in lightening the labours and furthering the successes of those comrades who had borne the brunt of danger in Central and Northern India. Sir Colin Campbell himself, the newly-arrived Commander-in-Chief, was busily preparing with larger means and fairer prospects to relieve Outram's garrison at Lucknow, and to crush rebellion wherever it might still show a determined front.*

The rebels indeed were slow as yet to accept the teaching of late events. Their leaders, fighting as it were with halters round their necks, strove to keep up the spirits of their followers with tales of imaginary successes and with promises of speedy help. While the fight was still raging round Delhi, for many days even after the fall of that city, the inmates of Agra Fort were following with anxious eyes the movements of hostile troops between Gwáliár and Dhólpur. At the latter place, about thirty miles away on the northern or British side of the Chambal, lay several thousand mutineers from Mhau and Indór, strengthened by a body of soldiers who had been induced to join them on their way through Gwáliár. In Sindhia's own capital the mutinous Contingent seemed ripe at any moment to cross the Chambal, do what the Mahárája and his able Minister, Dinkar Rao, might to hold them back. Happily, for some while longer they stood fast. But the Indór rebels, having idled away their chance of worrying Wilson's troops before Delhi, began to threaten Agra just as Greathed's

* Trotter.

flying column came within aiding distance of that place. On the 9th of October Greathed was at Hátrás, speeding towards Cawn-pore, when an urgent message from Agra turned his steps thither in all possible haste. A forced march of forty miles in twenty-eight hours brought his troops into camp on the Agra parade-ground soon after sunrise on the 10th.

Erelong the baggage streamed into camp, and the men began pitching their tents for a few hours' welcome rest. Many of their officers had ridden away to the Fort on leave warranted by the news received from the Agra officials. Suddenly from the fields of tall maize on their front and right a fire of roundshot opened on Greathed's scattered soldiers. The sounds of mus-ketry and the clatter of charging horsemen soon proved how utterly the Agra officials had been taken in. Instead of being ten miles away, the Dhólpur insurgents were pouring into the British camp. Taken by surprise, with the enemy's cavalry close upon them, amidst a wild rush of camp-followers and baggage towards the fort, Greathed's men had but a few moments to don their accoutrements, spring into their saddles, fix their bayonets, and stand by their guns. But those few moments were enough. The British guns were soon playing on the foe ; the 9th Lancers and the Panjáb Horse made short work of their assailants, scatter-ing them in some splendid charges, and taking several guns at the first onset. The skirmishers of the 8th Foot and the 4th Panjáb Infantry stood their ground like men. In spite of a strong resistance, the enemy, numbering about 7,000, were driven back from village to village by the advancing British line, now strengthened by a battery from Agra and six companies of the 3rd Europeans. Gun after gun was taken, and presently the rebel camp. Here, after a five-mile chase, were halted the British infantry.

'For five miles further, up to the Káli Nadi, our cavalry and horse-artillery kept up a keen and murderous pursuit. Before the beaten rebels got across the stream, they had left behind them all their twelve guns, their camp-furniture, and five hundred dead. The well-planned surprise had ended in utter failure, at a cost to the victors of twelve slain and fifty-six wounded or missing. No small share of the victory was due to Colonel Cotton, the com-mandant of Agra, who had come up during the fight, and himself ordered the final pursuit. That night Greathed's soldiers, of whose excellent conduct their brave young leader found it "im-possible to say too much," took out their hard-won rest in the captured camp. About a fortnight later one remnant of the beaten force got finally scattered at Fathipur-Sikri, by a few hundred of Cotton's troops.*

Some weeks before Greathed's victory, one prominent figure had passed away from the eyes of the Agra garrison. On the 9th of September died Lieutenant-Governor Colvin, whose health, long undermined by the cares of a time so stormy, had given way at last to an attack of dysentery. Less brilliant than James Thomason, Lord Auckland's able but disastrous private secretary had lately done much, as Governor of the North-Western Provinces, to justify the good opinion which Dalhousie conceived of the sometime Commissioner of Tenasserim. Under Colvin's administration some marked improvements took place in the processes of criminal law, in the general efficiency of judges, magistrates, and police, in the character and working of the village schools. Upright, sensible, painstaking, slow of speech and reserved in manner, "King John," as they who knew him least were wont to call him, would have won a higher place among Anglo-Indian statesmen but for the formidable outbreak which overtaxed his mental no less than his bodily powers. It was for himself and others a great misfortune that talents eminently suited to a time of peace failed in the midst of unwonted troubles to carry a burden for which strength and energy of the highest order were especially needed. All that a zealous officer of fair abilities and ripe experience could do at such a crisis John Colvin certainly did, struggling manfully to the last against disease and mental suffering; nor were there many of his countrymen and compeers who did not share the grief, expressed by Lord Canning, for the death of "one of the most distinguished among the servants of the East India Company."†

After a brief rest at Agra Greathed resumed his march upon Cawnpore. On the 19th of October, under its new commander, Hope Grant, the flying column entered Mainpuri, whose rebellious Rajah had fled elsewhere the day before. His property in guns and treasure was seized, and his fort blown up. A few more marches, one of them marked by a dashing fight of guns and cavalry, brought Grant's men with very little loss, by the 26th, into Cawnpore, whence, a few days later, it moved across the Ganges, as the vanguard of the army which Sir Colin Campbell was about to lead upon Lucknow.

* Trotter; Bourchier's "Eight Months' Campaign."
† Trotter; Kaye; Official Gazette.

From Delhi westward to the Satlaj, General Cortlandt, with a few troops gathered from Sirhind and the Panjáb, maintained the Government of his English masters. In Rájputána, with its ten million people spread over a hundred thousand square miles of land, Colonel George Lawrence, with the help of his native soldiery and a wing of the 83rd Foot, kept moving to and fro against small bodies of mutineers, and aiming frequent blows at all disturbers of the public peace. Against his failure in September to draw the mutineers of the Jodhpur Legion out of their strong position at Awah, may be set the defeat inflicted by Colonel Jackson and a few hundred troops on the forces of an insurgent Rajah, not far from Nasirábad. A few weeks earlier Captain Hall with a handful of Englishmen, mostly convalescents, had repulsed the sudden attack of a body of Jodhpur rebels who thought to carry the hill-station of Abu by surprise, and to murder every white man and woman in the place. On the 23rd of October, a few hundred troops, mostly native, set out from Nimach to attack a large body of Mandisúr rebels, strongly posted ten miles off at Jiram. The attack was so far successful, that the enemy that night abandoned the fort into which they had been driven. But the assailants lost two of their officers slain and five wounded; and during November the Nimach garrison had to defend themselves vigorously, for a fortnight, against four thousand rebels, who retired only on learning the approach of a relieving force from Mhau.*

The Rajput princes and statesmen, however loyal themselves, could not always reckon upon the faithfulness of their own men. In the first few weeks of the Mutiny the Jaipur soldiers, whom Eden himself had led across the Agra frontier, were found to be so far from trustworthy that Eden had to take them back again. A strong body of troops from Udaipur and Jodhpur had refused to attack the Sepoy mutineers on their march from Nasirábad. The rising of the Jodhpur Legion resulted among other things in the slaughter of Monck-Mason, who mistook a body of rebels for some of Lawrence's troops. Another political agent, Major Burton, was to fall a sacrifice to the sudden treachery of some Kotah regiments. He had returned from Nimach to Kotah with two of his sons, the younger only sixteen, on the 12th of October. On the 15th a crowd of armed soldiers and bazaar rabble entered the Residency grounds, cut down Dr. Salder with one or two other victims, and rushed into the Residency itself. Abandoned

* Trotter ; Chambers ; G. Lawrence.

by the guards and servants, Major Burton, his sons, and one faithful camel-driver, caught up their arms and fled for safety up to the roof of the house. For four hours they held their post amidst showers of bullets and the crash of roundshot from two guns. The roof of their hiding-place fell in, but the four were still unhurt. At last the building caught fire. The Resident proposed to surrender, if the assailants would spare his sons' lives. But the young men declared they would die with their father. After praying together for the last time, and helping their one servant to steal away in quest of succour, the hapless three calmly awaited the issue. In a few moments they knew that nothing could save them. With the help of ladders the mob climbed up into their lonely lair and slew them where they stood. The rebels paraded the head of their chief victim through the city, and the Kotah Rajah found himself a helpless prisoner in his own palace, until some troops from the neighbouring state of Karauli came to rescue him from his warders' hands.*

The little State of Rewah in Bundalkhand, after a fierce effort to shake off the stubborn Willoughby Osborne, who had one faithful friend in the Rajah himself, was awed into good behaviour by the timely advance of some troops from Mirzápur. From Rewah towards Bombay the roads through Jabalpur and Ságar were barely kept open in September and October by Major Erskine's succours from Madras, and the loyal 31st Sepoys serving under Brigadier Sage. At Bhopál, on the road from Ságar to Indór, the stout-hearted Sikandar Begam, Queen Regent of the little State founded by her Afghún ancestor, Dost Mohammad, had lately proved her loyalty in the teeth of menaces from her own family and followers, by escorting the fugitives from Indór and other stations to the southern bank of the Narbadda at Hoshangabad. She was now engaged in pacifying her unruly subjects, in suppressing mutiny among her troops, and in collecting soldiers and supplies in aid of the columns which Lord Elphinstone was sending forward from Bombay. Further westward at Dhár, near Indór, some three thousand mixed troops of the Málwa Field Force, under Brigadier Stuart, drove a strong force of rebels before them on the 22nd of October, with the loss of several guns, and after a few days' shelling found themselves masters of the timely-abandoned fort.†

Jabalpur itself—"the city by the hill" in the heart of the Narbadda Valley—had in September become the scene of one

---

* Lawrence ; Chambers.   † Trotter ; Chambers ; Malleson.

of those public executions to which Englishmen in that year of horrors were growing accustomed. A Ghond Rajah, Shankar Shah, and his son, whose plot for destroying all the white men in Jabalpur had been discovered by the Deputy Commissioner, Lieutenant Clark, were tried and sentenced to be blown away from guns. On the 18th of September they underwent their doom a few hundred yards in front of the Residency. The older culprit, whose snow-white hair and calm bearing, in the words of an eye-witness, "almost excited compassion," walked up to the guns with a firm stride, while his son stepped forward slowly with a downcast air. As soon as the guns were fired, kites and vultures pounced upon the scattered remains, but all that could be collected were handed over to the Rajah's widow. Undeterred by so fearful a warning, the 52nd Sepoys mutinied on that same day and marched off quietly towards Damoh. Two days earlier the 50th Regiment had risen at Nagódh, burned the bungalows, emptied the jail, and sent the English flying out of the place. The timely presence of five hundred native troops from Madras under Colonel Miller enabled the English at Damoh to march thence with their goods and the public treasure towards Jabalpur. On their way thither Colonel Miller, on the 27th, met and routed several hundred of the mutineers.* Erskine's prayers for help from any of the neighbouring provinces still evoked nothing but discouraging answers. No more troops could be spared at present, even though the advance of a few score British soldiers might stay the march of anarchy and revolt in Central India.

Far away to the east, near Azimgarh, eighty miles north of Banáras, on the 20th September, some twelve hundred troops, mostly Gorkhas from Nipál, were led by Captain Boileau and the brave planter Venables against a large body of Oudh insurgents. In a dashing charge, rewarded by the capture of three guns, much camp-equipage, and by the scattering of a badly smitten foe, Shamsher Singh and his sturdy soldiers proved once for all to their doubting allies that, even under their own officers, the half-disciplined highlanders of Nipál could follow up a long march by a series of swift yet skilful movements over unaccustomed ground. Jang Bahádur's short-legged infantry were found to be as active as they were bold.

Not less brilliant was the onset led by Major English with a wing of the 53rd Foot and a few score Sikhs on the Ramgarh mutineers, who, after some weary marches, were overtaken on the

* Chambers.

2nd of October at Chatra, about forty miles north-west of Haza-ribagh. With a boldness founded on late experience, the assail-ants raced all together on two guns which had troubled, without delaying, their advance. Halting to take breath after their first success, they saw the enemy bearing down with two more guns and undiminished numbers on their front and right. But the new danger was met by another lightning rush, which carried the little force into the rebel camp. "It was splendid," wrote Major English, "to see them rush on the guns." The routed enemy left behind them forty dead, four light guns, ten elephants, a great many bullocks, tents, and carts, much ammunition, and sixty thousand rupees. The price of such a victory was six men slain and fifty wounded.*

Major English was less successful in his pursuit of the mutineers of the 32nd, two companies of which rose at Deogarh in the Sánthál country on the 9th October, murdered an officer, and plun-dered the bazaar. The remaining companies mutinied later at other places. In spite of the efforts which English made to intercept or overtake them—he engaged them once in a moonlight skirmish —the mutineers made good their retreat across the Són on their way to join the camp of Kúnwar Singh. Nor could mere boldness avail at all times against skill and courage backed by superior numbers. A small body of Rattray's Sikhs, led by their brave commander himself, were driven back on the 8th of September by the 5th Irregular Horse, who had revolted in August at Bahrampur, and were roaming diligently about Bahár, intent only on plundering the villagers and destroying property, with-out much regard for race or creed. For some weeks after the defeat of Rattray's Sikhs they pursued the same tactics along the Són, with small hindrance from the few troops and police-men employed in guarding the main lines of road.†

All through September and October the provinces of Oudh and Rohilkhand remained a prey to anarchy, rapine, and rebellion. Many an ousted or impoverished landholder had seized the occa-sion to recover by force his ancestral holding, or to enrich himself at his creditor's expense. Many a villager had joined the rebels in the hope of somehow bettering himself, or from fear of the risks involved in adherence to the losing side. The Tálukdárs of Oudh were arrayed against us almost to a man. Between the Hindus and Mohammadans of Rohilkhand there was much less of concert for any common end. The two sections were often at

* Trotter; Chambers.   † Chambers.

open war; and the oppressive rule of Khán Bahádur Khán, who, as lineal descendant from Hafiz Rahmat, the "Protector" of Warren Hastings' day, styled himself Nawáb of Baréli and Viceroy to the Moghal Emperor, soon made the Hindu peasantry long for the return of those English masters over whose expulsion they had so foolishly rejoiced.*

It was about the middle of September that Khán Bahádur Khán despatched his nephew at the head of eight hundred men towards Naini-Tál, the well-wooded station by the lake in the Kamáon hills, where many a fugitive three months ago had found safe shelter from his murderous clutches. But the plans of the erewhile Deputy-Collector were speedily frustrated by Major Ramsay, who marched down the hill with three hundred Gorkhas and fifty volunteer horse, attacked the rebels at Haldwani, and dealt them a blow from which it took them several months to recover.

In the latter part of October, while Peel's Blue-jackets were hastening up to Cawnpore, their leader heard that the Dánápur mutineers were ravaging the country around Fathipur. A mixed force of infantry, seamen, and marines, with two guns, commanded by Colonel Powell of the 53rd Foot, hurried on to Fathipur, whence another march of twenty-four miles brought them on the 1st of November within reach of the enemy, strongly posted with three guns at the village of Kajwa. With only five hundred men against three or four thousand, Powell grappled with the foe. After a sharp fight of two hours, which cost the lives of Powell and twenty-six of his men, Peel, who succeeded to the command, at length gained a victory, which only the weariness of his troops prevented him from following up. Two of the guns, however, were taken, the camp destroyed, and the enemy for a time debarred from further mischief.†

November, indeed, was a month of unwonted bustle, of memorable events for India. The troops from England, which had been sent round the Cape in hired sailing ships, as if time were no object and the great steamers of the Royal Navy were non-existent, were at last pouring by thousands into Calcutta after a voyage unusually slow. Their help was needed in many places, but the bulk of them held their way towards Cawnpore. While some good judges were calling for the preliminary re-conquest of Rohilkhand, others for an advance into Oudh by way of Banáras, Sir Colin Campbell was bent on mustering at Cawnpore a force

---

* Malleson.   † Trotter; Chambers.

sufficient to relieve and bring away the long-beleaguered garrison of Lucknow. At the beginning of November, Hope Grant's column was already on its way to the Alambágh, where a few hundred of Outram's men had lain besieged and isolated from the main body ever since the glorious 25th of September.

On the 9th of November, Sir Colin himself, who had just reached Cawnpore, set off to join Grant, then posted a few miles short of the Alambágh. By the 12th he was ready to begin work with 5,000 men of all arms, and thirty guns. It was not too soon to think of moving forward, for Outram's garrison were running short of food, and the Gwáliár Contingent, having finally broken loose on the 15th of October, were already within threatening neighbourhood of Cawnpore. An easy march brought Campbell into the Alambágh. After a day spent in changing the garrison of that post and blowing up a neighbouring fort, the troops began their movement against the city itself.

Instead of following the road taken by Havelock, Sir Colin preferred advancing slowly but surely by the south-eastern suburbs of Lucknow. A running fight of two hours left him master of the park and palace of Dil-Khushá, or Heart's Delight, and of the Martinière College, founded by the Frenchman, Claude Martin, who had risen high in the service of a former King of Oudh. Planted firmly on the canal which there joins the Gúmti, Colonel Hope's brigade, flanked by Bourchier's battery and two of Peel's heavy guns, defied all efforts of the enemy to recover their lost ground. A day's halt in the gardens of Dil-Khushá ushered in a day of hard fighting about the Sikandar-Bágh, a strong walled square that frowned across the canal from numberless loopholes pierced through the masonry of sides each a hundred and twenty yards long. Some 2,000 picked men lay within its formidable circuit. A hundred yards to one side of it stood a loopholed village full of musketeers. Further away rose a range of fortified barracks. Against these barriers Sir Colin had to hurl his men.

While Blunt's six-pounders galloped through a hail of fire from village and walled garden to open the battle within shot range of the latter, Hope's infantry dashed forward, carried the village with a rush, and then turned all their fire upon the Sikandar-Bágh. By that time, two of Travers's eighteen-pounders had begun to play their part in the attack. Erelong, companies of the 53rd Foot and the 93rd Highlanders, aided by two of Blunt's guns, pushed back a large body of rebels on their left front, cleared them out of the barracks, and followed them in skirmishing order across the plain.

Still the fight roared fiercely around the Sikandar-Bágh. At the end of an hour and a half a small breach showed itself in the massive wall, and a part of Hope's brigade rushed forward to storm the place. Some mixed troops under Major Barnston followed in close support. The sight, as witnessed by Campbell himself, was magnificent. Sikhs and English, veterans and recruits, vied with each other in surmounting all obstacles, in smiting down or scattering all who opposed them. Once inside the inclosure, they let their bayonets drink deep of Purbia blood. Like cats hunted down by trained bulldogs, the rebels died hard by the hands of men still maddened with bitter memories of Cawnpore. More than 2,000 of their corpses were afterwards borne out of that human slaughter-house in ghastly witness to the hate-accented prowess of their foes.*

The next point of attack was the Shah Najaf, a domed mosque in a garden surrounded by a loopholed wall, and covered at the entrance by a mass of strong masonry. For three hours the British guns kept pounding at this new obstacle. At last the 93rd Foot, supported by Barnston's companies, were let loose for the final assault. The outer defences were soon stormed, but the mosque itself stood out defiant still. Then it was that Peel's Blue-jackets came up to their comrades' help. Covered by a scathing fire from the Highlanders, they laid their heavy guns within thirty yards of the great building, as coolly as though they were laying the *Shannon* herself alongside an enemy's ship. A few rounds opened a way for the stormers, and that day's work was fitly consummated by the capture of the Shah Najaf.

Two more fortified posts still parted Campbell's troops from those which Outram had meanwhile launched successfully against some buildings in his front. On the 17th the Mess-House, a large building protected by a loopholed wall and a broad scarped ditch, was heavily pounded for several hours by Peel's guns on the one side and Vincent Eyre's batteries on the other. At 3 P.M., this post also was carried with a rush by a storming party from the 53rd and 90th Foot and the troops whom Captain Guise commanded in place of the wounded Barnston. One more charge drove the enemy out of the Moti Mahal or Pearl Palace; and then the Lucknow garrison, fresh from their own victorious onsets on the common foe, once more exchanged greetings with the outer

* Trotter.

world. Outram and Havelock were the first to congratulate their brave old chief on the thoroughness of his late achievements, in which the tried courage of British soldiers had been directed by the skilful strategy of their commander. After all that heavy fighting against positions carefully fortified and stoutly held by many thousands of good troops, Sir Colin's admirers might point with just pride to a blood-bill of a hundred and twenty-two killed, three hundred and forty-five wounded. Ten of the former and thirty-three of the latter were officers.[*]

Among those who helped to forward Sir Colin's enterprise, one name at least deserves passing mention. Mr. Cavanagh, a clerk in the Company's service at Lucknow, stole out of the Residency on the 9th of November, disguised as a native, bearing a letter, some plans, and a string of verbal messages from Outram to the Commander-in-Chief. After two days of perilous wandering through streets full of armed men, through a country bristling with rebel pickets, Cavanagh and the faithful spy who guided him, fell in with a British outpost, and were soon in close talk with Campbell himself. From Outram's letter and his emissary's own lips, Sir Colin was enabled to gather much useful information as to the best way of ordering his own advance. By means of a semaphore erected in the Alambágh he and Outram exchanged signals informing each of the other's plans and movements, so that both might act together in furtherance of a common end.

On the evening of the 17th of November the relieving army found itself holding nearly all the river-side of the city from the Dil-Khushá up to the iron bridge beyond the Residency. The next day was spent in strengthening the chain of British posts, in driving the rebels back to their last defences, and in cannonading the Kaisar-Bágh, whose massive walls still frowned defiance on the Farangi. Outram and Havelock were eager to attack this stronghold, the capture of which would have placed all Lucknow at our feet. But Campbell deemed himself weak in infantry; his ammunition was running low, and the Gwáliár rebels might any moment attack Cawnpore. For the present he would content himself with carrying off the Lucknow garrison and holding the city in check by means of a strong force entrenched at the Alambágh.

On the evening of the 18th the sick and wounded in the Residency were quietly borne away to the Dil-Khushá. During the next two days the women, children, and non-combatants had

[*] Trotter; Marshman.

to make the best of their way to the same shelter; many trudging painfully on foot through five miles of heavy sand; others drawn slowly along by horses too weak almost to carry themselves. More than once they had to run for their lives from a shower of grape or bullets; at other times a block in the narrow road kept them waiting for long minutes in sharp suspense. A few hours' halt in the noisome neighbourhood of the Sikandar-Bágh strengthened them for the latter and less dangerous half of a journey which the darkness, the danger, the crowding, and the many delays had protracted to a painful length. After all their past sufferings, however, in spite of their buried dear ones, of the worldly wealth they had been forced to leave behind them, their first night's quiet sleep under the canvas roofs in the Dil-Khushá was an event to remember with special thankfulness in after years.[*]

One only of the women and two or three of their attendants were hurt on the way by hostile shot. Meanwhile the rest of the garrison under Outram's masterly management were busied in preparing for their own departure. Of the guns they had served so well some were burst on the spot, others taken off to the camp. The ordnance stores, the treasure, the remaining supplies of grain, the State-prisoners, were all carried quietly away while the enemy's attention was drawn off by a steady cannonade of the Kaisar-Bágh and other strong posts in the city. At length, on the night of the 22nd, silently, and in perfect order, the last body of Outram's soldiers stepped forth from the lights and fires of the battered Residency into the darkness of the long winding lane that still lay between them and comparative safety. Campbell himself, riding with Adrian Hope's brigade, covered the retreat which Outram had so skilfully planned. Not a hitch took place in the course of a movement whose success depended on the intelligence and the discipline of all concerned. Not a man was lost in that critical night-march through the midst of forty thousand armed foes. One officer, indeed, who had somehow been overlooked, awoke to find himself alone in the abandoned entrenchment. Wild with horror, he ran from deserted post to post; then, hardly knowing which way to turn, sped on and on as fast as fear could bear him, until, breathless and well-nigh crazed, he came up with a part of the British rear-guard. By four in the morning of the 23rd the last of our soldiers had reached the Dil-Khushá. Some hours later the enemy were still firing away at the abandoned

---

[*] Trotter ; Chambers ; Lady Inglis's Diary ; The Polehampton Memoirs.

posts, and repairing the breaches which our guns the day before had made in the Kaisar-Bágh.*

To each and all concerned in the work thus happily consummated Sir Colin Campbell dealt out a liberal measure of just praise. Outram's able strategy, Hope Grant's untiring diligence, Peel's happy daring, the splendid rivalry of the Royal and Bengal Artillery, the steady zeal of the officers of the 9th Lancers and the Irregular Horse, who " were never out of the saddle during all this time," received from Sir Colin's pen no heartier tribute than did the fiery courage of the troops that stormed the Sikandar-Bágh, the soldier-like watchfulness of Brigadier Russell's column, and the matchless heroism of the whole force, which for seven days had formed " one outlying picket, never out of fire, and covering an immense extent of ground."

Admirable also had been the defence of the enlarged position, as maintained by Outram for nearly two months between the first and the second relief of Lucknow. The way in which a straggling, weakly-guarded line of gardens, courts, and dwelling-houses, mixed up with the buildings of a hostile city, had been held against " a close and constant fire from loopholed walls and windows," and a fitful storm of grape and roundshot from guns mostly within pointblank range, was a marvel of sturdy soldiership and engineering skill. Such a game of mining and countermining could hardly be matched in the annals of modern warfare. Against twenty of the enemy's mines twenty-one shafts had been dug by Napier's engineers. Of the former five only had been burst by the rebels, two of them quite harmlessly; while seven had been blown in by our men, and the enemy had been driven out of seven more.

As for the old garrison who had fought and suffered under Colonel Inglis, all England rang with stories of their prowess and with heart-felt pæans over their success. All Europe hailed with half-envious admiration the victorious issue of a defence which Lord Canning might well place beside the most heroic recorded in history,† a defence which Campbell himself called magnificent, and which, to Outram's thinking, demanded the use of terms " far more laudatory," if such were possible, than those once applied to the " illustrious garrison " of Jalálabád. To all

---

* Trotter.

† " There does not stand recorded in the annals of war," he wrote, " an achievement more truly heroic than the defence of the Residency at Lucknow."—Lord Canning's " Order in Council."

engaged in it honours and rewards were meted out with no grudging hand. The son of Sir Henry Lawrence was made a baronet for his dead father's sake. Colonel Inglis became Major-General Sir John Inglis of the Bath. Most of his officers were promoted, decorated, or publicly praised; every man in the garrison, whether soldier or civilian, was to receive six months' batta or its equivalent, and Mr. Cavanagh, Captain Aitken, and one or two others obtained the still rare honour of a Victoria Cross. Every British soldier was allowed to count a year's service in memory of Lucknow; the 32nd Foot became light infantry; and a new regiment of Lucknow was formed out of the faithful remnants of the 13th, 48th, and 71st Sepoys. On every native officer and private was bestowed the Indian Order of Merit, with a promise of early promotion, and with leave to count three years of service in return for a loyalty proof to all threats and bribes of his own countrymen, even of his own kin.

Nor were the heroes with whom Havelock, Neill, and Outram clove their perilous way to the side of their beleaguered countrymen forgotten in the general award. A knighthood and a baronetcy for Havelock; the rank of knight's lady for Neill's widow, with fitting pensions for both; proportional honours and preferments for such officers as Eyre, Napier, Lugard, Brasyer, Stisted, with batta and prize-money for the troops at large, attested the nation's gratitude for services hard indeed to overrate. For Outram himself and many of his bravest subalterns there remained yet a long course of splendid achievement, to be crowned in due time with further rewards, of which mention will be made in their proper place.[*]

On one foremost leader in that glorious struggle death was already closing fast. Worn out with toil, anxiety, exposure, and hard fare, Sir Henry Havelock fell ill of dysentery on the 20th of November. Two days later he knew himself to be dying, and on the 24th he breathed his last, calmly and contentedly, in the camp at Dil-Khushá. On the low plain by the Alambágh his body was buried the next day with all the honours that a crowd of mourning comrades, headed by Campbell and Outram, could bestow. The sorrow caused in every Indian station by the news of his death seemed weak in comparison with that displayed by his countrymen at home, who had come to worship him as their typical hero, clad in all the virtues of a Christian soldier as well as all the endowments of a great military chief. Statesmen,

[*] Trotter ; Malleson.

journalists, preachers, all hastened with one accord to pay homage
to the memory of him whose last achievements had crowned a
long life of noble duty, rewarded till very lately with comparative
neglect. A handsome pension was conferred on his widow and
his brave son. It seemed as if the tears of a whole nation
bedewed the grave of the soldier-saint whose worth they had too
late discovered, whose "antique grandeur" and irreproachable
name fired the eloquence of Montalembert, one of the most
eloquent and high-minded Frenchmen of his day. Nor was it in
England only that Havelock's death was lamented as a national
loss. Perhaps the most touching tribute to his memory came
from our English-speaking kinsmen across the Atlantic. At the
cities of New York, Boston, and Baltimore, the flags of the
shipping and the public buildings were hoisted half-mast high
from morning to sunset in honour of the dead hero whose name,
six months before, had been unknown to the people of the New
World. Such a tribute had not been paid before, even to the
memory of the great Duke of Wellington.*

The ill wind, indeed, of the Great Mutiny had blown to Havelock rich compensation for the struggles and discouragements of
forty years past. He had landed in Calcutta at the right moment
for asserting his claim to conduct the great enterprise which Neill
had so vigorously begun. That officer's splendid labours had prepared the ground for his own victorious advance to Cawnpore.
The very nature of Havelock's errand drew towards him the
tenderest sympathies of his countrymen at home, while their
hearts were stirred by the spectacle of a leader whose calm
courage, cheerful fortitude, and stainless piety recalled to
Montalembert the noblest traits in the great Puritans of the
seventeenth century. His brilliant though Pyrrhic victories on
the road to Lucknow took stronger hold of the popular imagina-
tion, than the more crowded but less dramatic incidents of the
long fight waging before Delhi. To the bulk of his countrymen
Havelock seemed to stand forth as the central figure of a war to
which his own exploits formed in fact but a brilliant episode.
Most fortunate of all for his new-risen fame was the deed of
generous self-denial by which Outram forbore to take from Havelock the command which Havelock had taken as a thing of course
from Neill. The march that ended in the relief of Inglis's
garrison gave a dramatic completeness to the campaign that
opened with the march from Allahábád. Havelock's star had

* Marshman.

been allowed to reach its zenith before it "shot on the sudden into dark." As one bright point in the galaxy that lights up the tale of the Indian Mutinies, the name of Henry Havelock will shed its own peculiar lustre on the minds of English readers in ages yet to come.

NOTE.

The services of our civil officers in the troubled districts deserve a chapter to themselves, instead of the few lines I have been able to give them. With rare exceptions, their conduct under sharp trial was worthy of their race and class. "Most of them," says Mr. H. G. Keene—himself conspicuous for his management of the Déra Dhun—"had to work as military officers, and often as officers without men. Their staff consisted, for the most part, of their official assistants and a few planters—some, like Venables and Dunn, men of great resolution and energy; but of the rank and file little was to be expected. A few Sepoys, of doubtful fidelity, unless they were Sikhs or Gorkhas; a half-disciplined jail-guard, often in sympathy with the convicts in their charge; a handful of messengers, often faithful fellows, but with no discipline at all: such was the material with which the fiercest passions of thousands were to be stayed, and the occasional raids of disciplined mutineers to be encountered, on pain of loss of life and honour, and of disaster and disgrace to the State."[*] Mr. Robert Dunlop, the active and daring Collector of Meerut, tells us, that out of 153 civil officers present when the mutiny began, about one-third were killed or wounded. "Twenty-nine have been murdered, killed in action, or died of wounds; three died from cholera or exposure on service, and several have been wounded."[†] In his "Fifty-Seven," Mr. Keene himself has recorded with just pride the adventures and achievements of such men as Robert Spankie at Saharanpur, Edwards at Muzafarnagar, Dunlop and Cracroft Wilson at Meerut, Sapte, Ross, and Lyall at Bulandshahr, Mark Thornhill at Mathra, Arthur Cocks at Aligarh, Power at Mainpúri, Hume at Etawah, John Sherer at Cawnpore, Court at Allahábád, and several other men of like mettle elsewhere. Some of them had charge of districts each as large as a good-sized English shire, with an average population of about one million. Of these districts several were successfully held during the worst days of the mutiny.

[*] Keene's "Fifty-Seven."
[†] Dunlop's "Service and Adventures with the Khakee Risalla."

CHAPTER II.

LAST WEEKS OF 1857.

On the 25th of November Outram brought into the Alambágh the rear-guard of the force which the day before had escorted the long train of sick, wounded and non-combatants thus far on its down-ward journey. Every one looked forward to some days of un-wonted rest, of easy marching towards Cawnpore. But the evil star of the Lucknow garrison seemed still to follow them. On the 27th Sir Colin Campbell, leaving Outram with nearly four thou-sand men to hold the Alambágh, made a short march thence to Banni with Hope Grant's division and the convoy from Lucknow. The sounds of heavy firing as if at Cawnpore decided Campbell, who had heard nothing lately from that quarter, to push on the next morning, convoy and all. On the morrow news came from Wind-ham of so dark an aspect, that the march continued into the night; Campbell himself riding ahead into Cawnpore, while his troops and their precious charges halted not far from the left bank of the Ganges, wondering at the din of battle that greeted them from the opposite side.

Campbell had not returned an hour too soon. He reached the intrenchment he had left in Windham's charge to find everything there in disorder; the hospitals filled with wounded, the camp strown with cattle, stores, and baggage, just saved from the grasp of a victorious foe; the troops themselves worn out with three days' fighting against some twenty thousand well-armed soldiers, mainly of the Gwáliár force. By the middle of November Sindhia's in-surgent troops, swollen by bodies of recruits from other quarters, were known to be drawing very near the intrenched post where General Windham, of Crimean celebrity, kept guard with some two thousand men over the bridge of boats and the city of Cawn-pore. His orders were to keep the road open between Allahábád and Lucknow. Puzzled by the prolonged silence of his absent Chief, Windham at length resolved to act upon his own judgement.

On the 26th of November he led forth some twelve hundred foot
with eight guns and a hundred Sikh horse to meet the first division of the enemy on the Pándu Nadi, a dry river-bed about eight
miles from Cawnpore.*

A vigorous onset of all arms soon drove the enemy back in swift
flight with the loss of three guns. Then seemingly for the first time
made aware of his nearness to the enemy's main army, Windham
gave the word to fall back upon the canal that ran through the
south-eastern corner of the city up to the intrenched post. The
enemy followed him as far as the canal bridge. About noon of the
next day he found himself suddenly assailed on his front and right
by a fierce fire from heavy guns planted behind a screen of brush-
wood and forest trees. Other bodies erelong threatened his left,
which lay nearest to the city. For five hours his little force held
out manfully against overwhelming odds. But at length it was
known that Windham's left had been outflanked, that the city was
filling with hostile troops, and the intrenchment itself exposed to
great peril. A retreat begun in order to save that precious post
turned at last into a crowded rush of soldiers, guns, camp-followers,
doolies, carts, and baggage-cattle, pellmell towards the common
goal. Scores of tents, cartloads of private baggage and public
stores, enriched the hands or fed the night-fires of the elated foe.
Of the flying troops few failed to reach the intrenchment, but one
gun, upset in a narrow lane, was only rescued in the middle of the
night by the stealthy advance of a few bold seamen and a company
of the 64th Foot.

Thus far things had gone badly enough with Windham; but a
day of yet worse disaster was to come. On the 28th some twenty
thousand Pandies with forty guns, with the Nána himself for one
of their leaders, advanced on the several posts still held outside
the intrenchment by Windham's force. Walpole's brigade, which
defended the slice of town to the left of the canal, fought with its
wonted courage, drove back the assailants, and took two of their
guns. But everywhere else the fight went against troops heavily
outnumbered, nor always rightly handled. A bold but isolated
dash by Colonel Wilson with a few companies of the 64th on a
battery some way in front of Carthew's post ended in a bloody retreat from overwhelming numbers, after two of the guns had been
fairly spiked. Wilson himself and several of his officers paid with
their lives for an act of daring which Carthew could not or would
not support. The important post held by Brigadier Carthew on

* Trotter ; Chambers.

the Bithúr road was abandoned at the close of that mournful day; and the enemy, enriched with fresh plunder, began next morning to bombard the intrenchment and the bridge of boats.*

All this, wrote Sir Colin, "appeared disastrous enough." A few hours more and the bridge itself might have been swept away. But the timely appearance of Campbell's troops gave a new turn to the course of events. The fire of our heavy guns from the Oudh bank, aided by that from Windham's post, soon opened a way for the crossing over of Hope's brigade, presently followed by the convoy from Lucknow. By the night of the 30th Campbell's whole force was safely encamped between the old dragoon lines and the spot made tragical by the sufferings of Wheeler's garrison. Hope Grant's division, thrown out on the left rear, commanded anew the road for supplies from Allahábád.

Before proceeding to pay off the enemy for their late successes; Campbell's first care was to secure the swift departure of his precious convoy or. the road down to Calcutta. On the 3rd of December, while the Gwáliár army was still making a show of besieging the intrenchment and annoying Campbell's outposts, the Lucknow garrison with a number of the wounded set forth on their way to a quieter resting-place in a city where, greeted by the harmless thunders of a royal salute, and steeped in an atmosphere of rest and comfort too long unknown, amidst the kindly ministry of friends, old or new, and the many tokens of a public sympathy at once deep and unobtrusive, the wanderers might look back with softened bitterness on the nightmare past; might brace up their spirits and ease their nerves awhile for the life-tasks that lay before them in the unknown future.†

At length, on the 6th of December, Campbell unleashed his troops against the foe who had thought to beard him as they had bearded Windham. The rebel line stretched in a loose disjointed semicircle from the old cantonments near the river round the eastern side of the city to a point on the canal westward of the road to Kalpi. At the enemy's right, which lay along the canal, Sir Colin resolved to strike his hardest, trusting to roll up one-half of that straggling array before the other could hasten to its support. A heavy continuous fire from the intrenchment against the enemy's left kept their attention diverted from the true point of danger, while Sir Colin's troops, covered by a screenwork of old barracks and stables, were quietly taking up their allotted posts. At length, about eleven o'clock, the word was given for an advance. Little's

---

* Trotter ; Chambers.   † Trotter.

cavalry brigade, with Blunt's and Remington's light guns, galloped off to outflank the enemy's right, while the infantry of Hope and Inglis, deployed in parallel lines, tramped gaily forward towards the canal. A rattling rifle-fire from the 4th Sikhs, followed by the thunder of Peel's, Crawford's, and Turner's guns, was answered by a hot cannonade from the foe in their front. The Sikhs, aided by the 53rd Foot, soon drove the rebel outposts across the canal. In line with our foremost skirmishers might be seen the sailors of the *Shannon*, bowling their twenty-four pounders along like so many playthings at a pace which fairly astonished their veteran Chief himself.* Their own leader, Peel, was the first man over the bridge on the main road to Delhi.

The rest of the troops soon gained the further side of the canal. Again unrolling their well-ordered lines, they pressed forward in eager chase of a foe already beaten. Their right centre hurled back upon their right by Walpole's infantry, their right breaking up before the steady advance of Hope's brigade, with the noise of Little's cavalry surging on their flank, the right wing of the rebels turned and fled towards Kalpi. But the pursuers were hard upon their heels, hunting them without respite as far as the fourteenth milestone from Cawnpore. The camp with all its contents, seventeen of their guns, and a great heap of ordnance stores, fell into the victors' hands.

Meanwhile to Major-General Mansfield, Chief of the Staff, had been assigned the duty of looking after the enemy's left wing, still posted about and beyond Cawnpore. Starting in the afternoon from the captured camp with two regiments of foot and twelve guns, he pushed his way through the broken ground, among gardens still held by the Nána's men; emerging at last on the plain by the old cantonment in time to see, in some measure to hasten, the retreat of the enemy's guns along the Bithúr road. Here Mansfield halted for the night, rather than risk an advance at so late an hour through a mile of old buildings in which a large remnant of the beaten army with a few guns were still sheltering. During the night this remnant quietly disappeared. When the morrow dawned, not an enemy was visible in the neighbourhood of Cawnpore.†

In all the movements of the last few days Campbell had lost no more than thirteen slain and eighty-six wounded. Yet smaller

---

* "On this occasion," wrote Sir Colin, "there was the sight beheld of 24-pounder guns advancing with the first line of skirmishers."

† Trotter ; Chambers.

was the price which Hope Grant was to pay two days later for his final scattering of the beaten foe. On the 8th of December that able officer led out from camp a force of 2,800 men and eleven guns, in hopes of catching the wrecks of the Gwáliár army on its way to Sarai Ghát, a ferry about twenty-five miles above Cawnpore. Next morning he found his prey within easy reach of him by the river-side. After a toilsome and perilous passage through heavy quicksands, Remington's and Middleton's guns played upon the hostile batteries to such purpose that the rebels at length sought to save their own guns by hurling a body of horsemen at their assailants. But Little's cavalry saw and thwarted the bold attempt. Onvry's Lancers sent the enemy reeling back from the mere thunder of their terrible onset. Younghusband's swart troopers of the 5th Panjáb Horse never drew rein until they had slain eighty-five of the foe and borne off three of the rebel standards. Before Walpole's infantry could strike a blow, the enemy fled out of reach, leaving our men to gather up the fruits of a victory which, in spite of nearly an hour's hail of grape and roundshot, cost the victors only one horse slain and not a single man hurt. Well might the Brigadier-General call it a "marvellous" event, enhanced as it was by the capture of fifteen guns, as many waggons, and a large stock of ammunition.

Cawnpore thus happily saved from further harm, and the great Gwáliár bubble blown into the air, Sir Colin Campbell was free to carry out his plans for the reconquest of Oudh, Rohilkhand, and the adjoining districts. While Franks at Banáras was mustering troops for a campaign on the southern frontier of Oudh, in concert with the 9,000 Gorkhas whom Jang Bahádur was leading against the rebels about Gorakpur and Azimgarh, bodies of British troops under Hope Grant, Walpole, Seaton, and Campbell himself, scoured the Ganges valley from Fathipur up to Farokhabad. Seaton's column, which left Delhi late in November to look after the rebel Rajah of Mainpúri, marched to and fro between Aligarh and Etawah, hunting the rebels from place to place, and routing them with heavy slaughter wherever they tried a stand. The recapture of Mainpúri on the 19th of December crowned a series of brilliant successes in which Hodson's troopers and Kinleside's gunners played a conspicuous part. Twenty-one guns and heaps of other booty were taken in the course of one week. From Mainpúri Seaton moved on to Bewár, awaiting orders from Sir Colin Campbell, whose own column by the end of December was only a march or two from Farokhabad.	Towards the same point the columns of Hope Grant and Walpole, which had been settling the country north and west of Cawnpore, began marching upward in the last days of this eventful year.[*]

Almost everywhere the year closed on brighter prospects, on events that spoke as hopefully for the future of British rule as the breadths of ripening tillage that well-nigh overspread the marks of recent havoc spoke for the likelihood of a bounteous harvest in the coming spring.	From his lonely post at the Alambágh, Outram watched every movement of the Lucknow rebels, and thwarted every attempt to sever his connections with Cawnpore.	His sudden raid upon the foe on the morning of the 22nd of December resulted in their utter rout and the capture of four guns.	On the 26th, at Majauli, on the eastern border of Oudh, Rowcroft's small column of sailors, Sikhs, and Gorkhas, attacked and routed four or five thousand followers of Mohammud Hussain, a rebel Tálukdár.	The insurgents strewed their flight to the Rápti with sixty or seventy dead, and one of their four guns was taken.	All further danger on that side of Oudh was averted by the sound of Jang Bahádur's advance across the Gandak upon Gorakpur.

Gerrard's defeat of the Jodhpur mutineers at Rewári in Gurgáon, if bought with his own and other precious lives, still proved for the enemy a disabling blow.	In the country between the Jamna and the Ganges rebellion was melting into peaceful order beneath the suasive energies of Eld and Riddell aiding and following up the work done by Seaton and Walpole.	The hill stations of Almora and Naini-Tál still held their human treasures harm-free, in spite of frequent threatenings from the armed banditti of Rohilkhand.

In Rewah the daring Osborne, aided by Colonel Hinde, had at length gained a series of victories over the rebels who infested the Jabalpur road.	He hunted them into their den at Mailier, stormed that town on the 28th of December, and six days afterwards became master of the citadel in which they had taken their last stand.	The Dháka mutineers roved forlorn in the jungles of Bhotán, while the mutinous remnant of the ill-famed 34th had broken away from Chittagáon only to fall before the year's end into the deadly clutches of Major Byng's Silhet Battalion. The followers of Kunwár Singh still lurked in the jungles of Jagdíspur; but from Dánápur down to Calcutta and eastward to the

Burman frontier armed resistance was either dead or dying out, when Lord Canning forwarded his last budget of that year's news to the gentlemen still held responsible for the Government of British India.

Even from the four hundred miles of country stretching south from Hánsi to Indór "nothing new" was the burden of Lord Canning's tale. Only about Chapra, in Málwa, was armed anarchy still rearing a defiant head. In the Ságar district the loyal 31st Sepoys and the 3rd Native Cavalry were giving a good account of any insurgent bands that crossed their path. In Holkar's capital the presence of the Mhan column on the 15th of December enabled the young Mahárája to gratify the English Resident, by disarming three of the regiments which had led the attack on the Residency in July. Lastly, from Nimach came news of the rout and final dispersion of the strong rebel force, which, after vainly hurling itself against the Nimach garrison, had been heavily punished in two days' fighting with Brigadier Stuart near Mandisór.*

Stuart's brilliant campaign in Málwa demands more than a passing sentence. Starting in July from Aurangabad, and picking Durand up at Asirgarh, Stuart brought his column by the 1st of August into Mhau. After two months of forced inaction owing to heavy monsoon rains, Stuart and Durand set out to chastise the rebels, who swarmed along the roads from Nimach down to Dhár. The little State of Dhár, on the Narbadda, nominally ruled by a boy of thirteen, had lately joined the revolt. On the 22nd of October Stuart's soldiers dealt a heavy blow on the insurgents posted outside the strong fort of Dhár. Three guns were taken in brilliant style, and turned against the enemy by the 25th Bombay Sepoys ; and a dashing charge by the 14th Dragoons and the Nizam's horse drove the rebels back with much slaughter into the fort. After a siege of six days that stronghold was carried by assault before daybreak of the 1st of November; but its defenders had an hour or two earlier made good their escape. After demolishing the fort, under orders from Durand himself, Stuart held his way towards Mandisór, while Major Orr with a few hundred of the Nizam's troops followed up and routed a strong force of rebels, who had just been plundering the station of Mahidpur. A fierce fight, in which Orr lost nearly a hundred of his men, was rewarded by the capture of eight guns and a heavy slaughter of the foe.

* Trotter.

Pursuing his march upon Mandisór, Stuart, on the 22nd of November, caught the enemy trying to turn his left as he halted for breakfast within easy reach of his goal. The attempt, however, was soon thwarted by a steady advance of the British line, by a murderous fire from Woollcombe's guns, and a timely charge of the Haidarábád Horse. Still harder and more decisive was the fight which raged on the 24th around the village of Goraria, where a host of the Nimach rebels had taken their stand with five guns. Their left and centre were gradually driven back upon the village itself; but there the enemy, consisting largely of Rohillas, stood out so resolutely that Stuart shrank from sending his brave infantry to carry the place by storm. Next day his heavy guns reduced the village to such a wreck that the 86th Foot and the 25th Sepoys were allowed to storm it in the afternoon. By that time Prince Firóz Shah, of the Delhi family, with his two thousand Afgháns had fled from Mandisór, and Durand, who shared with Stuart the honours of success, found himself free to return to Indór and welcome Sir Robert Hamilton back to his old post.*

Before the close of the year 1857 a large slice of country from Ambála southward to Gurgáon was transferred from the Government of the North-Western Provinces to that of the Panjáb. The new frontier of Lawrence's old dominion thus included the great city of Delhi itself. Erelong the great Commissioner who had saved India through his hold on the Panjáb was speeding down from Lahór to breathe new life into the political ruins of the province whose capital he had just helped to save from virtual erasure; for a cry had gone forth that Delhi, the accursed city, the nest of so much treachery and disaffection, the scene of so many triumphs over English helplessness, the late centre of a dangerous revolt against our rule, should be razed to the ground, should become at least as desolate as the ruins of older Delhis that still surrounded it. Why should a swarm of mere traitors be let back into their old haunts, to swagger about the Chándni Chauk, to wax rich on the rescued remnants of their forfeit wealth, to worship in the temples of a priesthood always ready to preach a holy war against the Farangi? The Government itself seemed half to sanction the popular demand by ordering the entire destruction of the city walls.

Sir John Lawrence, however, at once protested against so

---

* Malleson; Chambers.

extreme a measure, which would involve not only a heavy drain
upon a low exchequer, but even a serious bar to the future government of a city surrounded by a chain of robber villages. Thanks
to his strong remonstrances, the work of undoing the former
labours of our own engineers became restricted to the filling up
of the moat and the partial lowering of the lofty walls. By the
end of 1857 the affrighted citizens were once more filling the
streets and alleys of the war-beaten city, as fast as they could
purge themselves before the ruling powers of all complicity in the
massacres of May, or the misdeeds of the ensuing months. Once
more, within the great square of the Jamma Masjid, saved by
British clemency from Sikh defilements, could be heard the drone
of the Maulvi reading from his Korán; while the stream of busy
life flowed more and more freely along thoroughfares still marred
by ruins, past the tottering walls of the Bank, whose officers had
been swept away in a common massacre; past great bastions
knocked out of all shape, and heaps of rubbish that had once
been gateways; past the shot-riddled church, now serving as a
hospital for English sick; past the press-house whence the con-
ductors of the *Delhi Gazette* were already striving with new types
and invincible energy to gain the ear of a yet wider public than
before.

But the traces of recent warfare were not confined to shattered
woodwork, bare, gaping walls, and unsightly rubbish. Vengeance
hungered for more victims. Stern justice loudly demanded, cool
policy was swift to sanction, the judicial shedding of much guilty
blood. For weeks, for months after the storming of Delhi, the
gallows were fed with culprits who had been summarily tried
and sentenced by the special and military courts. One man, the
murderer of Simon Fraser, was cut to pieces by his captors,
without form of trial. Other victims of more or less note seem to
have been hanged in batches of five or six a day. On one day in
November, twenty-four of the king's kith and kin paid with a
shameful death for their share in the massacres of May. In the
course of the next two months a doom as exemplary overtook the
captive lords of Gurgáon, Jhajar, Balabgarh, and Farokhnagar,
all convicted, if not of murder, at least of plotting with the
shedders of English blood. Numbers of Englishmen gloated over
the death-struggles of these and other leading rebels, from whom
the sympathy, the mercy, the common justice owed by brave men
to defeated opponents was withheld, in part by the white man's
brutal scorn for the dark-skinned stranger, but chiefly by the

blinding memory of wrongs that could only be expiated in a sea of blood.

Some of the doomed men, like the Nawáb of Jhajar, met their fate with manifest dread. Others, like the Mir Nawáb, died as bravely as they had fought. The latter criminal proved himself worthy of the general who fought so hard at the Hindan, who commanded the rebels at Badli-Sarai, who planned many a fierce onslaught against our troops before Delhi. This " hardened villain," as he seemed to English eyes, helped with his own hands to remove his fetters, scoffed at the clumsiness of the smith who struck them off, and sneeringly advised the officials to make a greater show of him by hanging him outside the Ajmir Gate. With a parting prayer to Allah he gasped his way into the unknown world. One of his fellow-sufferers being a lean old man, was tied up with a silken rope, which broke and let him down. Again he was tied up; but the hangman bungled as the smith had done, for the noose slipped towards the old man's chin, and his death-struggles were painful to witness.[*]

The forfeiture of estates went hand in hand with the execution of their owners. Many lakhs of rupees thus found their way into the public coffers, in partial quittance of the losses caused by the rebellion. As a sop, however, to the conquerors of Delhi, much of the personal property taken from the rebels was set apart as their lawful prize. Another sop, for which many Englishmen still cried aloud, was still denied them by the wisdom of India's rulers. Ever since his surrender to Captain Hodson, the hoary old King of Delhi, who was said to have sanctioned the slaughter of his English captives, had been awaiting in close, in mean confinement the orders of a Government which, having spared his life, had still to arraign him for his alleged misdeeds. For many weeks the noise of a baulked revenge surged up on all sides against Hodson, against Wilson, against all who had borne any part in saving the nominal leader of the rebels from a violent death. Meanwhile the royal captive had little cause to rejoice in the clemency which reserved him for a fate that seemed hardly preferable to death itself. A small, low, dirty room, whose only furniture, a common "charpoy," rudest of native bedsteads, served as a couch for the little, hook-nosed, keen-eyed, white-headed, toothless, old smoker of eighty-four, whose ancestors had filled the world with their fame, whose titles would have covered a page of print; another room yet smaller, darker, dirtier, where, on a common charpoy, sur-

* Trotter.

rounded by several women and a boy or two, lay the dark, fat, shrewd, and sensual-looking Zinat Mahal, mother of his darling Benjamin, Jama Bakht,—such was the picture of royal pomp and luxury that awakened a thrill of half-ashamed compassion in the breast of at least one lady, the wife of Hodson, whose eyes were allowed to gainsay the lying stories circulated by the Indian newspapers.[*]

The life thus led by the royal prisoner in a corner of the palace where he had so long ruled his overgrown court, and fiddled and made verses, and leered on his dancing-girls, and dallied with his many wives, might seem no common punishment even for so great a criminal. Beyond this length of pardonable rigour Lord Canning's Government would not go without some fairer sanction than the outcries of a public wild for blood. It was settled that Mohammad Bahádur Shah should be tried as a felon before undergoing the felon's lot. A commission of field-officers, headed by Colonel Dawes of the Bengal Artillery, was appointed to sit in judgement on a prisoner long since foredoomed by the general voice of our countrymen in India.

The Court met for the first time on the 27th of January, 1858, amidst the marble fretwork of the Dewán-i-Khás. Tottering forward on the arm of Jama Bakht, the feeble old man coiled himself up into a bundle on the cushion set for him at the president's left hand. To his left sat the official prosecutor, Major Harriott. A little behind them stood the king's favourite son, with a guard of the 60th Rifles further off. On either side of the president sat the four members of his Court. A sprinkling of ladies and gentlemen, curious to watch the prisoner, to hear the evidence against him, or at least to play their little part in so rare a drama, dotted the surrounding waste of marble floor.

With indifference, feigned or real, the poor old wretch heard himself charged on four counts with complicity in various acts of high treason and wholesale murder done between the 10th of May and the 1st of October, 1857. After feigning utter ignorance of an indictment which had been read out to him many days before, he at length deigned to plead not guilty; and then began the real business of a trial which lasted with intervals down to the 9th of March. In the course of twenty sittings evidence enough was brought forward to justify the Court in finding the prisoner guilty of aiding and abetting his son Mirza Moghal with other mutineers and rebels in waging war against the Government, of

[*] Trotter.

causing or conniving at the murder of forty-nine Christians within the precincts of his own palace, and of tempting others in various parts of India, by promises, rewards, and direct orders, to attack and slay our countrymen whenever they had the chance.*

All through the trial the old king's demeanour had been that of one whose thoughts seemed far away; whose chief desire was to dream or doze through the time spent on an inquiry which concerned no one less than himself. More than once he had to be roused from slumber to hear the reading of the day's evidence, or to answer a question put by the Court. Now and then he woke up to deny the truth of some statement, to declare his own innocence, to ask whether the Russians and Persians were not the same people, or to avow his faith in some astrologer of whom a few days later he denied all knowledge. At such moments a sudden look or gesture, some hurried utterance of surprise, dissent, or approval seemed to show that his ears could be more attentive than his eyes. But no amount of helpless-seeming apathy, no eloquence of those who defended him, no appeals to the pity, contempt, or generous shrewdness of his judges availed to deflect or mitigate the inevitable issue. The sentence of death, from which Wilson's guarantee had saved him, was necessarily exchanged for one of transportation. In due time, on the 4th of December, 1858, the white-haired convict was steaming down the Húghli, to end his days, not as many had hoped in the savage loneliness of the Andaman Isles, but amidst the less dreary surroundings of a quiet bungalow in Rangoon.† Two wives, his son, Jama Bakht, and a very small train of servants were allowed to share the old man's confinement and the wretched pittance thenceforth reserved for the pensioned squanderer of many thousands a year. If to the proud-hearted Zinat Mahal such a lot might seem worse than death, her discrowned lord with his hookah, his verse-making, and his youngest boy, seemed willing to console himself for the loss of all that pomp and splendour which, long before the taking of Delhi, had proved to him a very crown of thorns.

Touching the guiltiness of his favourite Queen public opinion in India had very small doubt. Against her and her darling son the cry for vengeance had risen long and loud. It seemed to many an enraged Englishman as if mercy shown to any one of the House of Bábar were a wrong done to the memory of his murdered friends, kindred, and countrymen. Whoever shrank from full acquiescence in such a doctrine was reviled as a White Pandy. But Canning's Government had early become proof to the calling of hard names.

* Trotter ; Chambers.   † He died there in 1862.

Having already shown itself not all implacable towards male sinners, it was not likely to betray a vindictive longing for the blood of disaffected women and proud-seeming boys. Whatever his shortcomings, Lord Canning declined to win a fleeting popularity by deeds of panic-driven revenge. So mother and boy, instead of undergoing a public trial, were allowed to pass out of Delhi and share the fortunes of Mohammad Bahádur Shah.*

If Lord Canning's policy was unpopular in the provinces, in Calcutta itself it had long become a byeword for everything weak and despicable. From July 1857 onwards into the next year, his name stank in the nostrils of the white community, whose goodwill he had lost still earlier by his slowness in accepting their proffered services, and yet more by his haste in muzzling the whole of the Calcutta Press. Thenceforth nothing was too bad to believe of a ruler who had honestly tried to do his duty and to deal justly with all classes alike. In their distrust, dislike, their absolute hatred of one who clearly would not trust the only loyal section of his subjects, the English in Calcutta grew ever readier to swallow the wildest stories, and circulate the grossest slanders against a Government that dared to take its own line on questions touching their personal safety or their national pride. Their demands for summary vengeance on the rebels were met by an edict narrowing and defining the penal powers which had been intrusted to civil officers by the special enactments of May and June. Their prayers for martial law in Calcutta and the neighbouring provinces were answered by an Act obliging all men, Europeans as well as natives, to yield up or register their private arms. Their cry for protection against Mohammadan turbulence and a powerless or disloyal police, drew forth only a polite assurance that the police, the few English troops, the volunteer guards, and the whole body of European residents, were quite able among them to keep order in the capital of British India. In revenge for the new restrictions on free printing they sent home letters and pamphlets teeming with abuse of the Government, talked openly of deposing the Governor-General, and even forwarded to the Court of Directors a petition urging his immediate recall.

It was not long before the hurricane thus roused in Calcutta began to awake answering echoes in the hearts of Englishmen at home. A fierce controversy raged everywhere over the policy pursued by Lord Canning and his colleagues. Popular journalists denounced his clemency; public speakers and ardent pamphleteers repeated

* Trotter.

without a misgiving the most slanderous stories received from
their distant countrymen. One of the wildest of these gained
ready credence even in quarters where a prudent scepticism should
have prevailed. Not a few persons fairly conversant with India
professed to believe that Mr. John Grant, the temporary Governor
of the Central Provinces, had actually set free a hundred and fifty
of Neill's prisoners; had even gone the length of punishing with
death some English soldiers guilty of assaulting the pardoned
rebels.*

Careless of defending himself, Lord Canning caught with indignant gladness at the first opportunity for disproving the charges
thus foolishly levelled against "one of the ablest servants of the
Government." Grant's reply from Banáras to a telegram of inquiry from the Governor-General was received by the latter in
time for the homeward mail of the 24th of December. One of
the stories, he wrote, was false, while the other "could not
possibly be true." He had never pardoned or released a single
prisoner by whomsoever confined, nor had any case in the least
resembling an assault of British soldiers on mutineers ever come
before him in any shape. To the best of his knowledge he had
never seen General Neill, had never corresponded with him or
about him, had never, in short, had any relations with Neill of any
kind. Far from finding fault with any of Neill's measures, he had
always spoken with heartfelt admiration of "the noble, soldierly
qualities" displayed by that lamented officer. He had never so
much as heard of any transactions at all resembling those laid to
his charge. Never since his arrival at Banáras, on the 28th of
August, had he any the slightest approach to a difference with
any military officer answering in rank or position to General
Neill. Moreover, the whole story was "badly invented," with reference to Mr. Grant himself, than whom no one "could be more
strongly impressed with the need of executing justice on this
occasion with the most extreme severity." †

By the same mail which bore home Mr. Grant's plain answer to
the fables so readily believed in England, Lord Canning forwarded
to the Court of Directors a minute of his own, which fully and
clearly vindicated the terms of his oft misquoted Resolution of
the 31st of July. The document thus defended now needs no

---

* The provinces thus placed for a time under a separate ruler comprised the
districts of Banáras, Allahábád, the Lower Doáb, Gorakpur, Bundalkhand, and
Ságar.

† Trotter ; Parliamentary Papers.

defence. But for many months after its first appearance the
noble, the statesmanlike clemency therein so manifest became in
the mouths of Canning's countrymen a synonym for ill-timed and
disastrous weakness. Words, looks, gestures of fierce scorn or
quiet mockery hailed every mention of an ordinance which merely
laid a hand of warning on the intemperate zeal of a few civil
officers entrusted with enormous powers of swift punishment in
districts each as large as Yorkshire or Devonshire. The ill-will
born of Lord Canning's earlier mistakes clung like a Nemesis to
one of the most righteous edicts that ever issued from the desk
of an Indian Viceroy. He was accused of tying the hands of his
ablest officers because he strove betimes to check the shedding of
possibly innocent blood, and the indiscriminate burning of villages
peopled perhaps by rebels, certainly by useful taxpayers and
food-producing tillers of the soil. Englishmen whose hearts had
been fired anew by the horrors of Cawnpore, by the blundered
issues of the Dánápur mutiny, by the tales that accompanied the
arrival of fresh refugees from the Upper Provinces, were seldom
in a mood to own the justice of sparing men who had shown the
least sympathy with rebels and mutineers, or to see the wisdom
of pardoning unruly villages by way of surety against future
famine and a ruinous dearth of State funds. In the blindness
of their wrath they seemed to regard it as a personal insult, as a
wrong done to the British name, that any native who had ever
witnessed, or been accused of profiting by an act of outrage upon
any man or woman of the ruling race, should live to prate here-
after of Farangi sufferings, or to brag of the merciful treatment
wrung from Farangi fears.

Yet the very strength of this feeling proved Lord Canning's
surest vindication. Amidst such a swirl of maddening influences
it was well alike for Englishmen and natives that one or two
master-heads should keep clear. When the gallows, the cat, the
torch, were threatening to blot out the last distinctions between guilt and innocence, to turn whole districts into grave-
yards, deserts, haunts of beggars and fear-stricken outcasts, it was
time for some voice of power to cry out upon the folly, the
cowardice of indiscriminate revenge. In thirteen days of June
and July one Commissioner had sent to the gallows forty-two
wretches guilty, all save one murderer, of nothing worse than
robbery, rioting, or rebellion. Some of these paid with their
lives for having goods or money—even bags of copper half-pice—
about which they could give no satisfactory account. In less than

six weeks before the 1st of August, 120 men, none of whom were
Sepoys, and very few of higher rank than villagers, policemen,
servants, were hanged by the special courts of one district alone.
In many cases the evidence against the prisoners could have
seemed strong only to minds that saw everything through a film
of blood. Of the numbers arrested not one in ten appears to
have escaped some kind of punishment, not one in five to have
escaped the gallows. If many guiltless may have fallen at first
under the blind rage of the English or the reckless greed of
the Sikh soldiery, it seems clear that some needless waste of
lives and property, sowing in its turn rich crops of fear and
hatred in the minds of people otherwise peacefully if not always
loyally disposed, must be laid to the rash zeal of those civil officers
for whose guidance Lord Canning and his colleagues framed the
Resolution of July.

In the reports of those gentlemen themselves, in the complaints
that reached Calcutta through various channels, official or private,
there were signs enough of reckless cruelty, of unsparing
terrorism, to justify an impartial ruler in striving his utmost to
prevent a partial insurrection from widening into a war of races;
to imbue those gentlemen who wielded special powers under the
decrees of May and June with "a more just sense of their duties
and responsibilities; to save innocent men from a shameful death,
and innocent families from the destruction of home and property;
to prevent the fields from remaining untilled and the crops un-
sown;" and to assure the people at large that "justice, and not
vengeance, was the policy of the British Government;" was the
one right way of strengthening our hold on "the respect and
attachment of the well-affected natives of India." For these
ends Lord Canning ordered the Special Commissioners to punish
as deserters none but armed Sepoys belonging to disarmed regiments; while unarmed deserters were to be forwarded for trial
to their several regiments, or else kept in prison pending instructions from the Government. In the second place, deserters from
regiments unknown, or from those which had mutinied without
murder or violence, were to be punished on the spot only if
taken with arms in their hands, or if charged with overt rebellion: otherwise they were to be sent to Allahábád or elsewhither
for trial by a military court. Thirdly, all Sepoys of regiments
whose revolt had been stained with blood might be tried and
promptly punished by the civil power, unless they could prove
their absence from the scene of outrage, or the earnestness of

their efforts to avert the outrage done. For all prisoners of the latter class the Government would hold out the prospect of a free pardon.

Furthermore, the civil officers in every district were warned against the evil effects of unsparing severity continued after the first need for terror-striking examples had passed away. They were bidden to wield their great powers discreetly; to refrain from unduly hindering the return of social order and well-being by a wholesale destruction of villages and punishing of minor criminals; to aid, without rash promises or misplaced clemency, in reassuring the better affected, in winning the people back to their old homes, pursuits, and allegiance; and whenever they safely could, to reserve "all minute inquiry into political offences," for the future decision of a Government strong enough to deal with such cases thoroughly in its own good time.*

In all this there is no trace of undue leniency, no attempt whatever to tie the hands of any civil magistrate, still less to meddle with the powers entrusted to military officers.† On the contrary, in all cases calling for prompt treatment, the burden of proving their own innocence still lay as heavy as before on the shoulders of the accused, while Sepoys charged with less heinous crimes were merely shifted over from the uncertain handling of a civil Rhadamanthus to the regular processes of a military court. Only against reckless punishments decreed by men armed with vast exceptional powers did the Government of India raise its voice. Had it not done so, wrote Lord Canning, " we should have miserably failed in our duty, and should have exposed ourselves to the charge of being nothing better than instruments of wild vengeance in the hands of an exasperated community."

* Trotter ; Parliamentary Papers.

† The slanderous stories about Mr. John Grant appear to have sprung out of the popular delusion that Lord Canning's "Clemency Order" was directed against the powers of military as well as civil officers.

CHAPTER III.

RECONQUEST OF LUCKNOW.

WITH the first days of the new year closed the life of one whose only warfare had been waged against spiritual foes, whose twenty-five years of episcopal work in India had been marked, in the words of Lord Canning, " by a zeal which age could not chill, and by an open-handed charity and liberality which have rarely been equalled." On the 2nd of January, 1858, Daniel Wilson, Bishop of Calcutta, died in his eightieth year amidst the unfeigned regrets of all who had known him, whether in the pulpit or in private life. In his youth an Oxford prizeman, the sometime Vice-Principal of St. Edmund's Hall became in 1812 sole minister of a chapel in Bloomsbury, where for twelve years with simple earnestness he preached the Gospel as it revealed itself to a friend and follower of the Evangelical Simeon. Eight years more of duty in a London vicarage brought him to the threshold of his Indian career. Without the scholarly refinement, the poetry, the sweet grace, the mild religious breadth of white-souled Reginald Heber, the new Bishop won to himself the hearts of his countrymen in India by the simple kindliness of tone, the almost childlike earnestness of manner, that tempered he formal harshness of his theology, and seemed half to sanctify his disregard for the minor courtesies of social life. No one had the heart to quarrel with the good old enthusiast who fought so bravely against what he held to be the devil and his works, and who certainly strove his best, without respect of persons, to mend the morals of a community by no means blameless from a Christian point of view. No small part of his goodly income was spent in noble almsgiving, while some of it went towards the building of that cathedral wherein, ten years after its consecration, his body was to be laid.*

Shortly before the good Bishop's death the Sepoys of the dis-

* Trotter.

armed 70th Native Infantry had been started down the Húghli in fulfilment of their own request for leave to go and fight the Chinese. Two other regiments of disarmed Sepoys presently followed in their track, and took some part in the closing stages of a war which ended in the opening of new ports to the trade of Europe, and in the formal admission of England's claim to plant an embassy at Pekin.

Meanwhile, in India, the new year opened promisingly for the final triumph of our arms. On the 2nd of January Sir Colin Campbell struck the blow which left him undisputed master of Farokhabad and the ruined station of Fathigarh, the southernmost point of Rohilkhand. In default of any human victims, save one "notorious malefactor" who was duly seized and hanged, his troops employed themselves in sacking and destroying the palaces of the rebel Nawáb and his chief adherents. For the next few weeks they had little else to amuse their leisure than short raids after insurgent bands along the Ganges, varied by one or two brilliant fights between Hope's column and the Baréli mutineers. On these occasions Hodson's Horse and the 9th Lancers chased the flying enemy in the usual style after our guns and infantry had done their work.

While the British general raised false hopes in rebel hearts by tarrying, as it seemed so idly, on the borders of Rohilkhand and Oudh, other officers were winning victories or gaining ground elsewhere. The hill-stations in Kamáon being once more threatened by the enemy in the plains below, Colonel M'Causland sallied forth from Haldwáni, the scene of Ramsay's victory, with 700 of the 66th Gorkhas, two guns, and 200 horse, to catch the rebels at a disadvantage. On the morning of the 10th of February five thousand of their number were suddenly attacked and brilliantly routed with heavy slaughter and the loss of all their guns. Some weeks earlier, on the 12th of January, a fiercer fight had ended in a yet more signal defeat inflicted by Outram's warriors on six times their number of trained foes. From sunrise until 4 P.M. did the men of Oudh swarm like hungry wolves around Outram's post, trying again and again to find some weak point in his defences. Repulsed at all points with terrible slaughter, they returned four days later to the attack. Once more, after a long day's fighting, they fell back cruelly shattered and swept down by hundreds beneath the unerring hail of lead and iron.[*]

* Trotter; Chambers.

Jang Bahádur's successful march into Gorakpur on the 6th of January paved the way for the full re-establishment of British rule on the south-eastern border of Oudh. More to the west-ward Brigadier-General Franks, an officer of no mean repute, attacked on the 24th, and bloodily defeated, a body of rebels strongly posted about Nasanpur, not far from Allahábád. Two guns were counted among the spoils. By the end of the month Franks' force of English, Sikhs, Gorkhas, and Madrassies, about six thousand in all with twenty-four guns, were in line with Jang Bahádur's Nipálese along the whole south-eastern border of Oudh from the Ganges to the Rápti.

In Rájputána the 24th of January was marked by a successful attack of Major Raines's Bombay Sepoys on the fortified village of Rówa. A few days later, on his way from Bhopál to the relief of Ságar, Sir Hugh Rose was making ready to storm the rock-perched fortress of Ráthgarh, on the river Bina, about thirty miles from Ságar itself. Some of his guns had just been dragged through heavy jungle up to heights that had seemed unreachable, when the enemy taking fright began to slip out of the stronghold they had made sure of defending for months to come. A strong attack next morning on Sir Hugh's camp was foiled by the steadiness of his troops, and requited by the keen pursuit of Captain Hare's horsemen from Haidarábád. The fort itself was soon won, and the British commander then became free to relieve the long-beleaguered garrison of Ságar. In the neighbouring province of Nágpur a partial mutiny on the 18th of January had been checked by the loyal conduct of the remaining troops and the timely punishment of the ringleaders.[*]

All through February the stream of British progress flowed full and broad over many a field of strife and disorder. From Cal-cutta, from Agra, from the Panjáb vast stores of guns, ammuni-tion, food, cattle, medicines, and other necessaries, with many reinforcements of Sikh and English troops, found their way to Cawnpore, to Fathigarh, and other places where portions of the new-formed army of Oudh lay waiting for the order to advance. Day after day the boat-bridges at Cawnpore and Fathigarh creaked and swayed under the weight of men, guns, and baggage passing over into the seat of coming war. Not till the end of February did Sir Colin himself leave Cawnpore to take command of perhaps the finest army that ever in British uniform stepped out on Indian soil. With the wariness of an old soldier bent on

* Trotter.

leaving nothing to chance, and patient of delays that fretted the souls of his subalterns, and evoked impatient growls from on-lookers stirred by the dashing feats of Showers, Seaton, M'Caus-land, and other leaders of like mould, the Commander-in-Chief determined to hold his hand until he had brought together the means of crushing out all armed resistance by a few well-planted blows.

If there was reason in so waiting, in drawing together for that last march on Lucknow the troops that might else have done good service in the old irregular way, reason also had the critics who murmured at the loss of two months about Fathigarh while an armed rabble waxed bold in law-forsaken Rohilkhand, while bodies of rebels passed unchecked across the northern frontier of Oudh, and the Gwáliár troops began once more to threaten the British rear from their strong position at Kalpi. With timely help from Seaton or Walpole, the victories won by M'Causland might have hastened by many weeks the reconquest of all the country between Almora and Shahabad. Had more troops been at hand on the 4th of February at Bhágnipur, the defeat of the Gwáliár rebels on that day by Maxwell's soldiers of the 88th Foot and fifty Sikh Horse led by Mowbray-Thompson, the Cawn-pore hero, might have entailed the early capture of one strong-hold on the Jamna and the isolation of another beyond the Betwa. But Sir Colin had formed his own plans in concert with Lord Canning, then staying at Allahábád, for a grand advance upon one particular point; and the watch-fires of unfriendly criticism soon died out in the full sunshine of his ultimate success.

More than one, however, of his generals had earned fresh laurels during the Chief's halt at Cawnpore. On the 21st of February the warworn Outram had again to meet the furious onsets of twenty thousand rebels on all sides of a position weakened by the absence of some of his troops on escort duty. The assailants got nothing but heavy slaughter for their pains. Dosed with grape from the British guns, their swarming cavalry checked by the bold advance of a few field-pieces and a few hundred horse, those threatening masses were chased back to the shelter of their own batteries with the loss of many hundred slain or wounded, against only nine wounded on Outram's side.

Two days later Sir Hope Grant had carried by storm the walled town of Miánganj on the road from Fathigarh to Lucknow. In fifty minutes Anderson's heavy guns had breached the wall, while Turner's nine-pounders kept down the musketry fire in their front. With a soldierly rush the 53rd Foot under Colonel English mounted the breach, and swept in two columns through the town. Of the two thousand who had thought to hold it, nearly half were slain or taken prisoners, for Grant's cavalry, guarding the main outlets, caught up those who got away from the British bayonets. Six guns fell into the victors' hands. This piece of dashing soldiership, which checked betimes the gathering of hostile bands on the left bank of the Ganges between Cawnpore and Fathigarh, cost the winners no more than two slain and nineteen wounded.*

The same day, the 23rd, was signalized by the last of several victories won by Franks in his upward march from the southern border of Oudh. On the 19th that brilliant officer had crossed the border from Singramau at the head of six thousand troops, half of whom were Gorkhas from Nipál under their own brave leader, Palwán Singh. Strong in guns—eighteen light and two heavy—Franks could only muster sixty-three horsemen, of whom twenty-five were mounted soldiers of the 10th Foot. His aim was to attack and rout in detail the force which Mohammad Hasan was employed in massing around Chánda. Learning that half of that leader's twenty thousand men were still some miles away from Chánda, Franks pushed on to that place. After a careful reconnaissance, his troops moved forward in fighting array over the breadth of jungle and tall maize that served to shelter their advance. The fire of his skirmishers soon forced an answer from the enemy's guns. At length the contiguous columns unfolded out into the long thin steel-pointed line that seldom threatens mischief in vain. In its front, behind a long row of hillocks, lay the village of Chánda, flanked by a large mud fort and a walled *sarai*, round both of which ran a ditch and breastwork armed with a battery of six guns. Following swiftly behind the skirmishers and light guns, our soldiers drove the foe in ever-quickening flight out of the intrenchments, through the village into the dense thickets bordering the plain beyond. Every gun was taken. The few cavalry used their sabres to good purpose, and deadly was the grape which Major Cotter's guns poured again and again into the flying masses.

Three miles beyond Chánda the pursuers halted. In the course of the afternoon Franks marched a few miles farther leftward on the road to Hamírpur. Still no enemy appeared. It was near sunset when Mohammad Hasan's array grew visible in front of the British left. With a swift change of its own front our line

* Trotter.

went forward to grapple with the new foe. His right soon broken
by a murderous fire from our guns and rifles, the Názim was not
more successful in his attempt to turn the British right. A
timely charge of Gorkhas soon cleared the mango-groves in their
front, and sent the last of the enemy flying in disorder back to
Wári, whence they had come. Only the darkness and the pace at
which they fled saved their guns from capture, and themselves
from utter ruin.*

The next day both armies halted; Franks waiting for his
baggage, the rebels drawing together for their next move. Cut off
from the straight road back to Lucknow, they might still succeed
in holding the strong jungle pass and fort of Badáyan against all
assailants. But the Názim had found his match. Too late he
discovered that Frank's feint upon Wári had screened the sudden
march of troops and baggage towards Badáyan. Master of the
pass and fort by the evening of the 21st of February, Franks
halted the next day in hopes of being strengthened by a body of
horse from Imhór. Meanwhile the Názim was taking up a new
position at Bádsháhganj, two miles beyond Sultánpur. What
with fugitives from Chánda and mutineers from all the neighbourhood, he mustered an army twenty-five thousand strong, with a
battery of twenty-five guns. Against his eleven hundred horsemen Franks could still set only a few score volunteers and
irregulars, for the two hundred and fifty fresh sabres were yet
many miles away when he marched out to battle on the 23rd.

Beyond a deep winding ravine that ran down to the Gúmti
stretched the enemy's array along the plain that parted Sultánpur
from Bádsháhganj. Their left rested on the Sultánpur bazaar,
their centre behind some ruined police lines, their right on the
village and strong-built *sarai* of Bádsháhganj, behind a range of
low hillocks. A strong battery guarded the road through their
centre from Sultánpur to Lucknow. Six guns were posted about
the *sarai* and village, three in a village on the extreme left. It
was a strong position, to carry which without heavy loss craved
wary generalship; but Franks proved equal to the need. A well-
planned reconnaissance showed him a way of turning the enemy's
right. A skilful movement brought his troops unhurt, well-nigh
unseen, to a spot where the heavy guns could pass the ravine in
safety. Once round the enemy's flank, the British general might
count on an easy victory. Swinging their left more and more
forward across the enemy's line of retreat his troops bore steadily

* Trotter.

down, like the rollers of a storm-ridden sea, on the flank and rear of an outwitted, a vainly-resisting foe. A brave stand amidst the heavy guns of the central battery checked for a moment their destroying onset; but a few minutes later the rebel gunners lay dead or wounded around their captured guns, while the bulk of Mohammad Hasan's infantry were flying in utter rout across the ravine. The rest with three guns held out a little longer by Sultánpur until two Gorkha regiments drove them also away from their artillery and the field.

Matheson's Horse and the mounted volunteers with a few of Middleton's guns did their best to harass and cut up the flying foe. Of the rebel guns only four got clear away, and among some hundreds of the slain was the son of Mohammad Hasan. This brilliant day's work, which left the victors free to march on to Lucknow, had cost them only eleven men. The whole British loss in the battles of the 19th and the 23rd comprised but two slain and sixteen wounded, a result mainly due to the tactical skill of a leader who had made his mark in the battles of the Panjáb.*

On the 1st of March Franks halted at Salimpur, eighteen miles from Lucknow. That day's progress had been enlivened by a daring charge of a hundred Sikh Horse under Captain Aikman on about seven hundred horse and foot with two guns, aided by the fire from a neighbouring fort. In spite of such odds the guns were taken, a hundred of the rebels slain, and the rest sent flying across the Gúmti. Four days later Franks' column lay encamped before Lucknow, having stormed the fort of Daurára on its way. Among the few wounded in this sharp little affair was Lieutenant Innes of the Engineers, who, in the battle of Sultánpur, had dashed ahead of our skirmishers at a gun still held by the retreating rebels, had shot down the gunner, whose match was already near the touchhole, and amidst a shower of matchlock balls, had kept back the remaining gunners until his own men could hurry up to his aid. For this piece of fortunate daring he received the well-earned honour of a Victoria Cross.

Meanwhile some two hundred and fifty seamen of the *Pearl* frigate under Captain Sotheby had steamed up the Gágra north-westward to Naurain, twenty miles from Faizabád, a former capital of Oudh, lying seventy miles eastward of Lucknow. Disembarking on the 20th of February, they marched inland to attack two forts which guarded the road to Faizabád. Colonel Rowcroft

* Trotter ; Chambers.

with two thousand Nipálese joined in the fray. In less than an hour the enemy saved themselves by a hurried flight, leaving their guns and ammunition in the victors' hands.

A few days later our Nipálese ally, who had taken his time in marching up from Gorákpur, sent some of his troops, under Brigadier Macgregor, to capture the little fort of Birozpur near Faizabad. It was a very "hedgehog of a fortification," as Lieutenant Sankey afterwards described a stronghold only sixty feet square. What seemed at first a mere clump of bamboos proved to be a work combining the twofold strength of a mud fort and a Burman stockade. Behind the outermost line of bamboos ran a deep ditch; behind that came another belt of tall bamboos, screening another ditch, behind which rose a mud wall fifteen feet high, very thick at bottom and loopholed at the top for musketry, with round bastions at each corner. After a vain attempt to carry by assault a place defended by about thirty men, Captain Holland at length got one of his six-pounders across the outer ditch into a good position for breaching the wall. Numbers and perseverance in due time unrolled the hedgehog. A small breach offered a perilous opening through which Sankey forced his way. The Gorkhas, who had fought like heroes under Jang Bahádur's own eyes and lost heavily in storming the stockades, scrambled after him as fast as they could climb; and erelong the thirty-one brave defenders lay dead within their ruined lair.[*]

On the 5th of March the leading division of Jang Bahádur's force, nearly four thousand strong with thirteen guns, attacked the remnants of the Názim's twice-beaten army at the Kándu stream. The enemy, who still numbered four thousand with only one gun, were strongly posted behind ravines and jungle. After a few rounds from his own guns, General Kharak Bahádur slipped his sturdy infantry at the foe. Erelong the latter were flying through the jungle, hard pressed by the pursuing Gorkhas, who exacted a bloody reckoning with their rifles and "kukris," or hunting-knives, for their own trifling losses.

Westward of the Jamna several columns of troops from Bombay and Madras were sweeping in February through the disordered states and provinces of Málwa, Ságar, Rájputána, and Bundalkhand. From Nasirabad a serviceable force of more than six thousand men with thirty guns was preparing to march under General Roberts on the rebellious town of Kotah, whose loyal Rajah was besieged in his own capital by the Sepoys who had

* Trotter; Chambers.

been concerned in the murder of Major Burton and his sons. Before the end of March the Kotah rebels had been driven out of all their defences with the loss of fifty guns. General Whitlock's Madras column, after pacifying the country around Jabalpur, was about to pursue its march north-eastward through the troubled districts of Bundalkhand. In the country around Rewah and Nagódh, whose chiefs had stood faithful amidst strong temptations to revolt, the native troops raised by Captain Osborne and drilled into decent order by Colonel Hinde had in two months taken six forts, forty-two guns or mortars, and a host of prisoners; had disarmed, in short, a strong rebellion, re-established the police, the post-houses, and made travelling safe between Rewah and Jabalpur. Such results, achieved mainly by one or two bold Englishmen with the smallest means, richly deserved the warm thanksgivings with which Lord Canning recounted them in the *Gazette.**

About thirty miles east of Ságar lay the strong fortress of Garakót, which forty years before had defied the pounding of twenty-eight siege-guns backed by an army of eleven thousand men. Placed between two rivers that served for moats, its thick stone walls were further guarded by dense jungle and a chain of villages held by bodies of mutineers. Before this stronghold Sir Hugh Rose presented himself on the 10th of February, at the head of one of his brigades; the other under Brigadier Stuart being employed elsewhere. That evening his troops had gained a footing close to the walls, from which the enemy tried in vain to dislodge them during the night. Next morning he made a strong reconnaissance, driving the rebels back from their outposts and filling their places with his own men. Scared by movements which threatened to cut off their retreat, and dismayed by the marvellous shooting of Lieutenant Strutt's guns, the enemy that night stole away from a stronghold which Sir Hugh's weak force could not else have taken without heavy bloodshed. Early in the morning a troop of the 14th Dragoons and one of Haidarábád Horse followed the flying Sepoys beyond the Biás, cutting them down by scores while daylight lasted.†

On learning that Whitlock had set out from Jabalpur, Sir Hugh advanced northwards into the highland district of Shahgarh, whose rebellious Rajah had thus far successfully braved his fate. With his one brigade Sir Hugh attacked and drove some five thousand rebels, after a sharp fight on the 3rd of March,

---

* Trotter ; Chambers.   † Trotter ; Malleson.

through the strong pass of Madanpur. Owing to the panic caused by this fresh defeat a number of forts, towns, and fortified passes, including the strong pass of Máltún and the rock-fortress of Tál-Bahat, fell without a struggle into the victors' hands. By the 10th of March, Sir Hugh's guns proclaimed the hoisting of the British flag on the strong fort of Maraura, only twenty-five miles from the blood-recking citadel of Jhánsi. Meanwhile, on the 6th of March, Sir Hugh's trusty lieutenant, Brigadier Stuart, had forced his way through thick jungle up an intrenched hill into a walled garden lying near the commanding fortress of Chandairi, on the left bank of the Betwa.

On this great stronghold, the centre of a district once ruled from Gwáliár, Stuart presently turned his guns to such purpose that an assault was delivered on the 17th. In a twinkling the 25th Bombay Sepoys and the 86th Foot were pouring through a breach in the sandstone walls, while the enemy promptly availed themselves of an unguarded outlet to escape for the most part from impending doom. In the front rank of the stormers moved the political agent, Captain Keatinge, who had won a name for special daring in the fight of the 6th. Leaving one of Sindhia's officers in charge of the captured fort, Stuart resumed his march northwards to Jhánsi.*

While all eyes were still turning eagerly towards Lucknow, and Lord Canning was overlooking the course of events from his temporary abode at Allahábád, bodies of rebels in Oudh and Rohilkhand kept plundering towns and villages, making raids on weakly-guarded posts, and otherwise daring their fate at British hands. Ever watchful for the safety of Kamáon, Colonel M'Causland on the 3rd of March had despatched two hundred Gorkhas, with two hill-guns, under Captain Baugh to drive some thousands of rebels out of Sitaganj. Only the tail of them, however, were caught next morning, for the main body had retired betimes with their guns to a position safe from present attack.

At Gorakpur on the 5th the rebels became the assailants. Ten or twelve thousand Sepoys and Irregulars, led by the oft-beaten Mohammad Hasan and some other chiefs who still hoped for victory or despaired of pardon, attacked Colonel Rowcroft, whose little force of fourteen hundred men included two hundred of Sotheby's Blue-jackets and as many of volunteer horse. The assailed had but four guns against the enemy's twelve. Four hours' fighting ended in a signal victory for the fewer numbers.

* Trotter ; Malleson.

Chased seven miles back to their intrenchments, the enemy lost several hundred men and eight of their guns. The moral effect of such a victory was soon to be weakened by Colonel Millman's forced retreat upon Azimgarh, where Wynyard, of the Civil Service, had long maintained the same bold front he had first displayed at Gorakhpur. On the 22nd of March, Millman led a small force of English, Gorkhas, and Madrassies with two guns against a body of insurgents, chiefly of the Dánápur Brigade, posted in mango-groves near Atraulia. These were scattered at the first onset, but soon the word came that thousands of Kúnwar Singh's men were close at hand. Millman declined to follow the bolder example set by Vincent Eyre. His men fell back upon their former camp, erelong upon Azimgarh itself. A panic among the camp-followers crowned the day's mishaps with the loss of many tents and much baggage. Emboldened by their cheap success the rebels for a few days invested Azimgarh, and even talked of marching on Banáras.*

Another mishap occurred about the same time within thirty miles of Allahábád. Throughout this rebellion, as in the Sikh wars, nothing was more remarkable than the number o guns brought out against our troops. They seemed to start up every-where, like Jason's crop of armed men. Not a fort, however small, but had its fair complement. Not an armed band, however motley, how often soever routed, but still managed to confront or check its pursuers with a fresh array of guns. Some of these were mere tubes of wood clamped with rings of iron, fit only to fire a few rounds ; others, of brass or iron, had been wrought by native workmen careless of the nice adjustments, the evenness, and the finish which science and long training alike demand. Others again were old pieces rummaged out of odd corners and trimmed up into some poor show of fitness for present use. The remainder, mostly of modern date and choice workmanship, had either fallen at first into rebel hands, or been recovered and patched up anew after their English captors had left them spiked, or buried them out of the way. That almost every batch of armed rebels should have guns of some kind came to be a thing of course; but the fact of a hostile band moving about with six field pieces towards the end of March, 1858, within easy reach of Allahábád, proved an unwelcome surprise for the two or three hundred troops whom a certain magistrate had taken out with two guns on the road to Gopiganj. As the men passed on after

* Trotter ; Keene.

their promised prey, the jungle in front suddenly grew alive with rebels, and the shot from their six guns came bounding into the pursuers' ranks. In an hour's time the magistrate's party had lost so many killed or wounded that nothing remained for them but a swift retreat.*

By that time the last great stronghold of rebellion in Upper India had fallen to our arms. The British Fabius had dealt a blow so crushing that few cared to ask whether it might not have been struck sooner. On the 2nd of March Sir Colin Campbell with the van of his fine army passed near Alambágh on the way to his old camping-ground at the Dil-Khushá. Four strong divisions of infantry, including that of Franks', two good brigades of Sir Hope Grant's cavalry, three splendid brigades of artillery under Sir Archdale Wilson, and one of Engineers, made up an army of twenty-five thousand men, two-thirds of whom were British-born. Outram, of course, commanded the first infantry division, which included the heroes of so many bloody fights between Fathipur and Lucknow—Neill's own Fusiliers, the 78th Highlanders, and Brasyer's Sikhs. To the second division, under General Lugard, belonged the 93rd Highlanders and the 4th Panjáb Rifles. Conspicuous among the regiments of Walpole's division were the 1st Bengal Fusiliers and the 2nd, or Green's, Panjáb Infantry. The warworn 9th Lancers, Hodson's swarthy horse, and the dashing volunteer cavalry formed the pick of Hope Grant's powerful array. The Engineer Brigade might well be proud of such a leader as Robert Napier. In the long roll of battery-commanders the names of Turner, Tombs, Olpherts, Remmington, Middleton, Bishop, recalled many a great deed done before Delhi, or on the way to Lucknow, by the soldiers of an arm renowned for matchless services in every field. Major Henry Norman, the Adjutant-General, had won no small distinction during the siege of Delhi. As Chief of the Staff, General Mansfield was in his right place. Dr. Brown, the Superintending Surgeon; Major Johnson, the Assistant Adjutant-General; Captain FitzGerald, of the Commissariat; Captain Allgood, the Quartermaster-General, were all officers of known worth in their several lines. Joti Parsád himself, the great contractor, came over from Agra to supply the means of feeding and moving Sir Colin's troops.

After a sharp skirmish, in which the enemy lost a gun, Campbell's force got firmly planted around the Dil-Khushá, its right resting on the Gúmti, its advanced pickets holding the Dil-Khushá on

* Trotter.

its right, the Mohammad-Bágh on its left front. Both points were strengthened with heavy guns, which kept down the fire from a line of outworks along the canal. The next two days were spent in bringing up the remainder of the troops, guns, and stores of all kinds from the rear. Colonel Campbell's cavalry brigade guarded the left of the camp, and scoured the country in front of the Alambágh. Hodson's ubiquitous troopers kept diligent watch towards the fort of Jalálabád beyond the British left. On the 5th General Franks, true to the day appointed, was ready to fill up the gap which Outram's march across the Gúmti would leave on the morrow in Campbell's line.[*]

With the morning of the 6th began the turning movement which Sir Colin had rightly entrusted to the foremost soldier in his army, the first deliverer of Lucknow, the stubborn defender of the Alambágh. While the Commander-in-Chief prepared to crash his way forward through a triple line of works held by a foe at once strong and resolute, his trusty lieutenant was to press onward up the left bank of the Gúmti, to block the way of escape on that side of the great city, and to storm or rake with his heavy guns the eastern and northern faces of the enemy's works.

It was no light task indeed that awaited the powerful Army of Oudh. Whatever a brave, resolute, and cunning foe could do to strengthen a strong position, had been done by the seventy or eighty thousand Sepoys, volunteers, and armed retainers, whom national pride, fanaticism, or hope of plunder, had rallied to the colours of the manly-hearted Queen Regent, Hazrat-Mahal, or to the green flag of her suspected rival, the Maulvi of Faizabád. Besides the natural strength of a large city full of narrow streets, tall houses, and great palace-squares, each forming a separate stronghold, its defenders had gained ample time to repair past damages and to throw up new defences at points that seemed open to future attack. The canal itself formed a wet ditch to the outermost line of works whose kernel consisted of the cluster of courts and buildings known as the Kaisar-Bágh. A fortified rampart stretched along the inner side of the canal. The midmost line of works covered the great pile of the Imámbára, the Mess-House, and the Moti-Mahal. Each of these lines ended at the river, which swept sharply southward as it passed the neighbourhood of the dome-crowned Imámbára. Their inner flanks rested on the streets of a crowded city, through which no general would choose to force his way. Outside the canal, in the

---

[*] Trotter ; Chambers ; Malleson.

bend between it and the river, stood, amidst fair gardens and stately groves, the building once known as Constantia, and since called after its founder La Martinière. From this post the rebels for the first few days kept up a fire not altogether harmless. But it was not Sir Colin's cue to take one step forward until Outram had fairly turned the defences of the canal.

On the 6th of March, therefore, Sir James led Walpole's infantry, a picked brigade of horse under Hope Grant, and five batteries of guns under Brigadier Wood, across two bridges which Napier's engineers had fashioned out of beer-casks, ropes, and planking in two or three days. That night he rested near the racecourse, on the left bank of the river. The next day was spent in repelling the enemy's attacks upon Outram's pickets. On the 8th his men were employed in preparing batteries for the heavy guns sent over that morning for his use. The dawn of the 9th was ushered in by the thunders of a crushing fire poured into the enemy's works at the Chakar Kothi, or Yellow House, from eight heavy guns and three howitzers. Erelong the Chakar Kothi was stormed by a part of Walpole's infantry aided by a few of Wood's guns. Pressing hotly on the heels of a retreating foe, Outram carried with ease the strong walled inclosure of the Pádshah-Bágh or King's Garden, and began with his heavy guns to rake the lines of works behind the Martinière. .

Meanwhile, from the opposite bank of the river, Sir Colin's heavy guns and mortars kept pounding into the defences in their front. Peel's rockets scared the rebels out of corners still spared by his shells. The storming of the Yellow House became the signal for Lugard's advance on the first line of works. Without firing a shot, the Highlanders and Panjábis of Hope's brigade stormed the defences of the Martinière; then with another magnificent rush they clomb up the lofty ramparts lining the canal. Their steps were quickened by the sight of an English officer waving his sword atop of the rampart, a mark for the muskets of many foes. It was the bold Lieutenant Butler of the Bengal Fusiliers, who had swum across the river to acquaint Hope's skirmishers with Outram's success in turning the first line of works.[*]

That evening the line of the Canal as far as Banks's House was safe in British hands. The next day was spent by Lugard's column in battering and storming Banks's House and in making ready for a flank march to the left of the Kaisar-Bágh, while Outram was bringing his guns and mortars to play upon the same

---

[*] Trotter ; Chambers ; Innes.

post from his camp across the river, and Hope Grant's horsemen were busy scouring the plain between the river and the old cantonments. On the 11th, from both flanks of the besieging army a furious storm of shot and shell crashed down on the remaining defences of the doomed city. The Sikandar-Bágh, scene of so much slaughter in the past November, was carried easily that morning. Other buildings to the right were won as swiftly by storm or simple cannonade. One massive pile of buildings, known as the Begam Kothi or Begam's Palace, held out for several hours under a merciless pounding from Peel's howitzers. While Napier was yet watching for the moment when bayonets might take the place of cannon, Sir Colin and some of his officers were engaged in the less congenial task of exchanging courtesies with Jang Bahádur, who had just brought his Gorkhas, some days after time, into the field.

In honour of his coming, Campbell had mustered a choice array of officers brilliant in scarlet, blue, white, and gold; the whole forming a strange contrast, whether to the grim realities of the fight in front, or to the natural tastes of the war-furrowed, mild-looking veteran, who, in the splendour of an uniform tight-fitting and unbearably hot, stood uneasily awaiting the approach of his tardy visitor. At last, amidst the clang of welcoming music, the Nipáleso warrior drew near; his dark face showing dim through the blaze of gorgeous apparel, brightly-waving plumes, and lavish jewellery—his train of followers only less gorgeous than himself. While the leading actors in this scene were politely asking through the interpreter after each other's health and wellbeing, a strange voice was suddenly heard from outside the circle. It was soon followed by the war-grimed figure of Hope Johnstone, bearer of happy tidings from the front. As soon as he announced the storming of the Begam Kothi, all further forms and ceremonies were laid aside. In another moment Sir Colin Campbell and Jang Bahádur were grasping each other's hands and making up with friendly smiles for their want of a common language. Every one looked happy, and so the meeting came to an end. Pleased to hear that some of his Gorkhas had shared in that day's success, the Nipálese chief went off to take the place allotted him in Campbell's further proceedings.*

The fight whose issue had been thus opportunely announced, was described by Campbell himself as " the sternest struggle which occurred during the siege." After a fierce bombardment

* Trotter ; Russell's " Diary."

of eight or nine hours, ending in a practicable breach, Napier resolved to carry the Begam's Palace by storm. About 4 P.M. Adrian Hope led forth a column of the 93rd Highlanders, 4th Panjáb Rifles, and a thousand Gorkhas to the attack. The Highlanders mounted the breach first, but their comrades were close behind. At every turn some fresh work had to be carried, some fresh group of rebels to be overpowered. But the dread bayonet clove its way through all barriers. Erelong the whole pile of buildings, itself a powerful fortress, bastioned, loopholed, filled with men and guns, begirt with tall ramparts and a broad deep ditch, had been swept clean of its living garrison. Of the rebel dead five hundred bodies were afterwards counted up. The victory would have been cheaply won but for the death of the far-famed Hodson, who, having joined the fight as a volunteer, fell shot through the liver by one of the Sepoys lurking in an outer room of the great courtyard. Some of his troopers cried that night like children over their dying hero, whom those rough Eastern warriors had loved and worshipped as their ideal of perfect soldiership, the model captain of light horse, the matchless swordsman, the wise yet daring counsellor, the born leader of men, who would have followed him anywhither to the death.*

" I trust I have done my duty," were the last words which the dying hero spoke to his sorrowing friend Napier. On the evening of the 12th, the day of Hodson's death, his body was buried in the grounds of the Martinière. At the moment when it was lowered into the grave, Campbell himself, the veteran Commander-in-Chief, burst into tears over the loss of " one of the finest officers in the army," the man whom Robert Napier was proud to call friend, to whom Montgomery could find no equal for his rare combination of talent, courage, coolness, and unerring judgement. It had been alleged that Hodson was cruel beyond most men, that he loved plunder yet more than fighting, and that proved peculation had caused his removal from political service in the Panjáb. But Dr. William Russell, the war correspondent of the *Times*, bore trustworthy witness to his " humane and clement disposition ; " nor did John Lawrence himself plead more boldly than Hodson for the need of a general amnesty after the fall of Delhi. His alleged thirst for plunder is belied by page after page of his published letters, by the testimony of those who knew him best, and by the circumstances which compelled his widow to accept from the Compassionate Fund the means of paying her passage home. As for the

---

* Trotter ; Russell ; Hodson's " Life and Letters."

causes which reduced him from the command of the Guide Corps to the rank and pay of a subaltern in the 1st Bengal Fusiliers, it is enough here to say that a careful scrutiny, conducted by Major Reynell Taylor, issued in a Report which entirely acquitted Hodson of anything like foul play. On the strength of this very document General Anson at once took him by the hand, and started him afresh on the path which duty and ambition alike urged a man of his rare brains, energies, and hardihood to follow out.

Outram also had been gaining ground this day. While his heavy batteries pounded the Mess-House and the Kaisar-Bágh, his infantry flanked by the horse swept onwards through the suburbs on that side of the Gúmti, seized a mosque commanding the iron bridge above the Residency, and drove the enemy as far as the stone bridge by the Machhi-Bháwan. At this point Outram sounded a halt. Strengthening his hold on the iron bridge, he resolved to await the coming of some more heavy guns, which might help in raking the defences of the Kaisar-Bágh. On the 13th these new allies spoke to such effect that the enemy, placed between two raging fires, fled despairing on the morrow from their last great stronghold in Lucknow. In all these movements on the left bank of the river Outram's loss, apart from the cavalry, amounted only to twenty-six slain, a hundred and thirteen wounded.

Meanwhile, on his own side, Sir Colin had been steadily tearing his way to the heart of the rebel defences. On the 12th Franks's division relieved Lugard's. While Napier's sappers kept blowing up the lines of building between the Begam Kothi and the Kaisar-Bágh, the infantry with some of the mortars moved gradually forward, and a strong battery of heavy guns thundered against the fair-fronted Imámbára, the great Moslem cathedral of Lucknow. At last, on the morning of the 14th, this light and graceful monument of Moorish art was carried with a rush by Brigadier Russell's infantry. A minute later Brasyer's Sikhs had followed the flying Pandies right through the open gateway of the Kaisar-Bágh. Other troops came up close behind the Sikhs; but their help was hardly needed, for no stand was made save where a knot of rebels, driven into a corner, had to sell their lives as dearly as they could.

Still the conquerors pressed forward, the more eagerly for that last success. One after another the Mess-House, the Téri-Kothi, the Moti-Mahal, and the Chatar Manzil, all scenes of hard fighting in the past November, fell into their hands. It was a hard day's work for all concerned; but the elation of repeated victories upheld them marvellously to the end. That evening Campbell might fairly deem himself master of Lucknow, might well be proud of a conquest achieved on the whole so easily, at a cost of only nine hundred killed and wounded, over an enemy of thrice his own numbers, intrenched along a range of massive palaces and wide-walled courts whose like could hardly be found in Europe; every weak point strengthened to the utmost, each outlet carefully guarded by works that displayed a marvellous industry and no common skill.[*] But for the enemy's comparative weakness in guns and ordnance stores—they had only a hundred guns and mortars, while Campbell's siege-train alone numbered nearly ninety—the siege might have lasted for weeks instead of days; and Sir Colin, balked in his efforts to sap and batter a passage for his splendid infantry, might have been driven to avoid the dangers of a long delay by means involving a fearful outlay of precious blood. Had the rebels fought with all their olden spirit under generals fitter to cope with ours, the flank march across the Gúmti could hardly have proved so swift, so decisive a success; nor would British daring on that eventful Sunday have been rewarded by the bloodless capture of the Kaisar-Bágh.[†]

On the scenes that followed the entrance of our troops into those stately palaces, where untold treasures of Eastern art, luxury, and magnificence lay mingled here and there with heaps of weapons, clothing, accoutrements, and such-like traces of Sepoy tenancy, the historian cannot touch, however lightly, without a blush for the Vandalism which war too often brings in its train. When revenge had sated itself with hacking and hewing at rare wood-work, statues, pictures, mirrors, chandeliers, divans, at whatever costly or beautiful thing met its glance in that long succession of halls and corridors, the inevitable thirst for plunder began to riot in its turn amidst a world of treasures hitherto overlooked. Shawls, laces, pearls of price, rare broidery in gold and silver, caskets heaped with gems and jewellery, vessels of jade and agate, swords, pistols, saddle-cloths blazing with gold and jewels, all the rich spoils of princely zánánas, the long-stored relics of lordly households, of chiefs erewhile renowned in arms or council, were rummaged, tossed about, scrambled for by successive groups of curious or greedy warriors, whilst a host of camp-followers rushed in to gather up their shares of meaner, bulkier, or less attractive spoil.[‡]

[*] Sir C. Campbell's Despatch.   [†] Trotter; Chambers; Russell.
[‡] Trotter.

But the full fruits of victory were still to reap. The beaten
foe had to be cleared out of their last refuge within the city. On
the 16th of March, Outram carried one of his brigades across
the Gúmti to the Sikandar-Bágh, and, strengthened by two more
regiments, pressed on to attack the Residency and seize the iron
bridge. Easily successful in both attempts, he lost no time in
carrying the Machhi-Bháwan and a group of buildings hard by.
The way of escape by the stone bridge being at length cut off by
Hope Grant's cavalry and Walpole's foot, the enemy sped up the
right bank of the river; some making straight for Rohilkhand,
others halting for a last stand in the Músa-Bágh, another of those
walled gardens that everywhere skirted the city. Meanwhile,
another body of rebels made a bold but fruitless dash upon the
Alambágh, where Franklin's small garrison stood quite ready to
receive them.

Letting the Músa-Bágh alone for the present, the British generals busied themselves for the next two days in driving the enemy
out of their last posts within Lucknow, and in bridling with a
firm hand the lawless greed of their own followers. Stern edicts
were issued against further plundering; pickets posted about the
city compelled many a native soldier and camp-follower to leave
his bundle of forbidden booty in their charge; all native soldiers
not on duty were to be confined to camp until further orders, and
commanding officers were held accountable for any acts of violence or indiscipline done by their men. To turn Lucknow into a
desert was no part of Sir Colin's plan. Every citizen who had
not borne arms against him was invited under a reasonable pledge
to return to his former home and occupation. Meanwhile, Outram
steadily clove his way through the north-western quarter of the
city. At the same time Jang Bahádur, having dislodged the
rebels from the neighbourhood of the Alambágh, advanced along
the southern side of Lucknow, clearing the neighbourhood of the
Hazrat-Ganj, the great street which led from the Char-Bágh
bridge up to the ruined Residency.

The movements of the Nipálese Chief hastened, if they did
not alone ensure, the deliverance of two English ladies from the
doom which four months ago had overtaken their fellow-sufferers.
Enraged at the safe withdrawal of the Lucknow garrison in
November, the insurgents had murdered all their English captives
save the sister of Sir Mountstuart Jackson and the widow of Mr.
Orr. After four months of sickening suspense, these two were
now rescued from further peril by Captain McNeil and Lieutenant

Bogle, who, with a small party of Gorkhas, hurried through the city to the spot pointed out by their friendly guide. In a minute the lorn pair, hard to recognize in their Eastern garb, were borne away from a neighbourhood still beset with armed foes. A mob of ruffians once threatened to stay the passage of their palanquin. But the foremost soon fell back before the Englishman's pointed revolver and the bayonets of his fearless escort. At length, all perils left behind, the rescued ladies entered the Gorkha camp, to enjoy at their leisure the full bliss of recovered freedom, and the company of their fellow-countrymen, after the bitter sufferings of nine months past.*

On the 19th of March a combined movement was made, under Outram, against the 5,000 rebels still intrenched within the Mússa-Bágh. The task allotted him was soon accomplished. Position after position fell with hardly a struggle, until the enemy were sent flying in headlong rout before the sweeping rush of Colonel Campbell's horsemen. Of their twelve guns two were at once abandoned, four were taken by Outram's pursuing force, and the other six fell into the hands of Campbell's lancers, who kept up the chase for several miles. But two or three hundred horsemen could not annihilate so many thousand Sepoys fleeing through cornfields, enclosed gardens, and ground cut up by ravines. Most of the fugitives, therefore, got away to brew fresh mischief anon in other places.

One of the rebel leaders, the Maulvi of Faizabád, was still lurking in the heart of the city with a few hundred of his bravest followers. On the 21st, Sir Edward Lugard was sent to dislodge him. A stout resistance was at last overcome by a successful charge of the 93rd Foot, who took three guns and slew more than a hundred of the flying foe. But, in spite of a keen pursuit, the Maulvi himself again made good his escape. By that time the few small parties who had lingered in odd corners of the city had been routed out and slain or scattered afar. Two days later, Hope Grant broke up a body of insurgents, twenty miles away on the Sitapur road, with heavy slaughter and the seizure of more guns.

With this last achievement ends the reconquest of Lucknow, and the short but memorable career of the army of Oudh. The last great centre of armed rebellion, eastward of the Jamna, had fallen wholly into Sir Colin's power. Paralyzed by the loss of Lucknow, by the defection or the quarrels of their foremost leaders, one of whom, Mán Singh, was already making terms with

* Trotter ; Chambers ; Malleson.

his former masters, the insurgents of Oudh could henceforth be attacked and crushed in detail by smaller columns moving each under its own-commander. In the great city itself was left a powerful garrison under the fit command of Sir Hope Grant, himself subordinate to Chief Commissioner Outram. Lugard's division, thenceforth known as the Azimgarh Field Force, hurried off southwards to deal with the rebels who, under Kúnwar Singh, were still threatening Azimgarh. Walpole led his own brave soldiers northwards into Rohilkhand. Jang Bahádur, with the pick of his Nipálese, marched off to Allahábád, where the Governor-General was waiting to thank his magnificent ally for services which, though tardily accepted, and somewhat haltingly rendered, were destined to reap no grudging reward. The rest of the Nipálese army hastened to begin their march back to their native highlands beyond the sunstricken plains of Oudh.*

* Trotter ; Chambers ; Malleson.

NOTE.

In his concise and admirable Memoir, " Hodson, of Hodson's Horse," the Rev. George Hodson has, I think, succeeded in clearing his brother's fair fame from most, if not all, of the shadows which threatened to obscure it. Hodson's widow died last year, in poor circumstances, as I am informed, in the quarters assigned her by the Queen at Hampton Court.

CHAPTER IV.

EARLY in April Sir Colin Campbell paid one more flying visit to Allahábád and the Governor-General. All through the siege of Lucknow he and Lord Canning had held daily, almost hourly, talks together by means of the electric wire which, laid at first to the Alambágh, kept uncoiling itself with each fresh advance of Sir Colin's head-quarters. What came of that last meeting was soon to show itself in various ways. Lucknow indeed was safe in British keeping; but a trying hot-weather campaign had been made inevitable by past delays and by the flight of insurgent troops and leaders from the conquered city into the surrounding districts. The centre of resistance was now shifted from Lucknow to Baréli, where the ambitious Khán Bahádur Khán still held some kind of sway over all the disaffected classes in Rohilkhand. Round the green flag of the grey-haired pensioner were now mustering all who had shared the guilt, or resolved to share the fortunes, of the Nána of Bithúr, the Faizabád Maulvi, the Begam of Oudh, and Prince Firoz Shah of Delhi. The bulk of the Hindu Rohillas, however disinclined to the new rule, had hitherto found small encouragement to make head against the armed zeal of their Moslem neighbours. For many months past one of the fairest provinces in India had been given over to virtual anarchy, tempered here and there by the presence of Khán Bahádur's magistrates or his troops.

At last, however, the time had come for restoring the old order with the least possible delay. While Hope Grant's column was forcing the Begam and the Maulvi to quicken their flight across the Gágra, Rohilkhand became the field of movements, more or less successful, made by the war-hardened soldiers of Jones, Seaton, Walpole, and Campbell himself.

On the 17th of April Brigadier Jones crossed the Ganges below Hardwár, with three thousand good troops and fourteen guns. In four days he twice routed the rebels in the Bijnaur district with heavy loss in guns and men. Then hastening down to Muradábad, he brought that city once more under British rule. The able Collector of Bijnaur, Alexander Shakespeare, at once returned to the post from which events had reluctantly driven him ten months before. Earlier in the same month Seaton, from his post at Fathigarh, swooped down upon several thousand insurgents, at a place called Kankar, and scattered them with heavy slaughter and the loss of two guns. Walpole's column, starting from Lucknow on the 9th of April, and marching under hot suns, over a roadless country, met with a disastrous check on the 14th, before the mud walls of Rádamau. Not all the courage of his Sikhs and Highlanders availed to atone for their leader's rashness in hurling infantry against works hastily reconnoitred and unassailed by a single gun. A few hundred rebels beat them back with cruel slaughter, with the loss above all of their young brigadier, Adrian Hope. Too late the heavy guns were brought into play, and the enemy vanished during the night.[*]

Some days later, on the 22nd, Walpole took his revenge on a large body of rebels encamped at Sirsa, a few marches from Baréli. Their guns, their camp, fell into his hands. In wild haste they fled across the Rámganga, leaving the bridge of boats intact for Walpole's use. On his way towards Baréli Walpole was joined by the force which Campbell himself had led on the 18th out of Cawnpore. The two columns, about ten thousand strong, marched on together to Shahjahánpur, where the Maulvi, it was hoped, might stand at bay. But at the last moment that worthy had got away, with all his followers, from a place on which the Nána had but lately left his desolating mark. By the end of April the British colours were once more waving over the ruins of a cantonment wrested eleven months before by Sepoy treachery from British keeping. Baréli itself was still to take, but troops were closing round it from all sides. On the 2nd of May Brigadier Jones and Sir Colin Campbell began their march thither, the one southward from Muradábad, the other northward from Shahjahánpur.

Four days later Jones had just driven the rebel outposts back into Baréli, when he heard the guns of Campbell's column announcing its arrival on the other side of the city. As Campbell's infantry were marching through the suburbs on the day before, a sudden volley of matchlock-balls caused a moment's

* Trotter ; Chambers ; Russell.

wavering in their front ranks. Then from the neighbouring houses burst forth a body of fanatic Gházis, their waists girt in thick folds of green, their heads stooped behind small leather shields, their right arms brandishing the sharp, curved *talwár,* or native sword. With loud cries of *Din, Din, Bismillah,** they charged like angry bulls upon Walpole's men. Some of them even got behind the advancing 42nd, and but for the ready bayonets of the latter, Walpole himself and one or two other mounted officers would have been cut to pieces. In another minute a hundred and thirty-three Gházis lay dead amidst a score or so of wounded British.

Later in the day a sudden dash of insurgent horsemen on our rear threw into panic disorder the mass of servants, cattle, and camp-followers that formed the inevitable tail to Sir Colin's army. This onset duly repelled, the British General halted for that night on the plain outside the wood-fringed town of Baréli. On the morning of the 6th his heavy guns began playing upon various points in the city itself. This became the signal for Jones's advance on the other side. On the 7th of May Baróli was once more safe in British keeping. Plenty of guns and ammunition were found in its abandoned workshops and magazines. But the chief prize had slipped through Sir Colin's hands. The rebel leaders with the bulk of their followers had disappeared, some making off for Oudh, others gone to swell the force which, ever since the 3rd of May, had been besieging Colonel Hall's weak garrison in the Shahjahánpur Jail.†

Hardly had Campbell turned his back on Shahjahánpur, on his way to Baréli, when some eight thousand rebels with twelve guns attacked the garrison he had left behind him—a wing of the 82nd Foot with four guns and a few score of De Kantzow's Horse. Driving Hall's troops into the jail, they plundered the town, killed many of the chief citizens and turned their guns upon Hall's intrenched post. On the 8th of May Brigadier Jones, with a picked force of all arms, was hurried off from Baréli to Hall's relief. After a march that cost it many lives from sunstroke, the relieving column fought its way on the 11th into the still beleaguered jail. Four days later the baffled enemy, led by the Maulvi and the dauntless Begam, returned to the attack in numbers so great that Jones could do little more than hold his ground. To his aid

* *Din,* " the Faith "; *Bismillah,* "in Allah's name." That is, "For God and the Faith."

† Trotter; Chambers; Russell.

at last came Sir Colin himself on the 18th, driving the rebels before him towards their main stronghold at Mohamdi, on the Oudh frontier. Thither on the 22nd he followed them up. But again the Maulvi proved too quick for him. One or two half-dismantled forts and a few guns were all the trophies of Campbell's last success in that scorching month of May. Rohilkhand, however, had now been virtually reconquered, and many a war-spent soldier could take his hard-earned rest in some pleasant station of Upper India.*

Meanwhile Sir Hope Grant had not been idle in Oudh. Through the greater part of April his troops were marching hither and thither through a hostile country under a cruel sun, scattering the rebels in two or three encounters, and trying hard but vainly to overtake the Begam and her chief allies. In May he again moved out of Lucknow, destroying one or two jungle-forts, and dealing on the 12th a crushing blow at 17,000 followers of Beni Mádhu, a leading Tálukdár, who ventured to withstand him at Sirsi. On the 25th he again started in quest of that chieftain, who was said to be threatening the Cawnpore Road. Still failing to catch his prey, Sir Hope Grant returned with the bulk of his column to Lucknow. Once more, in the night of the 12th June, he led forth a strong brigade of horse, foot, and guns, to attack some 16,000 rebels strongly posted behind jungle at Nawábganj, on the Faizabád Road. Good generalship, backed by disciplined courage, ensured his troops a full if hard-won victory over a foe impelled to stouter resistance by the prayers, the promises, and the daring zeal of many hundred Gházis, to whom death in battle with the unbeliever was the surest passage into eternal bliss. Six guns were taken and 600 rebels slain; but thirty-three of our men died from sunstroke, and the heroic Begam was erelong rallying her broken forces for another stand upon the Gágra.†

One of her staunchest friends had by that time ceased from troubling his Farangi foes. Hunted from place to place by his keen pursuers, the Faizabád Maulvi, Ahmadullah Shah, turned his arms in the middle of June against the Rajah of Powain, who had given signs of forsaking a worsted cause. In the fight that ensued the Maulvi was shot dead. His head, cut off by the victorious Rajah, was sent off to the Commissioner of Shahjahán-pur; and the reward offered for the living rebel was paid over, not without demur, to the double-dealing trader in a harmless corpse. The death of a leader at once brave, able, and widely

---

* Trotter; Chambers; Russell.   † Trotter; Malleson; Chambers.

revered, did more than many defeats to hasten the collapse of a rebellion doomed to failure through the cowardice, the treachery, the weak or divided counsels of its chief promoters. Surrounded by curs like the Nána, by triflers like her paramour, Mámu Khan, the high-hearted Begam appealed in vain for help to her powerful neighbour Jang Bahádur, to her powerful countryman, the time-serving Mán Singh. One by one her old friends, her dearest hopes, were failing her. Still even at the end of June her means of resistance were not few. Thousands of armed rebels, with many guns, were lying massed around Sultánpur, or distributed among a cluster of jungle-fastnesses between the Gágra and the Gúmti.

The Gorakpur district was still infested by one of her boldest partisans, the oft-beaten Mohammad Hasan. During April, May, and June, his troops had several encounters with the small force commanded by Colonel Rowcroft, who invariably got the better of his assailants. On the 9th of June a few hundred soldiers and seamen of his brigade marched out under Major Cox, to attack the enemy in their favourite post at Amorah. Some brilliant fighting issued in the rebels' retreat to a safer lair. On the 18th a somewhat larger force set out to drive them yet further away. The heat was frightful; but nothing could check the headlong valour of Cox's heroes. Dashing with their guns across the waist-deep Gágra, they drove 4,000 rebels back for some four miles, and gave up the pursuit only when tired nature could do no more.[*]

There had been hard work also for Lugard's column, which left Lucknow about the end of March. Not before the 16th of April did it succeed in reaching Azimgarh, and scattering the rebels whom Lord Mark Kerr with a few hundred horse and foot had already taught to respect the prowess of British soldiers properly led. One body of insurgents commanded by the tameless Kúnwar Singh was brought to bay by Brigadier Douglas after a five days' hunt over a hundred miles, and driven with much slaughter on to Beriya in the Gházipur district. Still pressing on the enemy's heels, Douglas on the morrow dealt him another blow as he was crossing the Ganges. Safe for a while from his tired pursuers, the wounded old chief held his way towards Jagdispur, crushing on the 23rd a small force of Sikhs and English whom Captain Le Grand had brought out from Arah to intercept him. Once more was seen the spectacle of a small but well-appointed column flying in wild disorder, without its guns and baggage, before 2,000 beaten, worn, disheartened rebels, who had left their last guns on

[*] Trotter.

the other side of the river. In Le Grand's own regiment, the 35th Foot, a hundred men were killed or wounded out of 150 engaged.[*]

Douglas, however, was not far behind. By the beginning of May the whole of his column had reached Arah, ready in spite of the fierce heat to beat up the enemy's camp in the jungles of Jagdispur. On the 8th, Lugard himself, with the rest of his force, came in sight of the rebel outposts. After driving the enemy out of Jagdispur he followed them deeper and deeper into their forest haunts, smiting them hard at Dhúlipur and Chitaura with one part of his force; while Corfield's soldiers and seamen baffled their efforts to break through the opposite line of attack. But Lugard's work was not yet over. Like the toils of Sisyphus, it seemed to have no end. His brave soldiers fell fast from sunstroke and other forms of disease, or became helpless from sheer exhaustion. If the fearless Kúnwar Singh was dead at last, his brother Umar Singh still kept his followers together. Routed in one place to-day, they would turn up on the morrow ripe for mischief in another. Fighting, plundering, burning, now in large bands, anon in scattered parties, now hiding in the depths of a pathless jungle, anon carrying their ravages up to Arah or to Baksár, these desperate outlaws contrived for many weeks, with the aid of a faithful or frightened peasantry, to foil the watchfulness, elude the attacks, and overstrain the endurance of Lugard's seasoned troops. The last days of that fiery June found the men of the 84th Foot, in the words of Brigadier Douglas, "quite unfit for active service." They were so exhausted that they could neither eat nor sleep. Their comrades of the 10th were hardly in better plight. Lugard himself had to make his command over to the more enduring Douglas, who some months later, in more congenial weather, was to become master of a district cleared of rebels and scored through its diminished jungles with several broad military roads.[†]

During those months of hot weather, when the dry west wind blew like a fiery furnace over the plains of Upper India, and crashing storms tempered the moister heats of the Southern Provinces, there was little rest for our soldiers in other regions than Oudh, Bahár, and Rohilkhand. All about the Gangetic Doab bands of rebels came from time to time across bodies of troops commanded by Showers, Seaton, Riddell, or Carthew, each of whom dealt blows more fierce than fatal at his ubiquitous opponents. In the neighbourhood of Kotah General Roberts

[*] Trotter ; Chambers.   [†] Ibid.

found much employment during April and May in following up a beaten soldiery and restoring order under the Rajah's rule. In May the province of Nágpur was worried by bands of freebooters, who, headed by a few insurgent landowners, slew stray Englishmen, destroyed much property, plundered many villages, and, deep in the shelter of frequent woods, managed for a time to escape their doom. Like disturbances so harassed a part of the Nizam's country, that a small force was sent from Bombay to aid Sálar Jang in bridling his unruly Rohillas. On the Panjáb frontier General Cotton and Colonel Edwardes were out among the hills in April and May with about 4,000 men and twelve guns, enforcing anew the old lessons of order and obedience on certain tribes of aggressive mountaineers.

Whitlock's march through Bundelkhand, in concert with Sir Hugh Rose, was marked by a victory won on the 19th of April over the rebellious Nawáb of Banda, whose army, 7,000 strong, fled from the field after six hours' fighting, with a loss of 500 slain and seventeen guns, leaving the town of Banda and a palace full of treasure in the victors' hands. After some weeks' rest at Banda, Whitlock's column set out on the 2nd of June for Kirwi, which was occupied without a struggle on the 6th, the day after the two young Ráos or chiefs of that place had sought pardon for their late offences by yielding up their swords and themselves into Whitlock's hands. The mercy shown to those young descendants of Marátha Peshwas—these mere tools of older and craftier rebels—extended only to their lives, for the bulk of the enormous treasures found within their palace was awarded as prize to their nominal captors, the officers and men of Whitlock's force. Sir Hugh Rose, whose recent victories had cleared the way for Whitlock's advance to Kirwi, could obtain no share in the forfeit plunder for his own men.*

Meanwhile, in the Southern Marátha country, from Púna down to Sáwant-Wári and Belgaum, fresh stirrings of disaffection taxed the watchfulness of Colonel Le Grand Jacob and the civil officers under his control. At Kolápur, Jacob's head-quarters, all had been quiet since the disarming of the mutinous Sepoys in the previous August. But in the middle of May the country around Dhárwár was heaving with disorder; and the neighbouring Chief of Nargúnd had long been wavering in his allegiance to a Government which had forbidden him to adopt an heir, and reclaimed from some of his friends the lands which for many a year past they had

* Malleson; Chambers.

held without a question. Before the end of May the Rajah of
Nargúnd had sealed his open defiance of the British power by
the treacherous murder of Mr. Charles Manson, the new Political
Agent, who had set out from Belgaum in hopes of bringing the
refractory chief to reason. Unhappily for Manson, the Rajah saw
in him only a member of the Inám Commission, and therefore a
foe of whom he and his countrymen would be well rid. But
swift punishment overtook the murderer. While Hughes's column
of Madras troops attacked and stormed the fort of a rebel chief at
Kopaldrúg, Malcolm hastened with a few hundred horse and foot
and two guns against the defenders of Nargúnd. The town was
soon won, and on the 2nd of June Malcolm found himself master of
an empty fort, the strongest in that country. Caught on the
following night by Frank Souter of the Belgaum Police, the
fugitive Rajah was brought to trial and hanged at Belgaum upon
the 12th. His wife and mother had drowned themselves some
days before.*

But of all who marched and fought in that burning summer,
no troops did their work so brilliantly against enormous odds as
the little army which Sir Hugh Rose led from victory to victory
through the wooded highlands of Central India. In a former
chapter we left that army encamped before Jhánsi, in whose fort
the bloodstained Ráni had taken her stand in the midst of ten or
eleven thousand mutineers.

A dashing soldier and a bold diplomatist, Sir Hugh had lately
shown himself a skilful and resolute leader of the force entrusted
to his charge. On his way to attack Jhánsi his self-reliance was
sorely tested by an order from Sir Colin Campbell to turn aside
and hasten to the relief of a loyal Rajah whose stronghold was
besieged by a hostile force. Happily the Political Agent, Sir
Robert Hamilton, who had received a like order from Lord
Canning, saw the folly of obedience at such a time, and took
upon himself the responsibility of sanctioning Sir Hugh's advance
against Jhánsi.†

On the 25th of March Sir Hugh's two brigades entered on the
task of capturing a fortress rock-perched, granite-built, with walls
of vast thickness guarded by stone outworks of great strength and
skilful design, jagged with frequent embrasures, and specked with
tiers of loopholes; while all around these, save where the rock
rose sheer to westward out of the plain, ran a broad belt of city
girdled by massive, tall, bastioned walls, and covered at the

* Malleson ; Chambers.   † Malleson.

weakest points by a fortified mound and ditch. Woods, gardens, temples, and a ruined cantonment spread for some distance round this, the richest Hindu city, and the most important stronghold in Central India.   After a close reconnaissance, Sir Hugh selected a rocky ridge on the southern and a rocky knoll on the eastern side of the city as the best, if not the only possible spots for his breaching batteries.   His cavalry and light-horsed guns kept careful watch and ward around the city.

From the 26th to the 30th the British batteries kept up a damaging fire on the southern line of works, while parties of riflemen from behind their sandbags picked off the rebels moving about the parapets and embrasures.   In spite of a fierce and well-planned resistance, most of the enemy's guns on that side were at length disabled, their best gunners slain, the defences knocked out of shape; while a breach gaped visibly in the fortified mound. Taking counsel with his engineers, Sir Hugh resolved to carry the first line of defences in part by escalade, before his heavy batteries had spent all their powder and shot.   But a new enemy had to be encountered first : Tántia Topi, the Nána's kinsman, who had beaten Windham at Cawnpore, was hastening from Kálpi to the relief of Jhánsi at the head of more than twenty thousand men.   Leaving his heavy guns to play upon the Ráni's stronghold, Sir Hugh, with only fifteen hundred of all arms, prepared, on the 1st of April, to strike vigorously at his new assailant.   The enemy fought hard and long, but Rose at last turned their flank, broke up their formidable array, and drove them with fearful slaughter to the Betwah.   Eighteen guns were taken and fifteen hundred rebels slain, with little loss to the conquerors.   Tántia sought to baffle his pursuers and save the remnant of his guns by firing the jungle.   But still, through the widening smoke and flame, destruction in the form of guns and cavalry thundered close upon his heels.   More guns were taken in the retreat.   Only the river and the toils of a long, hot chase saved his troops from annihilation.[*]

Once more Sir Hugh was free to grapple with Jhánsi, against which his heavy guns had raged all through the fight of the 1st. On the 3rd of April his brave troops made their first lodgement within the city.   Brigadier Stuart's columns of the left attack poured swiftly over the breach, or clomb the Rocket Bastion to its left.   The columns of the right attack under Brigadier Steuart had to overbear a sterner, a deadlier resistance, before they too clomb their way inside the city walls.   In both divisions men dropped

[*] Trotter ; Malleson ; Official Papers.

fast in their efforts to gain the central Palace through streets filled with armed foes. But the 86th Foot and the 3rd Bombay Europeans soon clove a way through all barriers to the common goal, taking as they went a bloody requital for their fallen comrades. Here, among other officers, fell the brave Colonel Turnbull, who had handled his guns so fatally in the battle of the Betwah. After the 86th had stormed the Palace, Sir Hugh set his men to clear the rebels out of that quarter of the city, while his cavalry with some infantry and light guns, under the dashing Major Gall, disposed of several hundred runaways brought to a stand on a hill outside the walls. All this accomplished—and no quarter was asked or granted—our wearied soldiers could that day do no more.

There was little rest for them even then. That same evening a false alarm caused Sir Hugh to draw up a large part of his force on the recent battlefield near the Betwah. Next day the rest of the city was carried and cleared out; most of those who got away from it falling into the hands of our cavalry pickets, who spared not a man. Still from its rocky seat the citadel frowned defiance on the troops below. But the need of storming it was prevented by the Ráni's timely escape. On the morning of the 5th Sir Hugh Rose learned that the brave old tigress, with some hundreds of followers, had stolen away through his chain of outposts. Although some of his cavalry got sight of her after a chase of twenty miles, they succeeded only in cutting up a few score of her attendant horsemen.

Her flight was the signal for that of all who remained behind. Resistance was over, and our troops took quiet possession of a fortress whose real strength Sir Hugh then for the first time discovered. Five thousand rebels—nearly half the garrison of Jhánsi—were reckoned up as slain, while the victors' loss in actual fighting against men who fought for their lives proved remarkably small. From the 25th of March to the 5th of April it amounted only to three hundred and forty-three killed and wounded, of whom thirty-six were officers. But the havoc caused by overwork and exposure left wider gaps in their ranks than all the enemy's shot and shell. For seventeen days and nights had Scudamore's cavalry brigade been out on incessant duty, never taking off their clothes nor letting their horses stand unbridled. Only less trying had been the toils encountered under a fiery sun by our infantry, artillery, and engineers. Even so, however, the prize for which all had striven so nobly, the native troops vying with their white comrades, had not been dearly won. None knew until it was taken the full strength of a fortress which, guarded at its weakest point by two massive walls, could only have been carried—wrote Sir Hugh—"by mining and blowing up one bastion after another."*

The rest of that April was employed by Sir Hugh Rose in following up his victory, and in preparing for a march on the next great stronghold of rebellion, the fortress of Kálpi, which, rising above the right bank of the Jamna, commanded the road from Jhánsi to Cawnpore. From the middle to the end of the month his active lieutenants, Gall and Orr, were busy beating up stray bands of rebels, taking their forts, and clearing the roads between Mhau and Kálpi. Towards the end of April Sir Hugh himself again took the field at the head of his heroic troops. By the 7th of May his whole force came in sight of the enemy strongly posted in the woods, temples, and gardens surrounding the town of Kúnch, about forty miles from Kálpi. Here the bulk of the Kálpi garrison, already known as the Army of the Peshwa, had taken its stand under the ablest of the Nána's generals, Tántia Topi. Conspicuous among his allies rode the Amazon Queen of Jhánsi at the head of her few hundred horsemen. It was a very strong position; but Sir Hugh had laid his plans for taking it in flank—a move peculiarly fatal to Asiatic armies—and what he planned his officers seldom failed to carry out.

One brigade had already marched that morning fourteen miles. Giving his men brief time for dinner, Sir Hugh opened fire with his heavy guns on the town and the woods adjacent, while Gall's dragoons and Lightfoot's horse-artillery probed the enemy's right. Behind them presently skirmished the 86th Foot and the 25th Bombay Sepoys. Erelong the woods on that side were cleared of rebels, the town itself was entered, and the enemy, whose right had been thus skilfully rolled back upon their centre, were forced to retire without a struggle from their strong posts in front of the British right. Outmanœuvred, leaderless—for Tántia Topi, less brave than skilful, was again among the first to fly—they fell back for a time in beautiful order, as became Sepoys drilled by English officers. But our cavalry and light guns pressed them with a rage so ruthless, mowing them down with grape, breaking up their ranks with frequent charges, and capturing gun after gun, that the rebels at length lost heart and streamed off in helpless mobs along the road to Kálpi. For eight miles the pursuit was pressed

* Trotter; Malleson; Sir H. Rose's Despatches.

beneath a blazing afternoon sun by men who had kept their saddles since two o'clock in the morning. Many even of the rebel Sepoys fell dead or dying from heat along the road, while their pursuers were beaten into a mere walk, at last into a helpless standstill. Sixteen hours of marching and fighting had done their work upon horses and men. But the enemy had little cause for self-congratulation. They had lost nine guns, heaps of warlike stores, and six hundred men slain, including nearly all that remained of the mutinous 52nd. For a time it seemed as if Kálpi itself would be surrendered without a blow.*

Sir Hugh's own loss was very small, for he had halted his infantry on the other side of Kunch rather than add more victims to those whom the sun had already stricken down. Twelve deaths from sunstroke in one weak wing of a regiment warned him against urging his splendid infantry too far. He himself was more than once laid low by the common enemy. A night's rest, however, was all that Sir Hugh could give his tired soldiers or himself. Nine days after the fight they were all encamped at Golauli on the Jamna, about five miles from Kálpi. On the 19th of May, after three days' preliminary skirmishing, Sir Hugh's mortars opened against some earthworks in front of the town. Emboldened by the timely aid of four thousand troops brought up by the Nawáb of Banda, Túntia's routed soldiery had resolved to " hold to the last their only arsenal, to win their right to Paradise by utterly destroying the infidel English." For a while their conduct was in keeping with the spirit of their leader's words, as revealed in a letter that fell into Sir Hugh's hands.

Their position of great strength was held by an array of more than fifteen thousand men, mutineers chiefly from Kotah, Gwáliár, and the Bengal Army. Guns in plenty and all needful resources were at their command. Rising on one side out of the rocky riverbank, the fort of Kálpi was covered elsewhere by a five-fold screen, the innermost being a chain of ravines between fort and town. Next came the town itself, girdled by another chain of ravines, outside which rose a formidable array of stone-built temples, each enclosed by massive walls. Outside all ran a line of strong intrenchments armed with plenty of good guns.

But Sir Hugh was not to be daunted by difficulties like these. On the 19th of May Colonel Maxwell's column from Cawnpore stood ready to fire on the fort from their side of the river. Another column under Colonel Riddell was nearing Kálpi from the north.

* Trotter ; Malleson ; Official Papers.

Next day the rebels made a determined effort to turn Sir Hugh's flank. Of course they failed. But the mischief threatened by Maxwell's guns urged them on to another attempt which, against a weaker general and troops a whit less heroic, might have proved successful. On the 22nd they sallied out in force against both wings of the British line, their courage inflamed by much opium, their advance sheltered by the broken ground. Leaving his left unaided to deal with the enemy's feint attack, Sir Hugh quietly waited for the full shock of battle against his right. The event proved the soundness of his forecast. So fierce anon, so fearfully critical grew the struggle upon his right, that he had to bring up the last of his reserves and leave the issue to his heroic infantry. One sweeping onset of the dismounted Camel Corps, led by Sir Hugh himself, hurled the assailants back from the guns they had nearly captured; then the whole line, dashing forward under cover of guns and cavalry, drove the discomfited masses back with dreadful slaughter into the town and fort. Gall's dragoons and Lightfoot's gunners completed the rout begun by the heat-spent warriors of the Rifle Brigade and the 88th Foot.

All through that night Maxwell's batteries kept up a scathing fire upon the fort and town. Before daybreak of the 23rd our tired troops were marching in two columns over deep ravines unguarded by a single foe. A few shots from one battery was all the resistance offered to either column. By ten o'clock Sir Hugh was master of all Kálpi, with its ample store of guns, ammunition, small arms, camp-equipage, its cannon foundries, its underground arsenal, its wealth of warlike tools. Signs of skilful workmanship and careful preparation everywhere met the eye, but no armed enemy remained within the fort. Gall and Lightfoot followed after the flying rebels for several miles, slaying hundreds, and capturing their last guns. Scattering by twos and threes across the country, their arms, their very clothes flung aside as they fled, the soldiers of the Peshwa's Army seemed to have neither heart nor strength left for any further mischief.[*]

After five months of toil, hardship, and fierce fighting, the work of the Central India Field Force seemed fairly over for that season. Strong in their able leader, in their own disciplined daring, Sir Hugh's brigades had marched without a check from one perilous enterprise to another, across rivers, over mountain passes, through intricate jungles, into the strongest forts, in the teeth sometimes of appalling odds, under the blaze at last of a sun

* Trotter ; Malleson.

surpassing the average even of Indian summers. They had fought
and routed again and again armies formidable from mere numbers
and warlike zeal, fairly disciplined, thoroughly equipped, nor
wanting in brave and skilful commanders. Not a man in that
heroic little army but stood in sore need of rest. Most of the
officers and men were suffering from some form of disease.
Brigadier Steuart had been too ill to march upon Kálpi. The
Chief of the Staff, Colonel Wetherall, was in a raving fever. Sir
Hugh himself, after five sunstrokes in yet fewer days, might well
plead his utter inability to write off at once despatches worthy of
the events he had to record, or of the troops whose signal merits
had brought those events to pass.*

In a kind of farewell order to his troops, some of whom were
on the point of starting for their respective summer quarters, he
thanked them all in justly glowing terms for the many proofs they
had given of " bravery, devotion, discipline," under every kind of
hardship, danger, and temptation. But, even as he wrote thus, an
event was happening which hardly one Englishman could have
foreseen, which threatened for a moment to spoil the fruit of his
late achievements, to open up a fresh vista of protracted toil and
struggle for soldiers already taxed beyond their powers.

An inkling of the coming storm had indeed been caught by
Colonel Robertson, whose flying column had tried hard to over-
take the scattered remnants of Tántia's force. The rebels, he
wrote, were heading off towards Gwáliár. But Sir Robert
Hamilton still believed in Oudh as the goal to which Tántia and
the Ráni of Jhánsi were inevitably tending. At length Sir Hugh
Rose himself awoke to the need for instant action. On the 1st of
June a part of Steuart's brigade was hurried off towards Gwáliár.
But the mischief was done already. On the 30th of May the fugitives from Kálpi were encamped to the number of eleven thousand
with twelve guns in the Morár cantonments outside the capital
of Sindhia's realm. Tántia's cunning and the Ráni's eloquence,
burning as that of Boadicea, soon did their work. On the 1st of
June the brave young monarch was fighting for his crown, an hour
later was flying for his life towards Agra. Treachery among his
own troops had left him powerless against the wrecks of his old
Contingent and the agents of a shadowy Peshwa demanding help
from his ancient lieges of Gwáliár and Indór. The rich treasures of
Jayaji Sindhia's palace, the gathered wealth of a populous city,
the whole warlike resources of a very strong fortress, lay at the

* Trotter ; Malleson ; Lowe's " Central India."

feet of men who seemed but a few days ago to have fought their
last fight against the British power. Another sovereign was set
up in Sindhia's stead under the new Marátha Peshwa, the infamous
Nána Sahib. All Sindhia's friends and followers were plundered
of goods or money. Most of the captured treasure was parted
among the successful soldiery; and in a day or two a powerful
array of seventeen or eighteen thousand fighting-men stood behind
their strong defences and their rows of guns, ready for the next
collision with their war-spent foes.

Once more Sir Hugh's warriors nerved themselves up for work
under a sun which sometimes marked a hundred and thirty degrees
in the shade. Leaving Whitlock to guard Kálpi, Sir Hugh himself
set off for Gwáliár with two of his old brigades led by Steuart and
Napier. A third, under Brigadier Smith, was hastening thither
from Rájputána. Nine days' marching brought the Kálpi force
within striking reach of Morár on the 16th of June. A swift and
sweeping reconnaissance preluded a sudden and successful attack
on that part of the enemy's lines. Before help could reach them
from other quarters, the defenders of the cantonments had been
driven back and chased with much slaughter across the intervening plain into the city. Sir Hugh's next movements waited on
those of Smith, who was marching on to the south-eastern side of
the enemy's position. By the evening of the 17th that officer had
fought his way, with the capture of several guns, up to some heights
overlooking the *Lashkar*, an old Marátha camp, since accreted
into a well-built city. The next day saw him master of the whole
crescent of hills that bars the approach to Gwáliár from the south.
In that day's struggle the bravest of the rebel leaders fought her
last fight. Dressed in her man's garb, the bold, the high-hearted,
if bloodthirsty, Queen of Jhánsi fell mortally smitten by sword and
bullet in vain flight from a body of hussars. With her fell the
last sure bulwark of a cause thenceforth depending mainly on the
cowardice of Tántia Topi and the despairing rage of Nána Sáhib.*

Meanwhile Sir Hugh Rose had marched off the bulk of his troops
from Morár under a sun which struck the white men down by
scores. That night he halted behind Smith's brigade. On the
19th the combined force went forward under a rattling shower of
shot and shell from the fort, the Lashkar, and the intrenched hill
nearest the city. Nothing could long withstand the resolute rush
of guns and infantry led by the 86th and the 95th Foot. In the
teeth of a murderous fire the British gunners brought their bat-

* Trotter; Malleson; Official Papers.

teries across the canal up a hill that rose beyond it. A short, sharp struggle ended in the crowning of the last height on the southern side of the fort. Every gun within reach was taken by our unfaltering infantry; the Bombay Sepoys fighting like Englishmen. Erelong the cavalry, white and black, were launched in keen pursuit of a broken and disheartened foe. Before sunset the Lashkar, the Phúl-Bágh or garden-palace, the old city, everything outside the far-famed citadel, had fallen, as Sir Hugh foresaw, into British keeping, at a cost of only eighty-seven men. The noble young Mahárája, who had ridden into camp from Agra the day before, might feel himself once more a king as he watched the progress of that day's fight, the achievement of a victory which enabled him on the morrow to pass with all kingly honour into his own palace through streets lined with crowds of smiling citizens.

It remained to follow up the routed foe, and to carry the fortress which still frowned defiance from its high thick walls and many towers, crowning an isolated rock that rose three hundred feet sheer above the plain. But a stronghold which, properly manned, might have held out for months, could offer small resistance with a garrison reduced to thirty men. Its capture on the morning of the 20th by a handful of Bombay Sepoys under Lieutenants Rose and Waller was a stroke of happy daring for which Rose, its real author, paid with his life. At his suggestion the two officers quietly marched their pickets up to the main gateway of the Fort. A lusty blacksmith broke a way for them through each of the six gates which barred their ascent. In the short but stern struggle which then ensued, the gallant Rose fell by a bullet which cut short a career of the highest promise. Waller avenged his friend's death on the mutineer who had fired the fatal shot, and erelong not one rebel was left alive in the captured stronghold.[*]

Not less bold than brilliantly successful was the stroke dealt upon the flying wrecks of Tántia's army by Brigadier Napier on the 21st of June. Starting on the 20th with about six hundred horse and Lightfoot's guns, Napier marched all night and far into the next day, before he got sight of the enemy strongly posted about Jaura-Alipur, fifty miles south of Gwáliár. To rush upon five thousand disciplined troops backed by twenty-five guns might have seemed mere madness to an average commander. But Napier

---

[*] Trotter; Chambers; Malleson. Rose had been twice mentioned in Sir Hugh's Despatches

knew his enemy and never stopped to count numbers. Covered by some rising ground, he hurled Lightfoot's battery against the enemy's left flank. After firing two rounds at five hundred yards from the foe, Lightfoot's gunners limbered up and thundered down at full gallop against the rebel guns. Straining after them, at their best pace, galloped the dragoons and native horse. Scared by that sudden onset, the rebels made small show of resistance, scattering in hot flight and leaving all their guns behind them with several hundred of their dead. Napier failed to overtake the nimble fugitives ; but thenceforth the army of the Peshwa ceased to be an organized whole. Broken up into flying bands, its residue might still give trouble to our wearied troops ; but as a source of serious danger its day was done.

The Central India Field Force could now go into summer quarters at Gwáliár, Morár, Sipri, and Jhánsi, for such rest as circumstances might allow. Sir Hugh Rose himself, as Commander-in-Chief at Bombay, was free at last to recruit the health long since shattered by the toils of a campaign second in dash and brilliancy to none ever fought by a British general—a campaign which, for the quick succession of telling blows, for the completeness of the victories, the greatness of the odds encountered, and the difficulties overcome; for the skill, the hardihood, the untiring pluck displayed by officers and men, may rank among the choicest masterpieces of modern warfare. If the conquest of Delhi was a marvel of heroic daring in the face of fearful odds, if the final capture of Lucknow seemed almost to justify the popular belief in Sir Colin Campbell's strategic prowess, Sir Hugh Rose's victorious march from Indór to Gwáliár, while it matched the former achievement in respect of soldierly endurance, raised its leader at one bound to a level with some of the first names in the military annals of all times.

With the recapture of Gwáliár the grim drama of the Indian Mutiny is fast nearing its peaceful close. Tántia Topi has yet to be run down. Rebellious Oudh has not yet learned the lesson of wise submission to the British yoke. Even in August of this year two more regiments of foolish or frightened Sepoys will rise in fierce mutiny at Multán, only to be slain in scores by the enraged men of the Panjáb Infantry and the Bombay Europeans. Rohilkhand has yet to be cleared of rebel bands. For several months to come bodies of raiders will ruffle the peace of the North-Western Provinces.

Umar Singh's men still haunt the jungles of Jagdispur. The

rebels in the country ruled by General Jacob will keep his troops employed into October. Calcutta itself will again be visited by a groundless panic. Both in India and in England the croakers will continue to prophesy evil things. But in plain truth the great storm is blowing over; the clouds once black with ruin are sailing off white and scattered under the broadening blue. What of ill omen may still meet eye or ear is but the farewell token of past calamity.

NOTE.

The summer of 1858 was remarkable even among Indian summers for its dreadful heat. If even natives were sometimes stricken down by the fierce sun of May and June, its victims among our own countrymen were all the more numerous for the need of marching and fighting at all hours of the day, sometimes in clothing utterly unsuited to the climate and the work in hand. In the fight at Kúnch, Rose himself was thrice struck down by the sun, thirteen of his men died outright, and many more were carried to the rear disabled. At Baréli ten out of nineteen stricken died. During Jones's march to Shahjahánpur thirty men of the 79th, according to Mr. William Russell, and more than forty of the 60th Rifles, were struck down or rendered helpless by the heat. "It was pitiable," Mr. Russell heard, "to see the poor fellows lying in their doolies, gasping their last." Few of the survivors could rejoin the ranks except after a long period of rest. We have seen how Lugard's and Hope Grant's soldiers suffered from the same cause. Some regiments wore a *kaki*, or grey uniform, but the black plumes of the Highlanders and the dark tunics of the Rifles could only aggravate the men's distress. In Bengal the heat proved quite as fatal. It was stated in a journal of the day that one clergyman in Calcutta buried in one day forty-eight Englishmen, chiefly sailors. "In one ship the captain, chief mate, and twenty-six men had all apoplexy at once." Nine men from Fort William were buried in one morning from the same cause. Many officers lost their lives or their health from sunstroke. One, at least, of the rebel leaders opposed to Sir Hugh Rose expressly ordered his troops never to fight the Farangi infidels before ten A.M., because fighting in the sun either killed them or sent them into hospital— (Malleson).

CHAPTER V.

THE LAST THROES OF REBELLION.

FROM his central watchpost at Allahábád Lord Canning had followed with expectant eyes the course of Sir Colin Campbell's final movements against Lucknow. To Sir Colin's camp before that city he forwarded, on the 3rd of March, a proclamation, of which Sir James Outram, as Chief Commissioner of Oudh, was to issue copies far and wide as soon as all Lucknow should have fallen into British hands. By the terms of this manifesto, as afterwards published, the whole proprietary right in the soil of Oudh, save in the case of six men—three rajahs, one tálukdár, and two zamindárs, who had stood faithful amid great temptations— was confiscated to the British Government. Of the rebellious chiefs and gentry those who should promptly yield themselves to the Chief Commissioner's commands were promised immunity from death or imprisonment, if only their hands were "unstained with English blood murderously shed." For any further indul- gence they must throw themselves on British mercy, which would be extended in the largest measure to all who should in anywise aid in restoring peace and order throughout the province. Those who had protected English lives would have especial claims to the kind and considerate treatment withheld from none but downright murderers of English men and women.

An explanatory letter accompanied the proclamation. But even this, as read by the Chief Commissioner, failed to mitigate the seeming harshness of the terms put forth by the Governor-General. Sir James protested against the sweeping sentence thus passed against a body of landholders not a dozen of whom but had given the rebels some kind of help. It was adding, he pleaded, one in- justice to another to press so hard upon a class of men who, smarting under the blows inflicted by the settlement decrees of 1856, had delayed taking up arms against us "until our rule was virtually at an end." Give them back their lands, and they will at once aid us in restoring order. Otherwise, driven to despair, "they will betake themselves to their domains for the carrying on of a long, bloody, and guerilla war." In reply to Outram's earnest remonstrances, Lord Canning instructed him to insert in the proclamation that qualifying clause above cited, touching the larger indulgence open to all who should help in re-establishing order. Beyond that concession to bare justice the Governor-General refused to go. He upheld the leniency of the terms offered, could see little injustice if much impolicy in the previous treatment of usurping tálukdárs, and argued that any concession of their old powers to insurgent landholders who had not laid down their arms would have seemed to the natives a confession of fear or weakness, a proof that rebellion against the British Government "would not be a losing game." It was mercy enough to exempt such offenders from death, imprisonment, and transportation. To concede all that Outram asked for would have been to treat the rebels not as honourable foes, but as foes who had won the day.*

Wise or unwise, this sweeping measure of confiscation could not be called unjust in respect of a country where absolute freeholds were things unknown, where no one had ever disputed the right of the *Sarkár* or Government of the day to derive the great bulk of its revenue from a rent-charge upon the land, or even to resume on good cause shown any *Inám* or freehold which had been granted for a certain time, or for some purpose no longer suitable. It was also true that some of the insurgent tálukdárs had made the Government an ill return for the liberal treatment of a day still recent; that others had merely been dispossessed of lands and villages to which fraud or violence had formed their only title, and that most of them had risen, as Lord Canning contended, in behalf of their scouted claims to arbitrary power and the privilege, once so dear to English barons, of unhindered fighting against each other. With regard to the forfeiture of estates for rebellion, such a punishment was clearly in keeping not only with European usage, but with the unvarying practice of native Indian States. It was a punishment which involved no loss of caste or personal honour, and which, under the proclamation, could be remitted wholly or in part to each offender according to his actual deserts; while it furnished the Government with the best means of rewarding faithful villages and gentlemen whose good services called for due requital.†

By this measure the Governor-General sought in fact to clear

---

* Trotter; Malleson; Official Papers. † Official Papers.

the ground for the rebuilding of our rule in Oudh on surer foundations by the light of a larger experience. For that end he was quite prepared to temper justice with the largest possible amount of mercy. But his good intentions were doomed to be misunderstood by others besides Sir James Outram. With the downfall of the Palmerston Ministry Mr. Vernon Smith had just given place to Lord Ellenborough at the head of the India Board of Control. A copy of the Oudh Proclamation passed among other official papers into the hands of the new President. Had he known what Mr. Vernon Smith forgot to tell him, that Lord Canning proposed to explain in a subsequent despatch the real drift and purpose of his new policy, he might perhaps have been saved from an act of hasty indiscretion. Reading the document by the light of his own preconceptions, Lord Ellenborough at once sat down to express, through a letter from the Secret Committee, his utter disapproval of an ordinance which seemed to " pronounce the disinherison of a people." Whatever instructions might have been given to the Chief Commissioner, the people of Oudh, he said, would " see only the proclamation ; " would learn that six men only were excepted from a sweeping forfeiture of rights concerning which the landholders of India were as keenly sensitive " as the occupiers of land in any country of which we have a knowledge." A decree that disinherits a whole people must wellnigh bar the way to an abiding peace by further enraging the aggrieved landholders, and driving to despair the bulk of a people whose national pride had first been roused through our harsh, our cruel overthrow of a faithful dynasty and a government which, " however bad, was at least native." Instead of being treated as lawful enemies rather than mere rebels, the people of Oudh were being made to suffer a penalty " exceeding in extent and severity almost any which has been recorded in history as inflicted upon a subdued nation." Other conquerors have punished the few and spared the many. " You," wrote the noble conqueror of Sind, " have acted upon a different principle," have departed from precedents, " conceived in a spirit of wisdom superior to that which appears in the precedent you have made." Contentment and general confiscation cannot go together, nor can any government long exist in " a country where the whole people is rendered hostile by a sense of wrong." The Governor-General must therefore " mitigate in practice the stringent severity " of his decree.[*]

Such was the pith and purport of the judgement recorded in

[*] Trotter ; Malleson ; Official Papers.

April, 1858, against the ruler whose manifest leanings to the side of mercy had already earned for him the scornful nickname of Clemency Canning. The undertone of insolent triumph ringing through every line of a despatch that went forth unread by any of the writer's colleagues would have sorely tried the temper even of Lord Canning's stoicism, but for the greatly comforting letters that reached him in June by the same mail. The Court of Directors declared anew their confidence in his general policy; the leading members of the late Ministry urged him to pursue his own line of action and on no account to resign his post. A fortnight later came a friendly letter from Lord Derby himself, excusing his colleague's indiscretion, and virtually asking the Governor-General to stay where he was. Ten days earlier, on the 17th of June, Lord Canning sent home a despatch in which he vindicated his own policy from the "taunts and sarcasms" hurled against it by Lord Ellenborough, and declined to lay down of his own act the high trust conferred upon him, unless his honourable masters should deem his policy erroneous in principle or futile in its results.

That policy, he maintained, had been "from the beginning merciful without weakness, and indulgent without compromise of the dignity of the Government." It was a policy which, if steadily pursued, offered "the best and earliest prospect of restoring peace to Oudh upon a stable footing." If the rebels in Oudh were to learn that his policy had been formally condemned at home, they would only be encouraged to fresh resistance; many who had shown no sympathy with the late king's family would be drawn to the Begam's side; and the probable union of all the rebel leaders would be "just what is wanting to give a national character to her cause." Declining to discuss the policy which had led to the annexation of Oudh, he protested against the language used in that connexion by a Minister of the Crown, a servant of the Queen, who was also Queen of Oudh, as tending to justify the people in their rebellion against the new rule.*

Meanwhile the official insult to Lord Canning had recoiled on the aggressor's own head. The offensive despatch became food for public comment of a kind which Lord Ellenborough had not foreseen when he imparted its contents to the philanthropic Mr. Bright. Early in May printed copies of it were laid on the table of the House of Lords. In both houses of Parliament hostile motions were at once threatened against the Ministry which had let one of their number indulge in such hasty, sharp,

* Malleson ; Trotter ; Official Papers.

ill-timed censure of a statesman deserving far other treatment at their hands. Whatever view might be taken of Lord Canning's proclamation, it was generally agreed that no time had been given him for a full explanation or a fair defence. Even after Lord Ellenborough's retirement from office the fight over his body still went on. The vote of censure, thrown out in the Lords by a small majority, was withdrawn from the other house by Mr. Cardwell's leave only after four nights of fierce debate.*

If public opinion in England was still divided on the merits of a question which even in India split our countrymen into hostile camps, Lord Canning could draw fresh encouragement from the approval of friends in power and from the steady march of events in Oudh. In the middle of May the Court of Directors passed a vote of continued confidence in the wisdom and large clemency of his measures for pacifying the rebellious provinces. Their covering despatch reaffirmed their belief in the merciful intentions that underlay Lord Canning's rigorous words. In Oudh itself, events were already proving the groundlessness of any fears awakened by the seeming sternness of Lord Canning's manifesto. When Outram left Lucknow in April to fill Low's seat in the Supreme Council, his meet successor, Mr. Robert Montgomery, proceeded to carry out the new policy with the mingled tact and vigour which had won for him in the Panjáb a name second only to that of John Lawrence. While Lord Ellenborough's rash letter was yet on its way to Allahábád, the new Chief Commissioner could tell of many an insurgent Tálukdár who had already thrown himself on the mercy of the "Sarkár," and received a new and surer title to his estates in return for his proofs of present, his promises of future loyalty. Under his skilful management the act of seeming confiscation became in fact what Lord Canning had always meant it to be, the groundwork of a plan for securing the rights and marking out the public duties of a landed aristocracy in Oudh. Slowly but steadily the work of pacification went forward, as one district after another passed with more or less of struggle into the hands of the civil power. Before the year's end nearly all the great landholders had made their peace on favourable terms with a Government whose right to rule them rested in their eyes on the best of all titles, its military strength. Assessed to the land revenue as lords of their respective manors, and further invested with magisterial powers, the reinstated Tálukdárs were thenceforward held responsible, not only for the

* Trotter ; Malleson.

State's share of the village rents, but for the maintenance of peace and order among their tenantry.*

From the middle to the end of 1858, however, the task of pacifying Oudh devolved in yet larger measure on the soldier than the statesman. At the end of May about two-thirds of the province were still to be reconquered. Hope Grant's progress in June we have already seen. Even the rains of July brought little rest for some of his troops. Before the end of that month his rapid advance had scared away and broken up a large rebel force employed in besieging Mán Singh's stronghold at Shahganj. After an interview with the wily Rajah whom he had thus opportunely rescued from his wrathful countrymen, Sir Hope and his lieutenant, Horsford, spent the greater part of August in following up and routing the rebels, fourteen thousand of whom with twelve or fourteen guns had massed themselves around Sultánpur. In the districts bordering Allahábád, a small column under Brigadier Berkeley captured a number of mud forts hidden away amidst broad belts of thorny jungle, while other troops were employed in punishing the armed bands that still troubled the peace of Rohilkhand, or endangered the new rule in Western Oudh.†

During the September rains our troops rested from the toils of war. Early in October the fighting was renewed in various places by Barker, Evelegh, and Seaton, who beat the rebels thoroughly wherever they awaited or began the attack. By the middle of the month Sir Colin Campbell, who had just been raised to the Peerage under the title of Lord Clyde, had matured his plans and issued his orders for the campaign, which was destined to quench the last throes of rebellion in Oudh. Before the end of November only two or three chiefs of any mark still cast in their lot with the untamable Bégam and outlawed Nána Sáhib. While the rest kept coming in by twos and threes to make peace with a Power as ready to spare the humbled as to beat down the haughty, Lord Clyde and his subalterns were pressing hard on the more obstinate rebels, taking fort after fort on their way, routing all who withstood them in the field, and leaving the enemy no way of escape save into the deadly jungles that bordered the hills of Nipál.

In this long but generally successful game Hope Grant, Troup, Evelegh, Horsford and Rowcroft maintained their old renown; Wetherall left his mark on Rámpur Kússia; while the young Sikh

* Trotter ; Chambers.   † Chambers ; Malleson.

Rajah of Kapurthala and his brother, Bikram Singh, led and handled their own troops on every occasion with a skill and courage which called forth the unstinted praises of their English comrades.

Lord Clyde himself, after a forced march of about sixty miles, caught Beni Mádhu's army on the 24th of November a blow which smashed to pieces the last rebel force on the southern bank of the Gágra. A few weeks later the Bégam herself was nearly hemmed in at Balrampur, and the coward Nána escaped across the Rápti but a few hours ahead of his pursuers. One more bootless stand made by the Bégam in the Naupára jungles, one last despairing effort of Beni Mádhu's to hold the strong fort of Majidia against British shells and bayonets, and the revolt in Oudh was fairly over. On the last day of December, 1858, Lord Clyde's infantry were just too late to help the 7th Hussars in arresting the enemy's flight across the upper waters of the Rápti. At another point nearer Gorakpur Hope Grant, four days later, overtook and routed some six thousand rebels led by the Nána's brother, Bála Ráo, driving them across the border with the loss of all their fifteen guns. Once safe within the jungles of Nipál, the Bégam and her allies could rest their hunted followers on neutral ground, until Jang Bahádur should give the hunters leave to track them down.

That leave was soon granted. On the 10th of February, 1859, Horsford's column came up with a few thousand wretches still holding together from choice or necessity, and sent them once more flying, with the loss of fourteen guns. Thenceforth the rebel remnants wandered miserably about the hills and forests of Nipál, or made fruitless efforts to break away from the pitiless pursuit kept up by Horsford and Kelly in concert with the less eager Nipálese. Many of the survivors threw away their arms and stole back one by one to their old homes. Others, more desperate, made sudden raids across the border, only to meet with heavy punishment at the hands of their watchful foes. At length, by the end of April, all semblance of an armed force had melted away. The last band of armed fugitives who dared trust themselves to British mercy had quietly yielded up their arms; and only a few of the more desperate chiefs and the blacker criminals, including the Nána and the men who aided in the massacre of Cawnpore, were left to face the terrors of the jungle or to enjoy the doubtful blessings of Nipálese compassion. It was deemed good policy to let them alone; but Hope Grant's pickets kept careful watch along the frontier against any attempt to break through.*

* Trotter; Malleson; Hope Grant's "Incidents of the Sepoy War."

By this time the civil power, as wielded by Montgomery and a staff of able assistants, had regained its old supremacy over all Oudh. In the previous autumn the Chief Commissioner had issued a decree requiring every one under certain penalties to yield up his arms, and every landed chief to dismantle his forts. In course of time the disarming process was carried out with results that strikingly attested the need for such a step. Of guns alone the number thus rendered useless was six hundred and eighty-four; while 186,177 firearms, 565,321 swords, 50,311 spears, and 636,683 weapons of other sorts were given up for destruction. As many as 1,569 forts were either dismantled or destroyed. By the end of 1858 the work of pacification had gone so far, that in the following January Lord Canning was able to hold at Lucknow a *Darbár*, or public reception, at which nearly all the Rajahs and Tálukdárs of Oudh came forward to have their sword hilts touched by the new-made deputy of the British Queen. To all there present he renewed by word of mouth the pledges they had already received through the Chief Commissioner. His impressive language dwelt in their memories like the formal charter of their newly-granted rights.*

The same month of April which saw the last flicker of armed strife beyond the Rápti, saw also the last throes of rebellion in the jungles of Central India. Ever since the great scattering of the rebel forces at Gwáliár and the rout of Jaura-Alipur in June, 1858, the Marátha leader, Tántia Topi, with a few thousand men and a large store of plundered treasure, had kept doubling like a hunted hare up and down the rugged plains of Rájputána and the adjacent provinces, now seizing an ill-guarded fort, anon paying dearly in men and guns for the satisfaction of once more baffling his tired pursuers. Beaten or turned again and again by Roberts, Napier, Michel, Parke, Showers, Smith, and other officers, the wily rebel still contrived, month after month, to save his plunder and put off his doom. By the end of August he had gained a new ally in the Rajah Mán Singh of Narwár, whom Sindhia had despoiled of his paternal domains. The quarrel with his own sovereign brought the Rájput chief into collision with Napier's troops; and thus drove him into active concert with the common enemy both of Sindhia and his English friends. Favoured by fortune and the goodwill or the inertness of their fellow-countrymen, these two kept their pursuers employed for several months in

---

* Chambers; Sir R. Temple's "Men and Events of my Time."

a task that seemed well-nigh as bootless as that of Schiller's pilgrim seeking to overtake the setting sun.

Hemmed in by half a dozen columns, Tántia's troops would suddenly dash across the Narbada, would turn up presently in Gujarát, be heard of next in Jaipur, and meet anon with heavy punishment not far from Jhánsi. Time after time they were caught up, surprised, and scattered with heavy loss by troops as nimble as themselves. The pursuing columns marched sometimes for days together at a pace which astonished their own countrymen. Bodies of infantry mounted on camels gave the enemy no rest. Gun after gun was taken from the flying rebels, and still they fled, carrying their treasure with them, to reappear in fresh places with numbers hardly diminished and a fresh array of guns. In November one of Tántia's lieutenants, the Nawáb of Banda, threw himself on British clemency. Some other chiefs soon followed his example, and many a Sepoy, "tired of always running away," left his arms behind him and passed into the surrounding peasantry. But Tántia and his comrade, Mán Singh, who had been undergoing his full share of hard blows and hair-breadth escapes, still braved the chances of a prolonged resistance against never so fearful odds.

In the first days of 1859 they were joined by the Moghal Prince Firóz Shah, who in the past December had cut his way with a few troops back from Oudh across the Ganges, baffled the efforts made by Hume, the bold magistrate of Etawah, to stay his course, outstripped a column sent in chase from Cawnpore, and made his way over the Jamna into Gwáliár before Napier came within striking reach of him. Escaping with heavy loss from that officer's clutch, Firóz Shah sped on to Indragarh, in the State of Tank, where Tántia found him on the 9th of January. By that time, however, the rebel game was nearly played out. The hunters were closing in about their prey, whose chances of escape grew daily weaker with each fresh defeat. Before the end of January Tántia and his new comrade had parted company. On the 10th of February another leader, Ráo Sáhib, was heavily beaten by the active Honner in a desperate effort to break through the guarded circle. Chased by Somerset into the Banswára jungles, the greater part of the rebels threw away their arms and made off to their own homes, while others, to the number of two hundred, gave themselves up to their pursuers. Very few remained to share the fortunes of their leaders, who, hiding away in the jungles, found safety in the thoroughness of their disguise, the loneliness of their haunts, and the sympathy or the forbearance of their rustic neighbours.

What became of Ráo Sáhib and Firóz Shah was never known, at least to English inquirers. Whether they died in the jungles or escaped elsewhither, no Englishman greatly cared. Mán Singh, on the 2nd of April, surrendered to Major Meade under guarantee of life and liberty and honourable treatment for his family and himself. Five days later, the Wallace of Central India had found his false Menteith. The treachery of Mán Singh enabled Meade to carry off the luckless Tántia Topi in the dead of night from his hiding-place in the Paron jungles, near Sipri. At Sipri, on the 15th of April, the ablest leader of the rebellion, who, at Agra, at Cawnpore, on the Betwah, at Kúnch, Kálpi, and Gwáliár, had shown every trait of good soldiership save steadfast courage; who for more than nine months had baffled the best-laid plans and eluded the fiercest onsets of his many pursuers, found himself tried by court-martial for rebellion and waging war against the British Government. Three days later, with surprising coolness, Tántia Topi underwent the felon's doom which even Canning's clemency could not bring itself to remit. Death by hanging was deemed the fittest punishment for a determined rebel who had not been formally accused of sharing in the darker crimes wrought by his master, the Nána Sáhib. If his own plea of innocence on that score may not count for much, it is certain that no attempt was made to prove his guilt. But the blood was still running hot in English veins, and the demands of stern justice overruled the pleadings of a generous if misplaced compassion.*

With the capture and death of Tántia Topi the last stirrings of rebellion died out in Central India. On the 8th of July, 1859, Lord Canning proclaimed the restoration of peace throughout the Empire which he ruled no longer in the name of the Company, but of the Crown. Of the rebel leaders whom it remains to account for, the Nána himself, his brother, Bála Ráo, and the dark-hearted Azimulla Khán all died during the same year in Nipál. Beni Mádhu was slain in November, fighting with Palwán Singh's Gorkhas. Khan Bahádur Khán of Baréli was hanged in March, 1860, on the spot whence he had given the signal for a rising crowned by deeds of fearful savagery. Imprisonment for life was the doom awarded to the less criminal Mámu Khán. On the 3rd of May, 1860, Jawála Parsád was hanged by the Ghát whence, as the Nána's subaltern, he had directed the massacre of our people

* Malleson.

in the boats. Driven by Douglas out of his native jungles, Umar
Singh at last fell into merciful English hands at Gorakpur. The
high-hearted Bégam of Oudh lived unmolested at Kátmandhu.
Banishment to Mecca, with the forfeiture of all his lands, satisfied
British vengeance against the Nawáb of Fathigarh.

Many rebels of less mark who escaped death in the field or in
the lonely forest were caught, tried, and punished or pardoned
according to their several degrees of guilt. Towards all, indeed,
but proven murderers and undoubted ruffians, British resentment
grew placable enough. A few hundred Sepoys had to linger out
their forfeit lives in the Andaman Islands; a few thousand worked
out shorter terms of forced labour in the local jails. Perhaps
twice as many more were allowed to go free. But of the once
powerful Native Army of Bengal, with its cluster of local contin-
gents, only a few weak regiments survived the mutiny from which
they had held aloof. The loss of life among the disloyal majority
through wounds, hardship, and judicial sentences, must have exceeded a hundred thousand within two years. Of other rebels
slain in that period the total must have been even greater, to say
nothing of those who perished by mistake. Nor had the conquerors come out of that long trial without cruel loss. Besides
many hundred victims of Sepoy treachery and Mohammadan spite, a
whole army of fighting Englishmen had succumbed to the wasting
influences of a struggle in which climate, numbers, position,
almost everything seemed against them save their own invincible
pluck. By their side also had fallen a smaller army of Sikh,
Hindu, and Mohammadan Sepoys and police, without whose help
our own countrymen would have fought in vain.*

In England, men's minds were still exercised with questions
rising out of the great struggle thus happily closed. The outburst
of 1857, was it a mutiny or a rebellion more or less widespread;
a popular uprising or a religious revolt; the expression of a passing frenzy, the outcome of political plottings, or the proof of a
deep-seated, long-smouldering discontent? What were the real
prompting influences of which the greased cartridge was the outward and visible sign? Commissions of inquiry on these and such-
like questions were ordered both by the old and the new Ministry;
heaps of books, pamphlets, letters, and leading articles were
written in support of this or that theory; but the multitude of
talkers went far to confuse the simple facts. Most of the causes,
direct or indirect, lay on the surface of the times. It was natural

* Trotter ; Malleson.

that a great Prætorian army which knew its own strength, had
ceased to care much for its alien officers, and saw its opportunity
in the seeming weakness of its European guard, should on fit
provocation break out into general revolt.   Behind that army,
itself a vast brotherhood bound together by the ties of kinship,
caste, a common grievance, and a common ambition, lay a mixed
multitude of plotters, fanatics, ruffians, rogues, ruined gentry,
and disaffected persons of every class, from the Nána Sáhib down
to his humblest follower.   At Delhi, Lucknow, Jhánsi, Bithúr, in
Oudh, Bahár, and Central India, wherever might be found a
dethroned or degraded dynasty, a body of disendowed chiefs and
discarded courtiers, a fanatic priesthood, or a turbulent populace,
there also lurked a possible danger to our rule.   In the event of a
Sepoy rising the flame would be sure to spread from one of these
powder-heaps to another.   But the great magazine of mischief,
the main seat of disaffection, was the overgrown Sepoy Army of
Bengal.   The great Sepoy rising, as Sir John Lawrence stoutly
held, "had its origin in the army itself," whatever advantage
other persons and classes took of it to compass their own ends.*

"It was the sense of power"—he was wont to say—"that
induced the Sepoys to rebel."   With numbers weighing more and
more heavily on their side, with all the fortresses, arsenals, magazines, and treasuries entrusted to their keeping, what wonder if
they had come to deem themselves masters of a Government
which strove too late to curb their insolence, and succeeded only
in fanning the flame of their discontent?   "For years"—said
Nicholson—"I have watched the army, and felt sure they only
wanted an opportunity to try their strength with us."   That
opportunity came at last in a shape and manner alike unforeseen.
The untoward incident of the greased cartridges brought the
seething disaffection to a head at a moment the most auspicious
for the plotters of revolt.   When the hot weather was fast approaching, when English succours on a large scale were impossible
for months to come, then was the time for a great native army to
rise up and overwhelm the weak English garrison scattered like
melting snow-patches over the breadth of Hindustan.   The flame
of mutiny, unchecked at Meerut, spread by degrees from station
to station, wherever a body of armed Sepoys obeyed the impulse
of mingled rage and fear, or carried out the promptings of Brahman and Musalman plotters within their own lines.   Out of the
mutiny grew as a thing of course a partial rebellion, the extent of

* Trotter ; Chambers ; Official Papers.

which varied always with the fortunes of the mutineers. There was no rebellion in any district where mutiny had not led the way. In most of the disordered districts outside Oudh the mass of the people, husbandmen, traders, artisans, gentry, maintained an attitude either neutral or friendly to the British power. South of the Narbada there was virtually no rebellion. Of all the leading native princes, Rájput, Marátha, and Mohammadan, from Kashmir to Travankor, from the Gaikwar of Baroda to the Nizám, not one made common cause with the mutineers, while some of them proved as staunch and helpful in the hour of our trial and of theirs, as if fealty to a foreign master were the strongest of all political and social bands. There was much significance also in the fact that among our foes were very few, if any, of those who had learned English in the Government or Mission schools, or had gained much experience of English ways. The rebels, it has been truly said, " would trust nobody who even knew English." The Nána himself, who had only a " smattering of English," was no real exception to this rule.*

The true lesson of the mutiny was to teach the folly of trying to hold India by means of a large Sepoy army of Brahmans and Rájputs unchecked by a due proportion of British troops. Owing to the mutual jealousies of the Company and the Crown, our native army, in 1857, outnumbered the English garrison by more than eight to one, while its ranks were chiefly recruited from one or two dominant castes in the Ganges Valley. The good old rule, " divide et impera," had been too long neglected ; we had failed to " keep our powder dry ; " and the fruits of our carelessness and false economy were gathered to the last sheaf. Happily the lesson has not been taught in vain. The excess of Brahmans and Rájputs has given place to a large admixture of Sikhs, Panjábis, Gorkhas, and Patháns ; our guns are manned and our strong places held by white troops, while the proportion of Sepoys to Europeans has been brought down by a twofold process of recruiting and depletion to the safe level of two to one.

* Temple ; Gubbins ; Sir C. Trevelyan ; Raikes ; Bourchier ; Norton.

CHAPTER VI.

THE DOOM OF THE GREAT COMPANY.

THE prophecy that foretold the extinction of the Company's *Ráj* in the hundredth year after the battle of Plassy was not wholly falsified by the event. Our Indian Empire survived the Mutiny, but the knell of its founders and nominal Lords, the East India Company, was rung in the massacres of Delhi and Cawnpore. Even before the final capture of Lucknow the chartered body of merchants and gentlemen trading to the East was already bowing its head for the blow that should consign it to the tomb of all bygone dynasties. Very slow at first to take in the full purport of the Sepoy revolt, the people of England in the course of a few months reeled through many phases of panic fear, rage, amazement, grief, vengefulness, perplexity, before their blind searchings after some convenient scapegoat brought them up beside the middle-class sovereignty enthroned in Leadenhall Street. Then at last there rose from every quarter an ever-loudening cry for the political death of the famous Company whose servants in a hundred years had conquered an empire wider than India itself. A hundred different theories touching the causes and character of the Mutiny would all lead only to one conclusion, the absolute need of removing so unsightly a barrier between the people of India and the British Crown. Whether the Company had or had not misgoverned their vast domains; whether their power for good or evil had been checked for worse or better by the Ministerial Board of Control; whether Mohammadan turbulence or Hindu discontent, the pride of over-petted or the fears of ill-used Sepoys, the absorption of native States or the steady undermining of native creeds and habits, the absence or the excess of Christian zeal among our countrymen, had most to do with the tragical uprising of 1857, every one save the Company's few friends agreed that the Queen of England should now stand forth sole mistress of an empire which the Crown in fact already wielded, under the mask of a directorate chosen by a few hundred owners of Indian stock.

Even they who felt most strongly the unfairness of punishing the India House for the shortcomings of Downing Street and Cannon Row, who believed that India was best governed by men of Indian experience untrammelled by party ties, in whose minds the name of the great Company had linked itself with a long roll of great deeds and glorious careers,—they, too, were borne unwillingly along the high tide of popular feeling, were driven at least to own the vanity of trying any longer to resist a movement which had gained in force and volume with each successive lapse and renewal of the Company's Charter. Ever since Pitt's invention of the Board of Control as a check upon the sovereignty of the India House, the doom of the latter had been foreshadowed more and more clearly in each fresh curtailment, whether of its commercial privileges or its political powers. In the great Sepoy rising most English statesmen heard only the long-delayed signal to let go the axe which for three-quarters of a century had been hanging over the heads of India's nominal masters. The bulk of their vast patronage already gone from them, their freedom of action more and more hampered by the Board of Control, their past services and present usefulness underrated or ignored, the magnates of the India House knew that their day was over; could do no better than await with the dignity of Rome's grey-bearded senators the blow that blotted them out of political being.[*]

To be wholly silent in view of impending fate might have taxed their fortitude overmuch. In December, 1857, they had learned from Lord Palmerston, then Prime Minister, that a Bill transferring the government of India from the Company to the Crown would shortly be laid before Parliament. This announcement speedily drew forth a plaintive letter to Lord Palmerston, in which the Court of Directors avowed their surprise at a step so hasty, founded on no sort of previous inquiry into the case at issue between the Directors and their opponents. "Even before the Mutiny was quelled," whilst the excitement in India was yet great, the Ministry had resolved upon the downfall of a body "entitled at least to the credit of having so administered the government of India, that the heads of all the Native States and the mass of the population, amid the excitements of a mutin-

[*] Trotter.

ous soldiery inflamed by unfounded apprehension of danger to their religion, had remained true to the Company's rule."*

The letter was followed by a solemn petition to the Parliament that met in February, 1858. In this masterpiece of careful pleading, dawn up by John Stuart Mill, the great English philosopher, who served as Political Secretary at the India House, the Court of Directors challenged the most searching inquiry into their past conduct, into the causes of the Mutiny, and the measures adopted for its suppression. If any of those measures had been wrongly taken, the blame, they urged, should lie chiefly with the Queen's Government, without whose sanction, against whose commands, nothing had been done or left undone. To believe that a Minister of the Crown would have governed India better without the aid of the Court of Directors was to believe that he had governed ill because he had been aided by "experienced and responsible advisers." Was it not absurd, they asked in effect, to try and remedy past failures by doing away with the secondary and therefore less blamable of the ruling powers?

Disclaiming all wish to shirk their full share of responsibility for the course of a government, "one of the purest in intention and most beneficent in act ever known among mankind," a government which, so far as they were concerned, might safely be left "to await the verdict of history," the petitioners could not but dwell on the mischievous impression which their impending fate would work upon the minds of their Indian subjects. To these the apparent change of masters—for as yet they knew only of the Company—would seem like the announcement of a radical change for the worse in the principles of our Indian policy. They would see but too good reason to believe that the new government would fling aside the pledges with the traditions of the old ; would no longer hold the balance fair between different creeds and races, or show due respect for the habits, feelings, and prejudices, social and religious, of the millions transferred to their charge. If such a belief should ever gain firm hold of the Indian people, then indeed would follow that general uprising which the wise forbearance of their old rulers had done so much to avert, even in the midst of a mutiny said to have sprung out of a blind religious panic.

With mingled pain and dismay the petitioners deplored the new-born temper of their countrymen against the natives of India,

* Official Papers.

and the wide growth of the doctrine "that India should be administered with an especial view to the benefit of the English who reside there." The ill-feeling towards the natives they held to be alike unjust and "fatal to the possibility of good government." As for the new doctrine, it was utterly at war with those principles of unselfish dealing which the rulers of India, allowing no such distinction as that of a downcast and a subject race, had always prided themselves on faithfully carrying out. Mainly for its faithfulness to those principles was the Company now assailed; and its fall would seem to the people of India like a first success achieved by its political foes.

Even if the change proposed were advisable, it ought not to be carried out until men's minds in England had cooled down, and the people of India had no excuse left for connecting the new reform with the late calamitous events. In all past changes tending to the common weal the petitioners had always willingly acquiesced, at whatever sacrifice on their own part. Even now they were ready to yield up the remainder of their trust without a murmur, if only a better system of governing India could be devised. Was it possible to devise a better system?

It might safely be assumed that no Minister of the Crown would be set to govern India unaided by a council of statesmen experienced in Indian affairs. Such a council must not only be fit to advise the Minister, it should also wield a certain moral control, as a counterpoise to the pressure of private interests and party claims backed by the organs of popular opinion at home. Without that moral check, without full power to press on the Minister their own opinions and to obtain his recorded reasons for overruling the same, such a council could only become his screen. And in respect of moral influence, what new council could ever equal the old historic Court of Directors? What freedom of action was likely to be found in the best-meaning body of Crown nominees? It was hard to see how such a council could maintain that happy independence of Parliament and party, which had hitherto saved India to the English nation by enabling the Directors to dispense their patronage freely among the middle classes at home, and to leave promotion in their Indian services to the unbiassed judgement of the local authorities.

Three things the petitioners deemed essential to the working of any scheme for the government of India. A majority of the Minister's council must "hold their seats independently of his appointment." To the council as a whole, and not to the Minister, should be assigned the duty of preparing the despatches, and the privilege of naming and controlling the officers on the home establishment. Lastly, the numerical strength of a consulting body, which ought to consist of men chosen from each of our Indian provinces, either for their general experience or for their special conversance with this or that branch of work, should rather outrun than fall short of the present limit of eighteen; especially as the larger body would be much more likely to press their joint opinion against the Minister than one of six or eight.

If Parliament believed that all these requisites of good government could anywhere be combined more largely than in the existing Court of Directors, the petitioners "humbly hoped" that Parliament would succeed in finding such a body. But if in the conditions thus set forth the petitioners had "in fact enumerated the qualities possessed by the present system," then they besought their honourable Houses to maintain the Directors in their existing powers.

It remained to deal with the cry of "double government" so often levelled against the present system, and so likely to be repeated against any system which might hamper a Minister with an independent council. Were the Court of Directors a purely executive body, there might be grounds for such a cry. But an executive body neither branch of the Home Government of India could fairly be called. "The executive government of India is and must be seated in India itself." The Court of Directors was in effect a deliberative body, with functions not unlike those of that "triple government," the British Parliament. "To scrutinize and revise the past acts of the Indian Government—to lay down principles and issue general instructions for their future guidance—to give or refuse sanction to great political measures which are referred home for approval"—these duties, common to both branches of the Home Government, were such as allowed and called for "the concurrence of more judgements than one." What gain could it be to make the double body single by cutting away its more efficient half?

But the Indian authorities are said to be less responsible to the nation than any other branch of the Imperial Government, because no one knows where to fix the responsibility between the India House and the Board of Control. That, however, was a notion very wide of the truth. The Home Government of India was doubly responsible, first, through the President of the Board of Control; secondly, through his official advisers, the

India House Board. As in other departments of State, the former must have either commanded or sanctioned everything done by his fellow-workers. On the other hand, his advisers, unlike those in other departments of whom the public knew not even the names, were by law "as much responsible for what they advised, as he for what he ordained." How then could the one form of government be called responsible and the other irresponsible?*

With a brief warning against meddling with the substantive character of that fine school for officers, the old Indian Army, and with one more prayer for a full inquiry and a wise forbearance from premature action, the petitioners brought their pleading to a close. A calmer, yet stronger statement of the case, as it lay between them and the Board of Control, it was hardly possible to put together. Had they deigned to descend to particulars, to make use of telling illustrations, the case for the Directors might even have gained in actual strength more than it lost in outward dignity. They might, for example, have shown how rightfully a former President of the Board of Control had claimed for himself the whole credit of that Afghán War which first demoralized the Bengal Army, weakened the old belief in British prowess, and hampered the Indian Treasury with a load of unaccustomed debt. And they might with equal justice have pointed to the low state of the British garrison in India on the eve of the Mutiny, as a proof of the power for mischief sometimes wielded by an English Ministry in spite of repeated warnings from Leadenhall Street.

Strong, however, as their case might seem from the standpoint chosen by the first logician of his day, and despite the suasive earnestness of their attempts to prove the complete responsibility of the double government, the Court of Directors failed to soften the hearts of statesmen and legislators eager only to carry out a foregone conclusion. Their demands for a fair trial, their arguments for reasonable delay, their warnings against crude reforms inspired by passion and panic rather than sober reflection, were drowned in the storm of popular prejudice evoked by the disasters of 1857. Because India had been nearly lost to us under the rule of the East India Company, every one agreed that the Company must cease to rule. Whether the India House or the Board of Control was most to blame for the late disasters, the British public knew not, neither cared to know. Their chief desire was to punish somebody for what had happened; and the Company,

* East India Company's Petition to Parliament, January, 1858.

as nominal rulers of India, and as the weaker of two rival powers, found itself offered up by statesmen of all parties as a convenient sacrifice to the popular wrath.

The statesmen of course had reasons of their own, more decent, more plausible, and better-founded, for their ready compliance with the popular demand. Their zeal against the India House botokened among other things the growing impatience of a system whose anomalies had become more glaring with each new term of years ; a system of makeshifts and compromises which had gradually turned the Court of Directors into a mere screen and mouthpiece for the Board of Control. For the Home Government of our Indian Empire they would henceforth have but one responsible head ; and that head could not of course be found in the boardroom of a merchant-company already far on the road to political extinction. The time had come, they felt, for getting rid of a clumsy anachronism, a transparent sham ; for clinching at one stroke the process which had gone steadily forward ever since Philip Francis and Chief Justice Impey first set foot on Indian ground. The sceptre of the House of Bábar must pass at once without further disguise or subterfuge into the hands of its rightful holder, the Queen of England.

Petitions to Parliament and debates at the India House notwithstanding, the Palmerston Cabinet pushed on their " Bill for the better government of British India." Its opening clauses proclaimed the transfer of all political power, of all rights and property therewith connected, from the East India Company to the Queen's Government.

As the one acknowledged Sovereign of India, Her Majesty was to vest her powers in a President and Council of Eight for Indian Affairs. The President would hold office like any other Secretary of State, and his vote on nearly all questions would be final. His council were to be appointed for unequal terms of years from among those who had either served ten years in India, or had lived there for fifteen years at least. This body was to wield the powers hitherto shared between the Directors and the Board of Control. As for the Indian Services and the local patronage, they would be left untouched.

In this manner, said Lord Palmerston, would the old " cumbrous machinery be reduced in form to what it was in fact," and the whole power rest in future where the responsibility already lay. These changes, remarked Sir Charles Wood, were merely a logical extension of those effected in 1853. Since India would hence-

forth be garrisoned by a large army supplied from England, the
political power, said Lord John Russell, must clearly go with the
military. Sir Henry Rawlinson, himself a Director, saw large
assurance of good in a measure which abolished the double government and proclaimed the Queen sole ruler of British India. The
native feeling in that country, now sore against the Company's
Ráj, would be soothed by a proclamation which held out hopes of
a happier future for the subjects of a new dynasty. On the other
hand, Mr. T. Baring's amendment against immediate legislation
for India gave birth to many speeches in defence of existing use
and wont. This was not the time for effecting a change so
sweeping, so sure to alarm the native mind, so unfair to the Company thus condemned without a trial, or even a specific charge.
Such a change would throw too much power into the hands of an
English Ministry. The double government was better than the
despotism of a Secretary of State. It was not the Company but
the Board of Control whose misdeeds stood out most salient on
the page of modern history. The new Councillors would be
chosen for their political leanings, and the whole course of
Government would be guided by party needs. Was it likely that
so many millions of Hindus and Musalmans would care to have
for their Queen a Defender of the Faith that was not theirs?
And the steady force of public opinion at home, would it not
urge the Minister for India perilously fast and far on the road to
reforms more or less conflicting with native ideas?*

To all such pleadings for arrest of judgement there could be but
one answer, couched in whatever form or phrase. It was too late
to extol the merits of a system which the Mutiny had already
shattered into pieces. Of what use to plead the past services,
real or imaginary, of the East India Company in bar of the sentence decreed by fate and sealed by the popular voice? It was
possible that India might become the battle-ground of political
parties, and that any change of rulers might in some respects
prove a change for the worse. But the change in this case was
inevitable; it meant only the removal of obsolete pretences; and
it involved no necessary break in our Indian policy. The transfer
of all power from the hands of an abnormal directorate to those
of a recognized department of the State would be no revolution,
but a mere piece of administrative reform, the last stage in a
process dating back to the days of Warren Hastings.

* *The Times ; Allen's Indian Mail, &c.*

Lord Palmerston's Bill, however, was not to become law. Carried through its first reading on the 18th of February, 1858, it shared the fortunes of the Ministry which found itself defeated next night in the Commons on a question arising out of Orsini's attempt on the life of the French Emperor, Louis Napoleon. The old British pride took fire at Palmerston's apparent readiness to play into the hands of a foreign tyrant under cover of amending our Conspiracy Laws. A Tory Government, headed by Lord Derby, stepped into power, and Lord Ellenborough displaced Mr. Vernon Smith at the Board of Control. Mr. Disraeli, as leader of the Ministerial party in the Commons, brought forward a rival Bill of his own or Lord Ellenborough's devising, which aimed at winning the votes of all parties, but succeeded in pleasing none. Its leading feature was the ordaining of a Council of Eighteen, whose special knowledge, experience, and distinction would invest them, said Mr. Disraeli, with a moral influence and authority before which even a despotic Minister must bow. In this council nine members appointed by the Crown would represent severally nine branches of the local government, from the Civil Service of Bengal to the Company's Bombay Army and the Queen's Forces in British India. Of the other nine, four were to be elected by the votes of all who had served ten years in India, or held a thousand pounds of India Stock, or twice that sum in Indian railways or other joint-stock public works. These four must have lived fifteen years in India, or else have served there in some capacity for ten years. The remaining five were to be elected by the voters in the five chief seats of English trade and industry from among those who had been for ten years engaged in some branch of our Indian trade.

The fate of Lord Ellenborough's bantling was soon sealed by the popular verdict. The Court of Directors deemed the new Bill at least as bad as its predecessor, while the Press in general laughed aloud at the intricate redundance of the projected Council. On the 23rd of April Mr. Disraeli, acting on a suggestion thrown out some days before by the veteran Whig leader, Lord John Russell, agreed to quash his own Bill and proceed by Resolutions towards the framing of another. Between the 30th of April and the 17th of June only five of these needful postulates had been affirmed by the House of Commons, after much debating, more than one party battle, and the long delay caused by Lord Ellenborough's rash interference in the affairs of Oudh. At length Lord Stanley, who had meanwhile taken up the post vacated by

Lord Ellenborough, proposed to waive further preliminaries, and to bring in a regular Bill founded on the bases already adopted.

On the 24th of June the new Bill was read a second time, after Mr. Bright had delivered a powerful protest, not against the second reading, but against the tendency to amass all local powers in the hands of one supreme Viceroy. On the 25th the House went into Committee on the Bill, of whose contents the following is a fair summary. A Secretary of State, armed with all the powers once shared between the India House and Cannon Row, was to be aided by a Council of Fifteen, chosen at first partly by the Court of Directors out of their own number, partly by the usual advisers of the Crown. Eight at least of the fifteen must have either served or lived in India ten years. After the first elections all future members of the new body should be chosen alternately by Council and by Crown. Each Councillor was to hold office "during good behaviour," with a salary of twelve hundred a year and a suitable pension when he chose to retire. No Councillor might sit in Parliament. The Minister-President could divide his council into committees for the better despatch of business. Once a week, if not oftener, he was to hold a general sitting, with five members for a quorum. When the numbers were equal he or his vice-president was to give the casting-vote; but in all questions save that of spending money his own veto could override any number of adverse votes. As representing the old Secret Committee, the President might forward or receive despatches unread by any of his Council. The old local patronage was to remain with the local authorities; what patronage in either country had belonged to the Directors being henceforth divided between the new Council and the Crown. A certain number of cadetships were reserved for the sons of those who had served in India. Competitive examinations for the engineers and artillery; the transfer of the Company's fleet, armies, property, claims, liabilities, all save the East India Stock, to the Crown; the placing of all Indian disbursements under the control of the Secretary in Council; the exempting of Indian revenues from all charges for wars unconnected with Indian interests,—such were the chief remaining items of Lord Stanley's India Bill, the only one that was destined to become law.*

Lord Palmerston's attempts in Committee to reduce the Council by three, and to claim the sole power of appointing to it for the Crown, were thwarted by large majorities. Other hostile

* Trotter; Chambers; Parliamentary Papers.

amendments met on the whole with small favour from a House impatient of further delay in finishing a tough and tiresome piece of legislative work. The retention, however, of the Secret Committee under a new form was carried only by twenty-four votes, against the ripe experience of Lord John Russell, the shrewd misgivings of the clear-headed Sir G. Cornwall Lewis, and the earnest remonstrances of Mr. Ross Mangles, then Chairman of the Court of Directors. A vain attempt to limit the term of office in the Council to five or ten years was followed by the defeat of a motion for enabling Councillors to sit in Parliament. With better fortune did Mr. Gladstone insist that, "except for repelling actual invasion, or under sudden and urgent necessity, Her Majesty's forces in India shall not be employed in any military operation beyond the external frontier of her Indian possessions, without the consent of Parliament."

At length, on the 8th of July, the new India Bill passed its third reading in the House of Commons. A few days later it was undergoing sharp criticism in the House of Lords. In the debate on the second reading Lord Ellenborough bewailed the difference between his own and the present Bill. The double government was not abolished; the presence of a responsible head was still lacking, besides many other faults which he could not help seeing. In Committee Lord Broughton, the Sir John Hobhouse of Lord Auckland's day, denounced the whole scheme of a Council as an useless clog upon the Minister. Lord Ellenborough again fell foul of the plan for opening the engineer and artillery services to public competition as "an act of homage to democracy." Lord Derby, for his part, failed to see why a clever youth should be shut out from an honourable career "because he happened to be the son of a tailor, a grocer, or a cheesemonger;" but a majority of the Peers resolved that none but "gentlemen" should compete for those services. In the last days of July the India Bill as amended by the Lords passed under review of the Commons. Most of the amendments were disallowed; but in spite of Sir James Graham's manly appeal from Lord Ellenborough's sneer against the John Gilpin class to the humble origin of such men as Clive, "the son of a yeoman," Munro, "the son of a Glasgow merchant," and Malcolm, "the son of a sheep farmer," the Government agreed for the present to accept the Peers' rule of fitness for the Engineers and Artillery.*

---

* Trotter ; Chambers ; *The Times ;* &c.

During the debates in the Upper House some few of the Lords Spiritual showed how hard it is for religious leaders to play the part of cool-headed statesmen. The Archbishop of Canterbury, for example, looked forward to the founding of a system which would bring about " the final conversion of India to Christianity ;" and he urged the Government no longer to recognize any claims of caste. The wisdom of utterances like these remained hidden from those who knew how much the spirit of Christian prose-lytism had to answer for the Mutiny itself, and how deeply rooted was the reverence for caste distinctions even among classes which had least claim to Hindu descent. It was left for uninspired laymen to handle these questions—from a higher plat-form than theological zeal. Even Lord Shaftesbury, the straitest of Puritans, could join with Lord Ellenborough in bewailing the mischiefs likely to flow from the bitter feelings which late events had left rankling in the hearts both of the conquering and the conquered race. In words that sounded like a grave rebuke to the blind zeal of clerical partisans, Lord Derby himself proclaimed how nearly it touched " the interest, the peace, the well-being of England, if not also the very existence of her power in India, that the Government should carefully abstain from doing anything except to give indiscriminate and impartial protection to all sects and all creeds." And the State, he added, could do nothing more inconvenient or more dangerous than the abetting openly and actively in any scheme for converting the natives from their own religious, " however false or superstitious."

Our statesmen had cause enough to preach a wise forbearance at a time when the furnace of theological bigotry had been fanned into stronger flame by the popular exultation over the failure of a formidable revolt. To many an ardent Christian who could see no other way to heaven than his own, it seemed as if Heaven itself had now marked out an easy road to the conversion of a con-tinent filled with heathens. Now, while the fear of the Farangi was great throughout India, while the foot of the conqueror was firmly planted on the neck of the conquered, should the banner of the Cross be openly unfurled in every city, market-place, school, canton-ment, by a host of missionaries eager for the fray. Government itself should become a missionary. Its officers should be allowed, encouraged, to mingle proselytism with their other duties. English-men must no longer be "ashamed of their Christianity." The Bible should be made a class-book in all Government schools and colleges. No more favour must be shown to heathens and idolaters. All grants of land or money for the maintenance of heathen priests and temples should be at once withdrawn. The last barriers of caste should be broken down, and native Christians encouraged to flock into the public service. Let us do all this, put down the native holidays, sweep away all native laws, forbid all offensive parade of native worship, and then the heathen millions will give up fighting against manifest doom, will turn with philosophic cheerfulness from the worship of idols and false gods, from the doctrines taught in the Puránas, the Granth and the Korán, to the one true faith professed by their English rulers.

Such was the vision of the future, as conceived by many an eager spirit who mistook his own fancies for the voice of experience. Among these modern imitators of Alfred and Charlemagne were some of those who had served their country well in her sore need. Even the strong mind of Sir Herbert Edwardes—he had now been knighted—got borne away upon the torrent of fanaticism let loose by the patrons and orators of Exeter Hall. In his scheme for governing India on Christian principles,* and in his subsequent addresses to a London audience, the brilliant Commissioner of Pesháwar betrayed a curious lack of sound statesmanship, an unchristian contempt for that form of justice which aims at treating others even as we would be treated ourselves. In this respect he differed widely from Sir John Lawrence, whose fervent piety was largely tempered by his stern love of justice and his sturdy common sense. In his letter of the 21st of April to Lord Canning, the ruler of the Panjáb dealt in the spirit of a Christian statesman with the various questions which Edwardes had just argued in the spirit of an all-daring missionary. He was willing to place a Bible in the library of each Government school, for the good of those who might care to study it; he upheld the duty "of doing Christian things in a Christian way;" he would debar no native from the public service by reason of his caste or creed. But he set his face sternly against all proposals to encourage the lower at the expense of the higher castes, to deprive native clerks and officers of their accustomed holidays, and to sweep away all native laws that sinned against English prejudices or beliefs. Religious processions, Sir John, indeed, desired to suppress, in the interests not of Christianity, but of the public peace endangered by quarrels between rival sects.† In the height of the

---

* "Memorandum on the Elimination of all Unchristian Principles in the Government of British India," 1858.

† Trotter; Chambers; Temple.

missionary fever he never forgot the claims of common justice, good faith, and enlightened policy towards the millions who obeyed our rule.

On the 2nd of August, 1858, the "Act for the better government of India" passed under the Royal hand, and the East India Company ceased to rule the empire founded in its name. On the 7th the Directors went through the process of electing seven of their number to seats in the new Council of India. Chief among these seven were Sir James Hogg, Elliot Macnaghten, Ross Mangles, and Captain William Eastwick : all names of note in past years. On the first day of the following month the Court of Directors held their last meeting in the noble-fronted pile which rose in 1796 on the spot where an older India House, reared in 1726, had marked the site of a building occupied by the Company's officers ever since the middle of the seventeenth century.* Two days earlier the Court of Proprietors, in special meeting, had voted Sir John Lawrence a handsome pension for his matchless services during the past year. On both occasions a spirit of kindly gratitude towards all their late dependents, of stately submission to their own fate, of cheerful trust in the wisdom of their successors, spoke out in the parting words and votes of those unseated magnates and disfranchised guardians of an imperial domain. From the masters of an empire nearly as large as Europe, the great Merchant Company sank thenceforth into the drawers of certain dividends on East India Stock. Only a few of their late directors remained to guard the interests of their former subjects in the new Council which met at the India House on the 3rd of September around the chair of its first President, Lord Stanley.†

Amidst the lull of a long parliamentary recess, and the general absence of holiday-making Britons from their ordinary homes and wonted business-haunts, the passing away of the world-renowned Company awakened less stir in England than it might else have done, even in view of the popular demand for its extinction. If leading journals chanted a Requiem for "the greatest corporate body the world has ever seen,"‡ the mourners around its grave were comparatively few. The Company had no friends about the Throne, and very few in the leading circles of political and commercial life. Even among its late servants the feeling evoked by its fate was commonly one of hopeful or contented

---

* Two years later the India House was pulled down and carted away.

† Trotter; Chambers.   ‡ *The Times,* September 1, 1858.

acquiescence in a change which involved no loss of former privileges, no disturbance of vested rights. The younger members of the great Indian Services found especial comfort in a process which transformed the officers of a merchant company into acknowledged servants of the Crown. Nor in its earliest issues did the change itself seem very great. It was rather as if an old business-firm had placed a new name upon its doors. A Minister of the Crown sat in Leadenhall Street instead of Cannon Row. His Council was composed either of old Directors or distinguished servants of the Company. Among the latter were the well-known names of Sir John Lawrence, Sir Henry Montgomery of the Madras Council, Sir Frederick Currie, and Sir Henry Rawlinson. Of the two Under-Secretaries one was the veteran Sir George Clerk. Under him Mr. James Melville still held his former office. Ill-health alone accounted for the retirement of Stuart Mill. The general staff of the old departments, both at home and in India, remained well-nigh untouched. In the whole machinery of government very little indeed was altered beyond the apparent relations of one particular wheel towards the rest. Whatever changes might come thereafter, nothing seemed for the moment to suffer except the mere romance of a glorious name.

Some words, however, of natural regret may well be spoken in memory even of a bygone romance. Looking back to the days before Plassy, Englishmen might well feel proud on the whole of the part which English enterprise had since played so brilliantly in the far-off East. A Service which, during the past century, had bred an unrivalled succession of names great in peace and in war; a Company which in the same time had grown out of a mere trading-firm into the rulers of thickly-peopled provinces held by an army of half a million men; a dozen great dynasties overthrown; two hundred millions of people kept on the whole in prosperous order by a few thousand white men leading twenty times their number of native soldiers, policemen, and law-officers,—the bare statement of results like these suggests a rich storehouse of romantic themes, over which the shadow of a catastrophe long feared, yet sudden in its coming, broods like the Nemesis of " Agamemnon " or " King Lear."

" Some men," says Malvolio, " have greatness thrust upon them." Little did the chartered Company of Queen Elizabeth's last years, little did the merchants to whom Charles II. gave up the island-dower of his Portuguese bride, little did Holwell and his fellow-sufferers in the Black Hole of Calcutta dream to what heights of seeming glory the magnates of the India House would rise even in the first years of the nineteenth century. From the day when Plassy avenged the insults and the cruelties endured by the prisoners of Suráj-ud-daula, greatness came upon the Company against its will. One step forward led to another; Hastings outshone Clive; the Marquis of Hastings bettered the teaching of Marquis Wellesley. Dupleix and Lally, Haidar Ali and Tippu, the Maráthas and the Nizám, all helped alike by their failures and their successes to hasten the consummation they least desired. The friendship and the enmity, the weakness and the strength, of native rulers alike served as stepping-stones to fresh conquests on the part of a corporation which still protested and even struggled against manifest doom. In spite of his own pledges and prepossessions, each new Governor-General plucked fresh clusters of the fruit that each successive Court of Directors ordered him, if possible, to let alone. It was the old tale of Roman conquests repeated, with certain differences, in a later age. Wars of self-defence begat treaties; breaches of treaty entailed fresh wars, fresh changes in the map of British India. At first as humble lieges, then as favoured subalterns, finally as all-powerful vicegerents to the helpless House of Bábar, did the Company's agents win their way, with eyes averted, with unwilling feet, with regretful utterances, up to the topmost peak of a sovereignty surpassing even that of Akbar and Aurangzib.

The first step taken forward involved the last. A score of arguments always sprang up to justify or excuse each fresh enlargement of the Company's domains. Policy, justice, honour, compassion, self-defence, one or another of these motives had been pleaded even in defence of the Afghán War and the conquest of Sind. Out of each conquest arose new entanglements. To stand still upon ground so steep and slippery was more dangerous than to go on. The storming of Seringapatam cleared the way for a decisive struggle with the great Marátha power. British failure in Afghánistán had to be retrieved by the overthrow of Sind Amirs and the final conquest of the Panjáb. Burmese insolence had to be requited by the loss of provinces which skirted the Bay of Bengal and guarded the outlets of the Irawádi. Fair-sounding pleas of justice and humanity covered alike the forfeiture of Berár, the absorption of Nágpur, and the establishment of British rule in Oudh. By whomsoever sanctioned, the Court of Directors or the Board of Control, the game of conquest went merrily forward; the Python of the India House was never long without its accustomed meal. The Company might continue to make wry faces over the feast thus set before it; but a cynical and unfeeling world mistook the emotion for something akin to crocodiles' tears. What reason could any one have for weeping over the growth of an empire whose greatness filled all Europe with wonder and unfeigned respect for the British name?

The Company, however, had cause for sadness in the most glorious moments of their career. In every pealing of bells for a great victory they could hear their own dirge sung anew. The broader grew their empire, the nearer drew the hour of their political death. Their sovereignty had long been undermined by the powers entrusted in 1784 to the Ministerial Board of Control. Each subsequent revision of their charter had but driven another nail into their coffin. Each fresh inroad into their old monopoly, whether of trade or government, had brought them nearer to their final eclipse. During the past quarter of a century the whole spirit of modern statesmanship, the whole force of popular English feeling, had overborne their efforts to avert the crisis which a sudden uprising of Sepoys, fanatics, and bazaar-rabble brought to a fateful head. The Company's patronage, their last remaining source of political life, was fast slipping out of their hands, when the great storm of 1857 swept away the last remnants of their former greatness. Shaken to its foundations by a fearful earthquake, the stately building they had helped to rear outstood the shock, but the ownership passed away into other hands. In that momentous struggle against appalling odds the Farangi triumphed, but the assailants had their revenge; for while the last of them were yet fighting, the old " Kompani Bahádur " had disappeared from the historic scene as utterly as the last prince of Bábar's line.

BOOK V.

THE NEW ERA.

1858–1868.

CHAPTER I.

FIRST DAYS OF THE NEW RULE.

On the 1st of November, 1858, when the steamy heats of the rainy season had vanished before the cool breath of an Indian autumn, a new era of peace and good government was proclaimed throughout British India by the reading of the manifesto in which Queen Victoria formally assumed the sceptre hitherto wielded by her trustees, the Honourable East India Company. This carefully-worded State-paper, drawn up by Lord Derby and retouched by the Queen herself,* teemed with every assurance of pardon, protection, goodwill, and tender treatment for all ranks and classes of Her Majesty's Indian subjects, save the convicted murderers of English folk. It proclaimed a policy of strong-handed peace, good faith, and enlightened efforts for the common weal; of respect for "the rights, dignity, and honour of native princes as our own;" of impartial tolerance for all forms of religious belief or worship. None should be "in anywise favoured, none molested or disquieted" on account of his religious creed under a Government which for the first time openly rejoiced in its own Christianity. Every native, of whatever race or creed, was to be freely admitted to any public office, the duties of which he might be qualified by "education, ability, and integrity duly to discharge." In all future legislation all possible regard should be paid to "the ancient rights, usages, and customs of India," especially to all rights connected with the holding of ancestral lands.

Her Majesty's Indian subjects were bidden to "be faithful and to bear true allegiance" to their new Sovereign, who declared Viscount Canning her first Viceroy and Governor-General. Every servant of the East India Company was confirmed in his present office, subject to the Queen's future pleasure and to any laws and regulations that might thereafter be enacted. Fresh offers of grace and amnesty, besides those already issued by Lord Canning, were held out to all who might comply with their conditions

* Sir Theodore Martin's "Life of the Prince Consort."

before the first day of the coming year. One last assurance of the Queen's desire to further the well-being of all classes by good government and useful public works ushered in this brief but solemn prayer, dictated by the Queen herself :—" May the God of all power grant unto us, and to those in authority under us, strength to carry out these our wishes for the good of our people ! "*

It was a memorable holiday all over India, the day when this Proclamation was read aloud, not only in the Viceroy's camp at Allahábád, but at the head-quarters of every province in the Empire, from the Panjáb to Pegu. At the great frontier outpost of Peshúwar John Lawrence himself delivered the royal message, as he sat on horseback amidst the assembled troops. In all the chief cities of British India the booming of guns, the clang of military music, the cheers of paraded soldiery, and the noise of admiring crowds acclaimed the new charter of Indian rights and aspirations. In the hill-girt harbour of Bombay, in the rising port of Karáchi, in the breezy roadstead of Madras, on the breast of treacherous Húghli, of deep-rolling Irawúdi, the flags that covered the shipping streamed bright in the clear November sunshine. At night, both on land and water, there burst forth everywhere a blaze of fireworks, blue lights, and the gleam of countless coloured lamps. Every public building, every street in the great Indian capitals was lighted up for hours. Mosque, pagoda, and Parsi temple vied with church and chapel in making night glorious in cities where gas was still unknown. Rejoicing crowds buzzed along the bazaars or blockaded with carriages the broader thoroughfares of the English town. There was feasting in the houses not only of our own country-folk, but of many a native gentleman in all parts of the country. Translated into twenty native tongues and reproduced in thousands of printed copies, the glad tidings proclaimed on that auspicious day speedily found an echo in the farthest corners of the Queen's new realm. Loyal addresses to Her Majesty, weighted with a host of native signatures, seemed to attest a feeling stronger than mere acquiescence in the new rule. Native journalists and native speakers at public meetings agreed in welcoming " with the highest hope and the liveliest gratitude " a manifesto which asserted in every line the broadest principles of humanity, mercy, and equal justice to prince and peasant, Brahman and Pariah.†

In the principles thus revealed there was after all no marked

* Trotter ; Chambers ; Martin.
† Trotter ; Chambers ; *Allen's Indian Mail* ; Martin.

divergence from those professed by the East India Company. It formed indeed one special merit of the Proclamation that, in seeming to declare a new policy, it held fast in effect to the good old ways. The voice was Jacob's voice, though the hands were the hands of Esau. If the new Government made a little louder profession of its religious faith, if it held out to the natives a little surer prospect of rising in the public service, in all other respects the official programme might have been taken for a condensed copy of the lessons continually instilled into their servants' minds by the well-meaning directorate of Leadenhall Street. It involved no question of a revolution, hardly even of a reform. No new principle really underlay the assertion of Her Majesty's resolve to govern her new subjects with a tender and scrupulous regard for the rights, dignities, usages, and well-being of each and all.

Nevertheless the Royal Proclamation held for many minds and many classes of people a very powerful charm. To all who had a grievance or a grudge against the Company, to all who feared for their religion, their property, or their lives, to all who had just been tasting the bitter fruits of anarchy and violence, it seemed like a happy waking out of a bad dream, a quiet sunrise after a night of storm and great peril. A certain sense of relief from past troubles, from secret fears for the future, inclined the people at large to see in any change of rulers some change for the better, to extract from this first utterance of their new Sovereign as rich a store of comfort and encouragement, as words of manifest kindliness and good faith could yield. Loyal princes feared no longer for their prescriptive rights and immunities; insurgent Tálukdárs hastened to recover by timely submission their forfeit lands; while everywhere, in town and country, the men of culture, energy, and social weight hailed the new edict as a timely message of peace and goodwill for all classes of the people; as the fitting prologue to a new tale of national progress under a ruler whom all men, high and low, Hindu and Mohammadan, were bound by custom and the force of circumstances to obey.

In close keeping with the spirit of the Proclamation were the measures taken by Lord Canning's Government to reward the services and confirm the loyalty of the chiefs and princes who had stood by us in our sorest need. In the spring of 1858, when the reign of law and civil order had been fairly re-established in the city of Delhi and the surrounding districts, Sir John Lawrence marched up the country towards Lahór. On his way through Sirhind he exchanged cordial greetings and friendly talk with the great Sikh Lords of Pattiála, Jhind, and Nabha, whose splendid services called for timely acknowledgement at our hands. To his proposals on their behalf Lord Canning readily gave the needful sanction. Titles of honour and symbols of precedence are very dear to Asiatic princes. Among the new titles bestowed on Mahárája Narindar Singh of Pattiála were those of Farzand Khás or "Choicest Son" of the British Government, and Mansúr Zamán or "Conqueror of the World." The grey-bearded Rajah Sarúp Singh of Jhind was greeted as "Most cherished Son of true Faith," and the number of guns in his salute was raised to eleven. "Noble Son of good Faith" was the title bestowed on the Rajah of Nabha, who was thenceforth to enjoy a salute of nine guns. Seventeen was the number assigned to Pattiála, who ranked among the Panjáb Chiefs as second only to Kashmir. A more solid token of British gratitude was the grant of confiscated lands and houses allotted to each prince in proportion to his rank and services; Pattiála's income being thus improved by two lakhs, or £20,000 a year. In the following year another true friend of the white stranger, the warlike Rajah Randhir Singh of Kapurthalla, obtained a goodly fief in Oudh, with a title of honour and a salute of eleven guns, in return for the zeal and gallantry with which he had fought against our foes. A smaller estate and a lower title of honour were conferred on his brave brother, Sardár Bikram Singh.[*]

The debt of gratitude which England owed to the Nizám of Haidarábád and his faithful Minister, Sálar Jang, was not long to be left unpaid. The Nizám bore no special love to the countrymen of Lord Dalhousie; but he knew which way his interest pointed, and Sálar Jang's zeal in his master's service was guided to the happiest issues by the wisdom of a statesman reared in the learning and the culture of the West. In 1860 the great Musalman potentate of Southern India received back from Lord Canning a large slice of the territory his father had yielded up to Lord Dalhousie in 1853. Besides the districts of Naldrúg, Dárascó, and Raichúr, he was placed in full ownership of Shorápur, a little State whose young Rajah had rashly rebelled against the Indian Government. The Rajah's death-sentence had just been commuted to imprisonment for four years, when he died,

---

[*] Temple ; Lepel-Griffin ; Chambers.

perhaps accidentally, by his own hand.* To crown all, the Nizám's debts to the Indian Government, still amounting to half a million sterling, were altogether wiped out. Among the costly presents which Colonel Davidson was charged to offer him were a jewelled sword and a splendid diamond ring. Gifts of honour to the value of £3,000 each, were also presented to Sálar Jang and the stately old Nawáb Shams-ul-Umra, the highest noble in Haidarábád.

In return for the helpful services of our Nipálese ally a large tract of forest land on the borders of Oudh was transferred to the kingdom of Nipál. For the strong-handed Minister of Nipál's puppet king was reserved an honour till then confined to worthies of another creed and of a less barbarian stamp. In the gazette which announced the bestowal of a Grand Cross of the Bath on Sir Hugh Rose, the name of Jang Bahádur figured oddly under the same heading as the victor of Jhánsi and Gwáliár.†

Sindhia's loyalty under the most trying conditions deserved the fullest possible recognition at our hands. If the removal of a British garrison from his fortress of Gwáliár was a boon that could not then be safely conceded,‡ the cost of maintaining an armed force commanded by British officers no longer fell upon Sindhia's treasury. His territory was enlarged by a grant of lands yielding a revenue of three lakhs a year; and erelong the Indian Government allowed him to raise the strength of his own infantry from 3,000 to 5,000 men, and the number of his guns from thirty-two to thirty-six. His able Minister, Dinkar Rao, was afterwards honoured with a knighthood of the Star of India. Durand's influence in the Viceroy's Council still fought against the claims of Holkar to any other reward than his exoneration from blame for past mishaps. The manly-hearted Sikandar Begam of Bhopál received a liberal grant of lands confiscated from Dhár, and a formal acknowledgement of her sole right to reign over Bhopál, with a guarantee of succession for her daughter and her daughter's heirs. Many other princes and chiefs, such as the Gaikwár of Baroda, the Mahárája of Kashmir, the Rájput princes of Jaipur, Udaipur, and Karauli, were rewarded according to their several deserts, by grants of land, by reductions of their yearly tribute, by some relief from State debts owing to the

---

* The story of his brief career and its strangely foreshadowed close, is given by Colonel Meadows Taylor in his "Autobiography."

† Aitchison's "Treaties"; Temple; *Allen's Indian Mail.*

‡ It was at last conceded in 1885; the year before his death.

Paramount Power, or from the burden of maintaining a contingent force.*

To the loyal princes of Sirhind Lord Canning restored that full power of life and death over their own subjects which had been taken from them after the first Sikh War. For twelve years before the Mutiny that power had belonged to the Political Agent, without whose sanction no death-sentence could be carried into effect. But of all the boons which Canning was empowered to bestow on our Indian feudatories, none perhaps was more widely coveted than the right of perpetuating a native dynasty imperilled by the failure of natural heirs. If the great sovereign States, such as Haidarábád and Gwáliár, had nothing to fear on this score, the recent fate of Satára, Jhánsi, and Nágpur showed how easily the Right of Lapse inherent in the Paramount Power might be enforced against any State of a rank below the highest. That right had from time to time been enforced by native as well as English rulers, before Dalhousie began to use it as a means of enlarging the British power. But the doctrine which he had made the fashion no longer held its ground. A new fashion born of the Mutiny supplanted the old. Gratitude for the loyal bearing of so many native princes gave new vigour to the growing belief in the usefulness, the necessity of Native States, as a counterpoise to the drawbacks, and a virtual pledge for the maintenance, of British rule. The policy of absorption was formally exchanged for a policy of strict regard for the rights and dignities of native rulers.

In the spirit therefore of the Royal Proclamation, Lord Canning in 1860 issued a series of *Sanads* or Letters Patent, which expressly granted to each feudatory chief the right of adopting an heir from among his kinsmen on the failure of male issue in his own line. In the case of Mohammadan princes like the Nizám and the Nawáb of Tank, succession to the Masnad was guaranteed " in accordance with Mohammadan law and the customs of the country." In the case of Pattiála, Jhind, and Nabha, the new policy went further still. These princes of the same Phulkian line were assured that if one of them died without even an adopted heir, the choice of a meet successor should devolve upon the other two.†

Honours and rewards of various kinds in land, money, office, and decorations were showered on a host of lesser worthies who

---

* Aitchison; Malleson ; Official Papers.
† Aitchison; Lepel-Griffin ; Temple.

had done the State good service in their several ways and degrees. Such men as the Rajah of Banáras, Rajah Dirg Bijai Singh of Balrampur in Oudh, the Nawáb of Rámpur, and many a gallant Sikh Sardár obtained their due shares of the landed estates which their rebel owners had justly forfeited. Many a native officer and soldier was pensioned, promoted, or decorated with the Order of British India. Many thousands of rupees were distributed in small sums among faithful villagers and trusty servants who had saved English lives or rescued English property from rebel hands. Sometimes a whole township would be honoured as one man. During the troubles in Bahár, for instance, the men of Sáswaram, led by their Patél or headman, Kabir-uddin Ahmad, attacked and routed a strong body of Kúnwar Singh's troops. In honour of their bold deed the Viceroy ordered that the town itself should thenceforth be known as " Sáswaram, the defender of the Rulers." *

Nor were those of our own race forgotten who had unofficially done good service to the State. Vicars Boyle, the railway engineer to whose happy foresight the defence of Arah House was mainly due, was rewarded with a handsome Jaigir in Shahabad. Among other recipients of landed estates was Paterson Saunders, the merchant, planter, and able journalist, who had played so brilliant a part in the work done by the Agra Volunteers. The brave planter Venables, of Azimgarh, who had helped to defend that place in the worst days of 1857, and had fought as a volunteer under General Franks in 1858, died in April of that year of a wound received in Lugard's brush with the soldiers of Kúnwar Singh. To honour the memory of "this brave, self-denying English gentleman," as Lord Canning called him, was all that his countrymen could do ; and a committee formed for that purpose in Calcutta met with the Viceroy's heartiest support. Nor did the Court of Directors fail to add their solid tribute of respect for one whose "great services and untimely death "—he had gone back at Canning's request to Azimgarh, instead of returning home —entitled him to be held in equal honour with the best rewarded officers of the Crown and the Company.†

A new order of knighthood for India was a measure earnestly supported, if not conceived, by Queen Victoria herself. In May 1859 she wrote of it to her Viceroy as "a means of gratifying the personal feelings of the chief number of the native princes,

---

* Chambers ; *Allen's Indian Mail.*
† Chambers ; Trotter ; Official Papers.

binding them together in a confraternity, and attaching them by a personal tie to the Sovereign." As sketched out in her own letter, the proposed order might consist of twenty or twenty-four members, with the Queen herself for its Sovereign and the Viceroy for Grand Master. Some time was to elapse, however, before the scheme thus dimly outlined took definite shape as the Order of the Star of India. One cause of delay was the difficulty of choosing an appropriate title. Many nice points of detail had moreover to be discussed, both in England and in India. The question of a title was not finally settled till February 1861, and the new Order was not instituted before the 25th of July in the same year. The number of Knights, Indian and English, was fixed at twenty-five. The first grand investiture took place on one and the same day at Windsor and Allahábád.*

On the 1st of November, 1861, a gorgeous gathering of princes, gentlemen, officers, and English ladies, blazed around the rich red gold-flecked canopy beneath which, on his throne of state, sat Lord Canning, whose fine clear cut features set off a pale but noble countenance and a form and bearing full of the quiet dignity that became a ruler of men. Beside him were seated the new Commander-in-Chief, Sir Hugh Rose, the Mahárájas of Gwáliár and Pattiála, the Begam of Bhopál, and the Nawáb of Rámpur. Mr. Edmonstone, the new head of the North-West Provinces, and Sir Bartle Frere, as a prominent member of the Viceroy's Council, took their seats also among the favoured few. Conspicuous among them all for his goodly stature, his noble-looking mien, and his splendid apparel was the faithful Lord of Pattiála, whose prime of manhood was doomed a year later to an untimely close. Queenly and gorgeous in her own half-manly fashion sat the high-hearted Begam of Bhopál. To each of the native grandees in turn Lord Canning presented the star, badge, and collar of the new Order. Sir Hugh Rose had received his investiture a few weeks earlier. On the same day the Marátha princes of Indór and Baroda, and a little later the Nizám and the ruler of Kashmir, were invested with the Star of India, each in his own capital, by the hands of the British Resident. At Windsor Castle, on the same 1st of November, the Queen herself bestowed the same honour on the aged Lord Gough, Sir John Lawrence, Lord Clyde, Lord Harris, late Governor of Madras, Sir George Pollock of Afghán renown, and the young Mahárája Dhulip Singh, who had lately settled

---

* Martin.

down to the duties and the amusements of a wealthy English Squire.*

Meanwhile a number of changes and reforms more or less noteworthy had been going on in various branches of the Indian Government. In 1858 the Panjáb was raised to the rank of a substantive province, ruled by a Lieutenant-Governor and a mixed staff of officers, civil and military, under a system of "non-regulation" law. Sir John Lawrence, the first Lieutenant-Governor, resigned his post a few months afterwards to recruit his jaded powers and shattered health in the comparative repose of a seat in the Home Council of India. His place, however, at Lahór was worthily filled by Sir Robert Montgomery; the supreme charge of Óudh being handed over to Mr. Charles Wingfield, who upheld the new policy of friendly alliance with the Tálukdárs. Mr. George Edmonstone, Lord Canning's able Foreign Secretary, became Lieutenant-Governor of the North-West Provinces, which Canning himself had been virtually ruling during his stay at Allahábád. Sir John Grant succeeded Sir Frederic Halliday in the government of Bengal.†

In 1860 Lord Elphinstone, whose ready statesmanship had done so much for the maintenance of order in his own province and the defeat of mutineers and rebels elsewhere, made over the government of Bombay to the veteran Sir George Clerk, and went home, as it happened, only to die. At Madras Lord Harris, who had also proved an able and fearless ruler in a time of need, had meanwhile been succeeded by Sir Charles Trevelyan, whose great abilities had for some years past been turned to good account at home. He had already begun to show himself one of the most zealous and competent of Indian governors, when his bold defiance of the Supreme Government cut short his new career. Not content with minuting a vehement protest against the "tremendous taxes" which Mr. Wilson as finance-minister sought to lay upon the people of India, Sir Charles allowed his protest to appear in some of the local newspapers. For this offence against official decencies the Home Government speedily recalled him from a post in which he bade fair to rival the services and the popularity of Sir Thomas Munro. In the same year (1860) the noble Outram resigned his seat in the Viceroy's Council, and, worn out with the toils, hardships, and anxieties of the last three years, left the scene of his many distinguished services to linger peacefully, but not without honour, through the short term of life that still awaited him in his native land.‡

* Trotter; Martin.   † Trotter.   ‡ Trotter; Temple.

Instead of the old Legislative Council set up under Lord
Dalhousie, and denounced by his successor and Sir Charles
Wood, the new Minister for India, as a little parliament that
talked much and did nothing, a larger, less independent Council
was called into existence by the Parliament of 1861. The new
scheme certainly showed small trace of parliamentary freedom.
It left no place for the Calcutta judges, whose free criticisms
were wont to vex the official mind. The remodelled Council
had less scope for free action than the Darbár of a native
sovereign. Besides the members of the Executive Council, it
was to consist of twelve councillors, half of whom should be native
gentlemen or Englishmen outside the public service. Among
the first of the non-official members who held their seats as a
rule for one year, were the Mahárája of Pattiála, Sindhia's
late Minister, Rajah Dinkar Rao, and Rajah Deo Narain Singh
of Banáras, who during the late troubles had been one of our
staunchest friends. Like councils on a smaller scale were established in Bengal, Bombay and Madras.*

At the same time another member was added to the Viceroy's
Executive Council, so that Law and Finance might have an equal
voice therein. In 1859 the place of the fourth or law member of
Council had been assigned, not as usual to an English barrister, but to a gentleman versed in the weightier business of
finance. It soon appeared, however, that the lyre of government needed another string, and so in 1861 a lawyer once more
took his seat in Council beside Lord Canning's Finance Minister.
In the same year the old distinctions of Supreme and Sadr
Courts were blotted out by an Act of Parliament which united
the rival jurisdictions of Crown and Company into one High
Court for each Presidency. Of the judges allotted to each
Court one-third were to be English barristers of five years'
standing, and another third were covenanted civil officers of ten
years' service, who had been district judges for three years.
Native pleaders were also declared eligible for these High
Courts, whose members going on circuit were to hear all appeals
and try all cases, civil or criminal, reserved from the lower courts.
To them were referred all death-sentences passed by district
judges, and they only had power to punish European offenders
for crimes of the graver class. The sting thus taken out of the
old " Black Act," no good excuse remained for delaying the formal

adoption of that Penal Code which, first taken in hand by
Macaulay, had at length been moulded into thoroughly efficient
shape by Chief Justice Sir Barnes Peacocke. In the last weeks
of Lord Canning's rule the Code became law throughout India.*

A new Code of Criminal Procedure, by which many old processes were simplified or shortened and some useful innovations
effected, was set working at the same time. One of its provisions
empowered any justice of the peace to commit for trial any
offender even of the ruling race. This was a bitter draught for
some of our own people, whose pride took fire at the very thought
of subjection to the orders of a petty magistrate who might even
be a native born. It was felt, however, that public interests
called for some such method of dealing with the European loafers,
whose increasing numbers and lawless ways involved a new danger
to the public peace. Discharged railway-servants, sailors unemployed or absent without leave, masterless and reckless vagrants
of all kinds were beginning to haunt upcountry towns and stations
in quest of alms from any one, white or black, whose fears or sympathies might be turned to passing account. When prayers and
threats failed them, these homeless wretches would steal or
plunder in the bazaars to save themselves from starving, or to
get the means of drowning care in strong drink of the worst and
cheapest kind.† For some of these outcasts the magistrate's
order might ensure their temporary lodgement in a Presidency
jail, with the chance at least of making a new start in life thereafter.

The "Indian Civil Service Act of 1861" held out to deserving
natives and to all "uncovenanted" servants of the State—to all,
that is, who passed into the public service through other doors than
Haileybury and the new competitive system—a fair-seeming prospect of admission to many of the posts hitherto reserved for their
"covenanted" betters. It decreed, in the spirit of the Proclamation of 1858, that all offices in India, except those of Collector,
Magistrate, Judge, Commissioner, and a few others of special importance, might be filled by any person of whose fitness due evidence had been furnished; while even the excepted offices were
declared open to any outsider who, after living seven years in
India, could pass the regular departmental tests. The hopes thus
raised, however, in many hearts were doomed to prolonged disappointment. The Act remained for years, if not quite a dead

* Trotter ; Chesney.   † "Indian Year Book."

letter—a letter at least of no virtue except in non-regulation provinces like the Panjáb.*

In 1859, when the great storm of the Mutiny had blown itself out, a new danger remained to encounter. The troubles of the past two years had increased by twenty-one millions sterling the public debt of India. To that sum nine millions would have to be added for 1859, and at least six millions more for the coming year. A deficit of thirty-six millions in four years, on a revenue yielding barely thirty-seven millions a year, might well disquiet the minds of statesmen alive to the weak points of Indian finance. The Indian Treasury during that period had to bear the cost not only of a native army almost as large as that of 1856, but of nearly a hundred thousand British troops, or thrice the number of those that bore the first onset of the rebellion. New loans had been opened at high rates of interest, and large gaps in the revenue had to be filled by new taxes on trade or heavy additions to all manner of customs and excise dues. The import duties were raised from five to ten and even twenty per cent., and an export duty of three per cent. was levied on all the chief articles of Indian produce. India, in short, was paying the full money fine for an outbreak largely due to the carelessness of her English masters, who refused to help her even by guaranteeing the interest on her growing debt.†

They were ready, however, to let her pay for the services of one of their ablest financiers. Before the end of 1859 Mr. James Wilson, late Secretary to the English Treasury, a learned writer and high authority on all matters of finance, had taken his seat as Finance Minister in the Viceroy's Council. In the following February he propounded his scheme for rescuing India from financial collapse. Three new taxes on income, on trades and professions, and on tobacco, were among the means selected by him to that end. The income-tax was fixed at four per cent. on all incomes above £50 a year, and at two per cent. on incomes ranging between £20 and £50. The licence-duty ranged from one rupee a head on artisans to four rupees on shopkeepers, and ten on merchants, bankers, and professional men. This tax was designed to hit those classes of the people which had reaped most profit from our rule at the least apparent cost to themselves. The duty on tobacco was fixed at nearly a hundred per cent. The export duties of the previous year were taken off as mere clogs on native

---

* Chesney ; "Indian Year Book.' In the same year Haileybury ceased to exist as a training college for Indian Civil Servants.

† "Indian Year Book."

industry; but an export duty of ten per cent. was levied on salt-petre, a product of which India then owned the monopoly. On the other hand her customs tariff, with a few exceptions, was lowered to an uniform rate of ten per cent.*

For a moment the new Budget was hailed, as Wilson said, "with something approaching to enthusiasm." Armed with the full support of his Chief in England, Sir Charles Wood, and with the sanction at first accorded by Lord Canning himself, cheered also by a chorus of approval from his countrymen in India, Wilson declared himself to be "the most fortunate of tax-gatherers." But his sky was soon to be overcast. On his way down country the Viceroy heard enough from many quarters to impress him with the danger of carrying the new taxation to the lengths desired by his Finance Minister. The native community, silent at first and puzzled, but far from satisfied, presently found a bold mouthpiece and a powerful champion in the new Governor of Madras. Sir Charles Trevelyan's zeal on behalf of "the tens of millions of natives upon whom three new taxes would be imposed without any compensation" brought him, as we saw, into disastrous collision with the higher powers in Calcutta and England. The noble rashness which cut short his official career secured for his clients a substantial victory. Trevelyan was recalled, but Wilson had to remodel his budget. The income-tax was enacted for five years, but the other two taxes were reserved for further consideration. The concession was not made too soon; for the popular feeling waxed sore against a Government which levied taxes the more hateful for their very strangeness; and the natives had begun to assert that their new Queen was far greedier than the old Company.†

Wilson died of dysentery in August, 1860, after seven months of hard, incessant work. A fit successor was presently found in Mr. Samuel Laing, a member of Parliament, and a financier of high repute, who reached Calcutta in the following January. In spite of Wilson's efforts to square accounts, the deficit for the past year amounted to five millions and a half. The cash balances were running dangerously low. Commissions of inquiry into the military and civil expenditure were still hard at work. Lord Canning had been driven to confess that the danger of reducing the strength of his British garrison would be less than the danger of imposing unpopular taxes upon the people at large. The new Finance Minister saw the need of adapting his fiscal and financial policy to the circumstances of the time. In his opening address

---

* Chesney; Temple; Trotter.   † Chesney; Temple; "Indian Year Book."

to the Legislative Council he avowed his conviction that India was "no place for a tax on incomes going as low as £20 a year." Any tax that held out so large a premium to fraud must tend, he said, to demoralize the people and to embark the Government in ceaseless warfare with a large section of its subjects. As for the Licence Tax, to raise by it even £600,000, "we must send the tax-gatherer to four million doors, or, in other words, affect twenty millions of our population."

Mr. Laing therefore resolved to limit the demand for income-tax to incomes of more than £50 a year; thus relieving the poorer multitudes from the burden of an impost which encouraged a crowd of native underlings to plunder and oppress their own countrymen. The salt-duties were raised a little, and the outlay on public works was cut down by half a million. An estimated saving of more than three millions and a half on the naval and military charges completed his scheme for restoring the balance between outlay and income. Wilson's plans for a paper currency were taken up by his successor, and moulded into the shape preferred by Sir Charles Wood. Notes of ten rupees and upwards to the total value of four millions were to be issued against Government securities from Bombay, Madras, and Calcutta. Against all issues above that sum bullion was to be held in reserve. For the first time in Anglo-Indian experience it became possible to travel about the country with bits of paper money instead of bags of cumbersome rupees.*

Owing to an unforeseen decline in the opium revenue, the small surplus which Mr. Laing had hoped to show at the end of his first year's labours transformed itself into a trifling deficit. But the net result of those labours promised well for the future. At the beginning of 1862 the financial disorders caused by the Mutiny had well-nigh disappeared. The land-revenue was yielding two millions and a half more than in 1856. On taxes old and new there had been a total gain of two millions. About half a million was saved upon the civil services; and the army charges, which, in 1859, were little short of twenty-one millions, had in two years been cut down to less than thirteen millions. For this last saving Mr. Laing was mainly indebted to the successful zeal of Colonel George Balfour and his colleagues in the Department of Military Finance. Before leaving India in 1862, Lord Canning knew that the financial sky was fast clearing, that the storm-beaten ship of State was once more sailing easily with a fair wind.

* "Indian Year Book;" Temple; Cheaney.

CHAPTER II.

LAST YEARS OF LORD CANNING.

ONE of the problems that called for early settlement in the days that followed the great Mutiny was the reconstruction of the Indian armies. In July, 1858, a Royal Commission of Queen's and Company's officers, headed by three Ministers of the Crown, had been ordered to discuss and report upon twelve questions all bearing on the same great issue. Of these the most important were the question touching the due proportion of European to native troops in india, and the question whether the former should belong wholly or in part to Her Majesty's regular army. Before 1857 British India had always maintained a separate force of engineers and artillery, European and Native, sufficient for all her needs. Nine regiments of white infantry had made up the rest of a local force enlarged during the Mutiny by several regiments of horse and foot. Of these troops it is enough to say that they were always ready and fit for the hardest service, and did their duty in every field of warfare at least as thoroughly as any troops in the world could have done. In cantonments their discipline was certainly as good as that of any Royal regiment serving in India, and they never broke down on field service as their comrades of the Line were sometimes known to do. Every circumstance of training, habitude, and long tradition combined to render "the Company's Europeans" the true backbone of India's British garrison.

The Commissioners erelong decided that, for some years to come, India should be garrisoned by eighty thousand white soldiers, that what remained of the native artillery should be done away, that the proportion of native troops to English should be as two to one in Upper India, and three to one at most elsewhere. On the other point opinion was for some time sharply divided. On the evidence mainly of Queen's officers, the majority advised that the local white troops should be absorbed into the regular army; while the minority, backed by the powerful pleadings of many old Company's officers, held fast to the principle of a separate local army, side by side with a certain number of Her Majesty's regular troops. Behind the advocates of the former course stood the Sovereign herself, strongly seconded by one of her weightiest councillors, the Prince Consort.*

Hardly had the Commissioners got through their task, when the so-called "White Mutiny" began to rage. In 1859 it was rumoured throughout India that the Company's European troops, who had upheld their country's honour in a hundred fields, who during the late troubles had even surpassed their old renown, were beginning at last to follow in the steps of their old Sepoy comrades. The rumour was not wholly unfounded, although, like most rumours, it assumed as it flew a rather mythical shape. At several stations something of a mutinous spirit displayed itself in the language and even in the acts of men who sought only peaceful redress for what seemed to them a grievous wrong. Without a question asked or a choice offered them, these soldiers of the old local army had just been handed over "like a lot of horses" from the service of the Company to that of the Crown. Their moral if not their legal right to some voice in the matter had been brushed aside by the technical ruling of a few Crown lawyers. Remembering how Lord Palmerston as Prime Minister had, from his place in Parliament, declared that all who objected to serve the Queen would "of course be entitled to their discharge," they resented with a bitterness free from all disloyal motive the doing of a great injustice crowned by a manifest breach of faith. It was not that most of them had any thought of leaving the new service. They contended only for the right to choose for themselves between a free discharge and re-enlistment in the regular way. Nearly all were willing to accept a moderate bounty and serve again.†

A timely offer of two or three pounds a man would have satisfied the murmurers and profited the State. But once again Lord Canning failed to do the right thing at the right moment. Fortified by the quibbles of law officers in India and at home, he missed a golden occasion of yielding with a ready grace to a just demand. In some few stations the seething discontent boiled over in acts of passing insubordination. Lord Clyde saw the danger—saw reason also for the prevailing excitement. He knew that English soldiers were not likely to wax so turbulent without good cause. Courts of inquiry held during May of that

---

* Trotter ; Martin.   † Trotter ; Temple.

year 1859 brought out the real strength and bitterness of a grievance which expressed itself alike in the noisier utterances of the younger men and in the quietly scornful attitude of their older comrades.

The results of these inquiries drove the Viceroy to reconsider his first conclusions. But the old ungracious spirit that marred so many of his public acts spoke out again in the General Order of June 20th, by which every soldier enlisted for the Company's service might claim his discharge at once with a free passage home. None, however, of those who accepted his offer of discharge would be "permitted to enlist in any regiment in India," whether local or of the line. What Lord Canning expected from such a compromise it is hard to see. The aggrieved men had for the most part no special desire to leave the ranks. They had asked only for a small bounty in acknowledgement of their right to go or stay. They now saw themselves free to go on conditions which cut them off from all chance of re-enlistment in India. Their minds were quickly made up. As if to put their new masters thoroughly in the wrong, some eight thousand British soldiers from all three branches of the Indian service at once accepted their discharge. From the veterans of the old artillery and fusiliers down to the recruits of the newly-raised horse and foot, about three-fifths of the local white army gave up pay, preferment, prospects, everything, and with sullen glee sailed off as fast as ships could be found them on their voyage home. The public service paid dearly for the unwisdom of its chiefs. Between the display of ill-timed firmness at the outset, and the scant concession afterwards, eight thousand men were driven out of the service, and the price of a bounty for their re-enlistment was expended many times over in sending them back to England and filling up their places with fresh recruits.[*]

One body of malcontents were still debarred from the new indulgence, pending a full inquiry into their misdoings. The 5th Bengal Europeans, a new regiment quartered at Bahrampur, had carried their discontent to the pitch of downright mutiny. About half their number broke loose from all control, refused to turn out for any more parades, defied alike the orders, threats, entreaties of their own officers. Troops were hurried down to Bahrampur: for a moment it seemed as if Englishmen would have to fire upon Englishmen. At last the mutineers gave in, all but forty, who were seized and marched off to jail. Erelong, however,

[*] Trotter.

the viceregal clemency was extended to these men also, and in due time 700 of the Bahrampur garrison were struck off the strength of her Majesty's Indian Army. Of all the thousands who thus took their discharge, only a few score afterwards volunteered for service in China. The bounty proffered on that occasion had come too late.*

The storm died off, but the lesson which some minds were quick to draw from it added a show of weight to the arguments of those who sought to abolish the local European force. If a few thousand British soldiers were thus ripe for mutiny, what sort of trust could England place in a separate contingent forty or fifty thousand strong? It was loudly declared in many quarters that an army which had never once been wanting in any real need, might some day prove at once a danger and a burden to the Crown. Ten or twelve years' soldiering in such a force was suddenly found to be a system fatal alike to the health, the discipline, and the loyalty of British troops. The anomaly of two distinct armies under one head became suddenly visible to many who but yesterday had seen in the rivalry between two services the best means of maintaining the efficiency of both, and had pleaded for a strong local army as India's true mainstay in the event of an European war. Prince Albert's cry for "simplicity, unity, steadiness of system, and unity of command," was taken up by the members of Lord Palmerston's Ministry. And so, in the summer of 1860, after a vain resistance from all who still preferred the old two-handed system to the kind of unity embodied in the Horse Guards, the Ministerial Bill for amalgamating the two armies finally became law.†

In the next two years the work of amalgamation was carried out. Nine new regiments of Royal foot, three of horse, new brigades and companies of artillery and engineers, absorbed the residue of the Company's European troops. At the same time a new native army, made up partly of loyal Sepoys, mainly of Sikh, Gorkha, Pathán, and other levies, with only six English officers to each regiment, took the place of the old native army of Bengal. Its officers were furnished from the new Indian Staff Corps, which absorbed the great mass of those who had served on the general staff, civil or military, of their respective Presidencies. A certain number of old officers were invited to retire on special pensions suited to their rank and length of service. It was natural that the new arrangements should fail to satisfy every

* Trotter.   † Trotter; Martin.

member of a body several thousand strong; but a fair attempt at least was made to treat the old services in liberal agreement with the spirit of recent Parliamentary votes. In the native armies of Bombay and Madras no organic change was deemed necessary.*

A native army on a reduced scale involved the transfer of some of its former duties to an improved body of police. In most parts of India the native police had never been trusted to furnish guards for treasuries, court-houses, and jails, or to escort prisoners, treasure, and public stores from one station to another. All such duties had devolved on Sepoys, to the loss of their proper discipline, at much needless cost to the State. The task of remodelling the police of his own Presidency had been vigorously begun by Lord Harris, and carried on with like spirit by Sir Charles Trevelyan, before Wilson summoned the head of the Madras Police, Mr. William Robinson, to aid him in establishing a reformed police-system over the rest of India. A Commission sitting in Calcutta wrought out the details of a scheme which, framed on the Irish pattern, promised not wholly in vain to secure the highest efficiency at the lowest possible cost. The reformed police, under skilled European leading, has proved on the whole a fair success.†

In 1861 the strength of the British garrison in India was reduced to 76,000 men; that of the native army to less than 120,000. In the interests of economy and centralized rule a death-blow was struck at the old Indian Navy, whose many and brilliant services in Eastern seas had been enhanced by a long career of peaceful enterprise that taxed to their utmost the skill, courage, and endurance of officers and men. The same body which had so long furnished the police of the Indian seas, which had fought with so much honour against foes of many nations—Arab, Marátha, Dutch, French, Burman, Chinese, Malay—which during the Mutiny had dared and suffered heroically in the common cause; this same body had sent forth its choicest members, year after year, through storm, heat, sickness, perils and hardships of many kinds, to carry on the work of surveying the coasts, rivers, harbours and creeks of the great Indian continent, the Red Sea, and the Persian Gulf. The little Indian Navy had become a terror to all pirates and slavers in Eastern waters; while the exploring zeal of its officers had filled the library of the India House with valuable maps, charts, and other records of successful

* Trotter; Chesney.   † Temple; "Indian Year Book."

labour in new or half-studied fields. But the claims of this old Service to prolonged existence counted for nothing against the reasons, or the pretexts, urged by the powers at home for its abolition. Its officers were pensioned off, and the seamen discharged or admitted into the Royal Navy, which thenceforth undertook the duty of guarding our Indian coasts, and repressing violence and disorder in the adjacent seas. But for some years afterwards the marine surveys were virtually cast aside.*

The union of Arakan, Pegu, and Tenasserim under one administrative head was one of the questions which occupied the last years of Canning's rule. In 1861 those three provinces of British Burma were brought under the sway of a Chief Commissioner, Colonel Arthur Phayre, who, as Commissioner of Pegu since 1853, had won the confidence, respect, and love of his Burman subjects by the mingled strength and tenderness of a noble nature, by the union of a clear head and an upright heart with a sweet temper, an unfailing courtesy, and an energy that never tired. About the same time the Nágpur province and the Ságar and Narbadda districts were formed into the Central Provinces, with Colonel Elliot as Chief Commissioner. He had hardly taken up his duties when ill-health drove him away to Europe. Lord Canning then offered the post to Mr. Richard Temple, whose zeal, talents, and ambition had shone forth in the work achieved by him under the Lawrences in the Panjáb. The erewhile Secretary to the Panjáb Board accepted an offer which placed him far on the road that still lay before the future Governor of Bombay.†

In 1859 Lord Canning's Council passed a law which aimed at rescuing millions of Bengáli ráyats from the unforeseen consequences of the powers entrusted to a few thousand zamindárs by the famous Regulations of 1793. In surrendering to the zamindárs the rights possessed by Government in the produce of the soil, Lord Cornwallis had no desire to ignore or diminish the prescriptive right of the peasantry to the lands which their fathers had tilled before them. In order to secure the ráyats in their ancestral holdings, the zamindárs were bound to grant them leases at the customary rates. Other steps were also taken to restrain the new landlords from encroaching on their weaker neighbours. But from one cause and another these good intentions had borne sorry fruit. Himself hard pressed at times for the means of paying the Government demand, the zamindár was

* Low's "History of the Indian Navy"; Markham's "Indian Surveys."
† Chesney; Temple.

not slow to take his compensation out of the ráyat. The leases were withheld on various pretexts, and the zamindár lost no opportunity of raising his rents, or of levying illegal cesses from a peasantry well-nigh powerless for self-defence. The growth of a population living wholly by the land brought new and poorer soil under the plough, and gave the landlords fresh pretexts for enhancing the rents of older fields. The clearing of jungles drove the husbandman to burn bullock's-dung instead of firewood, and to raise scanty crops from fields no longer fertilised with any kind of manure. The village grazing-lands were ploughed up, and the cattle, stinted of their proper food, grew ever weaker and more liable to epidemic disease. The zamindárs of Bengal in the long run waxed rich and prospered with the help of money squeezed out of a patient, rackrented peasantry, most of whom could barely keep body and soul together by ceaseless toil, on holdings that averaged three acres to each family.[*]

It was in order to remedy a state of things which had grown in some measure out of our own neglect to secure equal justice between the tillers of the soil and the men who furnished the land-revenue, that Lord Canning's Government passed the Bengal Rent Act of 1859. The new law decreed that every ráyat who had held his land at the same rent for twenty years should be treated thenceforth as if he had held it ever since 1793. His holding, therefore, was secured to him and his family for ever at the rent then payable. Another class of tenants who had held their lands for twelve years were endowed with full rights of occupancy, and their rents could only be enhanced for certain reasons, after due inquiry by a court of law. Fixity of tenure at fair, if not always fixed, rents was thus ostensibly assured to every husbandman who had occupied the same holding for a given term of years. This was certainly a boon of the highest value for all who might succeed in holding it fast. But many of those who claimed it were still doomed to feel the difference between a declared right and counterworking facts. By various forms of evasion and obstruction the zamindárs contrived in very many cases to raise their rents and replenish their purses in defiance of the new law. And they were still free to work their pleasure on the multitudes of rackrented tenants at will whom the new law left entirely to their own devices.[†]

[*] Kaye; Trotter; Hunter's "England's Work in India"; "Report of the Famine Commission."

[†] Hunter; Act X. of 1859.

Hardly had Act X. of 1859 become law, when the peace of
Bengal was ruffled by a bitter quarrel between the indigo-planters
of that province and the ráyats who raised their special crop.
For some years past the growing of indigo had been fruitful of
ill-blood between the rival interests of capital and labour. The
English planters had been wont to bind down their ráyats by certain money advances, to furnish yearly so many bundles of a
crop which the ráyats found it yearly less profitable to grow at the
price offered them. Only a wild belief in the rumoured concert
of the Government with the planters had withheld them from
refusing to furnish indigo at a rate which, in comparison with
other staples, was found to be a decided loss. In his travels
about the country Sir John Grant, the new Lieutenant-Governor,
took note of the popular belief. Seeking to dispel so mischievous
a delusion, he issued an order which the foolish peasantry mistook
for an indirect dissuader from growing indigo at all.

He had merely given them to understand that the Government
had no thought of compelling the people to grow indigo, or any
other crop, to their own ultimate loss. But he told them plainly
that all contracts made with the planters must be fulfilled.
Catching only at one-half of his explanation, the ráyats overlooked
the other. They refused to make good their pledges. Government came for the moment to the planters' aid. In March 1860
an Act was passed which made breach of contract on the ráyat's
part criminal for the next six months. A Commission, headed by
Mr. Seton-Karr, the able Secretary to the Bengal Government,
was ordered to inquire into the causes of the prevailing discontent, and if possible to suggest a remedy. Impatient of any
delay, the ráyats in some places rose, ravaged the planters' lands,
assailed the factories, and spread abroad a terror which the
presence of troops alone could allay. Blood was shed on both
sides. The rioters felt aggrieved not only by the planters, who
had driven hard bargains with them, but by the Government
which punished breach of contract as a crime. A loud cry for
justice smote the ears of the Lieutenant-Governor himself as he
steamed down a river, both banks of which were lined by vast
crowds of men, women, and children, imploring his interference
in their behalf.*

That the rioters had cause for angry feeling against the planters
the Report of the Indigo Commission placed beyond a doubt.
That cause, said Lord Canning in his subsequent letter to Sir

* Trotter; Temple; "Indian Year Book."

Charles Wood, arose from the fact that "the manufacturer has required the ráyat to furnish the plant for a payment not nearly equal to the cost of production." He held that Sir John Grant had done no more than his duty in making known to the ráyats their exact position under the law. For the Government, he added, only one fitting and safe course remained open—" to speak the truth plainly and fully on both sides; to warn both; and to be prepared to enforce order with a strong hand."* About the same time Small Cause Courts were opened in the indigo districts for the purpose of rendering cheap and speedy justice to all concerned.

Before the end of 1860, however, the old quarrel had broken forth under a new shape. The planters agreed to pay more for their indigo, but demanded higher rents in return. One planter of Kishnagarh was quoted as a model of fair dealing, because he doubled the rates offered for indigo and nearly trebled his rents. The ráyats, emboldened by the new Rent Law, stood out everywhere against this new exaction, in spite of the evictions with which they were threatened, one and all. All through 1861 the quarrel raged. Fearful of impending ruin, the planters clamoured for martial law against tenants guilty in their eyes of combining to pay no rent whatever. Sir John Grant and some of his officers were covered with abuse by their angry countrymen, who resented all efforts to redress the grievances of a suffering peasantry as so many proofs of enmity towards themselves. The zeal of the missionaries on behalf of the poor neglected ráyats sowed fresh bitterness in the hearts of men who, strong in all the pride and power of a conquering race, looked upon their dark-skinned neighbours as mere cattle reserved for their own especial uses, and deemed it monstrous that the rights of any native should stand in the way of any privilege claimed by his English lord and master.†

The wrath of the planters and their friends waxed ungovernable when it transpired that a native satire on the English in Bengal had been translated, printed, and sent about the country at the public cost. The *Nil Darpan*, or Mirror of Indigo, was a Bengáli drama, the heroes of which, two indigo-planters, were painted as cruel tyrants whose conduct drove their ráyats into madness and

---

* Lord Canning's Despatch of 29th December, 1860.

† Trotter; "Indian Year Book." The natural feeling of English settlers in India towards the natives has been described with wonderful accuracy by John Stuart Mill, in his work on "Representative Government."

suicide. Their wives figured as foolish women who shocked native ideas of decency by riding about on horseback, and dancing with the district magistrate, "whose name occasions great terror." In the preface to this rude satire it was hinted that two editors of Calcutta journals had agreed to betray the cause of the ráyats for a bribe of a hundred pounds. The play was translated by Mr. James Long, one of the most upright, clever, and learned missionaries in Bengal. He had sent a copy of the original work to Mr. Seton-Karr, with whose sanction the translation was carried out. Unhappily the Secretary, misunderstanding the orders of his Government, had five hundred copies of Long's translation printed at the public charge, and posted nearly half of them under the Government frank.

This ill-timed blunder wrought up to white heat the fury of the planters and their friends. Dignity, decency, manliness, common sense, were all flung to the winds. There was nothing in the satire that an English judge in England could have defined as strictly libellous. But the English in Lower Bengal were beside themselves with rage. One of their leading journals shrieked against the Government of Bengal as vying in wicked purpose with that of Naples under King Bomba. From all the white town of Calcutta went forth a fierce cry for justice upon those who had spread abroad so foul a slander against the planters and journalists of Bengal. The men who thus owned how closely the cap fitted them resolved to strike at the Government through its reverend accomplice, Mr. Long. An English jury presently found that gentleman guilty of wilfully and maliciously libelling the owners of the *Englishman* and the *Harkára*, as well as all the indigo-planters of Lower Bengal. The judge himself, Sir Mordaunt Wells, had gravely declared his "horror and disgust" at certain passages which ought to have provoked neither feeling; and he had even raised the question whether a libel " so foul and filthy " on planters' wives was not in fact a libel on all English women of the middle classes.

The reverend prisoner found himself condemned to a month's imprisonment in the common jail, besides the payment of a considerable fine. A native gentleman at once stepped forward to pay the thousand rupees, but Mr. Long had to undergo the rest of his sentence in the steamy heat of an Indian August. His enemies had their revenge on Mr. Seton-Karr also, whose services were transferred to a less important post. Nothing, however, could save the indigo-culture of Lower Bengal from the fate foreshadowed by the late disputes. It was clear that an industry which had ceased to pay in the open labour-market must be given up. One after another the planters shut up their factories, sold their estates, and betook themselves to other fields of enterprise in India or at home.*

Meanwhile a cruel cloud of famine had been passing over the North-Western Provinces and a part of the Panjáb. The after-fruits of the disorders arising from the mutinies, a general failure in the rainfall of 1860, and an untimely hitch in the working of the Ganges Canal, all combined to bring about a lamentable dearth of food in the sun-parched plains between the Satlaj and the Jamna. The dearth was felt indeed beyond both rivers, and even eastward to the Ganges; but its worst ravages were mainly visible in the districts of Agra, Delhi, and Sirhind. Thirteen millions of people suffered more or less severely. For many months of 1861 millions of lean, hungry, half-naked wretches wandered to and fro in search of food or the means of earning it, or else with the apathy of their race let themselves quietly starve to death in their own homes. Relief works for the able-bodied, and relief shelters for the weak and sickly, were opened everywhere by order of the local Governments.

Officers of Government and volunteers, native and English, worked manfully together under the guidance of Mr. Edmonstone and Sir Robert Montgomery. But in spite of all their efforts and of the help in money furnished from private sources in India and England, five hundred thousand sufferers died of famine out of more than four millions reduced to their last shifts. Vast numbers of the weak and sickly were kept alive on wheaten cakes and *dall* given out daily by relief committees at stated hours. The Government laid out £250,000 on relief works and remitted £400,000 of land-revenue. The peasantry lost nearly five millions in cattle and produce. For six months human forecast, energy, and devotion of the highest order fought steadily, nor all in vain, against a scourge from which India can never be thoroughly safeguarded so long as the mass of her people live from hand to mouth on an overcrowded and impoverished soil.

At length, in June, the rain began falling so plenteously that all dread of further famine erelong died away. In its stead, however, came floods and cholera. Of those who had survived the famine thousands succumbed to the latter plague, which, never stopping to choose its victims, assailed also to deadly purpose some four

* Trotter; "Indian Year Book"; *Allen's Indian Mail;* Temple.

hundred English men, women, and children in Miánmir alone. In the Húghli district unusual sickness followed the unusual floods. But the death of Colonel Baird Smith in December, on his way home, touched the hearts of his countrymen in India with the sense of a great public loss.   The able and accomplished officer of Bengal Engineers, who after long service in the Canal Department had won so bright a name at the siege of Delhi, was Master of the Calcutta Mint when the drought and dearth in the Upper Provinces called him thither on special duty.   In a series of minute and exhaustive reports upon the famine districts he brought together the fruits of much painful toil, prolonged through most unhealthy seasons.   Ill, worn out, dying like so many others from overwork in a baleful climate, Baird Smith went on board the steamer in which, a few days afterwards, he breathed his last in the forty-fourth year of his age.*

Two men of like note and worth had preceded him to the grave in that same year 1861.   For the first time after sixty years of Indian service, half of which had been spent in governing Maisúr, Sir Mark Cubbon was voyaging home to England when death overtook him at Suez, in his seventy-seventh year. Of the work he did among the people of Maisúr some mention has been made in the chapters dealing with the rule of Lord Dalhousie. Of all the Company's soldier-statesmen few if any have left behind them a memory so justly dear to all classes, within the limits whether of his personal or his official sway.   Natives and Englishmen alike mourned him as their common father.   If Cubbon's death closed a career already complete, the death of George Barnes, Lord Canning's Foreign Secretary, cut short a life still full of promise, however mingled with much fruit.   A pupil of Thomason, he had helped as Commissioner of Kangra to suppress the Jalandhar outbreak in 1848.   As Commissioner for the Cis-Satlaj States in 1857, he had nobly justified his promotion to a post which, in that year of trial, demanded the highest qualities of heart and brain.   "Of all the officers in the Panjáb"—says Sir R. Temple—"there was none who commanded the confidence of John Lawrence more than George Barnes."   His zeal, energy, and tact in managing the princes of Sirhind resulted in placing all their resources at the command of his countrymen warring against Delhi.   Rewarded with the post of Foreign Secretary at an age still young, he saw the best prizes of the Civil Service within his reach, when his untimely death deprived

* Trotter; "Indian Year Book"; "Report of Famine Commission."

Lord Canning of "a sagacious, able, and experienced officer, equal to the most important services."[*]

Meanwhile the peace of India had now and then been ruffled by the clash of arms. A strange outbreak of Wághirs, a wild marauding race in the south-western corner of Gujarát, gave much employment to the Bombay troops in 1859 and 1860, before the insurgents, who fought boldly, were at last disabled from further mischief. In January 1860 the naked Kúki savages from the Tipparah hills on the Silhet border dealt murderous havoc on the neighbouring villages. About the same time Brigadier Neville Chamberlain was teaching the troublesome Waziri tribes on the Panjáb frontier a long-needed lesson of respect for the lives and property of British subjects. The same year witnessed the departure from India of several Sikh and British regiments, whom Sir Hope Grant led forth to fresh victories over the Chinese. Sikh soldiers shared in the storming of the Taku forts, so deadly in the former year to British infantry; shared also in the fighting beyond Tientsin, in the less noble sacking of the Summer Palace, and in the crowning march of "foreign devils" into the Imperial city of Pekin.

Before the year's end a mishap befell the small body of troops whom Dr. Campbell had despatched from Dárjiling northward, into the Sikhim mountains, to punish the refractory Rajah of Sikhim for deeds of outrage against British subjects. In the following year a larger force under Colonel Gawler soon brought the Rajah into a humbler frame of mind, and completed the act of annexation which Dr. Campbell had too hastily begun.[†]

In spite of the chaos caused by the Mutiny, great things in the way of roads, railways, and canals had been done for India before the close of Lord Canning's rule. In the first days of 1862 the East Indian Railway from Calcutta to Delhi was open as far as Allahábád, and was even then paying five per cent. on the capital outlay. Trains were already running over four hundred miles of the Great Indian Peninsula line from Bombay eastward to its future goal at Jabalpur. The line from Karáchi harbour to Kotri on the Indus, had been opened some months earlier. In March 1862, the Governor of Madras, Sir William Denison, opened nearly eighty miles of the Great Southern Railway from Nega-patam to Trichinápali. Out of 1,360 miles of railway then com-pleted, at a cost of forty-two millions, more than one-half had

[*] Temple; "Panjáb Administration Report."
[†] Trotter; Gawler's "Sikhim Expedition."

been laid out in the last two years. Three thousand more miles were already making. Travellers of all classes, including even high-caste ladies, filled the carriages, and swelled year by year the receipts of the railway companies. Of these receipts nearly a third was owing to the passenger traffic, especially to the millions of third-class fares.*

The Grand Trunk Road from Calcutta to Peshawar had at last been completed over a length of fifteen hundred miles. A tunnel at Atak beneath the swift-flowing Indus had been begun. Many hundred miles of metalled road had been opened in various parts of the country. A new line was in course of paving from Calcutta into Assam. A number of roads and canals were repaired, extended, or begun, in districts lately visited by famine or found suitable for the growth of cotton, in view of Lancashire's imperative needs. New branches had been thrown out from the great Ganges Canal, which by the end of 1861 fertilized an area of six hundred square miles, yielding food enough to maintain fourteen hundred thousand souls and all their cattle for one year. For the first time, in 1860, the income from this noble work exceeded the year's outgoings. In 1861 the Eastern Jamna Canal yielded twelve per cent. on the capital outlay. The Bari Doáb and the Western Jamna Canals were worked at a small but increasing profit. In Madras a guaranteed company was aiding the Government in opening out new lines of irrigation and water-traffic from the Tumbadra to Kistnapatam. Large sums were expended in the building of new barracks, fortifications, civil offices, lighthouses; in furtherance of the great Trigonometrical Survey, and in various smaller fields of public usefulness.†

In spite, to some extent in consequence, of the Mutiny, the foreign trade of British India during the last few years had steadily increased. The wants of a large English army, the demand for cotton in 'Lancashire to feed mills left empty by the civil war in the United States, the opening of new fields for native industry and English enterprise, all helped to stimulate the yearly flow of business between India and her foreign customers. At Bombay the exports and imports for 1861 were worth more by ten million pounds than those of 1857. The total value of India's foreign trade had risen from thirty-two millions in 1850, and sixty millions in 1857, to eighty millions in 1861; of which our own country absorbed one-half. Of the new wealth implied in these figures some share, however modest, fell to the industrial classes,

---

* Trotter; "Indian Year Book."   † Trotter; "Indian Year Book."

to the growers of cotton in Gujarát, Pegu, and the Dakhan, to the weavers of Bengal and the Panjáb, to the growers of tea in Assam, of coffee in Maisúr, of jute in Lower Bengal, of rice in British Burmah; to multitudes, in short, of toiling wage-earners and hungry tillers of the soil.*

The Himalayan uplands of Kángra, Kamáon, and Dárjiling were now becoming dotted with tea-gardens, the produce of which vied in delicate flavour with the best growths of China herself. Tea-planting in Assam and Kachar had already grown from a doubtful speculation into a stable industry, employing thousands of workmen under English overseers in the production of nearly two million pounds of tea a year. In all India some two hundred and fifty tea-gardens betokened the vigorous youth of an industry which has since gained a permanent footing in the markets of the West. To the Himalayan planters the Government still gave a helping hand, in the shape of seeds and plants distributed among them yearly cost-free.

On the wooded hill-sides of Maisúr, Kurg, and Wainád, English enterprise was clearing fresh ground year by year for the growth of coffee. In ten years the exports of the fragrant berry had risen from 35,013 cwts. to 165,816 cwts., worth £324,170, or one-fifth the value of the coffee then exported from Ceylon. As the Crimean War had given birth to a new and growing trade in Indian jute, so the war in North America threw the markets of England wide open to the native cotton-growers of Western India. Once made aware of Lancashire's needs, the peasantry of Kandésh and Berár were quick to learn their lesson; and in 1861 the exports of Indian cotton to Liverpool amounted to a million bales, or nearly twice the number exported in the previous year. In the same year a successful attempt was made to grow hops in the Déra Dhun, the wooded valley at the foot of the Masúri Hills.†

With the development of trade and industry was mixed up the question of utilizing the waste lands, of which every province had its share. Some of these lands were mere desert, others were uncleared forest belonging partly to the State, partly to private owners, single or corporate. As early as 1858 Lord Canning's Government had granted a thousand acres of land in the Kángra valley to a retired civil servant who wished to try his fortune as a tea-planter. But not till October 1861, when the pressure of the cotton famine in Lancashire gave strength and point to the cry for developing India's resources, did the Viceroy issue a formal

* Trotter; "Indian Year Book."   † "Indian Year Book."

Resolution touching the sale of waste lands. Under the rules therein embodied, any person was allowed to purchase up to three thousand acres of cultivable waste, free of land-tax, " at the rate of five shillings for uncleared and ten shillings for cleared soil." At the same time Lord Canning put forth his plan for redeeming the land-revenue at twenty years' purchase of the existing demand. Only ten per cent., however, of the land-tax in each district might thus be commuted at a rate which most persons deemed excessive for Bengal. Very few, at any rate, cared on such terms to buy the fee-simple of land then worth only six or seven years' purchase in the open market. The Waste Land Rules, on the contrary, succeeded in building up new and prosperous industries in the hills of Northern and Southern India.*

Before the close of Lord Canning's rule some steps had been taken to preserve the public forests from the havoc caused by fires and the reckless felling of trees for railway and other uses. As Conservator of Forests in Southern India, Dr. Cleghorn busied himself in replanting with teak the forests of Malabar, in covering many acres of the Nilgiris with good quick-growing Australian timber, and in checking private inroads on the lands reserved for the State. To Dr. Dietrich Brandis of Berlin was assigned the task of forest conservancy in British Burmah, where vast tracts of land are covered with the noblest teak-trees in the world. In 1861 Lord Canning summoned Dr. Cleghorn from Madras to explore the forests of Northern India and consider the best means of developing their wealth in timber.†

Another question taken up by Lord Canning was the cultivation of Cinchona, the quinine-yielding plant of Brazil, whose fever-healing virtues had first been made known to Europe by the Countess of Chinchon. Utakamand in the Nilgiris became the scene of an experiment destined in due time to yield plenteous fruit. In 1859 a few young plants were raised from seeds procured by Mr. Clements Markham, a clerk in the India Office who had once served in the Indian Navy. A few more were brought from Kew by Dr. T. Anderson of the Botanical Gardens near Calcutta, at whose suggestion the experiment had first been made. In reply to Lord Canning's personal request the Governor-General of Dutch India sent over a quantity of seeds and seedlings from Java to Madras. Dr. Anderson himself went to Java on a special mission from the Viceroy, and presently returned to India laden

---

* " Indian Year Book " ; Temple ; Norton.
† " Indian Year Book " ; Temple.

with four hundred plants of three species and half a million seeds. Before the end of 1861 more than eight thousand Cinchona plants were growing in the garden at Utakamand, giving good promise of a time when the Government dispensaries would supply cheap quinine to the fever-stricken millions of India.[*]

In the last years of Lord Canning's rule a marked improvement showed itself in the quality of the work done by the lower Civil Courts of Bengal. The proportion of cases confirmed on appeal by the High Court rose from two-fifths to more than three-fourths; and there was a marked decline in the number of false or litigious suits. The new Code of Civil Procedure swept away many an old hindrance to the despatch of business, and enabled the Courts to settle disputed claims without recourse to written pleadings. In the Panjáb the limit of actions for unbonded debts was lowered from six years to three: the registry of bonds for more than fifty rupees became compulsory; and every creditor had to produce his day-book as well as his ledger in support of his claim. In 1860 the chief landholders and feudal lords were entrusted with civil jurisdiction to the value of three hundred rupees; a duty which they discharged with praiseworthy zeal and fairness. Like powers to the extent of a hundred and fifty rupees were conferred on the leading landholders of Oudh. The same class of gentry in these provinces were empowered in criminal cases to inflict imprisonment for six months or under, and fines up to two hundred rupees.

The crime of Dakaiti or gang-robbery was steadily declining in Bengal, and Thaggi in the Panjáb was becoming an evil dream of the past. Murder was still rife on the Panjáb frontier, especially in Pesháwar, and robbery by means of narcotics had so increased in the North-West Provinces, that an officer of the Thaggi department was specially empowered to fight against it. When a number of murders happened in one district and no clue to their authors could be found, a large body of police was quartered on the neighbouring zamindárs and villages for a certain period at their sole cost. Sometimes the police themselves invented or committed the crime for whose detection they claimed a reward. A party of policemen in Oudh were tried and hanged for committing a murder, the blame of which they had endeavoured to throw on persons entirely guiltless. Nor had the old practice of torturing people to extract confessions of imputed crimes become quite obsolete, in spite of the efforts used by watchful magistrates to put it down.

[*] "Indian Year Book"; *Friend of India*; Markham's "Memoir."

Not far from Ahmadnagar one hapless peasant woman, wrongly accused of theft by the police, was beaten so shamefully twice a day with rods for three days running, that at last she drowned herself in a well. When the truth came out, the two policemen whose cruelty had driven her to despair were condemned to imprisonment for three years.*

In the jails of Bengal more than half of the prisoners condemned to hard labour were employed in manufactures which yielded in one year a net profit of £20,000. In four of these jails the earnings of each handicraftsman more than covered the cost of his keep. The convicts in the North-West made all the prison clothing, repaired jail-buildings, discharged all menial duties, and raised all the vegetables required for prison use. The labour of the convicts in the Lahór jail was let out to a contractor for three years. The yearly cost of each prisoner varied from twenty-one rupees in the Panjáb to eighty-nine in Pegu. The new practice of flogging prisoners instead of keeping them for long terms in jail, seems to have been carried sometimes to a dangerous length. In one jail alone at Faizabád several prisoners died in one year from the effects of a punishment always harder to regulate than to inflict.†

In the course of 1857 universities were opened in Calcutta, Madras, and Bombay, in which the standard of examination for a B.A. degree came quite up to that of our English universities. The number of State and State-aided schools of all classes rose steadily during the last three years of Lord Canning's rule. At Lahór a Medical College, and a school for the sons of Sikh nobles, were opened in 1861. Among the pupils in the latter was the son of Mulraj, whose treason had brought about the second Sikh War. Of the normal schools for training teachers that of Madras was declared to be the most complete. In the number of its schools and scholars the North-West Province ranked even above Bombay. Mission schools and colleges played their part in the work of popular instruction. Many hundreds of girls were learning their daily lessons in most parts of northern and western India. Many Parsi and Hindu citizens of Bombay gladly sent their daughters to schools founded and maintained by private enterprise alone. Some of the teachers were native ladies. Zanána Missions had lately opened a fair field of social improvement. A few brave women, English and native, had begun to visit the Zanánas or private rooms of several houses in Calcutta for the purpose of teaching the wives and daughters of Hindu gentlemen the arts of

* "Indian Year Book." † Ibid.

reading and plain needlework. Once a week Mrs. Mullens and two or three other English ladies went the round of some twenty households to see what progress had been made in the lessons daily given by native teachers of their own sex. At the house of a Brahman in Bangalór a zanána school was opened by Mrs. Sewell, in which a young Brahmani widow acted as daily teacher.*

Among the many English newspapers published in India were several written and conducted by natives only. Some of these in point of literary expression, high moral tone, and thoughtful reasoning would have done no discredit to their English rivals. The newspapers written in native languages were remarkable as a rule for the smallness of their circulation and the insignificance of their contents. Of published books in the native vernaculars there had of late years been a memorable increase. In 1857 three hundred new books were brought out for sale in Calcutta alone. Almanacs and schoolbooks had far the largest circulation; works of fiction and moral tales were very popular, but books on history, biography, law, and science, could boast a fair proportion of readers. A new literature in Hindi and Urdu was springing up amidst the classic growths of Sanskrit and Persian. In the Panjáb also had arisen a steady demand for books written in the language of the country.†

Only one or two of the great Indian cities had as yet been lighted with gas. The sewerage even of Calcutta was still in the experimental stage. Neither Madras nor Calcutta had as yet been refreshed with a regular supply of sweet water, such as flowed from the Vehar Lake into Bombay. In some parts of Calcutta the streets were still watered by *bihistis*, or water-carriers. Municipal improvements paid by local rates and town dues went forward in the capitals, where the ratepayers elected the Municipal Committees, and in a few score country towns, where an active English magistrate guided and stimulated the efforts of native helpmates slow to appreciate or unwilling to pay for the sanitary doctrines current in the West. The people at large, as Sir George Clerk affirmed, were ready as ever to "combine and pay handsomely to make a tank, a road, or a temple, from religious or purely benevolent motives, or to cleanse streets, or repair walls, or to provide corn and water for the hungry and the thirsty." But our English Conservancy they were prone to regard with a distrust, not wholly

* "Indian Year Book."
† "Indian Year Book"; "Selections from Government Records."

groundless, in the virtue of methods sometimes faulty, ill-chosen, or misapplied.*

The untimely death of Lady Canning, in November 1861, cut short her sorrowing husband's triumphal progress through Upper India, and presently hastened his return home after an eventful rule of six years. In March 1862 Lord Canning welcomed his successor from the broad steps in front of Government House. Farewell addresses from all sections of Calcutta society attested the flowing tide of a popularity which the departing Viceroy had never deigned to seek. On the 17th of June the heirless son of George Canning lay dead in Grosvenor Square. Him also had India slain before his time, for the years of his life were still short of fifty. In those last six years, however, he had lived a whole lifetime of experiences at once strange, awful, and unforeseen. Few men so circumstanced would have come out of the ordeal with greater, still fewer with equal, credit. While he was yet new to his work, before he had learned to swim without his official bladders, Dalhousie's successor had to battle with a storm which the might even of a Dalhousie could not easily have overcome. It would be absurd to blame him for his blindness to the mischief which none of his colleagues and advisers foresaw or feared. But after the storm had burst, a quicker, clearer intellect would at once have felt the danger, have risen to the need. Dalhousie would have quelled the mutiny in its first onset. But Lord Canning was no Dalhousie, only an upright, cool-headed, high-minded English gentleman of fair ability, slow perceptions, and unbending firmness. Few men could have been slower in framing their minds to any fixed resolve; but once let him see the way he ought to go, and nothing mortal could make him swerve from it. There is no finer scene in Indian history, since the days at least of Warren Hastings, than that presented by Lord Canning, as he stood forth, calm in the strength of his righteous purpose, stately in the pride of place and patrician training, amidst a roaring sea of hostile criticism, lashed into ever wilder rage by the gusts of an armed rebellion. Against that seeming marble the wildest utterances of British fury, baulked of its full revenge, dashed themselves in vain. His mental sufferings—for he felt keenly—were known only to himself and a few intimate friends.

In the darkest days of the mutiny, Lord Canning never lost his head, never yielded to the counsels of panic-stung revenge or ferocious folly. His cool courage commanded the respect of those

* "Indian Year Book"; Sir G. Clerk's "Minute on Municipal Institutions."

who most keenly resented the slowness of his movements. His strong sense of justice and his honest eagerness to do all his duty, to gain all knowledge needful towards that end, went far to atone for the statesman's inherent defects. Of administrative talent he had not a very remarkable share. His subalterns might respect, they seldom, if ever, worshipped him as Wellesley and Dalhousie had been worshipped by theirs. To inspire enthusiasm was neither his fate nor his forte. His very impartiality savoured less of the statesman than the mere lawyer. Slow to learn and to unlearn, he did few things thoroughly, not a few things too late. His Indian career might be called a succession of stumbles, retrieved not seldom by a happy recovery. In his last years the mistakes were fewer, the successes more appreciable. After all deductions, his name will stand fair in English memories as that of a fearless, true-hearted Englishman, who encountered, on the whole with credit, the twofold misfortune of a great Sepoy revolt and a predecessor unmatched in Indian history.

NOTE.

At noon on the 30th April, 1863, the "Company's Jack" was hoisted at the Castle flagstaff, in Bombay, to a salute of twenty-one guns from the Apollo Pier. As the last gun boomed, the old ensign was hauled down, "the broad pennant of Commodore Frushard and the pennants of all the Indian naval vessels in harbour were struck, and the Indian Navy ceased to exist." So wrote Mr. C. R. Low, a lieutenant in the old service, whose deeds he has worthily recorded in two thick volumes published in 1877, thus realizing the hope expressed by Mr. Clements Markham in 1871. For cool, heroic daring nothing in history—not even Sir Richard Grenville's feat on board the *Revenge*—could well surpass the fight which Lieutenant Pruen, commanding the Company's brig *Ranger* of twelve guns, maintained, in 1783, for four and a half hours, against eleven Marátha warships, three of which were larger and more heavily armed than his own small craft. Not till almost every seaman and soldier on board the *Ranger* had been killed or wounded, himself included, did Pruen consent to haul down his flag—(Low; Mill; Forrest's "Marátha Records").

CHAPTER III.

LORD ELGIN.

On the 12th of March, 1862, James Bruce, Earl of Elgin, took his seat as Viceroy and Governor-General of India. Son of the Ambassador who gave his name to the "Elgin Marbles," a direct descendant of the Royal victor of Bannockburn, a first-class man of Oxford in 1832, and a Fellow of Merton soon afterwards, he had sat but a few months in the House of Commons when his father's death in 1841 cut short the new earl's Parliamentary career, without bringing him a seat in the House of Lords. In the following March, however, Lord Stanley selected him to replace the popular and successful Sir Charles Metcalfe in the Government of Jamaica. So skilfully did the new Governor discharge his errand, that a few months after his return from Jamaica, in 1846, Lord Elgin was invited by Lord Grey to fill the higher and still more hazardous post of Governor-General in Canada. From this new ordeal he emerged in 1854 a statesman of rare excellence, equal to the gravest needs. In the spring of 1857 he was sent out by Lord Palmerston as Special Envoy to the Court of Pekin, for the purpose of exacting redress for insults offered to the British flag. His firmness, tact, and foresight, duly seconded by armed force, overcame all hindrances, made up for unforeseen delays and acts of untoward treachery, and finally gathered up the full fruits of Sir Hope Grant's victorious march to Pekin.[*]

Furnished with these credentials, Lord Elgin, at the age of fifty, once more embarked for the East. As he sprang lightly up the steps of Government House, his ruddy countenance, short, strong-built figure, and buoyant gait seemed to betoken a reserve of health, strength and energy, that contrasted sharply with the pale, wan, toil-worn aspect of his old friend and schoolfellow, Lord Canning. The new Viceroy took his seat in a Council the members of which were about to be nearly all replaced by new

[*] Walrond's "Letters and Journals of Lord Elgin."

men. The untimely death of the Law-Member, Mr. Ritchie, on
the 22nd of March, was followed soon after by the retirement of
Mr. Laing, and the promotion of Sir Bartle Frere and Mr. Cecil
Beadon, the former to the Government of Bombay, the latter to
the corresponding post in Bengal. Sir Charles Trevelyan became
Finance Minister in the room of Mr. Laing, driven prematurely
home by ill-health.* Of the old Council, Sir Robert Napier
alone remained.

The rest of that year Lord Elgin passed in Calcutta, diligently
studying his new part, quietly picking other men's brains of any
knowledge that might serve his purpose, and applying the fruits
of his large experience to problems none the less difficult for their
seeming clearness of form and feature. His own estimate of the
work cut out for the successor to Dalhousie and Canning was
modest enough. "I succeed "—he said—" to a great man and a
great war, with a humble task to be humbly discharged." But
no Viceroy has ever yet found the task of governing India to be
in any sense of the word an easy task ; and Lord Elgin never
spared himself, even in discharging the humble duty of "walking
in paths traced out by others." At the end of his day's work he
would often have two or three people to dinner, whose talk might
help him in the conduct of affairs, as much as it ministered to his
taste for social enjoyment. "If my bees "—he wrote—" have any
honey in them, I extract it at the moment of the day when it is
most gushing."†

To keep faithfully within the lines of Lord Canning's later
policy, so far as he could trace them out ; to foster all forms of
peaceful industry and productive enterprise ; to avoid all occasion
for levying new or maintaining old taxes that bore heavily upon
the people ; to afford equal protection to all classes and interests ;
to ensure fair play between the native princes and their subjects ;
to keep down the military expenses ; to suppress with prompt
severity any attempt at disturbance which might be made in any
part of India, such were the principles which Lord Elgin laid
down as the guiding points of his Indian policy. His letters of
this period show how early he began to judge and act for himself.
Ready as he was to go great lengths in aiding the ráyat to
extend the growth and improve the quality of the cotton which
Lancashire sorely needed, he refused to embark in any scheme of
rash interference with the natural working of economic laws. A

* Walrond ; Temple ; Prichard's "Administration of India."
† Walrond.

passing military panic in the North-West provoked from him a scornful comment on the man who "mistook the chirping of a cricket for the click of a pistol." Had the panic continued, he would have gone in the heat of June to Agra or Delhi, and, surrounding himself with native troops, have "put a stop to the nonsense by example."[*]

In the same month of June he had to deal with the case of a discharged English soldier who had been condemned to death in Calcutta for wantonly shooting a native in the Panjáb. A petition for a milder sentence was signed by a large number of the murderer's countrymen, who deemed the punishment too heavy for the actual offence. Instead of referring the question to the Government of the Panjáb, Lord Elgin took counsel with his law officers and the judge who had tried the case. Armed with their opinions, he refused to mitigate the just doom of a crime "committed in wanton recklessness, almost without provocation, under an impulse which would have been resisted if the life of the victim had been estimated at the value of a dog."[†]

In spite of the uneasiness expressed in many quarters, Lord Elgin refused to entangle himself in the intrigues and quarrels of his Afghán neighbours. Dost Mohammad, our good friend during the Mutiny, was now, in his eightieth year, engaged in fighting the turbulent ruler of Herát. The quarrel was none of his seeking, nor had he given us any excuse either for hindering, or helping forward, his march against Sultán Ján. But there were those in high places who pressed Lord Elgin to stay the Amir's advance, for fear of what might happen if Persia also drew her sword in defence of Herát. To all such counsels, inspired mainly by a secret fear of the Power that stood behind Persia, the Viceroy gave little heed. One step taken forward would involve the taking of many others, on pain of forfeiting our self-respect. "We should only speak"—he wrote in July to Sir Charles Wood—"when we have a case of self-interest so clear that we can speak with determination, and follow up our talk if necessary with a blow." He had no sort of toleration for "that prurient intermeddling policy which finds so much favour with certain classes of Indian officials." His ambition for England's sake rose far above the notion of trying to "play a great part in small intrigues," and scouted all interference for which "an unimpeachable plea of right or duty" could not be maintained.

One thing only at this juncture would Lord Elgin consent to do.

* Walrond. † Ibid.

The withdrawal of his Vakil or native agent from Kábul, in the event of Dost Mohammad's pushing on to Herát, would leave the latter free to follow his own devices, with no direct countenance from the Indian Government. As the aged Amir was bent on going his own way, the Vakil was ordered to withdraw. In June of the next year Dost Mohammad died, leaving the son of his preference, Sher Ali Khán, master for the moment of all Afghánistán. But two of Sher Ali's elder brothers had no mind to accept their father's choice of a successor, without a struggle for their own claims. The right of the strongest was the only right indeed which they and their countrymen would care to acknowledge. In the struggle which all men knew to be impending, which Dost Mohammad had long since foreseen, Lord Elgin steadily declined to interfere. A friendly answer to a letter from the new Amir, coupled with the despatch of his own Vakil to Kábul, were the only measures he could bring himself to adopt, and even these were delayed by his subsequent illness and untimely death.*

One of the lessons which Lord Canning had handed on to his successor was the prime importance of seeing for himself "as much as possible of men and things in all parts" of our Indian Empire. This wholesome lesson, drawn from Canning's own later experience, Lord Elgin speedily took to heart. In September, 1862, he declared to Sir Charles Wood, then Minister for India, that no man could govern India in ordinary times if he were to be "tied by the leg to Calcutta." The tour which he projected through Upper India was to be taken leisurely, even though it involved a long absence from the seat of Government. Travelling by easy stages to Simla, he would spend the next hot season in the Hills; and then marching in viceregal state through the Panjáb, would meet his Council some time during the winter at Lahór.

On the 5th of February, 1863, all legislative business ended for that season, and due provision already made for the year's expenses, Lord Elgin set out on the tour which he was destined never to complete. At Banáras, on the 7th, he held the first of those Darbárs which formed a salient feature in his official programme. At a dinner there given to celebrate the opening of a new section of the East Indian Railway, he dwelt upon the near approach of a time when private enterprise should come forward to replace the costlier system of State guarantees in the work of extending railways throughout the land. Four days later, at Cawnpore, the Viceroy

* Walrond; *Afghán Blue-book,* 1878.

took part in the solemn rites performed by Bishop Cotton over the graves of those who perished in the massacre of 1857. Above the well into which their bodies had once been tumbled now rose a sculptured angel, surrounded by a screenwork of mullioned arches, the central ornament of a fair memorial garden dotted with gravestones and bright with flowers. This spot, already hallowed by memories of a tragic past, the Bishop of Calcutta formally consecrated in the presence of Lord Elgin and all the English residents in Cawnpore.*

Travelling to Agra by rail, Lord Elgin spent six stirring days in the neighbourhood of Akbar's capital and of Shah Jahán's immortal dome. For miles around his own camp stretched the encampments of the many native chiefs and princes who had come thither from Rájputána and Central India, attended by thousands of armed retainers clad in the picturesque garb and varied colouring of the East, to exchange courtesies with the great Lord Sahib who, guarded by ten thousand of his own troops, represented the might and majesty of their common Pádishah, the Queen of England. A series of private interviews with the leading princes was followed, on the 17th of February, by a grand Darbár, surpassing in numbers and outward show even that which Lord Canning had held in 1861. Little as he cared at heart for the pomp and circumstance of such a gathering, Lord Elgin turned the occasion to good account in a short speech that might be heard distinctly from every corner of the vast Darbár tent. After assuring his hearers of the deep interest which their Royal mistress took in their welfare, and expressing his own desire to " promote the well-being and happiness both of rulers and of the people," he exhorted them all to aid his efforts to that end by founding schools and making good roads in their several provinces, and by doing their utmost to put down all barbarous usages and crimes. While he himself would not hesitate to repress disorder and punish all disturbers of the general peace, it was equally his duty to " extend the hand of encouragement and friendship to all who labour for the good of India," and to pledge the favour and protection of his Government to every Chief who made his own subjects contented and prosperous.†

From Agra the Viceroy and his party marched on by way of Delhi, Meerut and Hardwár, meeting-place of the old Faith " that washed itself in the Ganges " and the new Faith " symbolized in the magnificent works of the Ganges Canal "—to the great military

* Walrond; Life of Bishop Cotton.

† Walrond; Hovell-Thurlow's "The Company and the Crown."

station of Ambála, entered on the 27th of March. Here, on the following day, Lord Elgin addressed some words of wise counsel and just praise through his interpreter, Colonel Durand, to a strong gathering of Sikh princes and chiefs, headed by the youthful Lord of Pattiála, son of him who had helped to save India six years before. In the bracing air of Simla, whose verdure contrasted sharply with the bare brown ridges of Dagshai, the Viceroy returned with freshened spirit to his daily round of work and self-instruction; "gathering ever," says his biographer, "fresh stores of information, and forming ever clearer views of the problems that lay before him."*

During his stay at Simla a little cloud of war was rising among the hills on the western bank of the Upper Indus, above its confluence with the Kábul river. A large body of Wahábi fanatics and outlawed Sepoys from India had lately returned to their old haunts in the Mahában Mountain, whence they had been driven during the Mutiny by the hill-tribes with whom they had sought shelter. The craggy mass of the Mahában, jutting southwards like a vast wedge into the British frontier, formed a kind of natural outwork to the yet loftier masses of the Hindú Kúsh. From their stronghold of Malka and their outlying posts at Sitána and Jadún, these fierce refugees began raiding across the frontier, and drawing recruits to their side from among the Mohammadans of Bengal, Bahár, and the Panjáb. From Patna to Peshawár their friends and emissaries were engaged in collecting men, money, arms, and supplies for the holy war which the exiles of Sitána were about to wage against the infidel.

The need for a campaign against these enemies of our rule was urged so strongly by Sir Robert Montgomery, the Lieutenant-Governor of the Panjáb, that Lord Elgin at last agreed in 1863 to the course which, not a year earlier, he had resolutely forbidden. The arguments to which he yielded against his own judgement were no sounder than those he had hitherto set aside. One of the coolest and clearest heads in India, Sir William Denison, Governor of Madras, presently declared, after a careful study of the whole question, that "it was very impolitic to meddle with these hill-people at all," in attacking whom we had "nothing to gain and everything to risk." Lord Elgin himself had always hated the notion of a border war. He had small faith in the coercive policy then favoured at Lahór, and he held that "rising officials are instinctively in favour of a good row." But the statesmen at

* Walrond.

Lahór insisted on the need of forestalling Mohammadan plotters by a swift and telling blow at the Sitána fanatics, and all who had befriended them in the teeth of promises once made to the British Government. They warned the Viceroy against the dangers of delay, pleaded for prompt action as the best security for continued peace, and assured him that the projected movement would be little more than a brief military promenade.*

Dreading more than aught else the chance of entanglement in the maze of Afghán politics, Lord Elgin resolved, "in the interests both of prudence and humanity," to aim a speedy and decisive blow at the nascent trouble on his frontier. There were some who counselled him to delay that blow to the following spring, when Sir Hugh Rose himself—the Commander-in-Chief—might take the field at the head of a force strong enough to overawe the whole of the border tribes and to crush the hopes of our secret enemies throughout India. But to the Viceroy it seemed clear that the blow, if dealt at all, should be dealt as quickly as possible, before the supposed conspiracy had time to spread out its roots afar, and before many of the Afghán people had taken up their neighbours' quarrel as their own. He could see "no end to the complications" involved in such delay. It was therefore settled that measures should forthwith be taken to expel the fanatics from Jadún. If circumstances permitted, this blow might be followed up by the destruction of Malka and the punishment of those tribes who had harboured the refugees.†

By the middle of October, 6,000 good troops of all arms, with a battery of three nine-pounders and eight mountain guns, the whole commanded by Sir Neville Chamberlain, were in full march from Peshawar across the Yusafzai country towards the Pass of Ambéla, which climbs the mountain range that parts British territory from the highlands of Bunair and the Chamla Valley. On the 20th the main body entered the Pass, Colonel Wylde leading the way with his Guide Corps and a regiment of Panjáb infantry. A proclamation, issued only on the previous day, invited the neighbouring tribes to acquiesce in a movement which had no other object than the punishment of our enemies in the Mahában tract. Once clear of the Pass, our troops would only have to turn eastward along the Chamla Valley, and make the best of their way to the appointed goal.

But the invitation came too late. The Bunair tribes could see

* Walrond ; Sir W. Denison's "Varieties of Viceregal Life."
† Walrond.

only an armed force advancing over the border into their ground, and they naturally read our peaceful professions by the light of their own cunning practices. From the village of Ambéla, at the northern end of the Pass, they sent out bands of men who, on the evening of the 20th, swooped down from various points on the British camp, and kept our troops employed nearly all night in repelling their fierce though desultory onsets. To advance without due supplies and reinforcements in the face of these new foes Chamberlain saw to be impossible · and there was no braver man in his camp. Nothing remained but to entrench himself at the head of the Pass and post strong pickets on the adjacent heights.*

Day after day and night after night the Bunair men, strengthened by bands of Sitána fanatics and of hill-men from Swát, renewed their attacks with amazing courage, charging in hundreds up to our guns, surrounding our pickets, and taking heavy requital for their own losses. By the end of October nearly all the tribes between the Kábul frontier and the Indus had laid aside their own tribal quarrels to make common cause with the men of Bunair and Mahában. In spite of some timely reinforcements, Chamberlain could do no more than shift his camp to some higher ground, and employ his working-parties in making roads to guard his rear. For three weeks of November the fighting went on after a fashion which taxed to the utmost the courage and endurance of our troops. The Eagle-Crag post commanding the British right was twice in eight days carried by the enemy with an overwhelming rush which cost the lives of many officers and men. On the second occasion two officers and twenty-six men of the 101st Fusiliers† lay dead on the rock which Major Delafosse had vainly striven to hold with only fifty men, after an equal number led by another officer had too quickly found their way to the rear. On each occasion the ground so lost was speedily recovered—on the 13th by Colonel Salisbury and the 101st Foot, on the 20th by the 71st Highlanders under Colonel Hope.‡

On the same 20th of November many hearts were saddened by the tidings telegraphed over India from a secluded corner in the Kángra Hills. Lord Elgin had died that morning in the little hill-station of Dharmsála, amidst a landscape whose soft, rich beauty sets off the stern sublimity of the mountains that rise around it in petrified billows rolling upward to a lofty background of perpetual snow. He had left Simla on the 20th of September

---

* Prichard ; Sir J. Adye's "Sittana Campaign."   ·
† The old 1st Bengal Fusiliers.   ‡ Prichard ; Adye.

to plunge into the heart of the rugged heights through which the rock-walled streams of the Satlaj, the Biyás, and the Rávi cleave their way into the plains below. On his way towards Kángra, where he purposed halting to inspect the tea-gardens and to consider the prospects of trade with Ladák and China, the Viceroy scaled the Rhotang Pass, which rises 13,000 feet above the sea.

A still heavier tax upon his vital powers was the passage of the Chándra by means of a rude twig bridge that swung to and fro at every step he took, amidst frequent gaps through which many a sheep had fallen into the torrent foaming forty or fifty yards below. This, he said himself, was "about the most difficult job he had ever attempted;" and the effort needed to carry him safe across the river proved too much for a frame already shaken by the fatigues of travel in that keen mountain air. For some days he still rode his horse, reaching Sultanpur by the 18th of October. Four days later he felt so much worse that he had to be carried in a litter towards his last resting-place in the Kángra Valley. At Dharmsála, on the 4th of November, the death-stricken Viceroy was joined by his wife and the medical friend who had hastened up with her from Calcutta. Dr. Macrae soon found that his patient's days were numbered, that death from heart-disease was now very near. Lord Elgin calmly prepared for his end, bore his sufferings with cheerful fortitude, gave all the directions for his own funeral, requested the Queen by telegram at once to appoint his successor, and after one more night of pain and restlessness quietly breathed his last on the 20th of November, 1863, at the moment when his greatness seemed ripening for the harvest that in this world was never to be reaped. Only as "an unfinished *torso* in the gallery of our Indian rulers" was Lord Elgin's figure destined to remain. But the torso itself gives fair measure of the greatness to which, had life been spared him, he might have attained.[*]

Pending the arrival of a new Viceroy, Sir William Denison, as Governor of Madras, took up the duties of Governor-General. Landing at Calcutta on the 2nd of December, he found that the members of the Viceroy's Council had caught the alarm displayed by the Panjáb Government at the partial failure of their frontier campaign. As early as the 26th of November the Council had ordered the withdrawal of Chamberlain's force from Ambéla, as soon as that could be done without risk of military disaster, or of any grave blot upon our fair fame. Against so "cowardly a

* Walrond; Prichard.

policy " the acting Viceroy, a good soldier and a shrewd statesman, at once set his face.   If he could not bring the Council over
to his own views, which were those of Sir Hugh Rose also, he
was resolved to act upon his own authority and countermand the
orders issued to the Commander-in-Chief, then staying at Lahór.

In two days, however, Sir William had carried his point in the
Council itself, in spite of the resistance still offered by Sir Charles
Trevelyan.   The Commander-in-Chief found himself free to rein-
force Chamberlain with troops and supplies needful for a prompt
advance.   Sir Neville himself had been badly wounded in the
fighting around the Eagle-Crag; but the enemy had made no
further attacks on his position, and Major Hugh James, the
Political Agent, erelong persuaded some of the hostile tribes to
give up fighting and go home again.   General Garvock, an officer
of experience in Cape warfare, took command of the reinforced
troops in the room of Chamberlain, disabled by his wound.   As
negotiations with the leading tribes still hung fire, Garvock, on
the 15th of December, led forth one of his two brigades to dislodge the enemy from a high steep hill covering the village of
Lálu.   Wylde's brave troops, headed by the 101st, clambered
eagerly up the hill, leapt over the breastworks in their way, and
rushed with loud shouts and levelled bayonets on the disheartened
foe.   In a few minutes the hill from top to bottom was cleared of
its defenders.   Meanwhile Turner's brigade marched on against
Lálu, which was speedily carried and destroyed.*

Next day our troops drove the enemy before them out of
Ambéla, which soon underwent the fate of Lálu.   A murderous
sally made by the mountaineers against two of the Panjábi regiments was erelong beaten back with the help of the 7th Fusiliers;
and the crushing fire of Griffin's three guns left the enemy no
heart for any more fighting.   They had tried their worst against
us and failed.   Negotiations were once more opened with the
Bunair tribes, who, abandoned by their neighbours of Bajaur and
Swát, agreed to the terms they had once rejected.   A strong body
of their own people, accompanied by a few British officers and a
party of the Guides, was sent up the northern slopes of the
Mahában to destroy the head-quarters of the Indian fanatics at
Malka.   On the 22nd of December a broadening volume of smoke
and flame rolled up from the pinewood houses, workshops, and
powder-factory of the doomed settlement, in view of a gathering
crowd of dusky highlanders, scarce withheld by their own chiefs

* Denison; Adye; Prichard.

from falling upon the white strangers who had come to witness the crowning evidence of their defeat.[*]

The destruction of Malka, whence all its occupants had fled beforehand, closed a campaign which, in the words of Sir W. Denison, had "probably taught us a lesson as to the folly of interference with these tribes," while it certainly "read them a lesson which they would not forget for some years." Our troops had fought bravely in trying circumstances under a brave and experienced commander The Patháns in our ranks had stood nobly to their colours in spite of their kinship both in blood and religion with the border tribes. One object of the campaign, the destruction of Malka, had been carried out by the very men who had fought so hard to bar our way thither. We had also punished the tribes that harboured the Indian refugees. But it remains doubtful whether the campaign was politically worth its cost in blood and money; and it seems clear that the Panjáb officers failed to give the Bunair chiefs due warning of our real purpose in marching across their ground. From one cause and another the military promenade developed into a war which lasted two months among the hills where Akbar once lost a whole army. From one enemy at least our troops were fortunately saved ; the snow began falling a month after the usual time.

Malka reduced to ashes, Garvock's column quietly retraced its steps, emerging on Christmas Day from the mouth of the Ambéla Pass ; while the mountaineers, defiant if beaten, broke up the new road made by our working-parties, as if bent on removing the last traces of foreign invasion. On the 12th of January, 1864, Sir William Denison made over the seals of office to Sir John Lawrence, the Viceroy appointed in Lord Elgin's room. Two days afterwards he himself returned to Madras, well pleased to think that his timely interference had averted a serious danger from the North-West, and thus transferred to his successor an empire untroubled even by a frontier war.[†]

* Adye ; Prichard ; Denison.   † Denison.

CHAPTER IV.

SIR JOHN LAWRENCE AS VICEROY.

WHEN the news of Lord Elgin's mortal illness reached England, Sir John Lawrence was quietly doing his share of the work allotted to the Council of India, under the Presidency of Sir Charles Wood. He had already refused the Governorship of Bombay. No thought of returning to the scene of his former greatness ruffled the smooth flow of a life that found its chief happiness in the dear household circle and among private friends. But the hearts of his countrymen at once turned to him as the fittest man in all England to fill Lord Elgin's place at a moment of seeming danger both from without and from within. Their desire saw itself fulfilled in Sir John's preferment to a post which no member of the Indian Civil Service had held by regular appointment since the days of Sir John Shore. If there be some reason in the rule which reserves the headship of the Indian Government for home-trained statesmen of high birth and rank, Lord Palmerston needed no excuse for breaking the rule in favour of one whose qualifications spoke trumpet-tongued for themselves; who, unlike other Viceroys, would go out to India fully equipped at all points for any task that he might have to encounter; whose name alone would be a tower of strength for all well-wishers to England's sovereignty in the East.

Taking up his burden with cheerful readiness, the new Viceroy went on board the first mail steamer bound for Calcutta. The cheers that hailed him from all sides on his way from the Húghli to Government House told loudly of the hopes engendered by his reappearance on the scene of his old renown. And in many other parts of India the news of his arrival awakened a burst of unfeigned enthusiasm from all classes of his new subjects. Every one seemed to feel that, whatever happened, "Ján Lárans Sáhib" might be trusted to guide India safe through all dangers from whatever side, to govern her people with a light firm hand, strong to guard the weak from oppression, and heavy only against evil-doers.* The official classes felt for the moment proud of a Viceroy who had risen to that high eminence from their own ranks; and the mercantile classes hoped much from a ruler who understood the real wants of the country, and would aid heartily in every movement that promised to supply those wants.

The close of the Ambéla campaign marked the timely collapse of the plot which connected the Sitána colony with the Wahábi fanatics of the Panjáb and Bahár. Some of the arch-plotters, who had been tracked out and hunted down by the unwearied Captain Parsons, were tried at Ambála in 1864 by the Commissioner, Sir Herbert Edwardes, who had richly earned his knighthood by the part he bore in the events of 1857. Convicted of designs similar to those which William Tayler had defeated seven years before, they were shipped off for various terms to the lonely penal settlement in the Andaman Islands; a doom on the whole more terrible than death itself. Lawrence therefore entered on his new office unhampered by the fear of domestic troubles or the dangers of a frontier war. There was no need for his immediate journey to Lahór, and his mere presence in India, as his biographer has truly remarked, "was enough to remind the turbulent that their time was not yet."†

But there was no lack of regular business awaiting his attention; of business which in the past few months had fallen sadly into arrear. Setting to work at once, and working literally, as he said, ten hours a day, Sir John Lawrence managed in a few weeks to clear off all arrears, to keep abreast of the new business that daily beset him, and to breathe into all branches of the public service something of the energy and strength of purpose which had marked his government of the Panjáb. Day after day, from morning till dark, the ruler of India sat in his shirt-sleeves, going steadily through the contents of the red-leather despatch-boxes which arrived by every post from all parts of his broad empire. "No arrears" was his guiding principle. A very glutton for work, he did his own thoroughly, at a pace which few men could have equalled; leaving nothing to be done by deputy, seeing and judging everything for himself, and brooking no slovenly discharge of duty from any one who served under him. Superfine people and worshippers of mere show might sneer or shake their heads at a Viceroy who received a deputation in his slippers, who

* Denison ; Temple ; Prichard.
† Bosworth Smith's "Life of Lord Lawrence."

sometimes walked in public places instead of riding, who went to church attended by two troopers instead of eight, who chose to spend in private charities or on a Sailors' Home the money which others would have subscribed to races and theatres, or laid out in some fashionable field of viceregal magnificence.   The local press might misreport, ridicule, denounce him at every turn for social meannesses which he never committed, and for acts of sound policy, mere justice, or religious earnestness, which a ruler of his stamp felt bound to carry through.   But so long as he could do his own duty and see that others did theirs, the new Viceroy gave small heed to the silly, prejudiced, or ill-natured people who tried to weigh him in their Liliputian scales.   Highly as he valued the praise of praiseworthy men, and alive as he was to the power for good or evil of the newspaper press, he never deigned to defend himself from the attacks of the latter, nor would he stoop to seek popularity by any sacrifice of public interests to the clamours of a small but influential class.*

Among his colleagues in the Executive Council were men of tried capacity and of no common mark.   His old friend Sir Charles Trevelyan presided over the Department of Finance. That of Law-making was managed by Henry Maine, renowned already among jurists, scholars, and men of thought by his great work on Ancient Law.   The Military Member was Sir Robert Napier, the war-worn Engineer, whose fighting days were not yet over.   The management of home affairs and of public works was divided between Mr. William Grey and Mr. Henry Harington; while the Viceroy himself took special charge of all India's Foreign Affairs, which included the affairs not only of border kingdoms, but of every Feudatory State, large or small, between the Himalayas and Cape Comorin.   Over the other departments also he was free to exercise a steady control, bounded only by the extent of his own capacity for hard work and of the trust he saw fit to place in his fellow-workers.   As Commander-in-Chief, Sir Hugh Rose, of Central Indian fame, sat in the Council whenever his duties did not call him elsewhither.   Of all the Councillors Sir Hugh was to give his Chief the most trouble, from his zeal in debating questions of which he had small knowledge, and his pertinacity in renewing the fight over causes already lost.   " If every Councillor "—wrote the Viceroy some months later to Sir Charles Wood—" had been as pertinacious as Sir Hugh Rose, the work of the State would soon have come to a deadlock."†

* Bosworth-Smith ; Temple.   † Bosworth-Smith.

With the rest of his colleagues, especially Maine and Trevelyan, their President found himself in general accord. Between him and his Finance Minister, the "Indophilus" of the London *Times*, Macaulay's active helpmate under Lord William Bentinck, who had described him as "almost always on the right side in every question," there were many points in common which enabled them to work loyally together for the common good. Maine's varied learning, calm judgement, and statesmanlike breadth of view were to lend all their weight to the counsels of a ruler whose reforming energies were tempered by his native wisdom, and the teachings of an experience richer and riper than that of any Englishman then alive. If there was sometimes more of friction between John Lawrence and his brother Henry's dearest friend, Sir Robert Napier, who as Chief Engineer in the Panjáb had made some heavy inroads on the public purse, the Viceroy always spoke of his War Minister as "a noble fellow," differed from him with good-humoured frankness, and next year, by dint of hard pleading, obtained for him the chief command of the army in Bombay; a post which was erelong to become the stepping-stone to a peerage and the rank of a field-marshal.*

Both the Executive and the Legislative Council held their sittings once a week under Sir John Lawrence at Calcutta, during the season allotted to public business. Among the native members of the latter body were the Mohammadan Nawáb of Rámpur, the high-bred and accomplished Mahárája of Vizianágram, and the stout-hearted Sikh Rajah, Sáhib Dhyál Singh, all of whom had done loyal service in the darkest days of the Mutiny. The Nawáb, however, found the air of Calcutta so unwholesome that he turned his face homewards within a fortnight, but the other two held manfully on to their work in a climate to them as disagreeable as to the Viceroy himself.†

On the 15th of April Sir John Lawrence left Calcutta on his far way up to the hill-tops of Simla. By that time he had done some things worthy of special note. He had given such an impulse to the movements of the State machinery as went far to satisfy even Trevelyan's appetite for fruitful work. In his care for the public health he had taken sure steps to prevent the poorer Hindus from casting their dead into the Húghli instead of burning them to ashes on its banks. His sympathy with the

* Bosworth-Smith.

† Vizianágram is in Southern India, but the Mahárája had passed his youth at Banáras, while his estates were being nursed by the Indian Government.

humbler classes of his own countrymen had led him to select a
site for a new Sailors' Home in the best part of the city, to lay
the first stone of it with his own hands, and to contribute largely
from his own, as well as the public purse, towards the work of
rescuing our unemployed seamen from the snares that surrounded
them in their old place of refuge. He had taken a kindly interest
in the efforts then making at Lahór, Madras and Calcutta, to
reform the rude old practices of native agriculture; and had himself
opened the exhibition of steam-ploughs, threshing-machines, and
other products of Western science, wherewith the Lieutenant-
Governor, Mr. Cecil Beadon, sought to astonish and instruct the
native mind.*

In Sir John Lawrence the ráyats of Bengal had already found
a staunch champion of the rights secured to them by the Rent
Law of 1859. For their sake he had not only urged Mr. Cecil
Beadon to see justice done between the zamindárs and their
tenants, whose rights under the new law were virtually disallowed
by Chief Justice Sir Barnes Peacocke; he had also encouraged the
friends of the ráyats to fight their battle in the High Court of
Bengal against a ruling which defined a fair rent as the very
highest which a zamindár or a planter might succeed in obtaining
from any bidder. In due time Sir Barnes Peacocke was to see his
own judgement set aside by fourteen voices to one; and the ráyats
learned that their customary rents could be enhanced only in
strict accordance with the law as thus expounded by the great
legal Rabbis of Bengal.†

Another question which Sir John had taken up from the first
with eager energy was that of sanitary reform in the towns and
cantonments of British India. His efforts in this direction many
things combined to stimulate and inform. The Reports of two
Special Commissions had revealed a state of things which the
Viceroy, himself a soldier's son and brother, as well as a humane,
upright, clear-headed statesman, could not but set himself
straightway to improve. Barracks poisoned with the foul air
from long-neglected latrines; hospitals ill-built, over-crowded,
covered with filth, and reeking to the very punkah-ropes with
the well-known cholera stench; costly British soldiers dying in
ordinary years at the rate of sixty per thousand—such were some
of the horrors which Lawrence, before leaving England, had no
doubt discussed with Florence Nightingale, the noble lady who
had borne so memorable a part in the nursing of our soldiers

* Bosworth-Smith; Malleson; Temple. † Bosworth-Smith.

during the Crimean War. Both Sir Hugh Rose and Sir Robert Napier were eager to help the Governor-General in any scheme for bettering the lot of those who formed the real mainstay of our power in India. Thus seconded, Sir John Lawrence at once opened a vigorous campaign against the evil consequences of past neglect. Within a month of his arrival in Calcutta he had ordained a regular system of sanitary control—a Board of Health in fact—for all India. The new Sanitary Commission was headed by John Strachey, one of the ablest members of the Indian Civil Service, who, as head of the Cholera Commission of 1861, had gained an unwelcome insight into the causes of disease and suffering from his visits to Delhi, Morár, and Miánmir. In each Presidency a Sanitary Department under its own Commissioner was erelong at work, discussing, advising, and reporting on all questions that concerned the health of the Army, and conducting the needful measures of sanitary reform in barracks, hospitals, stations and the neighbouring towns. Every cantonment erelong had its Sanitary Committee, acting in concert with the cantonment magistrate for all purposes of conservancy and general health.*

In his care for the soldier's well-being Sir John Lawrence, for all his thriftiness, shrank from no outlay which public interests seemed to demand. The foundation of a proper sanitary system had in due time to be followed up by the building of new barracks, large, airy, and furnished with all needful comforts, at every station where our white troops would thenceforth be quartered. Even the barracks built by Dalhousie's orders were deemed by competent judges to have at least one fault; they only had one floor, and that for sleeping purposes too near the ground. In agreement with his military colleagues and the Sanitary Commissioner, Sir John decided to build by degrees a number of roomy, double-storied barracks, on the upper floors of which the men might sleep without risk of harm from the fever-laden night air. The ground floors were to be set apart for meals, amusements, workshops, reading-rooms, and even a room for private prayer. The whole cost of this great effort to save the soldier from the evils due to climate, bad housing, idleness, and the natural craving for a change, was reckoned at ten or eleven millions, to be defrayed partly out of income, and partly, if need were, by loans. Of this large sum nearly five millions were

---

* Temple ; Prichard ; Malleson ; Act XXII. of 1864.

expended with results by no means futile, before Lawrence returned home.*

At Simla the Viceroy was joined by his Council, who soon
learned that life in that fair Himalayan retreat was to be for them
no holiday, but a time of steady work. Lawrence had already
avowed his belief that he and his Council would do more work in
one summer's day at Simla than in five days down at Calcutta;
and the amount of work they were to get through yearly, during
the five or six months spent in the Hills, amply justified such a
prediction. The English dwellers in the City of Palaces might
grumble at the yearly flight of their Government from the great
centre of English trade, energy, and civilization. Anglo-Indian
journalists might declaim their loudest about the charms and the
perils of the Indian Capua in the North-West, and denounce the
costliness of a migration which for half the year robbed Calcutta
society of its official chiefs. But Lawrence was never thoroughly
well in Bengal; he had free permission from Sir Charles Wood to
pass six months out of the twelve at Simla, Dárjiling, or on the
Nilgiris; and he knew that without his Council the task of
governing so great an empire—a task much harder and heavier
than it had been twenty years before—could not be efficiently
carried on. The expense of such an arrangement would count
for little against the progress made in the despatch of public
business, and against the policy of shifting the seat of Government for half the year to a place so suitable as Simla for watching
the North-West Provinces, Oudh, the Panjáb and the Western
Frontier. A Governor-General, he rightly argued, who divided
his time between Simla and Calcutta, "would be seen and known
throughout our chief possessions." At the former place he would
have around him all the warlike races of India, all those on whose
character and power our hold on India, exclusive of our own
countrymen, depends.†

If he had no great love for the climate, moral and political as
well as natural, of Bengal, Sir John Lawrence was not one of those
who desired to transfer the regular seat of Government from the
banks of the Húghli to Bombay, Puna, or Jabalpur. Looking at
the question all round, he gave his vote for Calcutta as the winter
capital best suited to the character and conditions of our rule. It
lies within easy reach of the sea, on a river guarded by dangerous
channels from the approach of an enemy's fleet. It forms the
main outlet of a steadily-growing trade, the central link in the

* Temple ; Prichard ; Malleson.   † Bosworth-Smith ; Temple.

chain of intercourse with all parts of the country, the chief seat of European enterprise, and the safe head-quarters of a Government ruling over the oldest, wealthiest, and most populous of Indian provinces. For these and such-like reasons Sir John deemed it best to retain Calcutta as the seat of Government for a part at least of every year.*

During the five months of his stay at Simla in 1864, Sir John Lawrence gave clear foreshadowings of the policy he meant to follow. In September he issued a Resolution in favour of developing the municipal system on the lines which Lord Dalhousie had first marked out. The people of India, he said, "are perfectly capable of administering their own affairs. The municipal feeling is deeply rooted in them." Duty and policy alike bound us to "leave as much as possible of the business of the country to be done by the people, by means of funds raised by themselves ; " the Government for its part reserving to itself the right of "influencing and directing, in a general way, all the movements of the social machine."† Municipal committees had hitherto been started only in places where an active magistrate could persuade the people to follow his lead. In Bengal and Upper India they were still few and far between. The bulk of the natives looked with careless or suspicious eyes on a scheme which many of our own countrymen decried as premature, or derided as a mockery and a sham. It was true that the native members of these committees were appointed by the local Governments ; that they never thought of setting their own opinions against those of their president, the district officer ; and that no president could bear an independent brother, native or English, near his throne. Some of the methods used for raising municipal funds would have grieved the heart of a stern economist ; and the money thus obtained was sometimes expended on other objects than sanitary improvements and the repairing of roads. The *octroi* levied on goods entering a town tended to become a transit-duty, hurtful alike to traders and the towns that taxed them.

All such drawbacks notwithstanding, Sir John Lawrence clung fast to his old faith in the beneficial working of a system which, rightly developed, would train the people in every township to the proper management of their own affairs. Its due development might be slow, but he resolved to make it sure by helping it forward to the best of his power. If municipal committees could be formed only with the consent of the townspeople, many of the larger

* Temple.   † Government Resolution of September 14, 1864.

towns and villages might long continue undrained, uncleansed, and dangerous to the public health. It was not enough, he argued, to invite the people to tax themselves for local improvements which they would rather have let alone. They must be driven gently along the path selected by their official teachers; must go as it were to school for the purpose of learning practical lessons in the art of self-government. His efforts in behalf of municipal progress bore some fruit in the "Municipal Improvement Act of 1867," under which the Panjáb Government was empowered to form a municipal committee in any town which it might select, without reference to the wishes of its inhabitants. The members of the committee might be appointed either by the Lieutenant-Governor himself, or, if he so willed, by some kind of popular election. A similar Act was passed next year for the North-West Provinces.*

Another question to which the Viceroy had from the outset applied his vigorous mind was the dormant question of Tenant-Right in Oudh. Whoever had suffered by the reconquest of that province, certain it is that the Tálukdárs as a body had gained greatly more than their just deserts. Lord Canning had endowed them with full rights of ownership in lands the bulk of which had really belonged to village landholders and Zamindárs. Under the revenue-settlement of 1859 the rights of these ancient village folk were almost everywhere ignored, in favour of the new aristocratic idol which Lord Canning had set up. In Montgomery's successor, Mr. Charles Wingfield, the Tálukdárs of Oudh were to find a patron still more reckless than the Viceroy who had come to regard them as the rightful lords of the soil as well as the actual masters of the position. Far from sharing Lord Canning's belief in the Tálukdári system as "the ancient, indigenous, and cherished system of the country," Mr. Wingfield could point openly to the known proprietary rights of the village landholders, in the same breath in which he protested against any attempt to disturb the settlement already made with the Tálukdárs. Policy before justice was the principle that led the Chief Commissioner to carry out Lord Canning's purpose to lengths of which a Viceroy who sought to combine policy with justice could not entirely approve. In the process of building up a strong landed aristocracy in Oudh, Lord Canning had still left a door open for the claims of all who had any kind of vested interest in the soil. The *sanads* or title-deeds forwarded to the Tálukdárs were granted only on certain conditions, one of which ran thus:—"That you will, to the best

* Prichard.

of your power, try to promote the agricultural resources of your estate, and that, whatever holders of subordinate rights may be under you, will be secured in the possession of those rights."[*]

No such consideration, however, seemed to moderate the zeal of a Chief Commissioner bent, like the Earl of Strafford, on pursuing his policy of "thorough" at any cost. For some years Wingfield took his own way with hardly a check from any quarter; and the Tálukdárs took every advantage of the power which possession, rank, the Viceroy's ignorance, and Wingfield's partisanship placed in their hands for defeating the ends of justice and enlightened policy. There was small hope of justice for an "occupancy tenant" of never so long standing, from any court where one of the new-made landlords might sit in judgement on the merits of a case that directly impugned his right to rackrent or evict at his own discretion. "The Tálukdár," wrote one of Wingfield's settlement officers, "is in the saddle, and the under-proprietor has to unhorse him." As the burden of proof lay with the latter, and the Chief Commissioner lost no chance of strengthening the Tálukdárs, it is easy to see how often in such a struggle might would overcome right. In the course of 1863 Lord Elgin sounded a note of alarm at the policy pursued by Mr. Wingfield, who had ordered his settlement officers to omit from their records all distinction between the protected tenants and tenants-at-will. Such a policy, coupled with the judicial powers conferred on the Tálukdárs, would tend, he feared, to obliterate all those sub-proprietary rights which Canning himself had once formally acknowledged.[†]

His appeal to the Chief Commissioner seems to have met with no official reply. Sir Charles Wood's previous orders to the same authority remained a dead letter. But the following year saw Sir John Lawrence in the saddle, and against such a rider Wingfield and his clients could not long hold their ground. On the 17th of February Colonel Durand, the Viceroy's Secretary, wrote off a letter to Mr. Wingfield, declaring the views of the Supreme Government on the whole question, and requesting the Chief Commissioner to report with all speed what measures had been taken to record the rights of other classes of people in the soil besides the Tálukdárs. Wingfield's answer, denying the existence of occupancy rights in Oudh, and decrying any attempt to protect the peasantry as so much wrong done to the Tálukdárs, made Sir John Lawrence all the more resolute to enforce in Oudh some at least of the principles already established in Bengal and the North-

[*] Irwin's "Garden of India."   [†] Irwin; Temple.

West. He had no thought of undoing Lord Canning's work, of withdrawing from the Tálukdárs any right or privilege implicable in the terms of former covenants. But he could not stand by and see injustice done, if he could help it, to the mass of struggling peasants, the real backbone and lifeblood of an Indian province, for the sake of a few hundred landowners already honoured, enriched, and petted far beyond their utmost deserts. The Táluk-dárs should have strict justice according to past agreements, but nothing more. He was much too deeply impressed with the political value of a contented peasantry, too intimately versed in the history and science of Indian land-tenures, too honest a foe to wrong-doing under fair pretences, to put up with the clever sophis-tries of men who wanted to make Oudh a paradise for a few all-powerful, many-acred landlords of the old Cornwallis pattern.*

For several months the Viceroy argued with the Chief Com-missioner in vain. The latter would not give way on certain points which the former deemed essential to any compromise that he could accept, points which Maine and Trevelyan urged as strongly as their Chief. At last, on the 30th of September, Sir John Lawrence clinched his formal demands on the Chief Commis-sioner by appointing one of the ablest civil officers in the Panjáb, Robert Davies, to act as Special Commissioner in Oudh, with full power to direct the proceedings of the settlement officers and to decide all questions of tenant-right for the benefit not of one class, but of " all the people connected with the soil."

This attempt to "mitigate the evils of the Tálukdári policy," on behalf of the old peasant proprietors and tenants holding their fathers' lands, involved its author in a storm of hard words and angry epithets from the Tálukdárs' friends in Oudh, Bengal, and England. The Zamindárs and planters of Bengal swelled the out-cry raised in Oudh by the wily and fortunate Mahárája Mán Singh. Some of the leading Anglo-Indian journals raged unsparingly against their former idol, and enlisted on their side the voices of many a writer and politician at home, who rushed into the con-troversy with the haziest notions of its real meaning. In his own Council Lawrence had to reckon with more than one opponent, while three or four members of Sir Charles Wood's Home Council recorded their dissent from the Governor-General's views. He saw himself held up to public censure as a breaker of compacts, a destroyer of property, a foe to the established order of things.†

But he was not the man to flinch from doing his duty because

---

* Irwin ; Bosworth-Smith.　　　† Irwin ; Bosworth-Smith ; Temple.

the doing of it made him a target for all kinds of abuse. He had no wish to harm the Tálukdárs ; but in the interests of fair play he would stand to his guns. The inquiry he had ordered should not with his consent be dropped, nor would he modify the instructions he had given to Mr. Davies. " People in England," he said, " talk a good deal of truth and justice ; but when one desires to apply such principles, they are astonished and begin to complain." By the middle of 1865 he had learned from Mr. Davies that the old customary rights had practically disappeared in the long chaos of misrule and anarchy which preceded the annexation of Oudh. It still remained for him to " protect the interests of the under-tenantry, with due regard for those of their chartered landlords." The way before him might be rough and perilous, but go on he would, conscious of his own wise, upright purpose, and strong in the countenance afforded him by the Government at home.*

In the spring of 1866 the way was made easier for him by the retirement of his chief antagonist, Sir Charles Wingfield. With John Strachey as Chief Commissioner the Viceroy could work in fair accord. About the same time Sir Charles Wood retired in failing health, as Lord Halifax, to that asylum for invalid statesmen, the House of Lords. But in Lord de Grey, his too short-lived successor, the Home Council of India had a President to whom Lawrence could safely look for all due sympathy and support. Sir Hugh Rose, ennobled into Lord Strathnairn, made over his Indian command to Sir William Mansfield, who was soon to show himself one of the Viceroy's ablest allies in the Calcutta Council. Another of the new councillors, Noble Taylor, bade fair to fill up the gap left by the departing Trevelyan. In the course of 1867, after many conferences and much discussion, Strachey prevailed on the Tálukdárs to accept the compromise granted by the Governor-General. During his visit to Lucknow in November, Lawrence himself received further assurance to this effect from the lips of the leading Tálukdárs.

A Bill embodying the terms of this agreement had already been laid before the Viceroy's Council. It confirmed the present landlords in the enjoyment of all rights and privileges contained in the grants of 1859. It declared and defined the occupancy rights of those cultivators who had held their own lands within thirty years of the 13th of February, 1856. No such tenant could have his rent raised except on certain specified grounds, such as the higher

* Bosworth-Smith ; Temple ; Irwin ; *Edinburgh Review* (April, 1870).

rates ruling among tenants of the same class holding lands of a like character. No tenant who had improved his holding at his own cost, within a term of thirty years, could be ousted or compelled to pay higher rent, until he had been fairly compensated for his outlay, whether by money or a twenty years' lease. Under the head of improvements came all kinds of works that tended to increase the yearly letting value of the land.*

In 1868, after four years of struggle, the Oudh Tenancy Bill became law. Fixity of tenure with fair rents was thus in effect secured for a small section, not more perhaps than one-fifth, of the Oudh peasantry. The great mass of tenants was still left in the position of tenants-at-will, protected only by a milder law of distraint and by the right of compensation for any improvements of their own making. It was not much of a victory which Lawrence had won over the Tálukdárs. But he looked upon half the loaf as better than no bread, and he had at least succeeded in mitigating the worst evils of a policy which he felt himself bound in honour to uphold. It was something to have saved and restored, as Sir John Strachey has since declared, "such remnants of the ancient rights as had not been hopelessly swept away." Fighting as he did against tremendous odds, Sir John Lawrence had pricked with his Ithuriel spear some weak places in the system founded by Lord Canning; had taught the Tálukdárs that they also had duties to fulfil in return for the powers conferred upon them; and had paved the way for yet wider applications of the principles enforced by the Act of 1868.†

In the first year of his rule, Sir John Lawrence marked out the line he meant to take on certain grave questions of foreign policy. Owing to Lord Elgin's illness, it was not till December 1863 that Sir William Denison had formally acknowledged Sher Ali Khán as Amir of Kábul in the room of Dost Mohammad. When Lawrence arrived at Simla in the following year, the new Amir was already fighting for his throne against rival claimants of his own family. From many quarters the Viceroy was urged to throw his sword into the scale on behalf of the ruler whom Dost Mohammad had named his heir. But nothing would tempt him to swerve an inch from the path of patient neutrality on which his feet were set, in wise compliance with the late Amir's entreaty, that his sons, if they came to blows for the succession, should be left to "fight it out among themselves." Beyond offer-

---

* Irwin ; Prichard.　　† Bosworth-Smith ; Temple ; *Edinburgh Review.*

ing friendly assurances to the reigning Amir in return for his prayers for more active help Lawrence steadily refused to go. Sher Ali had his good wishes; but in the pending struggle for the Afghán throne no one should be allowed to meddle save the chiefs and people of Afghánistán.

CHAPTER V.

PAGEANTRY, WAR, AND FAMINE.

In the first days of October, 1864, Sir John Lawrence set out from Simla, journeying by way of Amritsar to Lahór. On the 14th he entered the capital of his old province, greeted as he passed along by a vast crowd of admiring natives eager to see or renew acquaintance with the Ján Lárans Sáhib of yore. His old lieutenant, Montgomery, who had met him at Amritsar, entertained him that night at Government House. Next day he gave private audience to each of the great Sikh chieftains in his turn. On Monday, the 17th, he paid them return visits, spent some hours in discussing with his chief officers the question of engineering works at Multán, talked for some time with 800 teachers and students of Government Schools, invested the gallant Rajah of Kapurthalla with the Star of India, and formally opened with a few words of kindly praise and regret the new Lawrence Hall, which Montgomery and other old friends had erected in memory of his former services.

On the 18th he carried out the main purpose which had brought him to Lahór; the holding of a grand Darbár on the plain where Ahmad Shah, the Duráni, had encamped on his way to Pánipat, and where Ranjit Singh had afterwards been wont to review his victorious Khálsa troops. Over this plain stretched the roofs of a tented city containing eighty thousand armed men, followers of the six hundred chiefs and notables who had flocked thither to pay their homage to the far-famed representative of India's Queen. That morning, at nine o'clock, every chief and notable took his allotted seat in the vast Darbár tent, on the right of the Viceregal throne. On the left sat Sir Robert Montgomery, Sir Henry Maine, Donald Macleod, and the various Commissioners of the Panjáb, while three hundred of Montgomery's officers took their places behind. Half an hour later, the whole assembly rose to their feet as, amidst the thunders of a royal salute, the

Viceroy himself, his tall figure clad in plain attire, walked through the tent to his seat on the richly-decked platform. In another moment he was addressing the brilliant throng around him in their own Hindustani tongue; the first Governor-General who could have done so since Sir John Shore. In words of simple earnestness he thanked the assembled princes and chiefs for their kindly welcome, given him after an absence of nearly six years. "I recognize," he went on, "the sons of my old allies, the Mahárájas of Kashmir and Pattiála; the Sikh chiefs of Málwa and the Mánjha; the Rájput chiefs of the Hills; the Mohammadan Maliks of Pesh`awar and Koh`at; the Sard`urs of the Derajat, of Haz`ara, and of Delhi. All have gathered together to do honour to their old ruler."

He then told his friends of the great interest which the Queen of England took in all things connected with the welfare, comfort, and contentment of the people of India; how kindly she had spoken of her Eastern subjects; how warmly she had bidden him watch over their interests; and how enlightened a counsellor on their behalf she had always found in her late husband. Then followed a quiet reference to his brother Henry's and his own earnest, unflagging labours for the good government of the Panjáb, and to the loyal services rendered in return by chiefs and people during the revolt of 1857. If it behoved the rulers of a country to understand the language and enter into the feelings of its people, it was not less important that the people should know something of their rulers, in order that both classes might live happily together. "To this end," said Lawrence, "I urge you to instruct your sons, and even your daughters."

After reminding his hearers how some of the ablest and kindest of his countrymen, such men as Sir Robert Montgomery, Mr. Donald Macleod, Mr. Roberts, Sir Herbert Edwardes, Colonel Lake, and Colonel John Becher, had been employed to excellent purpose in the Panjáb, Sir John Lawrence ended with a prayer to "the great God, who is the God of all the races and all the peoples of this world, that he may guard and protect you, and teach you all to love justice and hate oppression, and enable you, each in his several way, to do all the good in your power. May he give you all that is for your real benefit. So long as I live I shall never forget the years that I passed in the Panjáb, and the friends that I have acquired throughout this province."*

After this each prince and chief with some of their followers

* Bosworth-Smith.

was presented to the Viceroy, who touched their *nazars* or offerings, and shook hands warmly with those he had known of old. The chiefs in their turn received each his *khillat* or gift of honour from the Viceroy's hands; and by one o'clock P.M. the great Darbár was over. One of Lawrence's right-hand men in the days of the Mutiny, a form familiar to the wild Maliks of the frontier, was unavoidably absent. Sir Herbert Edwardes had been detained by illness at Ambála.

Among those who figured in this famous gathering were certain envoys from the Khán of Khokán, or Firghána, the Usbek kingdom on the Jaxartes, where Bábar, the future Moghal Emperor of Delhi, first saw the light. They had come all the way to India, seeking help against the Russians, who in eight years after the Crimean War had carried their arms from the Caspian to the river Sir or Jaxartes, and taken half of Khokán to themselves. True to the policy pursued on a like occasion by Lord Dalhousie, the Governor-General declined to interfere. He bade the Envoys tell their master to expect no aid from India against a Power with whom Great Britain had no cause of quarrel. At the same time he counselled the Khan to make the best terms he could with his formidable neighbour, and to restrain his subjects from all acts tending to provoke fresh hostilities and yet worse defeats. Three years later, when a Russian army was swooping down upon Samarkhand, an Envoy from Bokhára came to Calcutta with a like prayer for help against the common foe of Western Turkistán. Him also Lawrence could only answer with words of friendly counsel and frank warning.*

The great Darbár at Lahór was rivalled in pomp and splendour by that which Lawrence held at Agra on the 19th of November, 1866. On this occasion eighty-four princes and chiefs from Rájputána and Central India, including the heads of the oldest Rájput dynasties and the mightiest of the Marátha princes, Sindhia and Holkar, as well as the brave old Begam of Bhopál, besides some 250 from other provinces, flocked with thousands of their followers to the plain outside the imperial city of Akbar. An Investiture of the Star of India preceded by a few days the Darbár itself. One of the new Knights was the gentle and accomplished Donald Macleod, who had but lately succeeded Montgomery in the Government of the Panjáb. Another was Sir Cecil Beadon, whose recent blunders with regard to the Orissa famine had not yet been publicly recorded. Another was the

* Bosworth-Smith ; Temple ; Malleson.

Mahárája of Jodhpur, who would never have received that honour had Lawrence's protest reached England in good time. The Premier Prince of Rájásthán was governing his people so badly, that not long afterwards the Viceroy had to set up a Council of Regency in his stead. Unable to withhold the knight-hood, Lawrence took care to lecture the new knight, plainly but courteously, on the duties which a ruler of his long descent and prominent rank should make it his chief ambition to discharge. Several other gentlemen, native and English, were made Knights or Companions of the same Order, in reward for services heartily acknowledged by the Viceroy's own lips.

To the princes and chiefs assembled round him on the 19th of November Lawrence spoke in their own language, simply and weightily, at sufficient length. "The art of governing wisely and well" was the text on which he discoursed, the one lesson which he sought to impress upon his hearers. It was an art in which few Indian princes had ever trained themselves or their sons. Some of them had won transient fame as conquerors and heroes; but that fame alone, he said, is worth having and lasts for ever, "which is accorded to a just and beneficent ruler." English rule in India had conferred upon the people blessings unknown in the days when "neither the palace of the ruler, nor the cottage of the peasant, nor the most sacred edifices of Hindu or Mohammadan were safe from the hands of the plunderer and the destroyer." In some of the Native States, however, tyranny and oppression still prevailed, and crime too often went unpunished. It was the duty of every Chief to extend to his own people that peace and security from outward violence which English rule had conferred upon his own domains. "They have plenty of time to do all that is necessary, if they have only the will." No deputy can make up for the consequences of their own neglect. Instead of wasting their time in mere amusements or in quarrels with their neigh-bours and their own feudatories, they should devote themselves to carrying out good laws under well-selected officers, to improving their systems of revenue and police, to founding schools for the young and hospitals for the sick. Instead of vying with each other for precedence, let them "all try which can govern his country in the wisest manner;" for the British Government "will honour that Chief most who excels in the good management of his people; who does most to put down crime and improve the condition of his country."

To those who had done aught worthy of special notice, to the

ruler of Gwáliár and the Begam of Bhopál, to the deceased Nawáb
of Jaura, the nonagenarian Rajah of Sitamau in Malwa, and the
able Rajah of Katra in Jaipur, Sir John Lawrence paid the tribute of hearty and discerning praise. A few remarks on the new
but wholesome tendency of native princes to enlarge their minds
by foreign travel, and on the zeal which some of them had shown
in making roads through the length and breadth of their lands,
closed an address to which every one listened with a grave attention, deepened by a sense of mingled awe, esteem, and admiration
for the man who thus spoke.[*]

On his way down country from the Lahór Darbár, Lawrence
heard of the great hurricane which, after raging around Madras,
had swept up the Bay of Bengal beyond Calcutta even to Bardwán, leaving everywhere dismal traces of its power for destruction.
It drove before it up the Húghli a mighty storm-wave about
twenty feet high, which destroyed or wrecked everything that the
gale had spared. Village after village on the low river-banks
was swept away with all its living contents. Woods, cattle, houses
and growing crops were overwhelmed along a breadth of several
miles; and some forty good ships, to say nothing of the smaller
native craft, were sunk at their moorings, or dashed against each
other, or torn away to be flung bodily like mere playthings far up
the shore. Many a noble tree was uprooted or wrecked in the
park at Barrackpore and along the shady avenue planted in Lord
Wellesley's time between that station and Calcutta. The loss of
life alone from Calcutta to the sea was reckoned at 30,000 souls,
nearly 3,000 of whom perished on Ságar Island at the mouth of
the river. Another 30,000, according to Sir W. Denison, died at
Madras.[†]

By this time Lawrence had unwillingly embarked in a little
war with the rude mountaineers of Bhotán, a wild Himaláyan
country stretching eastward from Sikhim along the northern frontier of Bengal and Assam, to the south-eastern corner of Tibet.
This country, larger than all England and Wales, was peopled
only by a few hundred thousand Buddhist Tartars, ruled by Rajahs
who owned a loose sort of allegiance to the Grand Láma of Lhása.
Polygamy and polyandry had kept their numbers from increasing.
In 1772, when Warren Hastings ruled Bengal, their raids into
that province were checked by a small force of his disciplined
Sepoys, who drove the Bhotias back with slaughter into their own
hills. Their leader, the Deb Rajah, was glad erelong to make

* Bosworth-Smith.   † Prichard ; Bosworth-Smith.

peace with a Governor-General who not only gave him back his captured strongholds, but invited his subjects to trade freely with Bengal by way of Rangpur. Bogle's mission to Tásisudon in 1774 smoothed the way for a friendly intercourse which lasted during Hastings' time. After his departure in 1784 very little was heard of the Bhotias, until Assam passed into English keeping in 1826. At that time they held certain lowland Duárs or Passes at the foot of their own hills, for which they had paid the former masters of Assam a yearly tribute of yaks' tails, musk, gold-dust, ponies, blankets, and knives.*

In the first year of our rule in Assam the tribute fell into arrear, and the Bhotias met the demand for payment by raiding into British ground. Men, women, and cattle were carried off from time to time to Bhotán. Captain Pemberton's mission in 1837 having failed to secure redress for these outrages, the Indian Government annexed the Assam Duárs in 1841, but promised to pay the Rajah of Bhotán 10,000 rupees a year during good behaviour, as compensation for the loss of so much land. This arrangement worked, on the whole, successfully with regard to Assam. But on the Bengal frontier were other Duárs which the Indian Government rented from Bhotán; and into these the hill-men kept on raiding year after year, until in 1860 Lord Canning's Government enforced the demand for reparation by stopping their rents. As the Bhotán chiefs would neither restore their plunder nor refrain from fresh outrages, the Bengal Government persuaded Lord Elgin, in 1863, to despatch an Envoy to the Deb Rajah, the nominal ruler of Bhotán, in the hope that a little diplomacy might preclude the need of stronger and costlier measures on our part.

On the 4th of January, 1864, Mr. Ashley Eden, a civil officer of some repute, set out from Dárjiling on a mission foredoomed from various causes to ignominious failure. In his reply to previous overtures the Deb Rajah had clearly but politely declined the intervention of a British Envoy in matters which his own Government deemed unworthy of special notice. To subsequent letters from the Bengal Government and from Eden himself no reply had come from the ruling powers. Through other channels it transpired that some change of government had taken place in Bhotán. The Deb Rajah had been expelled from power, and two rival factions were struggling for the mastery. Sir William Denison however, as acting Viceroy, instructed Eden to

* Gleig's "Warren Hastings"; Markham's "Narrative of Bogle's Mission"; Chambers's "Encyclopædia."

go forward with the help of the Jangpen or Warden of Dhálimkót, in the belief that a new Deb Rajah would gladly cultivate the goodwill of his English neighbours.*

With Captain Godwin-Austen for his Assistant, with Dr. Simpson as medical officer, a native of Sikhim as interpreter, and an escort of a hundred Sepoys, Mr. Eden started on an errand which, as things stood, bore miscarriage written large upon its face. Delays and difficulties dogged his steps from the first. At the river Tista his party had to wait three days for fresh coolies in the room of those who had so soon deserted it. Fresh desertions took place daily. One chief shut the gates of his fort against our Envoy. The Jangpen of Dhálimkót proved his friendliness by exacting payment for all supplies at ten times the market rates, by drinking as much brandy as Mr. Eden could be induced to give him, and alternately bullying and cringing to his English guests. What with the need of waiting for fresh supplies from Bengal, with the flight of more coolies from the Mission camp, and with the game of obstruction privately played between the Jangpen and the new Deb Rajah, it was only on the 29th of January that Eden could resume his march from Dhálimkót into the Bhotán hills, leaving behind him half his escort and nearly all his baggage.†

Toiling onwards through lofty mountain passes sometimes blocked with snow, the Envoy gained continually fresh inklings of the dangers that beset a mission to a semi-barbarous country, then ruled by a number of chiefs under no acknowledged head. On the 7th of February one of these chiefs would have stopped by force the Envoy's progress, had he dared. Next day some messengers from the Deb Rajah to the chief of Dhálimkót showed Eden a letter in which the former personage threatened vengeance against the Jangpen for allowing the Mission to enter Bhotán. On the 19th another chief threatened violence until the Envoy bribed him into a friendlier mood. Still pressing forward, Eden received from the Deb Rajah a letter which ended by demanding payment of all arrears of rent for the Bengal Duárs. At Páro, the head-quarters of the Penlo or Governor of Western Bhotán, the Mission underwent a course of studied insults from the Penlo's officers, which might well have provoked the meekest of Envoys to throw up his errand and return home. Had Eden so acted,

* The real ruler of Bhotán seems to have been the Dharm Rajah, under whom the Deb Rajah acted as a sort of Prime Minister.

† Prichard.

Lawrence would certainly have held him blameless. The Viceroy, indeed, would gladly have recalled the Envoy from an enterprise in whose expediency he had no belief. But deference to the views and arguments of Sir Cecil Beadon, and trust in Eden's "*savoir faire* and judgement," stayed his hand until worse things than he had foreboded came to pass.*

Impelled by ambition or a mistaken sense of duty, the Envoy seemed determined to rush upon his fate. Even the long halt at Páro amid daily recurring tokens of native insolence, ill-will, and double dealing, failed to open his eyes to the folly of persistence in a bootless errand. On the 15th of March the Mission reached Punákha, the winter capital of Bhotán. Here the old tale of discourtesy and insult was repeated daily in various forms. On the 20th Eden and his officers were summoned to an interview with the Deb Rajah. After a few preliminary insults, they had to sit on mats in the sun outside a tent in which the Council of State were comfortably seated. Hustled thence through a jeering crowd towards the tent where sat the Deb Rajah, they had to stand uncovered in the hot sun, while the Bhotia prince read the Viceroy's letter which a common coolie placed in his hands. When the Deb Rajah had left his tent, Eden and his party were hustled on to another tent occupied by the mysterious Dharm Rajah himself.

After waiting another hour in the sun, the luckless Englishmen were led by the mocking Bhotia Sepoys before the Council, at the head of which sat the Tongso Penlo or Governor of Eastern Bhotán. When the Council had repeated their own demands against the Indian Government, the Tongso Penlo cut short the interview by crumpling up the draft treaty, declaring himself for war, and taunting the Envoy as a mere nobody, who had no power to treat on a question which a *chaprási*, or native messenger, might easily have settled. "I will have nothing more to do with you—Go," were the words in which this rude little potentate dismissed the Ambassador of a large and powerful Empire.†

Even this failed to break the neck of Eden's astounding patience. He agreed to attend another meeting of the Council. On this occasion the Bhotia chiefs made a show of accepting the treaty he laid before them. On the 24th of March were enacted the closing scenes in this portentous farce. Once more the Envoy stood before the Council, bringing with him the treaty which the Chiefs had agreed to sign. Instead of signing it, the

* Prichard ; Boswell-Smith. † Prichard.

Tongso Penlo demanded the cession of the Assam Duárs to Bhotán; and the rest of the Council laughed at the Envoy's protests against this unseemly renewal of a claim which they had already pledged themselves to waive. At last the rude barbarian closed the war of words by rubbing Mr. Eden's face with a piece of wet dough, pulling his hair, and slapping him on the back, amidst shouts of laughter from the assembled bystanders. Another chief bespattered Dr. Simpson's face with the *pán* leaf which he had just been chewing; while the interpreter, Chibu Láma, was forcibly relieved of his watch, a gift from the Viceroy himself. This was afterwards restored to its owner, and the Envoy's party were allowed without further molestation to withdraw.

One more drop in the cup of humiliation the Envoy had yet to swallow. On the following day the Tongso Penlo threatened the whole Mission with imprisonment, if nothing worse, unless Eden would sign a paper surrendering the Assam Duárs. Fearing the worst, for his persecutors began to cut off his food supplies, Eden on the 29th of March signed the requisite treaty, with the words "under compulsion" written above his own signature. After a few more formalities and threatenings the Mission was allowed to depart in peace.*

The Bhotia Chiefs had thus succeeded in playing a series of rough practical jokes on a British Envoy who seemed bent on provoking his fate. But the crowning insult offered to the Viceroy's official agent, Sir John Lawrence could not of course overlook, however deeply he might regret the policy whose failure had been thus scornfully proclaimed. The treaty which Eden had signed under compulsion was at once repudiated; the rent of the Assam Duárs was suspended; and the Ambári lowlands on the Bengal frontier were formally annexed. At the same time the Viceroy repeated the demands of which Eden had been the bearer, and gave the Bhotán Council three months to make up their minds for peace or war. No answer having reached him long after the term of grace had expired, he at length declared war in November 1864. Some six thousand troops, mostly native, marched in four columns against the five or six forts which commanded the several passes from Bhotán into the Bengal Duárs. Before the year's end each of these had fallen with hardly a struggle into our hands, and the force employed in taking them was broken up.

* Prichard.

Dewángiri, the easternmost of the captured forts, was held by Colonel Campbell and a garrison of five hundred men. To this post came a letter from the Tongso Penlo, threatening to attack the garrison unless they withdrew before seven days. As no one in the garrison could read the letter, Campbell forwarded it for interpretation to Dárjiling. Its true meaning, however, was first unfolded to him in the early morning of the 29th of January, 1865, when the Tongso Penlo well-nigh caught the garrison asleep. After the first surprise they drove the assailants back with a loss to themselves of five slain and thirty-two wounded. But the Bhotias cut off their water, their ammunition ran short, and the help they asked for never came. Campbell at length gave the word for a retreat, which, begun in the dark of the 5th of February, soon turned into a panic flight. The two guns, for want of men to drag them, were thrown down a precipice, and some of the sick and wounded fell into the enemy's hands. The rest of the garrison made good their retreat to Kumri Káta in the plains.*

Similar attacks had been made by the Bhotias on other forts held by our garrisons. But in no other case besides Dewángiri did the assailants gain any ground. Fresh troops marched in all haste to the Bhotán frontier; and Brigadier Henry Tombs, who had won the Victoria Cross at Delhi, took command of a field-force strong enough to drive before it any number of ill-armed, however brave and cunning, mountaineers. In due time Dewángiri was retaken with trifling loss, and the enemy were cleared away from the stockades they had planted in the neighbourhood of Dhálimkót and other of the forts we had captured the year before. In the course of this campaign the victors might well have learned a lesson of humanity from the vanquished. The Tongso Penlo had taken every care of the prisoners made by his troops during the disastrous flight from Dewángiri. But when that post once more fell into British hands, our well-drilled and civilized Sepoys could not be restrained from slaughtering even the wounded who lay across their path.†

With the recapture of Dewángiri the war was virtually over. In view of further resistance fresh troops were already gathering to complete the work of conquest, and to fill up the gaps which cholera, fever, and dysentery were making daily in our ranks, when messengers from the Deb Rajah and the Tongso Penlo announced their masters' readiness to treat for peace. The Vice-

* Prichard.   † Prichard; Bosworth-Smith.

roy's demands were moderate enough, too moderate to please the more fiery of his countrymen. The treaty which Eden had signed under compulsion was to be given up, as well as the guns which Campbell's men had abandoned. As a punishment for past and a guarantee against future offences, the Bengal Duárs must be formally ceded to the Indian Government; which promised in its turn to make up the consequent loss of revenue to Bhotán, by a yearly subsidy of 25,000 rupees, payable only during good behaviour. If the Bhotias adhered to their engagements this sum might afterwards be doubled. After some demurring, especially to the surrender of so rare a trophy as two British guns, the Bhotia Chiefs accepted the proffered terms, which received their final sanction in the Treaty of 1866.*

Thus ended what has well been called a "miserable chapter of British-Indian history;" a chapter of mishaps, mistakes, and shortcomings, retrieved at last by an inglorious success. There were some indeed who railed against the new treaty as a wanton sacrifice of the national honour. But all sensible men hailed it as the best means of escape from past entanglements, and the likeliest safeguard against future annoyances from Bhotán. The surrender of the guns was a point on which the Viceroy had strongly insisted, to the extent of ordering one of Tombs' trustiest officers to recover them, if need arose, by force. In promising the Bhotias a small yearly subsidy so long as they kept the peace. Sir John Lawrence sought not only to compensate them in some measure for the loss of those fertile lowlands which yielded the bulk of their poor revenue, but to bind them over to more peaceful habits by their knowledge of the power he retained to cut off their main supplies. While his hopes in this regard have since been fully verified, the land annexed by him has been dotted over with goodly tea-gardens, in which thousands of thrifty coolies are earning a fair day's wage.†

Hardly had this little storm of war blown over, when a worse storm of quite another kind burst upon the country, forming the south-western limb of Bengal. The province of Orissa, stretching southward from Midnapur to Ganjám, and eastward from Sambalpur to the Bay of Bengal, covers an area of 50,000 square miles, about half of which is peopled by Uriya Hindus, speaking a dialect of the old Indian tongue. Along the seaboard stretch the districts of Balasor, Katák, and Púri, over a surface of nearly 8,000 square miles. These districts make up the Katák Division

* Prichard; Malleson; Bosworth-Smith.   † Temple; Malleson.

ruled directly by the Government of Bengal. Outside this long narrow strip of alluvial soil, thrown out between the mountains and the sea by the waters of the Brahmani, the Baitarni, the Mahánadi or Great River, and several other streams, lie the Katák Maháls, a group of petty states ruled by native tributary chiefs; and beyond these again are broad tracts of hill and jungle in which various tribes of Kóls, Khánds, and other aboriginal folk find easy means of satisfying their simple wants. Here and there in the heart of the jungles and along the banks of the Mahánadi may be traced the ruins of cities great and populous in the centuries before Orissa passed under the Mohammadan yoke. Overrun from time to time by Pathán and Moghal armies, Orissa fell at last into the hands of the plundering Maráthas, who, with the help of floods, famines, and other physical agencies, reduced it to that state of utter wreck from which it is only now beginning to recover.*

Before the end of 1865 famine had begun to threaten the province of Katák and the adjoining district of Ganjám in Madras. The monsoon rains had fallen scantily, and in September had altogther ceased. The rice crops, which form the staple food of Orissa, were withering away for lack of the needful moisture; and the people were too poor to afford the high prices at which alone rice could be imported either by sea or land into a province shut in on the one side by roadless hills and forests, on the other by an almost unapproachable shore. The only road from Calcutta to Púri was seldom fit for anything but pack-bullocks, and even these in the rainy season were altogether stopped by some of the many streams that crossed their path. Of seaborne traffic there was not much at any time, and, owing to the stormy weather of the half-yearly monsoons, the only harbour, such as it was, at False Point, remained virtually closed to all vessels for the greater part of the year. Of the civil officers in the province one at least, the Collector of Púri, sounded the note of alarm, at the end of October, when all hope of further rain had died out, and the landowners of his district were praying for time to pay the revenue demand on their ruined crops.

Had timely heed been given to Barlow's warnings and the reports received from other quarters, the disasters of the following year might have been wholly or largely forestalled. But the Commissioner, Mr. Ravenshaw, made light of the coming scarcity, rebuked his subaltern for taking part with the croakers, and

* Hunter's "Orissa"; Thornton's "Gazetteer"; Prichard; Bosworth-Smith.

maintained that the grain-dealers had probably stores enough in hand to "supply the market for a couple of years." The Board of Revenue at Calcutta promptly rejected as "inadmissible" the prayer of the Púri landowners. A merchant firm in Calcutta urged upon Sir John Lawrence the need of buying rice on behalf of the Government and shipping it off betimes to Katák. But Lieutenant-Governor Beadon assured the anxious Viceroy that no official reports from Orissa warranted the course proposed by the Calcutta firm. The Revenue Board, for their part, scouted any course of action which sinned against "the laws of political economy." In reply to Mr. Cecil Beadon's questions, they advised the opening of a few relief works, and the forming of relief committees dependent on private charity for any funds they might be able to dispense. When the works were opened and the committees formed, about the end of 1865, it became clear to Mr. Ravenshaw himself that no amount of money would make up to the people of Orissa for the actual dearth of food. Of what use indeed could money alone be to hungry multitudes unable to exchange that money for the rice that was not there ? In vain did Ravenshaw, now thoroughly alarmed, plead the cause of common sense and humanity against the political pedants of Calcutta and Alipur. On the 1st of February, 1866, he received a telegram rejecting his prayer for State-aid towards the purchase of food-grains. "If the market favours," ran the message, "imported rice will find its way to Púri without Government interference, which can only do harm." So the people of Orissa were left to endure the doom of Tantalus in view of the plenty which a word from Calcutta would have placed within their reach.*

In spite of warnings and protests from many quarters, the Bengal Government still shut their eyes to the growing danger, still blindly trusted to the working of those economical laws whose virtue depends on conditions more or less wanting in this particular case. During the month of January the managers of the East Indian Irrigation Company were already feeding their native workmen with rice imported on their own account from Bengal. Colonel Rundall, the Company's engineer, and nearly all the white community of Orissa, declared in effect that famine was in their midst. The merchants and journalists of Calcutta re-echoed the same cry. It was known that the early spring crop must perish through failure of the cold-weather rains. Sir John

* Bosworth-Smith ; Blair's "Indian Famines".; Report of the Orissa Famine Commission ; Prichard.

Lawrence himself had strong misgivings as to the real state of things; but he felt loath without further inquiry to overrule the votes of his own Council in a matter which specially concerned the Government of Bengal. At his request, however, Mr. Cecil Beadon, accompanied by a member of the Revenue Board, set out in February on a tour of investigation through Katák.*

He returned erelong to Calcutta no wiser than before, having seen and heard nothing which led him to doubt the existence of a large reserve of food in the famine-stricken province. The result of Beadon's inquiries served for a time to convince the Viceroy that, with regard to Orissa, "all which appeared to be necessary had been done." But the old misgivings presently recurred to the Viceroy's mind. Towards the end of March the prayers of several merchants in Calcutta moved him to impress upon Mr. Cecil Beadon the urgent need of importing grain into Orissa from the Burman coast. Had his advice been followed even then, had he only ordered instead of advising, Orissa might yet have been saved from dire suffering. But Beadon again assured him that there was grain enough in the province to last till next harvest; and Lawrence in April went off to Simla, believing, or trying to believe, in the vanity of his late alarms. Mr. Cecil Beadon about the same time withdrew in quest of health to Dúrjiling.†

At last, on the 10th of May, two things happened which roused the Viceroy to swift and resolute action. A letter in the *Englishman* on "the starving poor of Orissa" caught his eye; and the shock it gave him was heightened by the reading of a letter which his private physician, Dr. Farquhar, had just received from a Calcutta merchant, the same Mr. Scott Moncrieff who, in the past November, had appealed through the same channel to the Viceroy's interference in the same behalf. His eyes thus rudely opened to the facts of which Beadon had meanwhile sent him not a word, Lawrence straightway telegraphed to the Lieutenant-Governor a strong demand for full and precise information, accompanied by an offer of certain funds for immediate use and a promise of liberal help in the future. In the same message he urged Mr. Cecil Beadon to go down at once to Calcutta and pour supplies of food into the suffering province.

Beadon went down to Calcutta, and soon learned enough from various quarters to convince him that Orissa was in sore distress. Not till the 29th of May, however, did he take the one step which, taken six months, or even three months, earlier, would have

* Blair; Prichard; Bosworth-Smith.   † Bosworth-Smith.

saved a multitude of lives. On that day he issued his orders for
the purchase of grain in British Burmah. Some precious days
elapsed before the first shipload of rice left the mouth of the
Irawédi on its way to Bálasor. While the vessel which Moncrieff
had chartered was speeding on its errand of mercy, the South-
West Monsoon burst in a sudden fury of rain and wind along the
Orissa coast. Starving multitudes saw the good ship tossing on
the waves outside the bar; "and for four months," says Dr.
Farquhar, "no living soul could open communication between
her and the shore." There were no boats at Bálasor fit for landing
grain in such weather. The overland road from Calcutta to Katák
would very soon be closed for some months to come. It was too
late, in short, to repair the mischief caused by a blind adherence
to inapplicable rules. The famine had fairly settled down upon
the land. Erelong the rain-swollen Mahánadi was running over
in floods that destroyed whatever crops the drought had spared.*

In the month of September 270,000 starving people were kept
alive on the food doled out to them daily by the Relief Committees. No efforts indeed were now spared to grapple with the
plague that kept on slaying its thousands for weeks and months
together. But all such efforts were as mere raindrops in the great
sea of human suffering. Disease followed, as ever, in the wake of
famine; and before the year's end cholera, fever, dysentery had swept
away multitudes of hunger-wasted folk. In the course of that
woful year nearly a million men, women, and children, or one-
fourth of the whole population of Orissa, were numbered among
the dead.† In the adjoining district of Ganjám the proportion of
deaths from famine was far lighter, thanks to the timely zeal with
which Lord Napier of Ettrick, the new Governor of Madras, threw
himself into the work of succouring the needy and saving lives.
Travelling through the district in the hot month of May, he learned
for himself how things stood, formed his own plans for dealing
with the trouble of the moment, and deputed some of his best
officers to see them carried out.‡

After his return from the Agra Darbár to Calcutta, at the end
of November, 1866, Sir John Lawrence saw himself confronted
not only by the cry for help from a starving province, but by an
outburst of popular feeling both in India and at home against the

---

* Orissa Famine Report; Blair; Bosworth-Smith; Temple; Hunter's "Orissa."
† Thousands of pilgrims to the famous shrine of Jagannáth, at Púri, were also
among the victims of famine and disease.
‡ Hunter; Bosworth-Smith; Prichard.

Government whose untimely inaction had borne such lamentable fruit. Lord Cranborne, who had lately succeeded Lord de Grey at the India Office, had already called upon the Viceroy to explain how things had come to so terrible a pass in a province so near the seat of our rule. Lawrence replied by deputing to Orissa a Commission of Inquiry, at the head of which was Mr. George Campbell, a civil officer of large experience, rare energy, and great mental power. Meanwhile Lawrence himself took the lead in planning measures of relief from further suffering. His appeal through the Mansion House to English charity drew little help from a country which at that time had little money to spare. In Calcutta and elsewhere he was more successful. Taking the chair at a large public meeting on the 12th of February, 1867, the Viceroy laid before his hearers the full extent of the havoc already wrought by famine, floods, and pestilence, and pleaded for their help towards rescuing the survivors by an importation of twenty-seven thousand tons of rice. He himself headed the subscription list with a gift of a thousand pounds from his private purse. Such an example found many followers, each according to his means; and kindlier seasons lent timely aid to the efforts of private charity and official zeal.*

Before the end of April, 1867, the Report of Campbell's Commission was on its way to England, accompanied by a minute from the Viceroy himself. Sir John agreed with the Commissioners in holding that "timely measures were not taken," and that "valid reasons were not adduced for the neglect." To him it seemed "beyond all doubt that there was a want of foresight, perception, and precaution regarding the impending calamity which was quite unaccountable, even when allowance has been made for the fact that the officers under the Government of Bengal had, with scarcely an exception, no previous personal experience with the character of famines." In the previous October he had written to Lord Cranborne, expressing his firm belief that the Lieutenant-Governor, the Board of Revenue, and the local officers "neither foresaw the famine and scarcity which were coming on, nor would admit them when pointed out by others." That Sir Cecil Beadon —"a man of decided ability and kindly nature"—should have failed so utterly in such a crisis, was a mystery which Lawrence in a subsequent letter sought to explain by a reference to his ill-health, and to the many years he had passed in the Secretary's office, where he had "learned to depend on others for information

* Famine Report; Prichard; Bosworth-Smith; Hunter.

and not to seek it out himself." Against such excuses, however kindly meant, must be set the Viceroy's own admission that Sir Cecil Beadon failed to attach due weight to the warnings received from Colonel Rundall, the missionaries and merchants on the spot, and other persons whose opinions differed from those of the Revenue Board.*

The broad facts of this great catastrophe speak for themselves. The Commissioner of Orissa makes light of the wiser counsel urged upon him by the Collector of Púri. The Board of Revenue take their tone from Mr. Ravenshaw, and refuse to believe in anything of which they have not been officially informed. Even after the Commissioner has clearly changed his note, they persist in bowing down at the altar of Red Tape and in muttering the shibboleths of a sham political economy. The Lieutenant-Governor of Bengal pipes on with emulous persistence to the same tune, heedless alike of the Viceroy's grave pleadings and of every warning uttered by unofficial lips. The Governor-General himself comes out of the business with no slur upon his character, yet not altogether free from blame. Sir George Campbell indeed has since declared that the Viceroy's "only mistake was in believing Beadon;" and a later Viceroy, Lord Northbrook, avowed that in like circumstances he "would have done exactly what Lawrence did." Lord Cranborne's successor at the India Office, Sir Stafford Northcote, assured Lawrence of the general sympathy displayed towards him in the House of Commons, a sympathy which "no one in England or in India more entirely deserved" than Lawrence himself. Many competent judges have held that in acting upon his own instincts, Lawrence would have outraged official decencies and the letter of established laws. But it is certain that, if he had so acted, the result would have been very much happier for the people of Orissa, and happier also for his own peace of mind. " I ought to have insisted on prompt action in the teeth of the Council and the Lieutenant-Governor, and I blame myself for not so doing "—was the burden of his letters home.†

* Famine Report; Bosworth-Smith; Prichard.   † Bosworth-Smith.

CHAPTER VI.

THE PROVINCES.

In the course of 1865 the Governor-General lost the services of his active and hard-working colleague Sir Charles Trevelyan, who, spite of lowering financial prospects and of Lawrence's anxious efforts to show a fair balance-sheet for the future as well as the past, had succeeded in getting the hateful income-tax shelved at the close of its appointed term. Lawrence himself would rather have renewed the impost for another year; but again he shrank from overruling his colleagues on a question which his old friend Trevelyan had set his heart on deciding in his own way. So he agreed, however unwillingly, to replace the income-tax by low export duties on jute, wool, tea, coffee, hides, and silk, by a small addition to the grain duties, and by a loan on account of public works. Trevelyan's proposal to increase the salt tax he utterly rejected as unfair to the poorer millions. As the new scheme of export duties was struck out of the Budget by Sir Charles Wood, in deference to the outcry raised by his countrymen at home, the Viceroy had to meet with diminished resources the ever-growing calls for fresh outlay. His new Finance Minister was Mr. William Massey, who had served some time as Chairman of Committees in the House of Commons, and had written a "History of the Reign of George III." In his Budget for 1866 Massey attempted no fiscal changes, beyond a further lowering of the duty on saltpetre to its old rate of three per cent. But in the following year he imposed a licence tax on trades and professions yielding an income over twenty pounds a year. It was a kind of graduated income-tax rising in its incidence from four rupees to two hundred, according to each taxpayer's apparent means. This new attempt to reach the pockets of those who had specially prospered under our rule awakened the loudest clamours in Calcutta. But the Viceroy stoutly upheld his colleague, and the India Office chimed in with both. In 1867 the tax was

renewed with amendments which relieved the many at the expense
of the few, by doubling the higher rates of assessment and
raising the level of exemptions to fifty pounds a year. In neither
year, however, did it yield much more than half a million sterling.*

In the same year as Trevelyan two other of Lawrence's best
officers quitted India never to return. There were many who
looked to see Sir Herbert Edwardes Governor of the province in
which he had so early achieved such high renown; and Lawrence
himself, who spoke of him as "a born ruler of men," had named
him as a candidate for that office second only to Sir Donald
Macleod. But ill-health was now driving him homewards, and
death a few years later overtook the brilliant soldier-statesman in
the flower of his manhood, while his fame was still fresh in the
memories of his countrymen. His last years were spent, among
other things, in writing the life-story of his old friend and master,
Sir Henry Lawrence; a work of love, knowledge, and literary
power, which another pen was unhappily destined to complete.
A lively companion, a daring and resourceful soldier, a shrewd
diplomatist, Edwardes had shown himself in the days before the
Mutiny "a steady counsellor in grave conjunctures, and full of
fire in the presence of danger."† During the Mutiny he had
been to Lawrence a tower of strength on the Panjáb frontier, and
an eager, cheery, undaunted helpmate in all his efforts to grapple
with a Hydra-headed revolt.

The other departure was that of Sir Robert Montgomery, who,
after five years of statesmanlike rule, made over his high post to
Sir Donald Macleod and went home to take his seat in the Council
of India. His services in the Panjáb before and during the
Mutiny had marked him out as the best possible successor to John
Lawrence in the government of Dalhousie's model province. The
first months of his rule had been disturbed by rumours of Sikh and
Mohammadan plottings, and by the sounds of incipient mutiny
among a portion of our white troops. The priests of Islám were
preaching sedition in the mosques of Lahór, and many of the old
Company's younger soldiers seemed ripe to dispute by force the
right of Lord Canning's Government to transfer them like cattle
from one service to another. But these clouds soon passed over.
Richard Temple, then Commissioner of Lahór, gave the priests
clearly to understand that mosques could not be used for political
purposes; and General Windham, working with Temple, succeeded
in bringing the incipient mutiny to a peaceful close. Nor were

---

* Prichard ; Bosworth-Smith ; Temple ; Chesney.   † Temple.

the minds of Montgomery's subjects stirred afresh to dangerous issues by the more untoward incidents of the Ambéla campaign. If the Lieutenant-Governor of the Panjáb went into that business with too light a heart, his general policy in those five years left nothing to regret. Under his strong yet wise and liberal rule the Panjáb made steady progress on the lines marked out by Dalhousie and the Lawrence brothers. In no other part of India did the people show such readiness to pluck the best fruits of Western civilization. Nowhere else could be seen a more thriving and contented peasantry, an official class more competent for all kinds of duties, or a landed gentry more loyal, more intelligent, more ready to act in furtherance of the public weal.*

In October, 1866, Dr. George Cotton, who had succeeded Daniel Wilson as Bishop of Calcutta in 1859, was cut off in the prime of his usefulness by a sudden death. He was making a pastoral tour by water through Assam, and his round of work in that section of his vast diocese was nearly ended, when on the evening of the 6th he made his way back from Kúshtia to the Lieutenant-Governor's steam-barge. In the darkness his foot slipped as he trod the plank that connected the steamer with the shore, and in a moment, before help could reach him, the swift rolling Brahma-pútra had sucked him down. The sad news, telegraphed to Simla, evoked an Order in Council, which declared the Viceroy's well-founded belief that there was hardly a Christian of any sect in all India who would not "feel the premature loss of this prelate as a personal infliction," and that large numbers even of the non-Christian population would join in lamenting the death of one whose great knowledge, sincerity, and charity they had learned to appreciate. Nor did Lawrence or his Secretary greatly exceed the truth in affirming that it had "rarely been given to any body of Christians in any country to witness such depth of learning and variety of accomplishments, combined with piety so earnest and energy so untiring." The whilom Master of Rugby and Headmaster of Marlborough had shown himself at all points worthy to fill the post once glorified by Reginald Heber. Every station in a diocese stretching from Pesháwar east to Pegu and south to Nágpur caught new life as it were from the ministrations of a bishop whose sound churchmanship went hand in hand with the large loving spirit of a Christianity which soared above all distinctions of church and party; a bishop who insisted not only on doing his own duty, but on seeing that all his chaplains did

* Temple ; Prichard.

theirs. Not less characteristic of the man was the lead he took in founding schools in the Himalayas for those European and Eurasian children whose parents could not afford to educate them in England, or even in Calcutta. The good Bishop's scheme had found favour with Sir Charles Wood and warm support from Lord Canning and his successors; and he himself lived long enough to see it fairly started on the hill-tops of Simla, Masúri, and Marri.*

Six months earlier, before the end of March, Sir William Denison had made over the government of Madras to Lord Napier, whose services during that year of famine were mentioned in a former page. Remarkable, as Sir Richard Temple has well said, for his "masculine common sense" and for "the tastes and ways of an English squire," Sir William had further brought to his Indian work the training of a Royal Engineer and the ripe experience of an able Australian Governor. The shrewd, hard-headed, soldier-statesman, who took the world as he found it, who had no taste for theories that conflicted with historic facts, who never allowed sentiment to override experience, set himself with quiet energy to the task of ruling thirty millions of dark-skinned strangers unlike in all points to their white masters, and demonstrably unfit as yet to govern themselves. In habits, character, and modes of thought he saw in the Hindu of his day "the genuine descendant of the Hindu of two thousand years ago." His new subjects he regarded as political children, towards whom the wisest and safest policy was that which Napoleon advised his brother Joseph to pursue in Naples. How, asked Napoleon, could a king, upheld on his throne by foreign bayonets, expect to win all at once the love and trust of his unwilling subjects? "Govern them; insist upon submission; show them that you are their master. Then, if you like, you may relax the reins; but you must not hope to govern by love for many a year."†

Feeling that the time for government by love was not yet come in India, and alive to the danger of "presuming too much upon our moral strength," Denison strove at any rate to govern his people well and honestly for their general good. Having no faith in the power of laws and legislative councils to make men morally better, he busied himself with trying as well as he could to improve their worldly prospects. In the first weeks of his rule he began to devise a scheme for draining and cleansing the filthy,

---

* Temple; Prichard; "Life of Bishop Cotton."
† Denison's "Viceregal Life."

foul-smelling, ill-drained, worse-watered city of Madras. No small part of his time was spent in travelling about the country, to see for himself what was doing or might be done for the development of its productive wealth by means of roads, harbours, canals, and railways. Wherever he went, he contrived to " pick up small bits of information," which might help him in applying "an Asiatic co-efficient" to every European formula. His reverence for facts drew him into sad disfavour with his coffee-planting countrymen in Maisúr and the Nilgiris, who accused him of neglecting the public interest whenever he failed to help them liberally from the public purse. If he looked upon English settlers as a source of anything but strength to our rule, if he begrudged alike to outside Englishmen and to all Natives any direct voice in the government of an Indian province, if he objected strongly to all schemes for transferring to private purchasers the State's share in the land, or even for settling the land-revenue on the permanent basis of Bengal, his zeal for improving the native agriculture led him to import from England a choice collection of steam-ploughs, threshing-machines, pumps worked by wind-power, and other appliances for saving labour and ensuring larger crops in a country where labour was remarkably cheap, and a plough that just scratched the soil had well served the poor easy-going ráyat's purpose for centuries past.*

With equal ardour and with more self-consistency he encouraged the people by his influence and example to send their children to the Government and Mission schools. He pleaded strongly for special instruction in mechanical science as a sure road to agricultural reforms. In the same spirit he upheld the need of utilizing those powers of wind and water which had hitherto in great measure gone to waste. In windmills and irrigation-works he placed his best hopes for the prosperity of Southern India. This was the lesson he impressed upon the most teachable and enlightened of Indian princes, the Mahárája of Travankór. For the due and speedy extension of irrigation-works he urged Sir Charles Wood to sanction a liberal outlay of borrowed money, instead of "dawdling" wastefully over such works at the rate of a lakh or two a year. Equal to all the duties of quiet times, Sir William Denison could show himself, as we saw, "a daring pilot in extremity," a statesman quick to decide what ought to be done, and strong in acting upon his own decision. Suddenly called upon to fill at a critical moment the place of a dying Viceroy, he had no sooner

* Denison ; Prichard.

grasped the true position of affairs on the Panjáb frontier, than he over-ruled the timid counsels of his Calcutta colleagues, and enabled his commanders to deal a blow which, in his own words, "finished the business, frightened the mountaineers, restored to our troops the prestige of victory, and secured us peace.*

In March of the same year Mr. William Grey exchanged his seat in the Viceroy's Council for the post vacated by Sir Cecil Beadon. Of the retiring Lieutenant-Governor it might fairly be said—"Capax imperii nisi imperasset." But for the ill-judged Mission to Bhotán and the wide-wasting famine in Orissa, Sir Cecil's name might have stood much higher in the list of Anglo-Indian statesmen. The plea of ill-health may be allowed in his favour for what it is worth; but even Lawrence, with all his liking and respect for Beadon, could not make that plea cover the whole of his friend's shortcomings in the hour of trial.

In the same year a far more noteworthy figure disappeared from the political stage in India. Sir Bartle Frere left Bombay in March to take his seat in Lord Cranborne's Council. As Governor of the Western Presidency, the brilliant nephew of the brilliant Hookham Frere had proved equal to the fame achieved by the erewhile Chief Commissioner of Sind. The same eager, fearless spirit which in 1834 had led young Frere to make his way as he best could through Egypt, down the Red Sea, to Bombay, the same tireless energy, prompt action, and enlightened zeal which marked his subsequent career as a settlement officer, as Private Secretary to Sir George Arthur, Governor of Bombay, as Commissioner of Satára and Civil Governor of Sind, shone out as brightly as ever in the last five years of his Indian service. Since the days of Mountstuart Elphinstone no Governor of Bombay had brought to his new duties so choice an outfit of special aptitudes, so fruitful an union of fine breeding, varied culture, far-reaching sympathies, and high mental power; none other had wielded so winning a charm of speech and manner, of mental and social graces, over all who came within his reach, from the Chiefs and gentry of the Dakhan to the scholars, placemen, and merchants of every class and colour in Bombay.†

"Beneath a gentle and composed demeanour, Frere"—says Sir Richard Temple—"had an ever-welling spring of enthusiasm." He threw himself with an ardour that brooked no hindrance and overbore all rebuffs into every scheme for developing the wealth and the well-being, moral as well as social, of Western India.

* Denison.	† Temple; Malleson.

The general dearth of raw cotton in Lancashire, which arose from the Civil War in the United States of America, had given a mighty impulse to the cotton-trade of Bombay. The price of " Surats " had more than doubled in a few months. Railways and roads were needed, among other purposes, to connect the rich cotton-fields of Nágpur, Berár, Kandésh, and Dhárwar, with the nearest ports on the Arabian Sea. Canals were needed to fertilize the parched plains of Kandésh and Sind. In the matter of railways, Frere's suasive influence did much to hasten the progress of the guaranteed lines leading from his own capital to Ahmadabad, Nágpur, and Madras. In the making of canals and roads, Colonel Fife and his engineers had to contend not only with the natural obstacles of ground and climate, but with scanty or uncertain resources in men and money. Without the sanction of the Viceroy in Council no provincial Governor could lay out a rupee of revenue on a new office, a new building, or a new road. Frere's zeal, however, in pursuit of a given object, spurned all barriers of official discipline. In his opinion, the best way of securing a timely grant of money for some desirable public work was, to carry the work on by his own orders to a certain point, and then forward his estimates and bills for sanction to the central Government. Lord Elgin seems to have winked at these irregularities of a statesman who knew at any rate the needs of his own province; but to Sir John Lawrence, with his scrupulous sense of duty, his zeal for economy, his sober judgement, and the cares of all India upon his shoulders, Frere's lawless raids on the Imperial Treasury were a source of frequent soreness, expressed in grave but kindly-meant rebuke. Nevertheless, victory, on the whole, remained with Frere, whose persistent daring covered the province with good roads, raised up a vigorous school of native engineers at Púna, and adorned Bombay itself with a group of public offices, markets, and other buildings worthy of a city ranking among the wealthiest and the most populous in the British Empire.[*]

Nor was Frere less eager in stimulating the higher classes of Natives to cultivate the arts of peace, and to train their children and their countrymen in the way he would have them go. In one of his addresses to the Marátha Chiefs of the Dakhan he descanted on the glorious if peaceful victories which those descendants of warlike forefathers might still achieve. " Though it is no longer necessary to build forts, you may rival the Pándu heroes of your early history by cutting roads over mountain gorges and building

[*] Temple ; Prichard ; Bosworth-Smith.

bridges over unfordable streams. You may emulate Asoka by works of irrigation, or of shelter to travellers, or by building hospitals for the sick and needy, and your name may be remembered with gratitude by future ages, when all traditions of the mere fighting chieftains of former days shall have passed away." These good counsels he followed up by opening a special school for the sons of native princes and noblemen, who afterwards endowed it with twenty scholarships in memory of its beneficent founder. Among the leading citizens of Bombay also Frere's persuasions and example fostered a fruitful rivalry in works of charity and public usefulness. It has been truly said by Sir Richard Temple, that "more hospitals, schools, and other public institutions were founded by private benevolence at that time than at any other before or since." Never, indeed, had Bombay been so prosperous; and her merchant princes, the Sassoons, the Jijibhais, the Jahángirs, the Raichands, vied with each other in working out the designs of a Governor who had the art of calling forth their noble qualities, of turning to good account the best traditions of a people inclined by nature and religion to all forms of almsgiving and munificence.*

One of these benefactors, the good old Pársi baronet, Sir Jamsatji Jijibhai, had in a few years laid out some £200,000 on schools, dispensaries, and hospitals in his native city. His son Rustamji subscribed £10,000 towards English-teaching schools in Bombay and Gujarát, besides £1,200 for the Bombay School of Art, which his father had founded, and of which Dr. George Birdwood was for some years the zealous, able, hardworking director. Mangaldás Náthubhai spent thousands of pounds on a chair of Economic Science and a travelling scholarship for Hindus in Bombay University, and towards the building of a College for Civil Engineers at Púna. David Sassoon at Púna, Chasatji Fardunji at Surat, Premchand Raichand and Kawasji Jahángir in Bombay were prominent workers in the same garden. Premchand Raichand alone gave £20,000 to the Bombay University. Many other natives of good culture and moderate means gave their best services to the cause of social enlightenment, and the relief of bodily suffering. Frere himself had an active helpmate in his accomplished wife, the daughter of that Lady Arthur who had been the first to carry the light of Western training into the homes of Indian ladies. It devolved on Lady Frere to carry on the work which her mother had begun, to draw native ladies

---

* Prichard ; Temple.

out of the privacy of their *zanánas* into social intercourse with their white friends, to convince them of the good which a little reading, writing, and ciphering might ensure to Indian as well as English girls. Under her leading, nobly seconded by Mary Carpenter, Manakji Kursatji, and other kindred spirits, many a school was opened for high-caste girls and their future teachers, while a few zealous Englishwomen gave lessons in their own homes "behind the Pardah" to the wives and daughters of Hindu and Pársi gentlemen.[*]

The work of municipal improvement went swiftly forward in Bombay under her active Commissioner, Arthur Crawford, who opened new streets through the crowded city, purified its filthy places, reformed its sewers, and made room for the noble markets which bear his name. No Roman Ædile could have worked more zealously in honour of the City on the Seven Hills. In the course of a few years he had gone far to transform the native town of Bombay from a huge den of "filth immeasurable," noted for its "foul and loathsome trades, crowded houses, foul markets, foul meat and food, foul wells and tanks and swamps, foul smells at every turn, unventilated drains, and sewers choked with animal and human ordure," into one of the cleanest, healthiest, best drained and watered cities in British India. In 1868 cholera had well-nigh died out, and the average death-rate had fallen from 35 to 20 per thousand.[†]

If Denison at Madras decried his Legislative Council as a mere clog on public business, Frere on the other hand seemed to delight in moulding the new instrument into serviceable shape. The native members of his Council seldom cared to thwart a Governor whose skilful courtesy flattered their self-esteem, and made them all the readier to mistake his counsels for their own. The course of legislation, therefore, ran smooth in the Western capital. Some of Frere's measures, such as the "Cotton Frauds Act" and the "Time Bargains Act," both carried through Council in the teeth of a strong resistance from the merchants of Bombay, aimed at repressing certain unfair and fraudulent practices which imperilled India's new-born ascendency in the cotton markets of the West. In another law were embodied the rules and principles, old and new, on which Frere proposed to resettle the land revenue of his province for a term of thirty years. Under this law, as administered by Colonels Francis and W. C. Anderson, the ráyats

---

[*] Temple; Prichard; Malleson; West's "Administration of Sir Charles Wood."
[†] Temple; Prichard; Malleson.

were assessed at rates which seemed low by comparison with the
ruling prices of food-grains and labour. To each was assured
the full benefit not only of his own improvements, but of any
rise in the value of farm produce before the end of his lease. At
that time a great deal of new land was yearly brought under the
plough, the seasons continued propitious, and thus in spite of low
assessments the land revenue increased steadily year by year.*

One measure taken by Frere's Government, the "Bank Charter
Act of 1864," proved fraught with ruin to a great many families
and with grave discredit to the Government itself. The civil war
in North America had produced a cotton famine in England; and
the ill wind that howled around the cotton mills of Lancashire
had blown a burst of marvellous prosperity to the Kunbis or
peasants of the Dakhan as well as the merchants of Bombay.
The price of cotton had quadrupled. The wages of labour rose
proportionally Cotton and railways brought sudden plenty to
millions who had been glad to earn their three or four rupees a
month. A golden stream kept flowing into Western and Central
India. The poorest ráyat became so rich that the high prices of
food-grains gave him small concern. His old mud hut was replaced by a roomier dwelling of brick or stone. His wife and
daughters decked themselves out in costly jewels. Earthenware
pots gave place to vessels of brass and copper and even silver.
Every coolie—said one who lived among them—"took to dress-
ing like a Brahman." Many an old barrier of caste-privilege was
broken down by the sturdy self-esteem that comes of growing
wealth. Even the Chamárs or leatherdressers no longer slunk
aside from any passing Brahman, whose sanctity their very
shadows might once have defiled.†

In the towns, especially in Bombay, the new prosperity gave
birth in 1863 to all manner of schemes for making fortunes out of
human wants, hopes, or weaknesses. The days of the South Sea
Bubble and the Railway Mania repeated themselves in Púna and
Bombay. New altars to Mammon rose in every street, in almost
every household. Joint-stock companies were got up for every
conceivable purpose, from the working of a coal mine or a tea-
garden to the reclaiming of new land from the sea. Some of the
shrewdest men of business lost their heads. English officers, civil

---

* Malleson ; Temple.

† Temple ; Trotter ; Official Papers. Out of the swift and wondrous rise in the
general well-being sprang the popular saying that every ráyat shod his bullocks and
bound his cart-wheels with silver.

and military, vied with merchants and brokers of every race in buying or selling the shares of some new company whose life, at best, depended on the turning of a hair. Cotton for a time was king; but how long would the American War last, and what would happen to India at the close of it? The answer which events gave to these questions differed widely from that which suited the self-deceiving speculators of Bombay. They hugged to their hearts the vain belief that, whichever way the war ended, Indian cotton would surely retain its sovereignty in the markets of the Old World.

Meanwhile the price of shares rose higher and higher, and the gambling fever showed no signs of abating. So far had it spread through the ranks of the public service, that in November, 1864, the Bombay Government formally warned its officers against indulging in the madness of the hour. Even then, however, the semi-official Bank of Bombay was plunging deeper and deeper into the mazes of rash speculation. In the spring of that year its charter had been renewed under conditions differing greatly for the worse from those which guarded the Banks of Bengal and Madras. Certain clauses of the new Charter Act empowered its managers not only to double their capital, but to advance large sums of money on securities other than those of the Government. The effect of these provisions in an Act passed by Frere's Government, and formally confirmed by that of Sir Charles Wood at home, became manifest in the disasters of the next two years. The year 1865, which saw the utter collapse of the Shareholders' fight for empire, and the ominous flow of American cotton into English ports, was a year of widespread ruin for the speculators of Bombay. With the fast falling prices of Bombay cotton, the value of all property in the Western capital fell apace. Passing through the city in the autumn of that year, Sir Richard Temple found her "in the very throes of trouble, her leading merchants ruined, many of her old-established firms in peril, her banking corporations in liquidation, her enterprises suspended." Seldom has so wide a ruin followed so quickly on the heels of a prosperity so great and sudden.*

For some months longer the help afforded by the Supreme Government propped up the tottering credit of the Bank of Bombay, which had already lost half its capital and owned two millions' worth of irrecoverable debts. Once more its shares rose to a high premium. But this was only the candle's expiring

* Temple; Prichard; Malleson; Report of Sir C. Jackson's Commission.

flicker. In the following year the Bank fell with a crash, which echoed throughout the Presidency. In answer to the outcry raised by the many sufferers who held the Government liable for their losses from a concern where Government owned many shares and supplied its quota of Directors, the India Office in 1868 sent out to Bombay a Commission headed by Sir Charles Jackson, a shrewd lawyer who had once sat as judge in the Supreme Courts, both of Bombay and Bengal. The inquiry yielded small comfort to those who had looked for any; but it turned an electric light on the dark corners of the Bank's recent history, and brought into sharp relief the blunders, the short-comings, the culpable carelessness of all concerned in the management of its affairs. To Frere himself must belong his share of the blame due to those who endowed the Bank with a charter so ill-suited to fulfil its apparent ends.*

In his views of foreign policy Sir Bartle Frere belonged to the Forward or Bombay school of General John Jacob and Sir Henry Green, the school that wanted to forestall a Russian advance on Herát, by pushing our outposts across the Sulaimán Hills to Kwatta. But against the rock of Lawrence's calm judgement Frere's eloquence dashed itself in vain. With a polite but plain-spoken negative the Viceroy brushed aside the rash proposals which emanated from Bombay and Sind. So long as he remained in India there was little fear that the Forward policy, which demanded unwise precautions against imaginary dangers, would get itself translated into fact.†

While Frere held the reins of power in Western India, the new-formed Central Provinces were steadily thriving under the vigorous sway of a Chief Commissioner who had made his mark under the Lawrence brothers in the Panjáb. In his new post at the head of a "non-regulation" province as large as England, Wales, and Ireland, Sir Richard Temple displayed a genius for hard active work, a zeal for acquiring all kinds of useful knowledge, and a keen personal interest in the lives and habits of all classes of the people, such as may hardly be matched in the records of Indian service. Like the great Akbar, he could under-go an amount of bodily exertion which the hardiest of his country-men would have shrunk from attempting. In one year alone, 1862–3 he travelled on foot, on horseback, or by boat, in the scorching winds of May, and through the drenching rains of the monsoon, over four thousand miles of pathless jungle, rugged

* Prichard ; Temple ; Sir C. Jackson's Report.   † Official Papers.

highlands, and lonely plains; exploring by turns the mines of Chindwára, the ruined temples of Mandla, the cotton-fields of Umrawati, the valley of the Narbadda, the feverish swamps and jungles of Sambalpur, and the haunts of primeval Gonds and Korkus in the Sátpúra Hills.

In the course of these journeyings the Chief Commissioner gained a good working acquaintance with the land tenures then prevailing in the different parts of his broad province. After a preliminary survey, field by field, the settlement of the land-revenue was carried out in careful accordance with ascertained facts, for terms of twenty and thirty years. The landholders, large and small, who had ousted the village peasantry under the Marátha rule, were confirmed in their prescriptive rights, and assessed at rates as low as seemed compatible with State-interests. At the same time all care was taken to restore, define and protect those tenant-rights which the Maráthas had ignored or swept away. Some classes of tenants became thenceforth entitled to hold for ever, at fixed rents, the lands which their fathers had tilled before them. To every tenant of twelve years' standing was assured the right of undisturbed possession, so long as he paid the customary or judicial rent. While every acre of land fit for tilling found its acknowledged owner, Temple took care to reserve for the State its full proprietary right over many thousand square miles of waste and unoccupied ground.

In 1862 there was no railway in the Central Provinces, and hardly a road fit for wheeled carriage other than the rude *hackery* or native bullock-cart. The traffic of the country was mostly borne on pack-bullocks owned and driven by Brinjáras, an old Gypsy tribe that once commanded the carrying trade of all India. In 1867 Temple's successor could tell of four hundred miles of good firm road opened in the last five years, besides a hundred and fifty more in progress. By that time one line of railway joined Nágpur to Bombay, while another placed Jabalpur on the Narbadda within easy reach of Calcutta by way of Allahábád. To carry a line eastward from Nágpur through the rich wheat-fields of Chatisgarh to Calcutta, was another scheme for which Temple pleaded many years before so great an enterprise could be set on foot. To Sir Arthur Cotton's scheme for making the Godávari navigable throughout its course Temple lent so hearty a support that the works, which Lawrence sanctioned, were well under way when Lord Mayo's Government saw fit, on economical grounds, to stop them altogether.*

* Temple; Prichard; Administration Reports for the Central Provinces.

What the Lawrence brothers did for the Panjáb, their old disciple may be said to have done in great measure for the Central Provinces. Under Temple's ubiquitous control a small but competent staff of English officers, most of whom were to make their mark in Indian history, worked with emulous zeal at the tasks allotted them by a ruler who aimed above all things to bring his young province "up to the high-water mark of Indian administration." Temple himself re-organized the police on the new system already working in Madras. Many of the native gentry discharged as honorary magistrates one-fifth of the magisterial business of the country " with credit to themselves and satisfaction to the people." The civil courts, over which Mr. John Strachey presided, became so popular that in five years the number of suits had risen from 19,000 to 45,000. In 1862 four schools were supported by the State. Five years later 1,570 schools gave instruction to 58,000 scholars. Other schools opened by missionaries and benevolent natives were maintained in part out of the public funds. In five years the number of dispensaries rose from sixteen to fifty-six, at which 150,000 patients were treated in one year. The sanitary rules enforced in towns and villages checked the growth of epidemic disease, and an active staff of vaccinators saved many thousands of children yearly from the inroads of smallpox. The wide tracts of forest that covered the Vindhya and Sátpúra Hills passed under the care of experienced officers, who strove with some success to wean the wild highlanders from the wasteful practice of firing the hill-side in order to raise with the least possible trouble a good crop of grain from the fertilizing ashes.*

In 1866, when Temple exchanged his post for that of Resident at Haidarábád, the Central Provinces were reaping the combined fruits of good government, propitious seasons, and a brisk demand for raw cotton. Landlords, husbandmen, and traders prospered greatly ; artisans and coolies drew good wages ; only pensioners and people of fixed incomes had much cause to complain. In five years the salt-revenue had doubled itself, the revenue from all sources had risen by one-third, and the foreign trade had swollen in value from two millions and a half to thirteen millions sterling. Barracks, court-houses, police stations, hospitals, churches, museums, covered the land ; numbers of new wells gave forth their water to thirsty fields ; and many of the wealthier natives opened their purses freely in behalf of local improvements and of the two industrial exhibitions which Temple got up at Nágpur

* Temple ; Prichard ; Administration Reports.

and Jabalpur, the political and the industrial capitals of his province. Of the many services rendered by its ubiquitous ruler not
the least memorable was the series of full, well-written reports on
the country, its people, and its resources, present and future,
which attested alike the thoroughness of his research, the range
of his bodily and mental energies, and his clear previsions of what
remained to accomplish in behalf of the people entrusted to his
charge.[*]

Under Mr. Edward Drummond,[†] the North-West Provinces
were fast recovering from the combined effects of the great Mutiny
and the famine of 1861. While railways, roads, cotton, and tea-
planting gave a new impulse to trade and labour, irrigation was
doubling and trebling the produce of the fruitful plains between
the Jamna and the Ganges. When drought once more visited
these provinces in 1868, its worst evils were averted by the recent
growth of railways and canals. The great Ganges Canal alone
saved nearly a million acres from drying up. A like service was
rendered on a smaller scale by the Eastern Jamna canal and the
various channels that water Rohilkhand and Déra Dhún. In
British Burmah the Chief Commissioner, Colonel Arthur Phayre,
could show a bright record of the progress yearly making under
his beneficent rule. In twelve years from the conquest of Pegu,
the provinces which Lord Canning afterwards formed into British
Burmah had doubled alike their population and their revenues. The
numbers of the former had been largely swollen by immigrants
from the kingdom of Ava, who were glad to exchange the tyranny
of their own rulers for the peace and prosperity that tempted them
across the border, into a country whose foreign trade had risen to
ten millions a year before Phayre retired from his post.

[*] Prichard ; Strachey's Administration Report for 1866-67.
[†] He succeeded Edmonstone in 1863.

CHAPTER VII.

PUBLIC WORKS AND SCHOOLS.

THE lessons of the Orissa Famine were not lost upon the rulers of British India. The cry once raised in Madras by Sir Arthur Cotton, "Water is gold in India," was caught up and passed on by the Viceroy himself to the Westminster Council, at the head of which a change of Ministry had just seated Lord Cranborne in the room of Lord De Grey. For some years past indeed the claims of irrigation by a general system of tanks, weirs, and canals, as a main bulwark against the inroads whether of drought or floods, had largely occupied the thoughts of earnest statesmen in both countries. Lord Canning in India, and Lord Stanley at home, agreed in calling upon private enterprise to aid the Government in carrying out a policy so helpful of India's needs. One English company undertook, mainly at their own risk, to water the low lands of Orissa with canals fed from the Brahmani and the Mahánadi. Another company, armed with a State guarantee of five per cent., undertook the same good office for the plains that stretch from Karnúl to Kadapa, by a waterway linking the Tumbadra with the Pannár. The Orissa works, begun in November 1863, too late to avert the subsequent famine, proved equal in 1867 to the task of watering forty thousand acres. From one cause and another, from want of capital, from the backwardness of the peasantry in using canal-water so long as they could do without it, from official dislike of private monopolies secured by a compulsory water-rate, these works made so little progress, that their authors were glad erelong to hand them over to the future management of the State.*

The Madras Company, first started in 1864, with a capital of a million sterling, and a guarantee for twenty-five years, spent all their money in preliminary surveys and in rearing a mighty stone dam or "anicut" across the Tumbadra. With the sanction of the

* Prichard ; Temple ; Thornton.

India Office more money was raised, and the works went slowly forward. But many years had yet to elapse before a canal was ready to enrich the harvests and bear the traffic of the country through which it passed.*

Meanwhile a number of questions had arisen which perplexed and divided the official mind both in India and at home. There were those who held that roads and railways were at least as necessary for averting famine as canals. India, it was said, grew food enough to supply all her millions, if the spare food of one province or district could only be brought at need within easy reach of another. Others held that canals would serve their main purpose only in districts where the rivers that fed them were not themselves liable to run low in times of drought. Others again preferred the old methods of irrigation by tanks and wells. Rival engineers in Bengal and Madras differed strongly, each according to his own local experience, on the best method of planning out a canal. Sir W. Denison argued with much force that no canal should be made to answer the twofold purpose of watering the fields and carrying the traffic. Sir John Lawrence and Mr. Maine alike objected to private enterprise in connection with waterways; the one because it tended to place the people at large in the power of a joint-stock company; the other, because it warred against the doctrine current in modern Europe that water, no more than light or air, could be treated as private property. Mr. Massey, on the other hand, pleaded strongly in favour of private enterprise as a lesser evil, if such it were, than delay in a matter of prime importance to the public welfare.†

Among those who held that the carrying out of irrigation works was a charge devolving specially on the State, it was still a question whether the cost of such works should be defrayed out of revenue or by means of State-loans. For reasons of sound policy, Lawrence himself earnestly counselled the latter course. It was impossible, he argued, to endow India with a proper system of canals if their cost was still to be defrayed as heretofore out of revenues wholly unequal to extraordinary needs. Justice, mercy, and common sense alike forbade the levying of new taxation from so poor a country, in aid of a scheme designed to benefit not one generation, but all. To arguments like these, enforced by the tales of suffering in Orissa, an encouraging answer came at length from the India Office, where Lord Cranborne held brief sway. Resolved to waste no more time in preliminary discussions, he sent the active Colonel

---

* Prichard ; Indian Progress Reports.　　　† Prichard ; Denison ; Thornton.

Richard Strachey, of the old Bengal Engineers, back to India as Superintendent of Irrigation, placed under his orders a numerous staff of civil and military engineers, and empowered the Viceroy to cut canals and dam rivers with the help of borrowed money, in every district liable to frequent drought or heavy floods.*

Having thus secured a separate service with a separate system of accounts for reproductive as opposed to ordinary public works, Sir John Lawrence, with Colonel Strachey at his elbow, was swift in turning his new powers to the best account. By the end of March, 1868, he could tell of the marked progress already made in cutting or surveying lines of canal for traffic or for irrigation through half a dozen of his fairest provinces." In every province a separate branch of the Public Works Department was organized under its own head, for the purpose of carrying on, year by year, the necessary works. There was reason to hope that, after a few years, the Panjáb, the North-West Provinces, and Oudh would be threaded by a waterway more than eight hundred miles long. In Bengal, British Burmah, and Madras, where floods were more to be feared than drought, the new works commonly took the form of tanks and embankments.†

In the progress of Indian railways Lawrence took a warm interest, bounded only by his sense of practical fitness. During the five years of his rule 1,556 miles of railway were opened at a cost of thirty millions sterling; the net receipts from all the lines had risen nearly sixfold; and the yearly payments from the Treasury on account of guaranteed interest had fallen nearly one-half. The difficult task of bridging the Són and the Jamna had been achieved by the perseverance of skilful engineers. Lahór was linked by rail with Multán, Jabalpur with Allahábád, Cawnpore with Lucknow. In November, 1868, the Viceroy formally opened the railway that joined Ambála to Delhi, and brought Calcutta within three days' journey of his summer capital in the Himalayas. The Eastern Bengal Railway was creeping on towards Dárjiling; and work was fairly begun upon a line connecting Banáras with Oudh and Rohilkhand. Had Lawrence's advice prevailed with the home authorities, the line of railway from Lahór to Multán would have been carried down through Sind to the rising port of Karáchi before a sod was turned of the railway leading from Lahór to Peshawar. But the commercial interests of the Panjáb weighed for nothing at Westminster against the duty of guarding a secure frontier from attack by a possible

* Temple; Prichard; Malleson.   † Prichard; Bosworth-Smith.

Russian foe; and so the making of a railway down the Indus Valley was postponed for years in favour of a purely strategic line to the foot of the Khaibar.[*]

While helping, so far as a Viceroy could, to carry out Lord Dalhousie's railway programme, Lawrence felt that the time had come when new lines of railway might be made more cheaply by the State itself, than by private companies armed with a State guarantee. With the work which those companies had undertaken he had no wish to interfere. It was theirs to complete within certain limits what they had begun. But outside those limits lay vast tracts of country to which the new principle might safely be applied. Before Lawrence left India the first State railway, the Northern Panjáb, had been begun. Nor was Sir John's influence wielded in vain on behalf of that large class of travellers from whom the railways drew their chief profits. To his strong remonstrances it was mainly due that the poorer millions were enabled to ride in greater comfort in carriages less dangerously crowded than of yore.[†]

In the improvement of the telegraph service the Viceroy's hand was yet more plainly visible. Five hundred miles of new line were opened during his rule, and the length of wire used on all the lines grew to a total of 22,567 miles, or nearly double what it had been. A marked change for the better took place in the working of these lines. In all parts of the country new stations were opened, messages travelled at greater speed, were delivered more punctually, and contained far fewer errors than of yore. Before Lawrence left India, he had so reformed the costly old tariff of charges, varying with the distance, that a message could be wired from any one station to any other, however remote, at an uniform rate of one rupee. And one of his very last public acts was the passing of a Bill which bettered even Dalhousie's postal reform by doubling the standard weight for all letters chargeable at half an anna, or three farthings each.[‡]

The formation in 1864 of a Forest Department for all India was a long step forward on the path which Lord Canning had been first to tread. Under the rules then issued by Sir John Lawrence a good working system of forest management, under an Inspector-General aided by an Inspector for each province and a staff of trained foresters imported from Europe, was set on foot. Assistants for service in the new department were sent from England to learn their business in the great schools of forestry on the

Continent. The marking out of forest domains, the planting of young trees in the place of those which had been cut down or hopelessly ruined, and other measures needful for checking further waste and ensuring a due supply of timber for railway uses, were carried forward from year to year, under the able Dr. Brandis, at a cost which seemed trifling in comparison with the ultimate gain.*

When the collapse of the Slaveholders' Revolt in America brought ruin to a crowd of speculators in Bombay, the cotton trade of India suffered partial eclipse. In one year the aggregate value of Indian exports fell by twenty millions. But behind the passing cloud Lawrence could read the promise of brighter days in store for a country which still exported more than a million bales of cotton from Bombay, and possessed a foreign trade worth nearly a hundred millions. Indian cotton, if ousted from its short-lived sovereignty in Lancashire, might still hold a prominent place in the markets of the world. Its manufacture might even in time become a source of profit to Indian merchants and artisans. By way of fostering healthy enterprise in an important trade, of helping the cotton-grower to obtain from the merchant fair value for the fruits of his toil, the Viceroy in 1866 appointed a Cotton Commissioner for the Central Provinces and Berár, whose duty it was to report on the extent and character of the cotton-crops in each district, to acquaint the ráyat with the prices ruling in the nearest markets, and thus to baffle the designs of commercial gamblers on the ignorance or the needs of honest men. So well did the experiment work that, two years later, the sway of the new Commissioner, Mr. Rivett Carnac, was extended to the cotton-fields of the North-West Provinces.†

In other directions also the Viceroy laboured not in vain to promote the interests of Indian trade. It was mainly through ·his influence that the Mahárája of Kashmir was induced to abolish some and diminish other of the tolls which beset the path of Indian traders journeying to Ladákh and Turkistán. Similar demands, urged again and again by Sir Arthur Phayre on the King of Burmah, evoked nothing but evasive replies, until in. November, 1867, that self-willed despot yielded to Phayre's successor, Colonel Fytche, all that Lawrence could reasonably have desired. In return for the goodwill shown by the Indian Government during a time of intestine struggle, the King agreed to reduce all his frontier duties to an uniform rate of five per cent.,

* Mal'eson ; Temple.   † Malleson ; Official Papers.

and to retain no monopolies except on earth-oil, timber, and precious stones. Colonel Fytche succeeded also in obtaining the King's consent to the passage of a British mission across Burmah for the purpose of reopening an old line of trade between India and Yunnan. Unhappily the royal promises in respect of the monopolies were to prove no better than idle words; and the tricks of Burman officials sorely delayed the progress of the mission which Captain Sladen, the British Resident, led from Mandalay towards the seat of the new Panthay kingdom in South-Western China.

The Panthay Mohammadans of Yunnan, descendants of old Arab settlers in that province, had lately risen in fierce and victorious revolt against their Chinese rulers, and a Panthay dynasty once more reigned at Tálifú. Visions of a prosperous trade with the new kingdom haunted the merchants of Calcutta and Rangoon. Colonel Fytche, the Chief Commissioner of British Burmah in the room of Sir Arthur Phayre, took fire from the prevailing frenzy, and persuaded Lawrence to send out an exploring party into the wild hill country that divides Northern Burmah from the plains of Yunnan. In the month of January, 1868, Sladen started up the Irawádi for Bhámo. After a month's delay at Bhámo, a delay for which Burman treachery was mainly answerable, the Mission struck eastward across the Shán country to Momain; their progress always hindered by the arts of their Burman guides and companions. At Momain Sladen halted for six weeks, hoping always to reach the Panthay city of Tálifú. But the way thither was reported dangerous for so small a party, and Sladen unwillingly retraced his steps to Mandalay, consoled by the manifest friendliness of the Shán people, and more impressed than ever with the golden prospects involved in the opening of a regular trade route from the Irawádi to the Yangtsi. For all practical ends, however, he might as well have staid at Mandalay. Ten years afterwards the Chinese reconquered their lost province; and all hope of a growing trade in that direction was quenched in the blood-reeking ruins of Tálifú.*

The cause of popular instruction gained a powerful and sturdy champion in the Viceroy, who was erelong to advance that cause among his countrymen at home. For the higher education, as supplied by three universities and forty-two colleges to about two thousand three hundred scholars, he begrudged no reasonable

* Malleson; Trotter; Allen's *Indian Mail.*

outlay in aid of local and private funds. But the spirit which pervaded Sir Charles Wood's Despatch of 1854 was the spirit in which the Viceroy laboured, for the mental and moral improvement of the many rather than the few. Under his auspices new schools for the humbler classes were opened yearly in fresh districts; normal schools for teachers sprang up here and there; and British Burmah for the first time saw a Director of Public Instruction and a proper staff of Inspectors added to her official strength. In the last months of Sir John's rule seven hundred thousand pupils were learning their lessons in nineteen thousand schools and colleges at an aggregate cost of £800,000 a year to the State. In five years the annual grant in-aid from the public treasury had risen by more than £200,000. If the percentage of pupils to population was still exceedingly small, the actual increase of schools and scholars in those five years had, all things considered, been very great. Every province now possessed its own staff of paid teachers, from the chief Director to the master of the humblest village school. The lower, middle, and high schools in each district were linked together by a system of scholarships which enabled the best pupils to work their way up from the village school to the provincial college. Special schools had also been founded for the teaching of law, medicine, engineering, and, above all, of agriculture.

Another part of the original programme Lawrence had set himself from the first to carry out. In 1864 he sanctioned a grant of £800 a year towards the maintenance of schools for girls in his old province, the Panjáb. In the following year he increased the grant to £1,800. Two years later he made liberal offers of State help to every province, the people of which desired to follow the example set by the Panjáb. In 1868 he granted £1,200 a year for five years to each of the provincial governments, for the purpose of founding in each province a normal school where Indian girls might be trained for the work of teaching scholars of their own sex and race. Before he left the country, fifty-four thousand girls were enrolled as pupils in two thousand schools maintained wholly or in part by public funds. It is true that the teaching in many of these schools was almost if not purely nominal, especially in Bengal, where half a dozen mere infants might be seen "sprawling about and inking their fingers in copying letters on strips of leaves," while one or two at most " could attempt a little reading." The lack of trained schoolmistresses was necessarily great; and an Inspector who could not see his pupils as they sat with their teachers behind the *pardah*, might well be puzzled to know "whether the girls answer the questions or their teachers, or whether they recite by heart what they are supposed to read." The custom of early betrothals and the frequent apathy of the people themselves fought against the progress of the new scheme. Nevertheless the new experiment was already bearing good fruit in Northern and Central India, and wherever else the people at large were encouraged by their Pandits to aid the Government in the war against ignorance and social tyranny.*

We have seen how warm an interest Lawrence took in the health and well-being of the British soldier. He was not less careful to forearm his countrymen at large against some of the worst dangers which had assailed them in 1857. Many a life had that year been lost or grievously imperilled through the almost utter lack of strong places guarded by white troops. Such defences, however slight and slenderly manned, might have saved some hundreds of English men and women from the sufferings that befell them at Meerut, Delhi, and Cawnpore. There were those indeed who held with Sir William Denison that any scheme for "dotting the country about with small forts" would be alike cowardly, expensive, and fraught with harm. But Lawrence, who was neither a coward nor a spendthrift, but a shrewd statesman endowed with a soldier's instincts and a large heart, had learned a different lesson from the events of a time the most critical in the history of British India. With the approval of Sir William Mansfield, he ordered the erection of fortified posts at certain places occupied by our troops, which posts would serve to protect our arsenals, magazines, and railway stations; to overawe the surrounding country; and to furnish shelter for the sick and helpless in time of need. At Multán, Peshawar, Rawal-Pindi, the new works assumed the character of strong fortresses.†

It was in 1866 that the first attempt at a general numbering of the people was successfully carried through in the North-Western and the Central Provinces. Before that year all our knowledge of the numerical strength of our Indian subjects had been gained from estimates supplied as best they could by district officers, who had to work often by stealth or artifice in the teeth of every obstacle that popular ignorance, mistrust, and superstition could

---

* Prichard ; Malleson ; Howell's "Note on Education."
† Malleson ; Denison ; Trotter.

throw in their way. To the average native mind the taking of a census for any purpose other than the laying of new burdens on the people seemed a notion altogether absurd. Estimates formed under such conditions could not but greatly err. The general Census of 1872 added fifty millions to the official reckoning for 1868. In Bengal alone the difference between the two sets of figures exceeded twenty millions.*

For the two provinces first-named, however, the numerical results obtained in 1866 were much nearer the mark. The census of the North-Western Provinces showed a population of 30,110,615, of whom only 4,105,206 were Mohammadans; the rest being nearly all Hindus. Of these the great bulk—more than three-fourths—were returned as Sudras, while the Brahmans numbered nearly three millions and a half, and the Rájputs somewhat less than three millions. Out of the whole population less than four millions belonged to the industrial classes, and a million and a quarter to the commercial, while 17½ millions lived wholly or mainly by the soil. The whole province contained only 5,069 Eurasians or half-breeds, and 14,126 native Christians. Under the head of trades and occupations were to be found 28 "pedigree-makers" and 226 "flatterers for gain," 18 "ear-piercers," 135 hangmen, 800 jesters, three fortune-tellers, and one "informer." Besides more than 400,000 beggars, 111 were set down as "alms-takers," 35 as "sturdy-beggars," 900 "badmashes" or town-loafers, and only one "vagabond." The proportion of males to females was as 16 to 14, and of adults over twelve years of age to children under twelve as two to one.

The returns from the Central Provinces showed a total population of more than nine millions, of whom only 237,922 were Mohammadans. Of the remainder not quite two millions belonged to the rude tribes that peopled the primeval forests. The proportion of children to adults was about two to three, while two-thirds of the people followed the plough. Although the two provinces were very nearly of a size, the great extent of mountain and jungle-land in the latter accounts for the wide difference between them in respect of population. While the fruitful plains and populous cities of the great Doáb had an average pressure of more than 350 persons to the square mile, the average for the Central Provinces fell some way short of a hundred.†

One noteworthy incident in the year 1867 may serve to illus-

* Prichard; Temple; "Statistical Abstract for 1869."
† Prichard; Administration Reports for 1867; Statistical Abstract.

trate the difficulties that beset the rulers of India in their attempts to deal with questions bearing on the usages, social and religious, of the people at large.   The twelve-year cycle for the great Hardwár fair had come round, and vast crowds of pilgrims were streaming from all quarters towards the spot where Ganga issued from her Himalayan cradle into the broad plains of Hindustan. Every Indian *méla* or fair is more or less of a religious gathering; and in point of numbers and sanctity the Hardwár fair was the greatest of them all.   Once in twelve years this yearly festival at the Gate of Ganges—Gangadwára was another name for Hardwár, the Gate of Vishnu—reached its highest tide.   In 1843, for instance, the number of those who went up to buy and sell, to bathe and drink of the holy waters, and to kiss the imprint of Vishnu's footstep on the Ghát, between the 10th of March and the middle of April, had been roughly reckoned at two millions. In the same weeks of 1867 three million people of all ranks and ages are said to have encamped around the same spot, where the great river, issuing from a gorge in the Sewalik Hills, parts off into several channels that meet again below Hardwár.   The numbers present on this occasion, whatever their actual sum, were swolien by a general belief that the sanctity of the Ganges would disappear as soon as its waters became absorbed into those of the Ganges Canal.

Hardwár and its neighbourhood had indeed been holy ground from a remote age for Hindus of every creed, from the ancient Buddhists to the disciples of Nának, and the rival worshippers of Siva and Vishnu.   There, in the last days of the fourteenth century, a vast slaughter of assembled pilgrims had taken place by command of the merciless Timur Lang.   Sometimes the pilgrims fought and slew each other.   In 1760, on the last day of the bathing, eighteen thousand men are said to have fallen in a long and furious fight between two rival mobs of Gosain and Bairági fanatics.   In 1795 the Sikh pilgrims attacked and slew five hundred of the Gosains.   Sometimes the headlong rush of the crowd towards the water ended tragically for many of those concerned. In 1819, spite of the precautions taken by the Government, 430 persons, including some of the Sepoys on guard, were crushed to death or drowned.   Sometimes the pilgrims on their homeward journey diffused the poison of some deadly disease, the germs of which had first revealed themselves at Hardwár.   From like causes several lives were lost in 1843.*

* Thornton; Hunter; Prichard.

In 1867, however, all went smoothly up to a certain point with the multitudes gathered to the great fair. Thanks to the untiring efforts of Major Watson, Superintendent of Police, of Mr. Robertson the Magistrate, and Dr. Cutliffe, Civil Surgeon of Saháranpur, the needful sanitary and police arrangements were enforced on the whole with marvellous success, throughout an encampment which spread for miles around the Sacred Ghát. Bodies of police from the Panjáb as well as the North-West Provinces patrolled the camps, and kept order along the roads that led through the large Island of Rori to the ten bridges which had been thrown at intervals across the river. Barricades for regulating the advance of the pilgrims were thrown up here and there along every approach to the river-bank. Hospital tents had been set up in every quarter, and a number of furnaces were daily employed in burning up the sewage and other refuse collected daily from the latrines and bazaars. There was so little sickness in all that vast assemblage of traders and pilgrims of all ranks, intermixed with horses, camels, oxen, mules and goats, that none of the hospital tents was ever full. Escorted by police and a few cavalry, each holy *mahant* or *jogi* led his throng of devotees across the river down the many stairs of the wide Ghát, whence all who bathed at the moment fixed by their astrologers might count on washing away their past sins. In the scramble to reach the water many a life would have been endangered but for the kindly vigilance of the police, who helped many a blind, infirm, or crippled person down to the water and back again up the steps. Women and children lost in the crowds were taken to the nearest police-station and restored in due time to their anxious friends.*

With the 12th of April the bathing came to an end, and the vast crowds began to disperse homewards. But on the very next day the cholera broke out among them, dogging their steps in whatever direction taken, and leaving its deadly mark on many a town and village of Upper India. On the true origin of this particular outbreak opinions differed, as they always will. The cholera poison is always lurking in the air, the water, or the soil of India. In one place and another it sweeps off a varying number of victims year by year. But the fact remains that, in spite of all precautions, the disease, from whatever source engendered, began its fell work a few hours after the close of the great Kúmbh-Méla at Hardwár. Wherever the pilgrims halted on

* Prichard ; Thornton ; *Delhi Gazette.*

their homeward journey, cholera forthwith began to rage. Between the Himalayas and the North-Western Frontier its progress from one town or village to another kept pace with that of the home-going pilgrim parties. Its dissemination in fact, if not its birth, was clearly owing to the vast number of human beings who flocked together at one time to wash themselves and their clothes, and to drink of the water thus fouled by their own act, in a kind of enclosed tank 560 feet long by 30 wide. What happened, in short, was one of those misfortunes which no amount of human forethought, skill, or watchfulness could have averted. As cholera had broken out after the Agra Darbár of 1866, so it broke out with yet greater virulence after the Great Fair of Hardwár.*

* Prichard ; Report of the Sanitary Commission for 1867.

CHAPTER VIII.

FOREIGN POLICY.

In the summer of 1867 England found herself drifting into a little war with the headstrong ruler of Abyssinia, who had kept an English Consul and some German agents of an English missionary society in close confinement for some years past. King Theodore had lately filled up the measure of his offences by including among his prisoners an Armenian envoy sent from London to demand the release of his prisoners. The war, which greater prudence and courtesy at an earlier stage of the quarrel might have averted, thus became inevitable; and erelong a compact force, collected and equipped in India, disembarked at a place near Massowah on the Red Sea, for the purpose of rescuing the captives and teaching Theodore a lesson of respect for the British name. For the leadership of that force the English Ministry selected Sir Robert Napier, the very man whom Lawrence himself had urged them to employ. On Napier's shoulders devolved the whole burden of planning and conducting a campaign which resulted a few months later in the capture of Magdála, the suicide of Theodore, the release of all his captives, and the safe return of our troops at the right moment to the shores of the Red Sea. The story of a war in which India had no direct concern need not be repeated here. But it is worth remarking that the troops whom Napier led to an almost bloodless victory were largely composed of Sikhs, that the task of equipping them and feeding them in the field devolved on officers of the Indian Government, and that some share in the achievement which won Napier his peerage may be credited to the Viceroy, whose helpful energy in preparing for the war enabled the British commander to fulfil his errand in one campaign.

. If England's honour was vindicated by the march to Theodore's stronghold in 1868, the Viceroy's sense of justice had been sorely wounded by the extent to which India was saddled with the cost of an undertaking that obviously concerned Great Britain alone. In several letters to Sir Stafford Northcote, who had meanwhile replaced Lord Cranborne at the India Office, Sir John spoke out bravely against the unfairness of charging India even with the ordinary expenses of troops drawn off for Imperial purposes from Indian ground. To him it seemed a question "neither of hiring nor lending, but simply one of payment by the country which employs the troops." It was right perhaps to make India share in the costs of the Persian War of 1856, but she had "not the slightest interest in the question at issue between England and King Theodore." Whatever happened to Theodore could make no possible difference to her. The principle of making her pay for England's advantage might be carried to any length, and applied on a larger scale. In point of fact she could ill spare the troops which had been sent off to Abyssinia. On what grounds, then, could she be fairly required to pay for them during their absence? India, moreover, was "really a poor country," in which the mass of the people could barely live; and their rulers were "at their wits' end" to devise new sources of public revenue which might be "remunerative and not extremely unpopular." To make her pay for troops withdrawn from her service seemed to the honest Viceroy "an arrangement which cannot be justified." Had he used yet stronger language, he would not have exceeded the mark.*

This piece of sharp dealing, so unworthy of a rich and powerful nation, yet so consistent with past usage, was formally sanctioned by the British Parliament. A curious instance of like contempt for vulgar rules of justice had occurred in the autumn of 1867, when the Sultan of Turkey was entertained in the new India Office at a magnificent State Ball, the whole cost of which was charged to the Indian Treasury. By way of excuse for this astounding meanness, the people of England were informed that the honour paid to the Sultan of Rúm would greatly please the millions of Indian Moslems who revered him as their true Khalif, the divinely appointed head of all Islám. It was easy to throw all that dust in the eyes of our countrymen at large, who were much given to confounding Mohammadans with Hindus, and knew nothing about the true relations between Constantinople and Delhi or Haidarábád. Nor were English tax-payers wont to inquire too closely into the justice of measures which transferred to other shoulders any of the burdens they might else be required to bear.

* Bosworth-Smith ; Trotter.

In the latter part of 1867 the peace of India was broken, for the first time since the close of the Bhotán War, by the outrageous doings of the Wághirs, a race of inveterate robbers who dwelt by the Arabian Sea in the north-western corner of Gujarát. The peninsula of Okhamandal, as their home was called, had a sparse population, a barren soil, and an export trade in conch-shells, which served as ornaments for Hindu maidens, or as wind-instruments for use in Brahman shrines. At Dwarka, on the western coast, rose the great, many-storied Temple of Krishna or Dwárkanáth, "the Lord of Dwarka," to which thousands of pilgrims had resorted yearly for centuries past. With the help of their offerings and the temple endowments at Dwarka and Bait, the Wághirs had been wont to eke out a livelihood won mainly by acts of piracy and plunder. Their lawless habits at length provoked the punishment they received from our troops in 1809. Six years later, in return for a few hundred pounds, their country was handed over to the Gaikwár of Baroda, who found little cause to rejoice over his share in that strange bargain. His new subjects drove away his officers, beat off his troops, preyed upon their neighbours' lands and goods, and held the fortress-temple of Dwarka against all comers. Dislodged thence by a British force in 1820, they continued to be a thorn in the Gaikwár's side, until in 1859 he was glad to let Okhamandal pass once more under British rule.

It was not without hard fighting that our troops succeeded in driving the Wághirs out of their last stronghold in the Isle of Bait. For some years these turbulent people ceased from troubling their new masters. But in 1867 they broke out again in deeds of violence and plunder which their new masters were forced to put down with a strong hand. A small body of horse and foot, commanded by Colonel Anderson, the Political Agent, came up with a party of Wághirs who had taken their stand on the top of an isolated hill about three hundred feet high. After a short but fierce struggle Anderson's Sepoys carried the hill, taking only two prisoners out of the twenty-five who had defied the attack. Of the remainder seventeen lay dead. But they had sold their lives dearly, for two of Anderson's officers, Hibbert and La Touche, were slain, and a third, Captain Reynolds, fell dangerously wounded.[*]

Early in 1868 our troops were engaged in quelling another outbreak in another part of the same province. A body of insurgent Bhils on its eastern border were attacked and routed by a squadron

[*] Prichard ; Thornton.

of the Gaikwár's horse and a few hundred Bombay Sepoys. A little later the Panjáb frontier near Kohát became the scene of some sharp fighting between our troops and the Bazóti clansmen, whose raids on British ground called for swift requital at our hands. Followed up into their hill-fastnesses, the Bazótis made a resolute but unavailing stand against larger numbers aided by higher discipline and well-served guns. In his eagerness to reach the foe a brave officer, of great promise, Captain Ruxton, lost his life; but the clansmen afterwards restored his body to his sorrowing friends.*

In the autumn of the same year a campaign on a larger scale was opened against the warlike tribes that people the Black Mountain, a lofty range trending north of Hazára, between the Indus and Kashmir. Nearly opposite, from the left bank of the river towered the Mahában, where our troops had fought and suffered in the winter of 1863. Below the southern slope of the Black Mountain lies the Agrór Valley. The village of Oghi, on the southern side of the valley, forms a frontier station for the Panjáb police. In the height of the hot season a band of Hasanzai Patháns swooped down upon Oghi, but the police fought bravely and drove them back. Such an insult, the last of several offered by the same tribe, could not be overlooked. There was reason to believe that recent outbreaks along the border had been directly inspired by the plots of Wahábi fanatics once more stirring on the Ganges. Itinerant Fakirs were again preaching in the bazaars, and plotters in Bahár were forwarding arms, money, and recruits to their exiled countrymen beyond the frontier. The lessons of the Ambéla campaign were not forgotten now. The Viceroy agreed with Sir W. Mansfield in the need of sending across the frontier a force strong enough not only to punish the Hasanzai raiders, but to overawe the neighbouring tribes.†

The troops designed for this purpose were moved up from their several stations during the month of September to their future base at Abbottabad. Some of them had but lately returned to India from hard service in the Abyssinian hills. General Wylde, who had shared in the fighting around Ambéla, commanded the whole force which advanced from Oghi on the 3rd of October in two strong columns, led respectively by Brigadiers Bright and Vaughan. Troops from Kashmir guarded the camp at Oghi and the pass that led into the Agrór Valley. On that same evening Bright's column had not only cleared the enemy out of Kun-Galli,

* Prichard.   † Prichard ; Bosworth-Smith.

a village on a hill commanding the northern end of the valley; but Brownlow's Panjábis lay intrenched at Nanna-ke-danna, four miles further up the hill. Baffled in their efforts to dislodge Brownlow's men by a series of night attacks, the enemy next morning fell back to their main position on the crest of the Black Mountain. From this they were speedily driven, after a brisk fight, by the fire of our guns and the steady rush of our infantry. That evening saw Bright's brigade in full possession of the Chatarbal Peak. On the morning of the 5th our troops carried the Machai Peak, which rises 10,000 feet above the sea. The next day was given up to road-making. On the 7th some troops were employed in wrecking the village of the Parári Sayads, who had been foremost in defying the British power. The burning of a few more villages reduced to zero the warlike spirit of the offending tribes. Their *maliks* or headmen came in to sue for peace, the terms of which were finally settled on the 10th of October. These terms included the expulsion of the Indian refugees as well as the payment of a moderate fine; and each tribe sent in its hostages for the due fulfilment of its bond. On the 13th the invading columns began their homeward march.*

Murmurs of discontent were heard throughout India at the seemingly poor results of a campaign opened on a scale so imposing. Many people had fancied that the Government were massing troops on the Indus in order to strike a blow that might be felt in Central Asia. Others predicted that the light punishment dealt upon the tribes of the Black Mountain would fail to deter them from raiding across our frontier at the first opportunity. Many an officer who had watched or shared in this brief and nearly bloodless campaign grumbled, as officers are prone to do, at the small results achieved in the way of bloodshed and burnt villages. Lawrence himself seems to have doubted whether the force employed was not too large for the work required. But it was not for him to refuse what Wylde and Mansfield both asked for; nor would he "run the risk of a second Ambéla campaign." That the expedition would "do much good," he had no doubt whatever. It certainly taught the fierce tribes on that frontier the folly of provoking a Power whose troops could find them out in the heart of their native hills, and beat them easily on their own ground. It inclined them to live in peace with the powerful neighbour who, after punishing, knew how to spare, and seemed so ready to shake

* Prichard ; *Allen's Indian Mail.*

hands with a humbled foe. And it forced the refugees and out-laws whom they had been harbouring to seek out new hiding-places at a safer distance from the Punjáb frontier.*

It was about this time that an embassy from the Mohammadan Amir of Káshgar made its way to Calcutta, in the hope of securing the Viceroy's aid against their Russian and Chinese neighbours. Like the famous Haidar Ali of Maisúr, the Amir Yákub Beg had risen to power by force of that mingled craft and daring which, under Fortune's favour, commands in its own sphere so large a measure of success. In 1862 Chinese Tartary, or Eastern Tur-kistán, stretching from Kashmir northwards to the Tian Shán Mountains, became the scene of a great Mohammadan rising against the odious Mánchu Government of Pekin. The struggle was long and desperate, and blood flowed on both sides without stint. Hard pressed in other quarters, the Chinese could send no more troops to the rescue of their beleaguered garrisons; while the Tungáni rebels, fired alike by patriotism and religious zeal, kept gaining ground until in the spring of 1865 the last Chinese soldier had been slain or driven out of Eastern Turkistán.

The people of Alti-Shahr—the land of the six cities—had shaken off the yoke of infidels, who would have made them wear long pigtails, pay new taxes, and cripple in Chinese fashion their daughters' feet. But their leaders soon fell out among themselves. Yákub Beg, the soldier of fortune who had led a few hundred troops from Khokán to the siege of Káshgar, no sooner found himself master of all that province than he hungered after the spoils of its neighbour, Yárkand. Before the end of 1867 his hunger had been allayed by the conquest, not of Yárkand only, but of Khóten also, and the remainder of the Alti-Shahr. From the Pamír Steppe eastward to the Chinese frontier, the people of a land where no white traveller before the luckless Adolph Schlagentweit had for centuries set foot, acknowledged as their sole ruler the man who thenceforth called himself Atálik Ghází, "Defender of the Faith."†

Beset by Russians on one side, and Chinese on the other, Yákub Beg turned for help against future needs to the great Southern Power, beyond the Kárakoram, whose fame may have reached his

---

* Prichard; Bosworth-Smith.

† Prichard ; Von Hellwald's "Russians in Central Asia."—Schlagentweit was murdered by command of the bloodthirsty Wali Khán Turra, merely in order that his head might be added to the pyramid of human skulls which the Khán was rearing outside his capital.

ears long before the bold traveller Johnson brought back from Khóten the story of his own adventures in 1865. But the Viceroy, who had reprimanded Johnson, as an officer in the Survey Department, for risking his life without orders on a dangerous errand, and had lately turned a deaf ear to the prayers of the Khán of Bokhára, was not likely to encourage the hopes conceived by a more distant potentate, whose reign might prove as stormy as his rise was sudden. The envoy from Káshgar was therefore dismissed with a polite assurance of the Viceroy's goodwill to his master, and with a plain, though polite, rejection of any alliance with a ruler so far beyond the range of Indian politics.*

Meanwhile Sir John Lawrence had kept a watchful eye upon the troubled course of affairs in the Persian Gulf, where the cruisers of the old East India Company had once been so active in suppressing piracy, in safeguarding the pearl-fishers of Bahrein, and strengthening the hands of the British Resident at Bushahr. For some years past their place had been taken—it was not quite adequately filled—by the warships of the Royal Navy. In 1865 our old ally, the Imám of Maskát, whose realms were washed by "the blue waters" of the Bay of Omán, was murdered, apparently by order of his son Salim, who was allowed by popular consent, or indifference, to fill the vacant throne. The Indian Government, as a thing of course, declined to dispute the ruling of accomplished facts. But Salim's uncle, the Sultan of Zanzibar, made the question of his nephew's guilt a pretext for withholding the tribute which Zanzibar had always paid Maskát, whenever the two States were under separate rulers of the same line. The Shah of Persia also prepared, on like grounds, to wrest from Salim the port of Bandar-Abbas, which a former Shah had leased for a yearly sum of money to a former Imám. But the Viceroy, through his agent, Colonel Lewis Pelly, brought the Shah's enterprise to an abrupt close; nor would he allow the Sultan of Zanzibar to withhold from Maskát, on any vain pretext, the tribute which Lord Canning had deliberately held him bound to pay.† When a successful revolution drove Salim from his capital, Lawrence contented himself with looking after the safety of British subjects and enforcing due respect for the British flag.

In the chronic feuds between the Khán of Khalát and his unruly barons, the Viceroy refused to interpose, so long as the peace of the Sind frontier remained unbroken. In vain did Sir Bartle Frere and other officers of the Forward school urge him

* Prichard; Temple. † Ibid.

to plant a British garrison at Kwatta, commanding the high road from Sind through the Bolán Pass to Kandáhár. By the Treaty of 1854 the Bilúchi ruler of Khalát had bound himself, if need arose, to let British troops hold some part of his territory. To occupy Kwatta would not only encourage trade between India and her neighbours, it might serve also to forestall a Russian occupation of Herát. So pleaded at least the friends of a Forward policy. Lawrence, however, could see in such a move nothing else than a great military blunder and a wanton menace to Afghánistán. Kwatta was the capital of a province still largely peopled by Afgháns, and for generations subject to an Afghán overlord. To the Afghán mind a British garrison in the Shál district would certainly seem the forerunner of a British advance on Kandáhár. In common with Sir W. Mansfield, Sir Harry Lumsden, Sir Henry Norman, and every officer of mark in the Panjáb, the Viceroy derided the notion of planting at Kwatta a British outpost, isolated from its nearest supports by two hundred and fifty miles of rugged, dangerous, and in many places waterless road. To his thinking, moreover, such a move would involve a needless and injurious drain upon India's limited resources in men and money; resources which, said Lumsden, "would be of immense value elsewhere."[*]

The whole course and spirit of his frontier policy ran directly counter to such a move. "Friendship towards the actual rulers, combined with rigid abstention from interference in domestic feuds," was the policy which, in frequent letters to the India Office, Lawrence declared himself resolutely bent on pursuing. It was a policy which, from first to last, he pursued with signal courage and complete success towards Afghánistán. So long as Sher Ali Khán and his brethren were fighting for their father's crown, Lawrence steadily refused to take part in the long and uncertain struggle. His sympathies might go with the heir of Dost Mohammad's own naming; but openly to support Sher Ali, even with a few thousand men and muskets, and a few lakhs of rupees, would have proved, he knew, a perilous and costly mistake. It would have turned against Sher Ali some of his warmest partisans. It would have drawn India into entanglements hurtful to her financial well-being. And it would have given Russia a convenient handle, if she were so minded, for fishing in the troubled sea of Afghán politics. Knowing the Afgháns better than any Englishman of his own day, Lawrence saw that strict

* Temple ; Afghán Blue-book, 1878 ; "Life of Sir H. Edwardes."

neutrality was the best way to disarm their suspicions, and to win so much of their goodwill as Afghán pride and prejudice might allow. Unscared by the spectre of Russian conquests, unswayed by the appeals of fire-eaters and alarmists, deaf to the pleadings even of his own heart, he kept loyally within the lines marked out by the Treaty of 1855, which bound us to respect the Afghán territories, and "never to interfere therein."[*]

Before the end of 1865 Sher Ali found himself losing ground apace on the side of Kábul. His long inaction at Kándahár, owing to the violence of his grief for the death of a favourite son, had told for the worse upon his fortunes. In 1866 Kábul fell into the hands of his eldest brother, Mohammad Afzul Khán. Lawrence rebuked his Vakíl or agent for congratulating the victor in the name of the Indian Government, and made Afzul Khán clearly understand the principles which the Indian Government were resolved to enforce. When the new master of Kábul asked the Viceroy to recognize him as Amir of Afghánistán, Lawrence refused to acknowledge him as ruler of those provinces where Sher Ali still held his ground. "If your Highness "—he wrote to Afzul Khán—"is able to consolidate your Highness's power in Kábul, and is sincerely desirous of being a friend and ally of the British Government, I shall be ready to accept your Highness as such, but I cannot break the existing engagements with the Amir Sher Ali Khán."

At that time Sher Ali still held his own in Herát and Kandáhár. In 1867 he was driven out of Kandahár also. Once more Afzul Khán urged Sir John Lawrence to acknowledge him as ruler of the whole Afghán realm. Once more the Viceroy refused to go back from his plighted word. He was ready to acknowledge Mohammad Afzul as actual ruler in Kandáhár and Kábul, but so long, he wrote, "as Amir Sher Ali Khán holds Herát and maintains friendship with the British Government, I shall recognize him as ruler of Herát, and shall reciprocate his amity." Mohammad Afzul dying a few months later, his brave and able son, Abdurrahman, to whom he had owed his late successes, waived his own claims to sovereignty in favour of his uncle Mohammad Azim Khán, whom Lawrence in his turn acknowledged as *de facto* ruler of Kábul and Kandáhár.[†]

The Viceroy's policy, in short, was one of careful waiting upon

---

[*] Wyllie's "External Policy of India "; Afghán Blue-book.
[†] Wyllie; Malleson; Afghán Blue-book.

events in the spirit of absolute fair play between the rival candidates for Dost Mohammad's throne. He had followed to the letter the old Amir's advice about leaving his sons to fight it out among themselves; taking good care that none else should interfere in a quarrel which concerned the Afgháns only, and that no act of his should embitter Afghán feeling towards the British name. The Saduzai head of Shah Shujá's family, then living in the Panjáb on a pension granted by the Indian Goverument, had besought the Viceroy's leave to fight for his own hand against his hereditary foes of the Barakzai clan. He even asked for a loan to aid him in his project. The Viceroy, in answer, warned the Saduzai prince that any attempt on his part, or on that of his family, to interfere in the pending struggle would involve the immediate withdrawal of his pension.*

It was rumoured that Sher Ali, as his prospects grew darker, had turned to Persia for the help denied him by his Indian neighbour. If such a step were taken, Lawrence held himself prepared to side with the party in power at Kábul against all assailants from without. In no circumstances would he depart from his settled policy of recognizing the *de facto* ruler, so long as he showed himself "not unfriendly" to the Indian Government. "In this way"—Lawrence wrote to the new Minister for India, Sir Stafford Northcote—"we shall be enabled to maintain our influence in Afghánistán far more effectually than by any advance of our troops—a contingency which could only be contemplated in the last resort, which would unite as one man the Afghán tribes against us, and which would paralyze our finances." It was clear that John Lawrence had not studied in vain the lessons involved in the story of the Afghán War.†

At last, in September, 1868, the fortune of war, which had lately blown so hard against Sher Ali, bore him back triumphant into Kábul, where, a few months later, after one last crushing defeat of Abdurrahman Khán, he saw himself firmly seated on his father's throne. Azim Khán and his brave nephew had fled to Balkh on their way across the Afghán frontier. By virtue of his latest victories, not of his father's choice, Sher Ali had become the rightful sovereign of Afghánistán. The time had come when Lawrence could exchange his attitude of strict neutrality for one of friendly support. Sir Stafford Northcote, in the name of the Home Government, had given him full leave to "pursue his own

* Malleson.   † Afghán Blue-book.

policy." In his letter of congratulation, written on the 2nd of October, he told the Amir that he was ready not only to maintain the old bonds of amity and goodwill, but, "so far as may be practicable, to strengthen those bonds." To help Sher Ali in securing his hard-won throne, six lakhs of rupees—£60,000—and several thousand muskets were placed at his disposal. In a subsequent letter, written just before his own retirement, the Viceroy informed the Amir that the six lakhs would shortly be doubled, as an earnest of the Viceroy's desire to see "a strong, a just, and a merciful Government" established throughout Afghánistán. All that the donor asked in return was "abiding confidence, sincerity, and goodwill."*

In the first flush of returning success the Amir had proposed to meet the Viceroy at Peshawar, or elsewhere, on the Panjáb frontier. But his enemies, though beaten, had not then been thoroughly routed; and before Sher Ali felt politically strong enough to leave his capital, the Afghán winter had set in, and Sir John Lawrence had gone down to Calcutta to employ the last weeks of his Indian rule in toiling as hard as ever for the general good. It was left for his successor to bind fast in the memorable Ambála Darbár that good understanding with Sher Ali for which the patient watchfulness of Sir John Lawrence had piled up the solid masonry. Whatever bitterness the Amir might have felt in the hour of his adversity towards the wellwisher who lifted never a finger on his behalf, he had learned to recognize the perfect fairness of a policy which left the Afgháns free to settle their own quarrels, and enabled the victor to reap the full rewards of his success. In the very fact that his own arms had won the victory, he could now see cause for gratitude to the powerful neighbour who had refrained from taking any, the least, advantage of his country's weakness and his own misfortunes. In thus fulfilling the pledges first given by Lord Dalhousie, and renewed by Lord Canning, the Viceroy had awakened in the minds of Sher Ali's countrymen a spirit of growing faith in the friendly purposes of the Power that ruled beyond the Khaibar. A conviction at last had dawned upon them that the policy of Lord Auckland and Sir William Macnaghten had given place to a policy of peace and goodwill towards the whole Afghán nation; that the tiger of their imaginings had become transformed into a very lamb. And Lawrence, for his part, could safely appeal from the warnings and reproaches of un-

---

* Wyllie; Malleson; Afghán Blue-Book; Trotter.

friendly critics, to the practical issues of a policy which had not only won the goodwill of his Afghán neighbours, but had saved for India's own advantage the large sums of money that might else have been thrown away in the attempt to guard her from imaginary dangers, through an ill-timed interference in the quarrels of Afghán chiefs.

NOTE.

Against the frontier policy of the Forward School Edwardes himself had always set his face. His ripe experience had brought him "very decidedly" to the conclusion "that our true military position is on our side of the Passes, just where an enemy must debouch on the plain." With regard to the Sind scheme for occupying Kwatta with a view to the taking of Herát, he wrote—"So vast a pile of impracticable schemes seems more like some dream of conquest than a sober system of Imperial defence."—(Life of Sir H. Edwardes.)

CHAPTER IX.

POLITICAL AND DOMESTIC.

THE same spirit that informed the Viceroy's foreign policy shone
forth in all his dealings with the Native Princes of the Indian
Pale. So long as they kept the peace within their own borders,
governed fairly well according to their lights, and broke none of
the treaties they had made with the Paramount Power, Lawrence
left them free to regulate their affairs, within certain limits, after
their own fashion. He stooped neither to flatter nor to bully
them. His agents at their respective Courts were enjoined to use
their powers of interference as sparingly as they well could. Of
his own advice, when needed, he gave freely, nor did he stint
his praise on fit occasion. If from some defect of sympathy on
his part, or rather from his long experience of native character,
he failed to inspire the ruck of the native princes' with the love
they afterwards felt for Lord Mayo, they learned at least to
respect him as an honest, plain-spoken friend, and to trust him as
a master who would never blame or coerce them without just
cause.

"The essence of native rule," said Lawrence, "consists in the
will and pleasure of the chief." Happy was the State which
possessed a ruler so enlightened as the Rajah of Jaipur, or
Ministers at once so able, wise, and upright as Dinkar Rao of
Gwáliár, Madhava Rao of Travankór, and Sálar Jang of Haidarú-
bád. Sindhia himself was an autocrat of the firmest grain, who
dispensed with the services of Dinkar Rao as soon as he felt himself strong enough to reign alone. During the Nizám's lifetime
Sálar Jang was almost a prisoner in his own house ; forbidden
without his master's leave to pass outside the gates of his courtyard, or even to hold an interview with the British Resident, and
seldom allowed to enter the august presence of a potentate whom
he worshipped with the blind devotion of a Chatham addressing
the Third George. It was only after the Nizám's death in 1867 that

the Minister he disliked for the very qualities which commended him to his English friends, was free at last, as Regent for the child-heir, to give his reforming energies full play, to travel into all parts of his young master's kingdom, to see with his own eyes many things of which he had hitherto been kept in ignorance or had learned imperfectly at secondhand, and to act in fair concert with Temple's successor on all matters that concerned the common interests of the Viceroy and the Nizám.*

As a check on the native ruler's mere will and pleasure, Lawrence sought to strengthen the influence of his Dewán or Chief Minister, whenever the latter showed himself worthy of such support. A capable Minister might save his State from much of the suffering entailed by the rule of a weak, vicious, or headstrong prince. Without the Viceroy's support Sálar Jang would soon have lost his place. When the young Chief of Dhár was allowed in 1864 to handle the reins of government, Lawrence bound him, among other conditions, to accept a Prime Minister of his Agent's choosing. In default of a native statesman fit to manage the affairs of Bhúwalpur after the death of its Nawáb in 1866, Lawrence appointed a British officer to act as Regent during the minority of the Nawáb's acknowledged heir. Sometimes the Viceroy had to take strong measures against a reigning prince whose misdeeds or follies it was impossible to overlook. Perhaps the worst of these offenders was Mohammad Ali Khán, Nawáb of Tánk, a small Mohammadan State in Rájputána, founded by his grandfather, the successful freebooter Amír Khán.

Mohammad Ali, in 1865, had taken arms in vain against one of his Rájput barons, the young Thákur of Láwa. The intervention of a British officer restored peace erelong between the combatants, on terms which appeared to satisfy both. But the young Thákur had an uncle, a brave old soldier, whose influence over his nephew stirred evil longings in the Nawáb's fierce heart. Dissembling his hatred of the man whose death he sought, Mohammad Ali in 1867 invited the Lord of Láwa to his capital to receive a *khilat* or robe of honour from his sovereign's hands. The Thákur came, attended by his uncle Rewat Singh and a small band of followers. On the evening of the 1st of August, in compliance with a message from the Nawáb's Minister, Rewat Singh hastened to the Minister's house, whence he was never to issue alive. In a few minutes he himself, his son, and two chief clerks lay dead in an upper room, while downstairs one only of his

* Bosworth-Smith ; Temple.

fourteen attendants escaped the death prepared for them by the Tánk Sepoys. Saved by the colour of his turban, he lived to bear witness against the murderers. After a three days' siege, the Thákur himself was starved into a surrender, and remained a prisoner in his own dwelling until the 8th, when the arrival of a British officer set him free.

So startling an outrage, so daring a deed of cold-blooded treachery, no Governor-General could have left unpunished. An inquiry into the whole affair was conducted by the Viceroy's Political Agent, who found the Nawáb guilty of the murders wrought by his command. In accordance with a verdict warranted by the clearest proofs, Lawrence decreed that the oldest son of Mohammad Ali should rule in his father's stead, that Láwa should thenceforth be separated from Tánk, and that Tánk's salute should be reduced from seventeen to eleven guns. The deposed prince was allowed to reside at Banáras on a pension of 60,000 rupees a year, while his Minister and tool was carried off a prisoner to the neighbouring fortress of Chunár. As the new Nawáb was young, ignorant, and the finances of his State had fallen into sad disorder, four of his leading nobles were formed into a Council of Regency under the headship of a British officer.*

Another offender in a less degree was the Jodhpur Rajah, of whom mention has been made before. In spite of Lawrence's grave rebuke at the Agra Darbár, the Rajah made no seeming effort to mend his foolish and oppressive ways. But for their fear of the Paramount Power, his nobles would have taken up arms against a ruler whose avarice knew no bounds, who slighted and oppressed them at every turn, who refused them the right of adopting heirs even to their private property, and endowed one of his own sons with a fief wrested from its rightful lord. For redress of these and other grievances they turned at last to the Viceroy, whose ears were always open to just complaints. In due time the Mahárája received from Lawrence a weighty reprimand, clinched by an order to mend his ways within six months, on pain of sharing the fate of the Tánk Nawáb. Happily for himself, the royal offender gave some earnest of a better spirit before his term of grace had wholly expired.

In the spring of 1868 died Krishnaráj Wodiyar, the titular Mahárája of Maisúr, thirty-seven years after the government of his kingdom had passed once more into British hands. It had long been a moot question whether Maisúr should remain for ever a

* Malleson ; Indian Blue-book.

British province or be once more handed back to native rule. Lawrence himself had seen too much of the evils wrought by native rulers of the common stamp, and believed too firmly in the general excellence of British rule, to accept without a murmur the policy which Lord Cranborne had resolved in the first days of 1867 to carry out. To give back into native hands the country which Mark Cubbon had ruled so prosperously for more than a quarter of a century, seemed to the Viceroy a change entirely for the worse. From the India Office, however, came the order which Lawrence felt himself bound to obey. On the death of the old Rajah his adopted son Chámrájendra, a child of six years, was proclaimed his successor in the sovereignty of Maisúr. During the boy's minority Maisúr was to be "governed on the same principles and under the same regulations as heretofore." If at the age of eighteen he should be found qualified for the discharge of kingly duties, the government of the country would be made over to him, "subject to such conditions as may be determined at that time." Meanwhile his little Highness was placed under the guardianship of a British officer, Major Malleson, who was to train him carefully in the way that he should go.*

This question as to the future government of Maisúr had formed in 1867 the subject of a debate in the House of Commons. On that occasion Lord Cranborne had dropped some remarks on the comparative merits of Native and British rule, which seemed to challenge one of the beliefs that lay nearest to the Viceroy's heart. "If our rule in India," he wrote to Sir Stafford Northcote, "was not much better than that of native chiefs, it would be indeed impossible for us to hold the country with the body of British troops allotted for the purpose." The shoe might pinch of course in several places, but the mass of the people, that is, all the industrious classes, were thoroughly alive, he contended, to the great and palpable benefits of a rule which prevented war and rapine, encouraged all forms of peaceful industry, and strove in many ways to promote the well-being of the people at large. And in proof of this he pointed to a number of facts which came within his own knowledge. In his younger days the Delhi districts were full of immigrants from the adjacent chiefships. As soon as the Panjáb became a British province its Mohammadan landholders flocked back to their old homes. Thousands of exiles from Oudh returned thither after annexation. In nearly all the large tracts of country which Lord Canning bestowed on native chiefs in reward

* Malleson ; Bosworth-Smith.

for good service during the Mutiny, the people were always complaining of their new masters, and imploring the Viceroy's interference on their behalf.*

Holding thus stoutly to his own convictions, Lawrence called on
the chief civil officers in every province to set out in writing the
genuine outcome of their own experiences and researches on the
question broached by Lord Cranborne. From each in good time
came an answer which justified the Viceroy rather than the erewhile Minister for India. Whatever flaws of design or failures in
practice took off from the merits of our administrative system,
however stiffly it sat upon native modes of thought and feeling,
however little it cared for the special interests of certain classes, or
even for the yearnings of a just ambition, the writers of these reports
agreed in bearing clear witness to the higher aims, the sounder
principles, the stricter methods, the far more solid achievements
of our own as compared with any form of native rule.†

Among the duties which our countrymen in India had long
since learned to recognize was that of relieving to the best of their
power the misery caused by famine. This duty they had striven
to discharge even towards the victims of administrative blindness
in 1866. Two years later, when famine threatened a great part
of Northern and Central India, Lawrence spared no effort to
minimize the evils he could not wholly avert. The failure of the
monsoon rains in July, 1868, gave timely warning of a danger
which the local Governments, mindful of Orissa and inspired by
the Viceroy's example, bestirred themselves at once to meet.
With Sir Donald Macleod ruling the Panjáb and Sir William
Muir the North-Western Provinces, there was little cause to fear,
so far as they were concerned, for the result. For the first time
in Anglo-Indian history Lawrence had warned the local Governments that he would hold them and their officers responsible for
every life lost through want of timely succour. At the same time
he promised to aid their efforts with all the resources that lay
within his reach.

Relief works were promptly opened for the able-bodied; and
relief committees distributed alms or food among the sick and
helpless. Timely remissions of land-revenue and "takávi" advances for the digging of wells or the buying of seed-corn enabled
many a husbandman to tide over the passing trouble. The Ganges
and the Jamna Canals poured their fertilizing floods over broad
belts of thirsty land, while the overflowing wheat-harvests of

---

* Bosworth-Smith.   † Official Papers.

Oudh helped to keep alive the dearth-stricken millions of the neighbouring Doáb. Thus it happened that the dreaded famine in our own provinces resolved itself into a partial scarcity, which ended with the next year's timely rains. Out of ten million possible sufferers in the North-West only sixty-two thousand appear to have died of famine, while the whole cost of relieving distress over an area of twenty-nine thousand square miles amounted only to four hundred thousand pounds.[*]

Among the sands and rocks of Rájputána, however, the famine-demon rioted for about two years. Fired by the Viceroy's counsels and example, the princes of that country vied with each other and with the neighbouring rulers of Indór and Gwáliár in carrying out the remedial measures suggested by the Residents at their respective Courts. Relief works were set on foot, transit-duties were suspended, remissions of land-revenue freely allowed, subscriptions opened and supplemented by timely grants from each prince's treasury. The Viceroy himself advanced loans for the purpose of making roads in a province where roads of any kind were few and ill-suited to modern needs. In the British town and district of Ajmir large sums of money were spent in relieving a host of sufferers who flocked thither from the surrounding country.

Far less fortunate were the people who fed their herds of oxen and camels on the sandy pastures of Márwár and Bikanír. Before the last blade of grass had withered up, the most of these roamed off with their herds and families, some towards Málwa, others for Gujarát. But Málwa also was suffering from drought, while the grass-lands of Gujarát lay drowned in floods of unusual extent. Of those who reached the former province numbers died there or on the way homewards. The bulk of their herds also perished by the way, or were sold to keep their owners alive. Nor did the wanderers in Gujarát fare much better in the long run. After months of vain roaming and the loss of very many beasts, they flocked homewards in the following summer only to find Márwár a bare desert under a cloudless sky. No signs of rain appearing by the end of June, 1869, they set forth again in quest of food and water elsewhere. But cholera strewed their path with dead and dying. Again they rushed homewards, believing that rain had fallen, and again they had to renew their wanderings into more favoured lands. But with cholera in their train

* Blair ; Famine Commis ion Report ; Gadlestone's "Famines in the North-West Provinces."

they found themselves shunned by the villagers who had once befriended them, and doomed to wander to and fro until death released the most of them from further suffering. Of the 750,000 men, women and children who first migrated from their homes, about half a million appear to have died in those two years. Out of two million head of cattle which shared their wanderings, only a small remnant returned to their own country. Of the people who remained at home in their own villages still fewer seem to have survived; thousands dying for want of food which no money could bring within their reach.

In the country around Jodhpur, the capital of Márwár, enough rain fell in the monsoon months of 1869 to give fair promise of a moderate harvest. The ráyats did their best, with means sadly straitened, to make that promise sure. But a new enemy undid their labours. While the grain-crops were yet growing, swarms of locusts began their destructive flight, eating up every green thing before them, and leaving only bare fields in their track. When they had done their work in Márwár, three-fourths of the standing crops were found to have been utterly destroyed.*

We have seen how bravely Lawrence fought the battle of tenant-rights in Oudh against Sir Charles Wingfield and the Tálukdárs. Before he left India he had won a decisive victory for the same cause in the province ruled by his old friend and trusty subaltern, Sir Donald Macleod. As the time drew near for reassessing the land-tax in the Panjáb, many of the landholders claimed sole ownership of lands which, under our rule, they had hitherto held as part proprietors. As such only had they been registered in the Record of Rights which gave birth to the settlement of 1853. Their claims found eager advocates with some of our ablest settlement officers in the Panjáb. There was doubtless much to say for a body of men who had learned too late the value of the rights they had once surrendered or failed somehow to assert. They had seen their country prospering yearly more and more under a rule which enabled thousands of thrifty husbandmen to reap a fair profit from the fields their labour had made so fruitful. While the land was everywhere rising in value, they had lost the right to rackrent tenants of a certain standing, to make money out of their improvements, or to evict any man from his holding without due notice and due cause shown.

To many of their number all this seemed utterly wrong. Such

* Blair ; Trotter ; Colonel Brooke's "Famine Reports."

a feeling was only natural on the part of those who had suffered in purse or prospects from the changes wrought by the settlement of 1853. The least blow dealt at one of their old privileges they resented as a crying injustice, a crime against social order. But the Viceroy, with his strong sense of justice, his honest care for the public weal, and his calm contempt for grievances based on class privilege, refused to sacrifice a crowd of protected tenants to the claims of a few landlords, whose rights, if any, had lain dormant for fifteen or twenty years past. He declined to remedy a small and shadowy by the infliction of a great and irreparable wrong. While the aggrieved landlords were at least as well off as in 1849, the settlement officers were already at work on a new settlement, which, but for his timely interference, would have reduced a multitude of protected tenants to the level of rackrented tenants-at-will. In the Amritsar District alone, out of 60,000 heads of families inscribed on the original Record of Rights, 45,000 might have been thus degraded, if the settlement officers could have had their own way.

Fortunately this was not to be. The "Panjáb Tenancy Bill," introduced by Mr. Edward Brandreth into the Legislative Council on the 17th of January, 1868, was the Viceroy's answer to the claims put forward by the landlords' friends. It embodied in clear and permanent form the principles involved in the land-settlement of 1853. The Bill once laid on the council-table, Lawrence allowed due time for the careful discussion of its contents. Among his own councillors were some of its sternest critics, from his old ally, Sir William Mansfield, to his old opponent, Sir Henry Durand. Soon afterwards Sir Henry went home on furlough, and his place was filled by Sir Henry Norman, who upheld the policy of the Bill. On the same side as Durand's successor were Sir Henry Maine, Sir John Strachey, and the new Finance Minister, Sir Richard Temple. At Simla, on the 19th of October, the Bill passed through Council, after a long and lively debate, in which Maine spoke out with a rare mastery of all details, and with a clear, close-grained eloquence that held his hearers throughout. Lawrence himself closed the debate in a speech full of pithy reasoning from a rich store of pertinent facts.

Before sitting down again he earnestly besought his hearers to pass the Bill that day. They passed it accordingly; but the "Panjáb Tenancy Act" had yet to be confirmed by the Council sitting at Westminster. Both in India and at home it still had enemies powerful enough to hinder, if not to undo, the good work thus verging on completion. From many quarters a loud cry went forth against a Viceroy who wanted to "sweep the landlords from the face of the earth" in order that their tenants might wax fat on the fruits of legalized rapine. At an early stage of the Bill the Anjumán-i-Panjáb, a club founded by native gentlemen at Lahór for the discussion of social and political questions, had protested against "any legislation which disturbed ancient rights, usages, and customs;" and their complaints were now re-echoed from the India Office itself. Stuart Mill, however, had not yet exchanged his post of Under-Secretary for India for a seat in the House of Commons; and his view of ancient rights and customs was not that of the Anjumán-i-Panjáb. The weight of his opinion helped not a little to turn the scale in favour of those who looked upon a thriving and contented peasantry as one of the strongest guarantees for national progress under a just, humane, well-ordered rule. In the last days of 1869 a despatch from the Duke of Argyll to Lawrence's successor, Lord Mayo, closed the controversy by confirming the new law.

Under the Act thus finally sanctioned the rights of occupancy tenants were carefully defined. No tenant who had held the same lands for twenty years could have his rent raised at the landlord's mere will and pleasure. The occupancy tenant's power of free sale was limited only by the landlord's right of pre-emption, a right claimable only within the month. The improvements for which he might look to receive compensation were also clearly specified, as in the Act relating to Oudh. Even those who had once parted with their proprietary rights, "otherwise than by forfeiture," might claim the full benefit of the Act, if they had ever since occupied as tenants their former holdings. All things considered, a large measure of justice, based on recorded rights and ancient usage, was thus formally bestowed on the great revenue-yielding classes in the Panjáb. Nor has later experience failed to justify the wisdom of the course pursued by a Viceroy who "never sold the truth to serve the hour." *

Before Lawrence left India, a Land Improvement Bill for the North-West Provinces had passed through its preliminary stages. With the Viceroy's sanction, it specified the sort of improvements for which a tenant might claim compensation on surrendering his farm. Under the law as it then stood, a tenant who dug a well or

---

* Prichard ; Temple ; Bosworth-Smith ; *Edinburgh Review* (April, 1870) ; *Allen's Indian Mail.*

planted a tree without his landlord's express leave was liable to eviction. This state of things the authors of the Bill proposed to remedy in the public interest, and under a new Viceroy the Bill became law. With Lawrence, however, justice to the tenant was no synonym for injustice to the landlord. He would help the one as readily as the other to improve his land for the general good. In the last days of his rule he carried through Council a Bill which enabled the Túlukdárs of Oudh to borrow money of the Government at moderate rates for the due improvement of their domains. At the same time their right to alienate their landed property was largely restricted.*

In the long list of measures drafted by the wise and learned Law-Member of the Viceroy's Council, there were not a few besides those already named, which owed their birth or their final enactment to the Viceroy himself. Among these may be noted the Act of 1866 which legalized the re-marriage of any native convert whose former wife refused to live with him after his conversion; an Act for the due protection of coolie emigrants to the British colonies; and two Acts for the prevention of venereal disease and for the medical treatment of its female victims. It was Lawrence also who first insisted on the need of levying cesses for roads and education from the untaxed Zamindárs of Bengal. These gentlemen raised their favourite cry of bad faith against the Viceroy who dared to tax them, however lightly, for the public good. But Lawrence refused to see any true connection between the maintenance of roads and schools for all classes, and the rights secured to one class by the Settlement of 1793.†

In another measure, which under his successor became law, the Viceroy aimed at repressing a serious nuisance caused by the recent growth of English enterprise in India. For some years past many Indian towns and stations had been haunted by white loafers, who lived from choice or necessity on the alms of their own countrymen, or on anything they might beg or pilfer in the native bazaars. Some of these lawless, masterless vagabonds were old convicts who had landed from Australia. Others were runaway seamen or soldiers who had been discharged or drummed out of their regiments. A few had been thrown out of employment, whether by mischance or their own fault. These outcasts, who preyed upon the weak and cringed before the strong, had become a terror to all respectable natives and a crying scandal to their own countrymen, if not a danger to the public peace. How to deal with this new

---

* Prichard ; Malleson.　　　　† Prichard ; Trotter.

heritage of evil was a question which sorely troubled the minds of Anglo-Indian statesmen. Under the existing law there were practically no means of abating a plague so hurtful to our moral supremacy. Before the end of 1868 the Viceroy had laid before his Council a Bill which made short work with vagrants of the customary type, while it offered a helping hand to those who were willing to earn their own livelihood if only they got the chance. Under the "European Vagrancy Act," as passed in the following year, any vagrant for whom no employment could be found in India might be shipped off to the country whence he had last come.*

A new set of furlough regulations for the civil and military services, the admission of qualified natives to posts formerly reserved for Europeans, the establishment of dispensaries and civil hospitals in British Burmah, the founding of a college for civil engineers at Rurki, the promotion of a scheme of weather observations along the Bay of Bengal, improvements in the police system, in jail discipline, and in the lower grades of the judicial service, inquiries conducted by a Currency Commission into various schemes for extending the use of gold and paper as money, —all these and such-like measures of public usefulness owed their inception or their advancement largely to the Viceroy's own prompting or to his powerful support. When Temple in 1868 succeeded Massey as Finance Minister, he found Lawrence eager to lower the salt-duties of Upper India down to the Madras level, and to turn the licence-tax into a tax of one per cent. on all incomes higher than fifty pounds. The Viceroy's desires on the latter point were destined to an early fulfilment; but India had to wait some years before any attempt was made to equalize those salt-duties which her statesmen find it equally hard to justify or to forego.†

During the last weeks of his rule the Viceroy and his Councillors were engaged in discussing the plans propounded by Sir Henry Rawlinson in order to "counteract the advance of Russia in Central Asia, and to strengthen the influence and power of England in Persia and Afghánistán." These plans Sir Henry had broached, as a member of the Home Council of India, in a memorandum which Sir Stafford Northcote forwarded to the Indian Government for its opinion thereon. In answer to a document which proposed to counteract Russian designs by making our influence paramount at Teherán and Kábul, the Governor-General

---

* Trotter ; *Allen's Indian Mail.*   † Malleson ; Trotter ; Temple.

addressed the Duke of Argyll, on the 4th of January, 1869, in a despatch protesting with rare dignity and quiet force against any marked deviation from the policy pursued by successive Viceroys. "We object," he wrote, speaking for his colleagues as well as himself, " to any active interference in the affairs of Afghánistán by the deputation of a high British officer, with or without a contingent, or by the forcible or amicable occupation of any post or tract in that country beyond our own frontier, inasmuch as we think that such a measure would, under present circumstances, engender irritation, defiance, and hatred in the minds of the Afgháns, without in the least strengthening our power either for attack or defence. We think it impolitic and unwise to decrease any of the difficulties which would be entailed on Russia, if that Power seriously thought of invading India, as we should certainly decrease them if we left our own frontier and met her half-way in a difficult country, and possibly in the midst of a hostile or exasperated population. We foresee no limits to the expenditure which such a move might require, and we protest against the necessity of having to impose taxation on the people of India, who are unwilling, as it is, to bear such pressure for measures which they can both understand and appreciate. And we think that the objects which we have at heart may be attained by an attitude of readiness and firmness on our frontier, and by giving all our care and expending all our resources for the attainment of practical and sound ends, over which we can exercise an effective and immediate control."

Having thus shown what ought not to be done, Lawrence proceeded, in few and fit words, to point out the true direction in which the energies of Anglo-Indian statesmen should be employed for the due safeguarding of our Indian Empire against all dangers, whether from without or within. Our true policy, our strongest security, he declared, in either case, would be found to lie "in previous abstinence from entanglements at either Kábul, Kandáhár, or any similar outpost ; in full reliance on a compact, highly equipped, and disciplined army stationed within our own territories or on our own border ; in the contentment, if not in the attachment, of the masses ; in the sense of security of title and possession, with which our whole policy is gradually imbuing the minds of the principal Chiefs and the native aristocracy ; in the construction of material works within British India, which enhance the comfort of the people while they add to our political and military strength ; in husbanding our finances, and consolidating and multiplying our resources; in quiet preparation for all contingencies, which no Indian statesman should disregard; and in a trust in the rectitude and honesty of our intentions, coupled with the avoidance of all sources of complaint which either invite foreign aggression or stir up restless spirits to domestic revolt."

By way of further precaution, Lawrence repeated the suggestion he had thrown out two years before, that some attempt should be made to arrive at a clear and friendly understanding with Russia, for the purpose of counteracting unfounded rumours and preventing unnecessary alarms. The Court of St. Petersburg should be told, "in firm but courteous language," that it must not interfere in the affairs of Afghánistán, or of any other State on the Indian frontier. And it would be well, he added, if our relations with the Persian Court were placed henceforward under the entire control of the Minister for India.*

Such were the words of weighty wisdom in which Sir John Lawrence summed up the recorded opinions not only of all his Council, but of the leading officers, civil and military, in the Panjáb; such men as Sir Donald Macleod, Mr. Robert Davies, Neville Chamberlain, and Sir Henry Norman. Nearly all the wisest statesmen and foremost soldiers in India were of one mind with the Viceroy on this matter. They preferred his policy of quiet watchfulness to the fussy, forward policy demanded by Rawlinson and Frere. It was not that they underrated Russia's power for possible mischief, but because they had taken careful measure of our own resources, and could see that, even in the unlikely event of a Russian invasion, the true danger to our rule lay nowhere across the frontier, but in India itself. To their thinking a Russian invasion of India was not more likely, and was still less feasible, than a French invasion of England. Nor could any one have seen more clearly than Lawrence himself the folly of trying to checkmate Russia on the Oxus by arousing against us the enmity of all Afghánistán. "Leave the Afgháns to themselves," he used to say, "for the first invaders of their country, whether Russian or English, will be received as foes, while the next will be hailed as friends and deliverers." With the strongest natural frontier in the world, guarded by deserts and rugged hills, with the sea at Bombay and Karáchi for our sure and ample base, with a powerful army well found in all warlike adjuncts, and ready to move by road or rail on any threatened point, with a people well governed, lightly taxed, and generally contented, he knew that we could afford

* Afghán Blue-book, 1878.

to wait behind our own defences for the first signs of danger looming a thousand miles away on the Oxus and in the wilds of Turkistán.

When Lawrence signed the despatch of the 4th of January, that last and noblest of his official utterances, the last hours of his rule were fast running out. Lord Mayo was already at Madras on the way to his future capital. On the 11th Sir John Lawrence took his seat at a farewell dinner given by a large and brilliant company of officers and civil servants, with Sir William Mansfield in the chair. The toast of the evening was fitly prefaced by the Commander-in-Chief with a graceful and eloquent summary of the Viceroy's claims to the admiration, esteem, and gratitude of his countrymen. In the course of his reply, Lawrence spoke with kindly warmth, in a voice sometimes broken with emotion, of the great help he had received in great crises from his fellow-workers and his countrymen at large. A storm of prolonged cheering re-echoed his appeals for justice and kind feeling towards the natives of India. In defending his foreign policy he declared that he "had never kept back from war when honour and justice required it." To the charge of following a supine and careless policy in Central Asia he gave an emphatic contradiction. "I have very carefully watched"—he said—"all that has gone on in those distant countries." He had set his face indeed against all projects which might involve active interference in the affairs of Central Asia, because such interference "would almost certainly lead to war, the end of which no one could foresee, and which would involve India in heavy debt, or necessitate the imposition of fresh taxation, to the impoverishment of the country and the unpopularity of our rule." Our true policy, he added, is "to avoid such complications; to consolidate our power in India; to give to its people the best government we can; to organize our administration in every department on a system which will combine economy with efficiency; and so to make our government strong and respected in our own vast territories." By so doing, and standing fast on our own border, we should be all the better prepared to repel invasion, if that should ever come.*

On the following day, the 12th, the retiring Viceroy stood before the grand entrance into Government House to welcome his successor, the Earl of Mayo, in due form. At the top of those broad stairs he stood, as Dalhousie and Canning had done before him, in full dress; overworn by incessant work and the cares of his high office, but upheld in spirit by the recollection of great

* Trotter ; *Allen's Mail.*

things achieved, of high duties loyally discharged. His eyes still shone with their old fire from out a countenance whitened with long service under Eastern suns, and he held his head erect as ever, though his tall figure seemed sadly shrunken from ill-health and overwork. At the bottom of the steps the incoming Viceroy, clad in "the easiest of summer costumes," with a burly figure and a ruddy face, sprang lightly out of his carriage amid the saluting of troops, and ran up the stairs to receive the usual greeting from the veteran whose place he was about to fill.*

On the 18th of January Lawrence received farewell addresses from the citizens of Calcutta, from the Bishop and clergy, and from missionaries of various sects. Early the next morning he passed through lines of troops down to Prinsep's Ghát, where a parting cheer, led by Lord Mayo himself, and warmly taken up by a large crowd of spectators, followed him on board the yacht waiting to bear his party down the Húghli to the mail steamer in which he had taken his passage home. His promotion to the Peerage, with the title of Baron Lawrence of the Panjáb and Grately, was the first mark of national gratitude that welcomed his return to England; an honour which the general voice of his countrymen would have bestowed upon him ten years before. As a means of helping him to support his new dignity, the Council of India converted his annuity of two thousand pounds into a pension for his own life and that of his next successor in the peerage. The cheers that greeted him from both sides of the House of Lords when, on the 19th of April, the new Peer rose to speak in support of a Bill prepared by the Duke of Argyll for reducing the tenure of a seat in the Indian Council to ten years, did less honour to the great man himself than to the august assembly which gave him so warm a welcome.†

The House of Lords might well feel proud of the new Peer whose services as Viceroy had, in the words of Sir William Mansfield, conferred new lustre, if that were possible, on the name he had won as Saviour of Upper India in the dark days of 1857. Lord Lawrence could truly say that he had "handed over the Government to his successor efficient in all its departments, with no arrears, and with all open questions in a fair way towards settlement." The five years of his rule had been years on the whole of peaceful progress in all things tending to promote the happiness and well-doing of all classes in his wide dominions. The foregoing pages have shown how earnestly and with what

* Hunter's "Lord Mayo." † *Allen's Mail;* Trotter.

success, in spite of many and great hindrances, he laboured, like another Bentinck, for the general good; how honestly he strove to keep down all needless expenditure, to avoid all pretexts for laying new burdens on the poorer millions, to preserve the customary and recorded rights of the peasantry in the land, to help the natives in managing their own municipal affairs, to develop sound schemes of popular instruction and sanitary reform, to provide new aids to commerce and agriculture in the shape of roads, railways, canals, cheap telegraphs, and cheap postage. And all this—as his biographer truly remarks—"he had done in spite of difficulties arising from weakened health, from differences of opinion between himself and some of the most influential members of his Council, from the persistent and malevolent attacks of a certain part of the Anglo-Indian press, and from the prejudices which had been aroused against him by the fact, now that he was a commoner, now that he was a civilian, now that he was a Panjábi, and now again that he was a genuine and devout Christian."*

In 1859, when Lord Stanley had charge of the India Office, the impression which Lawrence made upon him was one of "a certain heroic simplicity." He found himself "in the presence of a man capable of accomplishing great things, and capable also of leaving the credit of them to anybody who chose to take it."† Like the Victor of Waterloo, Lawrence was one of those who

> " cared not to be great,
> But as he saved or served the State. "

He was always ready to spend himself in his country's service, and no stress of circumstances proved too great for his strong will, his clear head, his prompt courage, and his vast capacity for work. Fortunate in his opportunities, he showed himself equal to the most splendid of them all. Detractors he had of course; but "malice itself"—as Lord Derby said of him after his death—"never fastened on his career the imputation of one discreditable incident or unworthy act." His sterling honesty, his sound judgement, his large heart, and his ripe experience gave their full leverage to that ingrained love of justice, rarest of all manly virtues, which Lord Lawrence displayed so strikingly in every passage of his public career.

* Bosworth-Smith.
† Lord Derby's speech at the Mansion House in February, 1880.

BOOK VI.

LORD MAYO AND LORD NORTHBROOK.

1869–1876.

CHAPTER I.

LORD MAYO AND HIS FOREIGN POLICY.

In the autumn of 1868 Mr. Disraeli appointed the Earl of Mayo to the post which Lord Lawrence was preparing to resign. As Chief Secretary for Ireland in three Conservative Ministries, the Vice-roy-Elect had given proofs of some special capacity for the task he was now to assay. Before he landed at Bombay, Mr. Gladstone's Ministry had replaced that of Mr. Disraeli; but the new Prime Minister at once confirmed the appointment which many of his own followers loudly urged him to annul. India had not yet become the battlefield for political parties of the English pattern; and Lord Mayo's management of Irish affairs had been marked by a rare freedom from party bias, and by a wise and genial tolerance of creeds and opinions differing from his own. Well knowing, as he wrote to a friend, that India was "a big thing," he felt confident that, with health and strength on his side, he would succeed in belying the predictions of those "bitter scribblers" who assumed that no statesman without Indian experience was fit to govern India. "I believe," he said, "that twenty years of the House of Commons, five years of labour in the most difficult offices, with two in the Cabinet, form as good training as a man could have for the work." In the new field that lay before him he asked only that men should judge him according to his acts.*

For some weeks before leaving England, he had worked hard day after day to arm himself with the mental equipment needed for his new post. He picked the brains of every one who had aught to say worth hearing on any Indian question. At every halting-place on his journey to Bombay he gathered new knowledge from every available source. At Bombay, Púna, and Madras he made large additions to his mental outfit, and by the time he landed in Calcutta his preliminary training was nearly complete.

* Hunter's "Life of Lord Mayo."

What of special guidance might yet be lacking, a few days' intercourse with Sir John Lawrence was certain to supply.[*]

At the age of forty-six, in the fulness of his lusty health and unbounded energies, the new Viceroy entered on his new career with every prospect of unalloyed success. Lawrence had left no part of the public business in arrear. The country was at peace and fairly prosperous; public works were making good progress; so carefully had Lawrence husbanded his yearly revenues, that after spending more than eight millions on barracks, irrigation, increased salaries, and the new troop-ships, the net deficit on five years' income was little more than three millions and a quarter; all of which might fairly have been placed to the capital account. Peace and order once more reigned beyond the Sulaimán Hills. Lord Mayo himself had a shrewd turn for all kinds of business, from the management of an Irish farm to the government of a whole nation. Of a bright, genial, generous nature; of frank manners and stately bearing; a statesman eager to learn and quick in grasping new facts, a keen sportsman, an active worker whose brain and muscle seemed alike untirable, he threw into his work the same power of enjoyment, the same glow of enthusiasm, which marked his play. That such a ruler would make himself popular with his own countrymen was a thing of course. But events showed that Lord Mayo was not less ready than his great predecessor to sacrifice popularity for the public good.[†]

One of the new Viceroy's first cares was the duty of clinching the arrangements which Lord Lawrence had carried on with the reinstated ruler of Afghánistán. The last of his enemies fairly driven from the field, Sher Ali was free to accept Lord Mayo's invitation to a friendly conference at Ambála. Towards the end of March, after settling with Sir Richard Temple the Budget Estimates for the current year, the Governor-General, attended by his Council and a numerous staff, made his way up country to the great plain where the Amir's party, a large body of British troops, and some native princes were already encamped, awaiting the Lord Sáhib's arrival. On the 27th of March the first meeting between Lord Mayo and his Afghán guest took place in the great Darbár tent. At Lahór the Amir had "begun to feel himself a king," so splendid was his welcome there. And now at Ambála the warworn heir of Dost Mohammad found himself received by the Viceroy of India with all the honours due to a sovereign of equal rank with the Queen of Great Britain. Lord Mayo pre-

---

[*] Hunter.   [†] Temple; Malleson; Hunter.

sented Sher Ali with six lakhs of rupees, the balance of the subsidy promised by Lord Lawrence. To this he added the gift of a richly jewelled sword, which the gratified Amir vowed that he would use only in defence of the British Government.*

On the 29th of March the Viceroy admitted the Amir and his trusty counsellor, Saiyad Núr Mohammad Shah, to a private interview, at which Sir Donald Macleod, Mr. Seton-Karr as Foreign Secretary, and Captain Grey as interpreter, were the only Englishmen present besides the Viceroy himself. A free and unreserved discussion of important topics then took place. Sher Ali wanted more than Lord Mayo could bring himself to grant. He had come to Ambála hoping to obtain a new treaty, a fixed annual subsidy, due help in arms and men whenever he asked for it, and the promise of our support to himself and his descendants in all emergencies and against all rivals. He would even have urged Lord Mayo to acknowledge Abdulla Ján, the child of his mature age, as heir to the throne of Kábul, in preference to the brave and able Yákub Khán, whose arms had borne him back in triumph to his capital. But on this last point the Viceroy would hear of no discussion; and the other four, after due discussion, he put aside with equal firmness and courtesy, as beyond his political scope. True to his own purpose and to the policy marked out for him by Lord Lawrence, he left Sher Ali no room for further grasping at vain shadows. The Amir was plainly warned that "under no circumstances should a British soldier ever cross his frontier to assist him in coercing his rebellious subjects; that no European officers would be placed as Residents in his cities; that no fixed subsidy or money allowance would be given for any named period; that no treaty would be entered into obliging us under *every* circumstance to recognize him and his descendants as rulers of Afghánistán." At the same time Lord Mayo promised to render him "all the moral support in his power," to supply him at need with money, arms, ammunition, and native workmen, and to correspond freely with him through the Commissioner of Pesháwar and our native agents in Afghánistán; the Amir on his part "undertaking to do all he can to maintain peace on our frontier, and to comply with all our wishes on matters connected with trade."†

For the Amir's contentment Lord Mayo, two days later, followed up his spoken word with a letter, in the wording of which his Council had borne their part. In this he informed

---

* Temple ; Hunter. † Afghán Blue-book ; Hunter ; Temple.

Sher Ali that the Viceroy's Government would "view with severe displeasure" any attempt on the part of Sher Ali's rivals to disturb his position as Ruler of Kábul and to rekindle civil war. "It will further endeavour," he wrote, "from time to time, by such means as circumstances may require, to strengthen the government of your Highness, to enable you to exercise with equity and with justice your rightful rule, and to transmit to your descendants all the dignities and honours of which you are the lawful possessor." Lord Mayo further requested his Highness to "communicate frequently and freely" with the Indian Government and its officers on all matters of public interest, and to believe that his representations would always be "treated with consideration and respect."

Two interviews between Núr Mohammad and Mr. Seton-Karr, dealing chiefly with questions of trade and frontier policy, brought the business of the Conference to an auspicious close. Early in April the Amír turned his face homewards, not wholly satisfied, perhaps, with the net results of his visit, but thoroughly pleased with the reception everywhere offered him, deeply impressed with all that he had seen and learned of the British power, charmed with the Viceroy's splendid courtesies, and firmly assured of our desire to act up to the spirit of the treaties made with his father in 1855 and 1857. If he had failed to win those guarantees of help and protection against all assailants for which he had pleaded, he returned to Kábul convinced that he had nothing to fear and much to gain from the assured goodwill of his powerful neighbours, so long as he followed their advice in all things pertaining to the peace, order and well-being of his dominions.*

Lord Lawrence's Afghán policy, founded on the good faith of former treaties, on a wise avoidance of all entangling alliances with semi-barbarous neighbours, and on a proud but reasonable contempt for the schemes of hotbrained panicmongers, had thus become the established policy of the Indian Government both in India and at home. The Ambála Conference, with all that came of it, was the necessary sequel to the Minute of January. In all he did or planned in this connection Lord Mayo was simply bent on working out his predecessor's designs. When the Duke of Argyll, writing in May to the Viceroy, betrayed some misgivings as to the extent of our new liabilities in Afghánistán, Lord Mayo hastened to reassure his Grace by reviewing the steps he had taken to carry

* Afghán Blue-book ; Temple ; Hunter.

out the very principles laid down in the Duke's despatch. He showed how entirely those principles harmonized not only with the views set forth in his previous letters to the India Office, but with each step in the course of business transacted at Ambála. So far from exceeding former promises or extending our liabilities in any way, he had done his best to "define and clearly explain" our true position towards the Amir, to limit rather than extend our supposed obligations, and to make Sher Ali understand that the fulfilment of our pledges would depend solely on his own persistence in well-doing, on his own success in maintaining a strong, just, merciful, and friendly rule. With these explanations the Duke of Argyll could not but own himself thoroughly satisfied.*

The lessons which Sher Ali had learned at Ambála bore fruit soon after his return to Kábul. He strove honestly, with some success, to show himself worthy of the Viceroy's continued support. He set up a Council of State, composed of thirteen members, who were to help him with their advice in the management of public affairs. He offered pardon on fair terms to several of his late foes. He remitted the savage penalties against several more. He established post-offices, organized a new police, remodelled his troops and drilled them after the English fashion, opened a new court for the hearing of civil suits, and tried to introduce the practice of paying public servants in cash instead of the old assignments on land or revenue. If his efforts in this last direction proved a failure, he was more successful in removing hindrances to internal trade, in keeping the peace of his own frontier, and in trying to settle disputes with his neighbours by diplomacy instead of arms. And the only help he sought or received from Lord Mayo's Government after 1869 came to him in the shape of moral sympathy and seasonable advice. His very extravagances betokened the strength of his new leanings. He made his officers dress, like himself, in an English costume, and he ordered the shoemakers of Kábul to deal thenceforward only in boots and shoes of the English pattern.†

Lord Lawrence had repeatedly advised the Home Government to come to a clear understanding with Russia as to her projects and designs in Central Asia. Her late advance from the Jaxartes to the Oxus, and the rumours so often circulated by the Press had engendered in the minds of Englishmen and natives "an exaggerated opinion of her resources and power." For the purpose of counteracting unfounded rumours and preventing unnecessary

* Afghán Blue-book.   † Hunter ; Sir J. Strachey's Minute of 1872.

alarms, he had urged the Gladstone Ministry to inform the Court of St. Petersburg, "in firm but courteous language, that it cannot be permitted to interfere in the affairs of Afghánistán, or in those of any State which lies contiguous to our frontier." To this policy Lord Mayo from the first had given his hearty support. He looked upon Russia's neighbourhood to India as a possible danger, only if English statesmen took fright at shadows and kept their eyes shut to plain facts.   Cool-headed and clear-seeing, he felt no uneasiness at the advance in Asia of a civilized Christian Power strong enough to overawe the surrounding tribes, and wise enough to forbear from troubling the friends of its English rival. If both Powers could only agree to lay aside their mutual jealousies and suspicions, there was no reason, he thought, why Russian interests in Asia need ever clash with our own.   Regarded as Asiatic powers, England in fact was the stronger, wealthier, better organized of the two.   If Russia "could only be brought to act cordially with us," he wrote to the Duke of Argyll in April, "to say that she would not obstruct our trade," nor encourage any hostile movements against our neighbours in Yarkand or Afghán-istán, she would greatly forward the work of civilizing wide tracts of country, and would do much to hasten the complete establish-ment of her own power.*

In this direction indeed the Home Government needed little prompting.   On the very same day that Lord Mayo opened his Darbár at Ambála, Queen Victoria's Foreign Secretary, Lord Granville, was holding friendly converse with Prince Gortschakoff on the desired agreement between the two Powers.   It is only fair to say that the Russian Government had sought five years before to enlighten Europe as to the true meaning, the "imperious neces-sity," of Russia's onward march through Turkistán; a march "where the greatest difficulty is to know when to stop."   Lord Granville's first interviews with Prince Gortschakoff served to dispel the misgivings which Sher Ali's visit to Ambála had re-awakened in Russian minds.   These interviews were followed by others, which led to nothing definite, until in November, 1869, Mr. Douglas Forsyth, of the Bengal Civil Service, who had made his mark during the Mutiny, was sent off to St. Petersburg at Lord Mayo's instance, to clear away the doubts and difficulties that still blocked the negotiators' path.   He did his errand so thoroughly, that the bases of a friendly understanding were laid down in the course of that winter.   The Russian Government agreed to acknow-

* Hunter ; Temple ; Central Asian Blue-book ; Strachey.

ledge Sher Ali's sway over all his father's possessions on the south side of the Oxus, and to abstain from all interference therein, so long at least as Sher Ali kept to his own side of the river and forbore from interfering in the affairs of Bokhára. The English Government, for their part, stood forth as sponsor for the Afghán Amir, promising to use their best influence in fulfilment of the pledges offered on his behalf; while Russia undertook the same office for the Amir of Bokhára, whose troops were even then raiding across the Oxus.*

It remained to settle the question of boundaries between Afghánistán and her northern neighbours. This was a process which would take some time and evolve some conflict of opinion by the way. General von Kauffmann, the Governor-General of Russian Turkistán, maintained, for instance, that the outlying States of Wakhán and Badakshán formed no part of the Afghán dominions, while Lord Mayo and his advisers held fast to the contrary belief. When other points of difference had been duly got over, this question still kept the field. The discussion was conducted on both sides with admirable courtesy and manifest goodwill. At last, in January, 1873, the Russian Government gave way; the Czar himself declaring that "such a question should not be a cause of difference between the two countries." On the principle that one good turn deserves another, he commanded his Ministers to accept the boundary-line laid down by the English Government.†

The policy thus consummated had already borne good fruit. Russian influence had constrained the ruler of Bokhára to recall the troops he sent across the Oxus in the winter of 1869. The same Power withheld the Afghán refugees beyond the river from disturbing the peace of Afghánistán. Abdurrahman Khán himself, the ablest of Sher Ali's foes, was plainly warned by General Kauffmann to expect no kind of help from either Russia or Bokhára in the prosecution of any design against his uncle, the Amir of Kábul, in whose welfare Russia and England were alike concerned. Abstinence from all political intrigues and projects was the one condition on which Russia could grant the homeless exile an asylum and a pension suited to his needs. In the spring of 1870 Kauffmann began a friendly correspondence with Sher Ali, in which he assured the Amir of his neighbourly sentiments towards a Government which enjoyed the protection of his English friends.‡

* Central Asian Blue-book; Hunter; Temple.
† Central Asian Blue-book; Temple; Hunter.
‡ Central Asian Blue-book; Strachey.

Nor did Lord Mayo fail on his side to use his best influence in strengthening the hold he had won upon the Amir. When the quarrel between Sher Ali and his son Yákub blazed into open war, the Viceroy's friendly counsels composed the strife and secured a timely concession to the just demands of Sher Ali's ablest and most popular son. In the long-simmering dispute between the Amir and the Shah of Persia touching the frontier province of Sistán, Lord Mayo interposed as the umpire accepted by both parties. His influence alone withheld Sher Ali from resisting Persian encroachments by force of arms. To Colonel Frederick Goldsmid, an able and experienced officer of Engineers, he entrusted in 1870 the task of adjusting the rival claims to a swampy desert watered by the Helmund, and famed chiefly as the birthplace of Rústam and other heroes of Persian song.*

Before Goldsmid could surmount the delays consequent on Yákub Khán's rebellion, his services were required for a like purpose elsewhere. Persia had been trying for years past to push her south-eastern frontier into the heart of Southern Biluchistán. Lord Mayo, however, brooked no such interference with his scheme for maintaining a belt of friendly independent States along the Indian frontier; and the invaded country, with its seaboard stretching from Sind to Bandar Abbas, belonged in fact to our ally, the ruler of Khalát. The Shah at length agreed to submit this question also to arbitration, and Colonel Goldsmid undertook for the Khán's western frontier the same office which he had yet to discharge for Sistán. The result of his researches, pursued for several months amid the dreary, thinly-peopled wastes of Makrán, enabled him in 1871 to draw up a convention which both Shah and Khán agreed to accept. In the following year a survey party, led by the active Major St. John of the Engineers, employed itself in tracing out the western boundaries of Khalát, from Gwadar northwards to the Perso-Afghán frontier. Meanwhile Goldsmid had returned to his old problem, the settlement of boundaries in Sistán. This, the harder problem of the two, he succeeded in solving by an award which neither claimant at first accepted with a good grace. Before that award was actually given, on the 19th of August, 1872, Lord Mayo had ceased to breathe.† His Com-

---

* Hunter ; Strachey ; Temple ; Trotter.

† Hunter ; Temple ; Afghán Blue-book. A full account of the proceedings of the Persian Boundary Commission will be found in "Eastern Persia," edited by Sir Fred. Goldsmid—(Macmillan, 1876).

missioner's patient services were duly honoured with a knighthood of the Star of India.

In Khalát, as in Afghánistán, Lord Mayo's soothing influence was not confined to the settlement of border disputes. He tried his best to allay those bitter feuds between the Khán and his barons, which continually ruffled the peace of Biluchistán. These feuds turned in effect upon the question whether the Khán was supreme ruler over the whole country, or only *primus inter pares*, the head of a confederacy of powerful and co-ordinate chiefs. If there was little hope of settling the question upon any clear ground of historic right or usage, the Viceroy's efforts might smooth the way to some arrangement which both parties would choose to accept. Lord Mayo therefore instructed Sir William Merewether, his Agent for the Sind frontier, to act as peacemaker between the Khán and his unruly Sardárs. Under Sir William's able management the distracted country enjoyed a long-needed rest from internal troubles.*

In his desire to strengthen the frontier States against the Shah, Lord Mayo was not less anxious to strengthen Persia herself against the Power that pressed upon her from the North. He had strong faith in " the good influence which an able and energetic Anglo-Indian statesman would exercise over the mind " of Persia's sovereign. Such men were always to be found in India, and there was no limit to the power they could wield for good over the minds of Asiatic rulers, if the charge of the British Mission at Teherán were only transferred from the Home Government to that of India. This was a measure for which successive Viceroys had vainly pleaded in the teeth of objections more plausible perhaps than sound. The English Government still refused to deal with Persia as a part of the Indian political system, even while it kept on charging the Indian revenues with £12,000 a year for the maintenance of a Mission over which the India Office had no control whatever.†

Among the frontier States with which Lord Mayo had friendly dealings was Eastern Turkistán, which Yákub Beg, the conqueror of Káshgar, had wrested, as we saw, from the Chinese yoke. In March, 1870, an Envoy from the Atálik Gházi, or Defender of the Faith, as Yákub now called himself, reached Calcutta to acquaint the Viceroy with his master's earnest desire for friendly intercourse between the two countries. In accordance with Yákub's own request, Lord Mayo selected Douglas Forsyth, who had just

* Hunter ; Strachey.   † Hunter ; Rawlinson.

returned to Lahór from his Russian errand, to accompany the Envoy homewards as far as Yárkand, his master's southern capital. Forsyth's mission was to be purely commercial. He was instructed to learn as much as he could of the history and resources of Eastern Turkistán, and to ascertain what sort of goods the people wanted in exchange for those which they could best supply. Beyond repeating the friendly advice which Lord Mayo himself had given the Atalik's Envoy, he was strictly forbidden to meddle in any way with the politics, internal or external, of the countries he might travel through.

Leaving Jalandhar on the 26th of April, 1870, Forsyth marched through Káshmir to Leh, the capital of Ladákh. From thence, in company with the Yárkand Envoy, he set out towards the end of June on a long and difficult march through the wild Himalayan region that divides Ladákh from Eastern Turkistán. Mounted on ponies or on foot, his little party had to climb ridge after ridge of snowclad mountains by passes rising eighteen and nineteen thousand feet above the sea-level. The last of these was threaded by the end of July, and the travellers pursued their way to Yárkand, where the Atalik's deputy received Forsyth with a hospitality which knew no stint. The Shahgassi, indeed, strove hard to detain his guest on one pretext or another at Yárkand, until Yákub Beg himself should have returned from the war he was waging in the west. But the British Envoy, true to his instructions, insisted on returning to India before the snow began to block the passes. With great reluctance the Shahgassi let him and his party go, laden with presents and well furnished with the information they had been sent to procure. So far, at any rate, the Mission had not proved a failure, while it paved the way for further negotiations, which Lord Mayo's successor was happily enabled to carry through.*

With the frontier State of Nipál, still ruled by the strong hand and busy brain of Jang Bahádur, the Viceroy had no difficulty in maintaining an intercourse as friendly as Gorkha pride and patriotism would allow. His influence kept the King of Burmah true to the engagements he had made with the late Viceroy. In 1869 Captain Strover entered on the duties of British Resident at Bhámo, and British steamers began to navigate the Irawádi between Bhámo and Rangoon. If Lord Mayo failed to wean his Majesty of the Golden Foot from his old faith in the fiscal virtue of royal monopolies, the King's long-cherished

* Hunter ; Sir D. Forsyth's Report.

distrust of those English neighbours who had robbed him of Pegu seems to have cooled down into a cheerful acquiescence in the benefits derivable from British trade.[*]

In the quarrels of petty potentates on the Persian Gulf, Lord Mayo intervened only when they seemed like to imperil the lives and property of British subjects trading in those parts. So long as these were safe under the watchful protection of Colonel Lewis Pelly and a few British cruisers, it mattered nothing to him that Azán-ibn-Ghás drove his brother-in-law from the throne of Maskát, or that rival Arab chiefs fought for power and plunder in districts outside the range of our diplomacy. If the actual ruler of Maskát would forbear from attacking Zanzibar and from doing aught to harm or hinder the peaceful traders in his ports, the Viceroy was content to acknowledge him as Sultan for the time being, and to keep due watch upon the movements of his ousted rivals who had found shelter at Bombay.

In dealing with the Pathán tribes on the Panjáb border, Lord Mayo preferred a policy of preventive vigilance to one of armed retaliation. Instead of punishing a border raid by the usual process of burning villages and destroying crops, he desired to avert all occasion for such reprisals by guarding the frontier with a strong, well-armed, and vigilant police. The notion of destroying villages and "killing people for the sake of prestige," he regarded as alike impolitic and unworthy of the British power. He held that every shot fired in anger within our borders confirmed our ill-wishers in the belief that our power was still disputed in Hindustan. A strong force of border police, ever on the watch against sudden forays and prompt to chastise evil-doers caught in the act, would teach the mountaineers what punitive expeditions never could, that "assassination, the attack on a defenceless village by night, or killing people in their beds, are not acts of war, but are esteemed by civilized nations to be acts of murder." It may be a question whether the new policy would have served our purpose in the past as well as that system of reprisals which many of Sir Donald Macleod's officers still favoured. The question had been raised some years before by Sir Bartle Frere in a despatch comparing the rival methods of dealing with the border tribes in Sind and the Panjáb. The milder method, he argued, had proved the more successful. But Lord Lawrence had clearly shown in answer, that the Panjáb system was the one best fitted to repress the murderous outbreaks of tribes far fiercer and more

[*] Hunter.

unruly than any of those on the Sind border. Of late years these outbreaks had been much less frequent, and the Viceroy had fair grounds for believing that a policy of "constant vigilance and defence" would better serve thenceforth the ends of civilized rule, than a policy of sharp and sweeping chastisement by fire and sword.[*]

On his north-eastern frontier, however, Lord Mayo found himself driven to punish deeds of outrage by armed force. In January, 1871, the peace of India was rudely broken· by bands of naked Lushai savages, who dwelt amidst the densely wooded hills and valleys that stretch along Eastern Bengal from Kachár southwards to Arakán. Their murderous inroads across the frontier spread havoc and dismay among the outlying tea-gardens of Kachár. Troops and policemen were at once sent off to guard the frontier from further ravages; but, owing to the lateness of the season, no attempt could then be made to pursue the raiders into pathless jungles, which the rains would erelong convert into poisonous swamps. The Viceroy, however, made up his mind to despatch an armed force into the Lushai country later in the year, "for the purpose of punishing the guilty where they can be traced and found, but more particularly for showing these savages that there is hardly a part of their hills which our armed forces cannot visit and penetrate." Lord Napier of Magdála, who had just succeeded Sir William Mansfield as Commander-in-Chief, conducted with his usual thoroughness all the needful arrangements for the coming campaign. In November two columns, formed mostly of native troops, led by Generals Bourchier and Brownlow, set out from Kachár and Chittagong on their toilsome march through a land of swamps and dense bamboo-jungle, broken by range on range of steep hills, each crowned by its stockaded village.

Both columns slowly but steadily pushed their way through all obstacles, beating the enemy wherever they attempted a stand, cutting roads through the jungle with infinite labour, and bearing hardships of every kind with the cheerfulness of soldiers who trusted alike in their leaders and in themselves. By the end of February, 1872, their work was over. The headmen of the Haulong and Sailu tribes had yielded at discretion; the captives carried off from Kachár were given up, two or three villages were destroyed, and hostages were taken for the good behaviour of the tribes concerned in the recent raids. Before the rains set

[*] Hunter; Temple.

in, our troops had recrossed the frontier on their way home. The Lushai borderers, having thus found their master, learned to lay aside their plundering ways, and began to reappear as peaceful traders on the scene of their former ravages.*

* Hunter; *Allen's Mail*; Woodthorpe's "Lushai Expedition." "The history of the expedition," wrote General Bourchier in his Field Force Order of March 19, "from first to last has been sheer hard work." In spite of the large scale on which the expedition was planned and conducted, it is shown by Lieutenant Woodthorpe that, "after deducting the guards necessary at the various stations to keep open communications, only a force of 400 men were available for the final advance on Chumfai—not by any means too many, supposing the Lushais had made a stand at Tulcheng."

CHAPTER II.

LORD MAYO'S FINANCIAL POLICY.

ONE of the first problems which the Earl of Mayo had to take in hand during the summer of 1869 was the question of financial ways and means. The last three years of Lord Lawrence's rule had been years of deficit, amounting in all to five and three-quarter millions sterling. In each year the Budget estimates from one cause or another had been greatly falsified by the actual results. In 1868 alone Mr. Massey's expected surplus of two millions issued in a deficit of the same extent. During the same period the cash balances in the Indian treasuries fell from thirteen and three-quarter millions to ten and one-third millions. In his Budget Statement on the 6th of March, 1869, Sir Richard Temple, warned by past misreckonings, laid his account for a modest surplus of £48,263 at the end of the current year. This surplus he hoped to secure by turning Massey's licence-tax into a regular income-tax of one per cent. on all incomes of more than fifty pounds a year. When he had seen his Budget safe through the Viceroy's Council, and proclaimed a loan of three and a half millions for "extraordinary" or reproductive public works, Temple returned to England for a few months on sick leave.

He had made his forecast to the best of his judgement on the information at that time within his reach. But India is a country of vast distances; the yearly accounts for so many provinces needed time to collect, examine, adjust; and the Regular Estimates on which the Finance Minister framed his Budget gave the actual figures only for nine months out of the twelve. The disturbing influence of a bad harvest, a declining trade, or a slack demand for opium, might sadly falsify the most carefully founded forecast of income and expenditure. And thus it happened that, soon after Temple's departure, Lord Mayo discovered signs of a startling discrepancy between the figures of Temple's Budget and those revealed in the full and final accounts for the past year.

Further inquiries conducted by Temple's substitute, Sir John Strachey, showed an actual deficit of more than two millions for the year which ended in March 1869. This was more than double the amount of deficit which Temple, guided by the Regular Estimates, had sought to make good. It was clear, therefore, that something must be done to avert the larger deficit for which no provision had yet been made. What ought to be done was a question which the Viceroy solved in his own resolute fashion. " I am determined," he wrote in August to Sir Henry Durand, " not to have another deficit, even if it leads to the diminution of the army, the reduction of Civil Establishments, and the stoppage of Public Works."

He had already exhorted the Local Governments to keep their expenditure within the narrowest possible bounds. He curtailed by £800,000 the projected outlay on ordinary public works. The usual grants for education and some other services were cut down by £350,000. These retrenchments might just suffice, if other things went well, to balance the accounts for that year. But certain other things, such as the opium and customs revenues, were not going well. The effects of past drought in Upper and Central India, of wide-wasting fevers in the waterlogged plains of Bardwán and Húghli, were still telling upon the trade of the country. Nothing but fresh taxation could avert another deficit. In ready answer to the Viceroy's inquiries Lord Napier of Ettrick proposed a moderate increase of the salt-duties in Madras. Sir Seymour Fitzgerald agreed to a like arrangement for Bombay. In spite of hesitating voices in his own Council, Lord Mayo was bent upon doubling the income-tax for the latter half of the year. On his return to Calcutta in November, Temple himself took charge of a measure which he would gladly have brought forward in March ; and the Legislative Council soon passed the necessary Bills, not only for doubling the income-tax, but for raising the salt-duties in Bombay and Madras. Half a million was thus added to the revenue for the financial year 1869–70, and the Viceroy's efforts to avert a deficit were rewarded at the year's end by a surplus of £108,000.*

In framing his Budget for 1870, Temple took care to keep his estimates of the year's income down to the level of apparent facts. In view of a declining trade, diminished receipts from opium, and a possible increase in various charges, he proposed to levy an income-tax at the rate of four per cent., or double the rate

* Hunter ; Temple ; Strachey.

fixed in the past November. Deferring, however, to the scruples or the fears of Lord Mayo and other of his colleagues, he contented himself with a less daring flight. His Bill for raising the rate of income-tax in the current year to three per cent., or sevenpence halfpenny in the pound, was strongly opposed by the commercial and native members of the Legislative Council. But the Viceroy and his Cabinet were of one mind on this matter, and the Bill was carried amidst a rising storm of popular malediction, which was to rage for months against Lord Mayo and his Finance Minister. The Viceroy's growing popularity suffered for the time a complete eclipse. No one outside the official circles would believe in the necessity of the new turn thus given to the fiscal screw. Whatever may now be the case in England after an experience of many years, in India an income-tax, however light, meant more or less of fraud, extortion, and sheer injustice in the process of collecting it. Every enhancement of such a tax would tend to multiply the attendant evils out of all proportion to the realized gains. For every rupee that reached the Treasury, one or two at least found their way into the pockets of native underlings, who traded on the fears, the selfishness, or the needs of their own countrymen. The rich gave bribes to avoid paying their full shares of the hated impost; the poor were frightened into compliance with unlawful demands, or punished for their resistance by the summary sale of their few goods. A great wave of popular resentment swept over the country. The Town Hall of Calcutta resounded with indignant or plaintive speeches. In nearly all the chief towns and stations of India public meetings were held against a tax which men of all classes and colours agreed for various reasons in reviling. Petition after petition went up to Simla from the Chambers of Commerce, the Zamindárs of Bengal, and other bodies representing European or Native interests; the newspapers teemed with instances of alleged hardship or extortion; and the Government found itself at issue with some of its ablest and most experienced subalterns, notably with Sir William Muir, who, having lately exchanged his seat in Council for the headship of the North-Western Provinces, had since gathered from the reports of his district officers detailed evidence of the mischief wrought by entrusting the collection of such an impost to native hands.[*]

That this was the real blot in his fiscal policy Lord Mayo himself was soon driven to confess. His letters to Sir William Muir,

* Hunter ; Temple ; Trotter ; *Allen's Mail.*

to Lord Napier of Ettrick, and to the Duke of Argyll, all express his growing conviction that no direct tax can be levied in India, especially on small incomes, through the agency of native officials, without opening "a wide door for oppression." As European agency was almost wholly out of the question, Lord Mayo felt that the time for imposing a permanent income-tax on the people of India had not yet come. But he could not bring himself to abolish the tax altogether at the end of the current year. The Regular Estimates for the year which ended with the close of March, 1871, revealed a surplus much larger than Temple had predicted, a surplus afterwards found to exceed a million and a half. For this surplus the receipts from opium, customs, and other old sources of revenue were mainly accountable. Nevertheless the Viceroy's old dread of a deficit was still to temper the force of his new convictions. He contented himself with renewing the income-tax for another year, with due restrictions, at the low rate of one per cent., or twopence-halfpenny in the pound.[*]

The exemption of the lowest class of incomes reduced by one-half the number of persons assessed; while the lowered rate and the new exemptions together implied a deduction of a million and a half from the next year's revenue. So fair, however, was the financial prospect, and so strict the economy enforced in every department, that Temple laid his account for the year ending in March, 1872, with a moderate surplus, which kept growing month by month until it reached the unprecedented sum of three millions. The clamour against the tax was still maintained by the wealthier classes, who chafed under burdens, however just and moderate, to which they had not yet become inured. These were the very classes whom Lord Lawrence had always desired to reach; and Temple, in common with Strachey and others of the Lawrence school, held that a light income-tax, limited to those classes, and carefully assessed on trustworthy returns, might in a few years become the mainstay of Indian finance. Time alone, he thought, was needed to prove its usefulness in ordinary seasons and its power of expansion in special crises. The Viceroy, however, seems by this time to have satisfied himself that the tax, however amended, would not work. In January, 1872, he declared himself bound to oppose any scheme which "might continue the bare chance of such injustice" as had lately come to light. But his untimely death a few weeks later prolonged the life of the doomed impost for yet another year.[†]

[*] Hunter; Temple.   [†] Ibid.

A conspicuous feature in Temple's Budget for 1871–2 was the new scheme of fixed yearly allotments for the Provincial Services. Hitherto the Local Governments had been wont to regulate their outlay by the sums which from year to year they might succeed in extracting from the Imperial Treasury. Their receipts varied less with the urgency of their demands than with the humour or the convenience of the Central Government. For every service a separate sum was meted out; nor could the money saved from Roads or Jails, for instance, be applied without special leave to some other service, such as Education or Police. The Local Government had to show cause for every item of its outlay, and to credit the Imperial Treasury with all unexpended balances; there was no distinction, in fact, between Provincial and Imperial revenues. In the sphere of finance the Provincial Governor was simply an agent for the collection and disbursement of Imperial funds. For every rupee spent in his own province he had to account to the keeper of the Viceroy's public purse. Without the Viceroy's sanction he could order no new outlay, however small, in any branch of the public service.

With the growth of our Indian Empire such a system became less and less tolerable for all concerned. It caused increasing friction between the power that held the purse and the powers engaged in spending the money. The Central Government groaned and fretted under the weight of responsibilities in which the minor Governments had no share. The latter had no motive for husbanding those resources in the management of which they had no voice. They were tempted to ask for much in order to obtain a little; and the greater their importunity, the more money they were likely to get. In the scramble which came off yearly for the public purse the largest share would commonly fall not to those provinces which needed it most, but to those which pressed their claims with loudest persistence on the notice of the controlling power.*

Various remedies had often been proposed for a state of things which successive Viceroys had agreed in deploring. No one had felt more strongly than Lord Lawrence the absolute need of endowing the Provincial Governments with enlarged control over their outlay on certain sections of the public business. It was no longer possible to keep a tight rein on strong-willed Governors like Sir Bartle Frere, if they chose to brave the displeasure of a Viceroy who could only rebuke them for past offences and warn

* Chesney; Strachey.

them not to offend again. One school of Anglo-Indian statesmen
had proposed to invest the Local Governments with power to raise
and spend their own revenues, on condition of remitting a certain
sum for Imperial purposes to the Imperial Treasury. Others,
including Sir Richard Temple, were for combining the principle
of a common fund with the concession to Local Governments of
enlarged powers of control over certain heads of administrative
outlay. In 1868 Lawrence accepted the principle of Temple's
scheme. But the last weeks of his rule were fast expiring, and
he had no wish to hamper his successor's free choice. In due
time Lord Mayo's mind was thoroughly made up. His resolution
of the 14th of December, 1870, proclaimed the right of the Provincial Governments to spend for certain purposes, at their own
discretion and responsibility, the sums yearly payable to each in
fixed proportions from the common fund. Under this new charter
of the Local Governments, as explained at greater length in
Temple's Budget-Statement of the following March, each Government was to receive thenceforth a fixed yearly allotment, ranging
from £207,000 for Oudh to £1,169,000 for Bengal, towards defray-
ing the cost of jails, police, education, printing, roads, civil buildings, and other local works, sanitary improvements, and some other
items formerly supervised by the Central Government. On these
services each Government was to regulate its own expenditure
within limits carefully defined. Without the Viceroy's sanction,
for instance, it might not make a new appointment worth more
than Rs. 250 a month, or raise the pay of any officer above that
sum.

If the money allotted to any province fell short of its actual
needs, its Government was empowered to make up the difference
as best it could by some form of local taxation. Each Government found itself free at last to frame its own Budget in accordance with certain plain rules. The yearly allotment to be shared
among the several provinces was fixed at five millions sterling.
Each Government was made responsible for the due management
of its own finances, and warned to expect no further help from
the Imperial Treasury in the event of its outlay exceeding
its income. By such means the Viceroy hoped to secure
due guarantees for thrift in provincial finance, to remove
one fruitful cause of disagreement between the Supreme and
Local Governments, to give the latter free room for developing
the fiscal resources and fostering the political growth of their
respective provinces. On the last-named points, indeed, the

Resolution of December laid strong emphasis in a passage penned by Lord Mayo himself:—"Local interest, supervision, and care are necessary to success in the management of funds devoted to Education, Sanitation, Medical Charity, and Local Public Works. The operation of this Resolution, in its full meaning and integrity, will afford opportunities for the development of self-government, for strengthening municipal institutions, and for the association of natives and Europeans to a greater extent than heretofore in the administration of affairs."*

Lord Mayo's great experiment proved erelong a genuine success. The Provincial Governments made no new demands on the Imperial Treasury, nor were they tempted to increase their revenues by new taxation without due regard to their actual needs and obligations. At the end of five years the Provincial Revenues from all sources, except the Imperial Grant, amounted only to about two millions, half of which was derived from new taxes on land, houses, and local trades. In some provinces the new system was at first regarded with deep mistrust, as a new device for extracting money from the greatest number of pockets for purposes which few people cared to comprehend. The landholders, especially in Bengal, kicked against any attempt to educate the people or improve the roads with the help of a small cess upon their lands. The people at large had not yet forgotten the smart of an income-tax at three per cent. In time, however, as these wounds began to heal, the tax-paying classes came to acquiesce in a system which brought the Provincial rulers into closer harmony with the ruled, impelling the former to adapt their measures to the bent of native habitudes, and encouraging the latter to make their voices heard a little in matters that specially concerned themselves.†

At the end of three years, by dint of careful economy, Lord Mayo had reduced to 47 millions the expenditure, which in 1869 stood at 50¾ millions. In 1868, the last year of Lord Lawrence's rule, it had risen as high as 54 millions. The revenue for 1871 amounted to 50 millions, or a million and a third below that of the previous year. The accounts for the last two years of Lord Mayo's rule showed an aggregate surplus of four millions and a half, three millions of which must be credited to 1871 alone. The Viceroy's strivings after economy, if not more earnest than those of his famous predecessor, proved more successful, partly because he came after Lawrence, partly because he had to reckon with fewer opponents, whether in India or at home.

* Hunter ; Temple ; Strachey.   † Temple ; Statistical Abstract for 1877.

Indian finance, he said, was "very sick;" but he hoped in two years to make it well again. His medicines, however nasty, would avert worse suffering thereafter, if taken in good time. In order to keep out of debt, he would stick at no retrenchment, however unpopular, that got rid of "useless people and unnecessary offices." No outcries, nor any regard for old use and wont, deterred him from carrying on the war against unthrift and extravagance, in whatever shape or guise.[*]

One of his heaviest onslaughts in this war was aimed at the Department of Public Works. This department, of which Colonel Richard Strachey was Chief Engineer, the Viceroy had early taken under his own charge. In every branch of a service which had spent twelve millions in two years on "ordinary" works alone, he found a number of defects, due either to a faulty system, or to the men employed in working it. Of the new barracks, which were costing so many millions, some were far too palatial for the needs of a dry soil and a good climate; others were built so badly, or on such weak foundations, as to prove unfit for human, if not for any use. In the same way some of the new civil buildings were either disastrous failures or costly redundances. In most cases the actual cost far exceeded the original estimates. The excess of actual over estimated outlay rose sometimes to a hundred per cent. In one case it grew from £18,000 to more than £100,000. Again and again had Lord Mayo to read the same "deplorable history of negligence, incapacity, corruption;" negligence on the part of superintending officers, incapacity in their subordinates, and corruption among the contractors who undertook the works. Again and again he had to deal out his stern but just rebukes of the waste, the blunders, the misdeeds, and the shortcomings which his own inquiries and the reports of competent witnesses brought to light. Of one great public work he declared that almost every fault which could have been committed in its construction was to be found there, from a bad design and an ill-chosen site to "estimates a hundred per cent. wrong." He could find "no word strong enough to condemn the utter recklessness" revealed in another case that seemed to him "little short of wholesale robbery." The report which he read on certain barracks was "quite dreadful. There is not a man referred to who seems to have done his duty, except one, who was unmercifully snubbed."[†]

From strong words the Viceroy proceeded to decisive action.

* Hunter.   † Ibid.

In the course of two years he cut down the expenditure on ordinary works by nearly two millions. The stoppage or the postponement of unnecessary undertakings, the abolition of useless appointments, and the enforcement of a wise economy throughout the great "spending department" were the visible fruits of this reform. He forbade the building of any more palatial barracks in the plains, because for one thing he hoped to see more regiments quartered in the hills. He ordered the Department to furnish proper estimates of every scheme which he might be asked to sanction. He insisted that many works should not be undertaken at one time under one management by a staff inadequate for such a need. No wonder, indeed, that so many things were done badly under a system which made it difficult to do even one thing well. It was impossible for the most active Engineer to be in two places at once, to toil all day over his accounts, his plans, and his correspondence, and yet fulfil the many outdoor duties of a working overseer. Lord Mayo himself had seen with his own eyes the marked difference in this respect between works conducted by a private company and some of those undertaken by the Public Works Department. In the one case might be seen two or three English gentlemen standing out in the hot sun to control and stimulate the labours of the native workmen; in the other he saw only a gang of workmen doing as much or as little as they pleased. The engineer in charge was away at his office, and his subordinate had other works to look after in the same district.

"Good supervision and one thing at a time" was Lord Mayo's avowed aim. For this end, in 1871 he decreed that a number of first-class military works should no longer be "carried on in different parts of the country at one and the same time." Such a system had been at the best a costly makeshift for the purpose of meeting a large and sudden demand. Thenceforth a few of the more important works were to be placed under a picked staff of experienced engineers, who, after pressing them rapidly to completion, might be transferred to some other undertaking next in order of importance. There remained some military works which the Local Governments would take in hand. To these also the Viceroy applied the principle of adequate supervision under one responsible head.[*]

While Lord Mayo's drugs and blisters were doing their work on the engineering service in India, the Duke of Argyll was en-

* Hunter.

gaged in furthering the same object by a course of tonic treatment applied from home. The supply of recruits from England to meet the growing needs of the Public Works Department had fallen of late years below the mark, in respect of quality, if not of numbers. Some of them had all their work to learn when they landed in India. Under the Duke's auspices a training college for civil engineers was founded at Cooper's Hill in Surrey, amidst the fair landscapes of which an English poet once sang so pleasantly. For its worthy President he chose Colonel George Chesney of the old Bengal Engineers, whose work on " Indian Polity " had already stamped him as a wise, weighty, clear-headed reasoner from a mass of carefully-digested facts. Before they passed out of college, his pupils had to undergo a careful training, which thoroughly fitted them, as the events showed, for their future career.*

Meanwhile, in India, Lord Mayo was cutting out work for his engineers on the new system of State Railways which he had resolved to take in hand. When Lord Lawrence left the country about 4,000 miles of railway had been opened by Dalhousie's guaranteed companies, at an average cost of about £17,000 a mile, or double that foreseen by Dalhousie himself. The balance of interest payable to the shareholders on account of the guaranteed five per cent. came up to a million and three-quarters a year. It is needless here to repeat the reasons which induced the Court of Directors to accept the principle of a State guarantee for undertakings that might have been more cheaply prosecuted by the State itself. But in applying Dalhousie's principle the Court withdrew the safeguards by which he set most store; and the guaranteed companies were not slow to profit by the door thus opened to unthrift and carelessness at the public cost. Another source of wasteful outlay was the joint control wielded by officers of railway companies and the State. In theory the Government Director at home and the Consulting Engineers in India overlooked and moulded every detail of railway management, from the planning out of a given line to the fixing of fares and times for running the trains. Other officers of Government were paid to examine and audit the railway accounts. For almost every step in the making or the managing of a railway the Government, in short, were outwardly responsible. But the difference between theory and practice was very great. As a rule the companies contrived to take their own way; and State control too often be-

* Thornton.

came a mere synonym for time and money wasted in vain efforts
to save both. In the conflict of rival interests the power which
claimed the right of veto was no match for the power that found
the money and carried on the business. Divided counsels resulted
only in untoward delays; the desired checks on waste and mismanagement proved nearly useless; and the country had to pay
for two sets of establishments employed in doing the work of
one.*

Lord Lawrence, prompted or encouraged by Colonel Strachey,
had strongly upheld the policy of exchanging a system so imper-
fect for the cheaper system of railways made and managed by the
State. Lord Mayo, in his turn, accepted the new principle as the
one most likely to avert "financial difficulties of the most serious
and dangerous character." The conclusion to which he came,
after much inquiry, he prepared with his usual vigour to carry
out. Leaving the guaranteed companies to fulfil their own mission
within certain specified bounds, he reserved for the State those
wide tracts of country for which no line of railway had as yet
been sanctioned or begun. His zeal for economy carried him yet
further out of the old tracks. The standard gauge of an Indian
railway, as fixed for good reasons by Lord Dalhousie, was five feet
six inches. For this, in agreement with Colonel Strachey, he resolved to substitute the "metre" gauge of three feet three inches,
on most of the lines undertaken by the State. "Cheap railways
or none" was the burden of all he wrote or said on this matter.
The prospect of saving several thousand pounds a mile, by means
of State railways lightly built on a narrow gauge, emboldened the
Viceroy to disregard the pleadings of merchants who deprecated
a break of gauge, of engineers who denied the essential cheapness
of any particular gauge, and of all who contended that the standard gauge was the best suited alike for military and commercial
needs. In spite of the resistance offered by some members of his
own Council, he carried the vote which enabled him, with the
Duke of Argyll's ready sanction, to decree the making of a cheap
railway line from Agra to Ajmir, and of another from Lahór towards
Peshuwar. By the end of 1871 nine hundred miles of State railway had been put in hand, mostly on the metre-gauge, in Rájputána, the Panjáb, and Berár.†

In the interests of a wise economy, of an economy which recognized
waste in excessive saving as well as in excessive outlay, Lord Mayo
strove to cut down the military charges to the lowest point compat-

* Chesney; Thornton; Hunter.　　　† Hunter; Thornton; Temple.

ible with the public well-being.   Out of a net available revenue of
about thirty millions he found that more than one-half was absorbed
by the net expenditure on the Indian armies.   The Duke of Argyll
himself was calling loudly for retrenchments to the extent, if possible, of a million and a half.   This, however, was easier said than
done.   What the Indian Government could do in this direction,
Lord Mayo and his colleagues, including Sir Henry Durand, Lord
Sandhurst, and his successor, Lord Napier, certainly did.   They
abolished a number of needless posts in the Army Departments
and the Staff.   They proposed to save half a million a year on the
cost of our British troops and batteries, without any loss of
numerical strength or military completeness, and without docking
the pay of a single officer or man.   " We have not one British
soldier too many," wrote the Viceroy, rejoicing in the prospect of
saving perhaps a million, " without giving up one of the little
white-faced men in red."   To this end he wanted to reduce the
number of regiments and batteries serving in India, and to increase
the strength in non-commissioned officers and privates of those
that remained.   Such an arrangement would involve no loss of
real efficiency in any respect.

In the same way he proposed to deal with the Native Army of
Bengal, not a man of which could be spared from the rank and
file.   With regard to the armies of Madras and Bombay, which
seemed too large for any existing need, he sought merely to reduce
their total strength alike in regiments and men.   The whole of
these measures taken together would have resulted in an aggregate saving of about a million a year.   But the Minister for India
could not see his way to accepting in full a scheme of retrenchment against which many powerful influences in the War Office,
the Horse Guards, and the Indian Council were sure to fight.
The claims of power, patronage, sentiment, vested interests, and
social privilege, were too strong for Lord Mayo and the Duke of
Argyll.   In vain did the Viceroy plead against compelling the
people of India to "contribute one farthing more to military
expenditure than the safety and defence of the country absolutely
demand."   The proposed reductions in the Staff and Army
Departments were allowed; but those in the British forces were
confined to two regiments each of horse and foot, with no addition to the rank and file of the remainder.   While the policy of
reducing the native armies was admitted, the mode of enforcing
that policy remained a vexed question at the time of Lord Mayo's
death.   It was something, however, to have succeeded in saving

even half a million for more peaceful purposes, with little, if any, loss of working strength.*

Another of his economic schemes involved a thorough reform of the Salt Department, and a gradual lowering of the salt-duties in Bengal and Upper India to the level of Bombay and Madras. The Salt Tax is a barbarous relic of the days when almost everything in India was taxed by the Moghals. In those days, however, the tax seems never to have risen above eight annas, or a shilling, the *maund* of 82 pounds. It was left for English statesmen of the nineteenth century to raise it higher and higher, until in some provinces it amounted to three rupees eight annas, and yielded in Lord Mayo's time five millions and a half clear. The average official mind looked with favour on an impost so easy to collect, so rich in assured profit, and so hard to replace by any other; on a poll-tax to which every one paid his share according to the amount of salt consumed by himself and his family. There were those, however, who held that the financial gains from such an impost were dearly purchased by a host of attendant drawbacks. The difference between the prime cost of salt made in India and the price which a struggling ráyat or a half-starved coolie had to pay for it often exceeded the difference between a shilling and a pound. So heavily did the burden fall on the poorer millions, that thousands of fishermen could not afford to buy salt for curing their fish, and myriads of ráyats had to stint their cattle, if not even their own families, of what for men and cattle seemed as necessary as their daily food. Lord Lawrence himself had often declared that the " enormous rate " of the salt-duties limited the consumption not only by human beings, but still more by the cattle, whose decimation by murrain he ascribed mainly to the want of salt. In 1871 the natives of Bombay petitioned the House of Commons for some relief from a tax which prevented large numbers of the people " from procuring more than half the quantity absolutely required for health." An eminent Scotch minister, Dr. Wilson, who had lived forty years in Bombay, declared before a Parliamentary Committee that, for want of cheap salt, many people were driven to use wild spices with their food, and to cure their fish by means of tamarind-juice. Even wild spices must have been less unwholesome than the saline earth with which many more have been known to allay their craving for the purer but less attainable condiment. For want

* Hunter ; Strachey.

of pure cheap salt not only cattle but human beings have died like flies, in seasons of unwonted sickness or distress.*

Nor was this by any means all the harm done. The Government monopoly had to be enforced by stern laws against smuggling and illicit manufacture of salt. To be guilty of extracting a little untaxed salt by the rudest process from the sea-wave or the salt-lake, from the floor or wall of a mud-cabin, or from the refuse of a saltpetre yard, was to incur the penalty of a fine, a flogging, or imprisonment for many days. The like penalties awaited him who tried to smuggle the cheaper salt of Madras across the frontier into Bengal. An impenetrable hedge of prickly thorns, stretching for eighteen hundred miles across India, and patrolled at all points by a preventive police, formed not only an effective barrier against illicit trade, but a serious hindrance to all kinds of internal traffic, and a source of untold annoyance to the people on either side. A whole army of revenue underlings preyed upon their helpless countrymen under cover of the powers entrusted to them for the service of the State. In Oudh our heavy salt-duties and sternly repressive laws killed the old local manufacture of salt, as soon as that province passed under our rule. The use of salt as manure had become impossible for the Indian husbandman, who would have to pay at least ten pounds a ton for that which cost the British farmer no more than fifteen shillings.† Both trade and agriculture were starved, and millions of men and cattle doomed to disease and premature death, in order that the Government might draw a net revenue of five millions.

Some, at least, of these evils Lord Mayo sought to redress at no cost to the Indian Revenues. His schemes for abolishing the inland customs lines and for equalizing the salt-duties all over India were left over for accomplishment under later Viceroys. But his attempts to lower the prime cost of salt, to cheapen its carriage and remove some of the hindrances to inland trade, were crowned with a certain measure of success. He improved the working of the salt mines in the Panjáb, and opened out new roads thence to the central marts. He tried to restore the salt-manufactures of Oudh. He persuaded the rulers of Jáipur and Jodhpur to grant his Government a lasting lease of the great Sámbhar Lake in Rájputána, whose boundless supplies of salt would erelong be carried cheaply across the Jamna by the new lines of State railway running from the Lake to Agra and Delhi. Such measures went

---

* *The Nineteenth Century* for July, 1883 ; *Allen's Mail.*

† Hunter ; Temple ; Pogson's "Agriculture for India."

some way towards lightening the burden of a tax which no sane Englishman would dream of imposing now for the first time, and which no honest Viceroy would shrink from repealing, if only something better, but not less productive, could be found to take its place.*

* Hunter; Strachey.

CHAPTER III.

EDUCATION AND PUBLIC WORKS.

IN the last days of 1869 the *Galatea* frigate steamed up the Húghli, bearing her commander, Prince Alfred, Duke of Edinburgh, thus far on his voyage round the world. It was the first time that a Prince of the English blood-royal had ever visited the broad empire which a trading company had won for the British Crown. The landing of our Sailor Prince in Calcutta on the 22nd of December marked the first stage of a truly royal progress which lasted about three months; a progress which, says Lord Mayo's biographer, "called forth a burst of loyalty such as had never before been awakened in the history of our rule." To such a guest no Viceroy could have played the host with more splendid courtesy and genial grace than did the frank, good-humoured, sympathetic Irish Earl who entertained him at Government House. Lord Mayo's taste for pageantry shone out at the great Darbár held on the Calcutta Maidán, where a splendid and picturesque array of Indian princes and high English officers was gathered from all parts of the country to see the son of their common Sovereign invested with the Star of India. The Prince was royally feasted by the native gentry of Calcutta. Hospitable Rajahs on his way up the country amused him with sport of various kinds. The great cities of Upper India received him with all befitting enthusiasm. His visit to Lucknow was glorified by a brilliant gathering of loyal Tálukdárs. On the 7th of March, 1870, Prince Alfred played his part at Jabalpur in the ceremonial opening of the railway line that links the commercial capital of the Central Provinces with Bombay and Allahábád. The rich and populous capital of Western India entertained him for several days with a splendour worthy of the occasion; nor was Madras at all behindhand in her efforts to amuse and honour the departing guest.*

* Hunter; Temple; *Allen's Mail.*

Viewed from the decorative side, as a piece of State pageantry, the Prince's visit to India was a conspicuous success. It pleased his countrymen also to read in the welcome which everywhere greeted him the manifestations of a growing loyalty towards the Sovereign whose living presence seemed for the time embodied in the form and movements of her son. His intercourse with the Native Chiefs and Princes would surely tend, they hoped, to strengthen the bonds of goodwill and common interests between the ruling and the subject races. How far such hopes were verified it is impossible to say for certain, in view of the gulf of habit, thought, and feeling which divides the Eastern from the Western world. Even princes cannot work miracles, nor have Irishmen learned as yet to love our rule. In India the multitude cherished a wild belief that their Royal visitor had come to remove the income-tax which Lord Mayo had so lately doubled. The wealthier and more educated classes may have accepted the Prince's visit as a fresh proof of his Royal mother's goodwill towards her Indian realms. The princes and the nobles may have found their loyalty quickened by renewed assurances of the friendly interest which India's Empress, speaking through her son, displayed in all that concerned their personal and political welfare. In grateful memory of Prince Alfred's visit the leading Natives in many parts of the country subscribed large sums for the founding of institutions such as the Sailors' Home at Bombay. Loyal effusions in prose and verse filled the columns of many a native newspaper. But the impartial observer will continue to doubt whether one-half of the good things predicted from the visit of an English Prince to India has ever come to pass. It is never safe to argue from the feelings of a people ruled by men of their own race, to those of a people who have nothing in common with their foreign lords. Nobody would think of judging the ordinary state of a man's health by merely feeling his pulse when it has risen to fever-pace.

In the spring of 1870 Sir Donald Macleod, the upright and widely-honoured ruler of the Panjáb, turned his face homewards, sped by the farewell blessings of a whole people. His place was presently taken by the soldier-statesman, Sir Henry Durand, whose varied services and high character had long since marked him out as worthy of any prize that Fate and the Indian Government might bring within his reach. But the new career thus opened to the Military Member of Lord Mayo's Council was too soon to to be cut short. In the last days of December the new Lieutenant-Governor lay dying at a lonely post on the Panjáb frontier. In the dusk of a December evening the elephant on which Durand rode was entering the gateway of the little fort of Tánk. The arch proved too low for so tall a beast, and Durand was violently thrown from his howdah to the ground. A lighter man might have received a smaller hurt, but the effect on Durand, with his tall broad figure and "grand appearance," was fatal. For a few days he lingered paralyzed with a broken neck; and on the first day of 1871 he ceased to breathe. His successor in the Government of the Panjáb was Sir Robert Davies, who had risen from one post to another in that province ever since the day when John Lawrence became its Chief Commissioner.[*]

In the latter part of 1870 Sir William Grey resigned the Government of Bengal. Lord Mayo's choice of a successor fell upon Sir George Campbell, a shrewd, active, hardworking, busy-brained Scotch gentleman, who had done good service in many parts of India, had conducted an important inquiry into the Orissa Famine, had sat in the High Court of Bengal, and governed the Central Provinces in a manner worthy of Temple himself. In this new field of usefulness Campbell's reforming energy soon had full play. The principle of Grey's policy had always been to let sleeping dogs lie, to rest contentedly on the old ways, whether they were bad or good. He had shrunk even from touching the question of local cesses for the maintenance of roads and schools. And he had made no effort to improve and extend the system of primary instruction for the millions of Bengal. To Campbell, on the other hand, no innovation seemed amiss that promised to abate or remove some manifest evil, or to supply an undoubted want. With the courage of his convictions, he hastened to pass through his Council a bill for levying those rural cesses which the landholders vainly denounced as oppressive, needless, and unfair. Under his strong impulsion a regular census of the oldest of our Indian provinces was successfully taken for the first time in the beginning of 1872. He founded in Calcutta a Medical School for the training of Native assistants in hospitals and dispensaries. He infused new life into every branch of the public service; lightened the work of the district officers by sub-dividing their districts and materially strengthening their Native staff; and compelled all Native candidates for civil employ to undergo a competitive examination, which tested alike their mental and their bodily powers.[†]

[*] Temple ; *Allen's Mail.* [†] Temple ; Hunter ; *Allen's Mail.*

Nowhere did the zeal and energy of the new Lieutenant-Governor yield more memorable fruit than in the field of educational reform. His efforts in this direction needed no prompting from Lord Mayo, who found him ready and eager to attack the problems which his predecessor had left untouched. The Viceroy and the Lieutenant-Governor were heartily at one in their dislike of the "filtration theory," under which a few hundred Bengáli Bábus, most of whom could have paid for their own schooling, obtained a good English education at great expense to the State. It was fondly hoped that the knowledge thus imparted to these gentlemen would somehow filter downwards into the untaught millions of Bengal. While the policy announced in the Despatch of 1854 was being steadily enforced in Bombay and the North-West, in Bengal the cause of primary instruction had been left almost wholly to shift for itself. For want of State-help, and of pupils who could afford to pay something for their schooling, the old indigenous *patshálas*, or rural schools, were fast disappearing before the growth of high schools and colleges; and the millions were starved of their mental food for the benefit of a favoured few who had little need of help from the State, and whose chief ambition, as Lord Mayo contended, was to "qualify for Government employ."

All this Sir George Campbell set himself forthwith to amend in the spirit of the Despatch of 1854. Of the money which had formerly been lavished on the higher education a large part was thenceforth reserved for primary instruction. With the further help derived from the local cesses he brought many an old patshála under Government control, founded a number of good village schools, and furnished them with schoolmasters properly trained for their work. In the course of three years and a half Bengal was covered with primary schools, and the number of pupils receiving help from the State had risen from 163,854 to 400,721. Meanwhile the higher education had suffered no real loss from a reform effected at a cost comparatively trifling; the whole yearly charge on State funds having grown from £186,598 to no more than £228,151.*

There was one large section of the people of Bengal which still reaped but little benefit from any system of State-aided schooling. According to the census of 1872 the Mohammadans of Bengal proper numbered nearly twenty millions against thirty-nine million Hindus and two million of other creeds. The bulk of these Mohammadans were sprung from Hindu or low-caste converts to

* Hunter; Temple; Bengal Administrative Report for 1873.

Islám. Only a few families here and there represented the old
Pathán and Moghal invaders of Bengal. In the northern and
eastern districts, from Bahár to the Bay of Bengal, Musalman husbandmen, traders, artisans, boatmen, fishermen, chiefly abounded.
Their religious training, such as it was, the frequent preachings
of fanatic Mullahs, and the memories of old Mohammadan greatness,
combined to keep nearly all classes of these people from sending
their children to Government schools where every teacher was a
Hindu, and where little if any of the learning dear to a good
Mohammadan was taught. From these and other causes it happened that Bengal could show no more than 14,000 Musalman
scholars against 100,000 Hindus. And, as few Mohammadans
below the highest class had the means or the energy to bring up
their sons on Arabic, Urdú, or Persian lore, it happened further
that the Hindus were fast expelling their religious rivals not only
from the public service, but from the lucrative professions of
medicine and the law.*

"In no Province," wrote Lord Mayo, "except perhaps in the
North-West Provinces and the Panjáb, do the Mohammadans
adequately, or in proportion to the rest of the community, avail
themselves of the educational advantages that the Government
offers." It appeared, moreover, that certain funds bequeathed by
Musalman donors for the special good of students of their own
faith had been applied to other than Mohammadan uses. To
many a devout believer in Islám the knowledge of these things was
embittered by a growing conviction that Fortune and the British
Government were leagued against him in favour of the once
despised and neglected Hindu. The flame of discontent was fed
by Wahábi plotters at Patna working through friends and emissaries in other parts of Bengal. Lord Mayo brought the strong
arm of law to bear upon a movement whose leaders the police were
engaged in tracking out. In the course of 1871 several of the chief
plotters, including Amir Khán, a Mohammadan merchant of great
age, were arraigned for treason before the High Court of Calcutta.
They were defended by Chisholm Anstey of the Bombay Bar, with all
the zeal, eloquence, and daring which nine years earlier had marked
his defence of Karsundás Mulji, the high-minded native gentleman
who dared to expose the bestial immoralities practised by the
Mahárája Brahmans of Bombay.† But the best efforts of a pleader

---

* Hunter ; Statistical Abstract.

† Karsundás was tried before the High Court of Bombay in 1862 for libelling the
"Mahárájas," a Hindu sect whose religion was a cloak for the most licentious

who carried his privilege of free speech to the brink of license, failed to avert or mitigate the doom of men convicted on fair trial of the crime alleged. Amir Khán and his accomplices were transported for life to the Andaman Islands, and Wahábi disaffection to all appearance soon died out.[*]

Before the trials were over, an event happened which startled our countrymen in Calcutta with strange foreshadowings of a new danger lurking in their midst. One morning in October Mr. Norman, the acting Chief Justice, was going up the stairs of the Court-House, when a native accosted him with a written paper in his hand. As the Judge stopped to look at the proffered paper, a knife gleamed in the air, and in another moment he fell stabbed to the death by a fanatic prepared to spend himself freely in the hope of saving his fellow-plotters from their imminent doom. Such at least was the murderer's confession before he underwent the last penalty of his bootless crime.[†]

In all such stirrings of Mohammadan disaffection Lord Mayo found but stronger reasons for just and generous dealing with a people who formed one-third of the whole population of Bengal; who possessed a classical literature of no mean order, studied and taught by a special class of learned men; and who numbered among them not a few gentlemen noted, like Saiyid Amir Ali, for choice and varied scholarship, or, like Abdul-Ghani, for zeal in diffusing knowledge and doing good. If he might not hope to win the loyalty of all his Mohammadan subjects, he would try at least to leave their leaders no fair excuse for plotting against our rule. As some concession to Mohammadan prejudices, he proposed in one of his Viceregal Minutes to give Arabic, Persian, and Urdu, the classical and vernacular languages of Moslem India, "a more prominent place in many of our schools and examination tests." He would offer grants in aid of Urdú as well as Bengáli schools, would open out classes and scholarships for Mohammadan students in Government colleges, and make room for qualified teachers of the same sect in some of the schools where English was specially taught. And he invited the Local Governments to consider how these and such-like reforms might best be furthered

practices. After a long trial Sir Joseph Arnould summed up strongly in favour of the defendant, whom he extolled as a public benefactor. The verdict of acquittal was hailed with approval by the native press of Bombay.

[*] Temple ; Hunter ; *Allen's Mail.*

[†] Temple ; *Allen's Mail.*

with due regard for "the fundamental principles of our educational system."[*]

His efforts in this cause were strongly seconded by Sir George Campbell, who applied to the maintenance of Mohammadan schools and colleges certain funds bequeathed by Mohammadans for the good of their own community. Lord Napier of Ettrick and Sir William Muir gave practical answers to the Viceroy's appeal on behalf of the Musalman minority in Southern India and the North-West Provinces. In due time the reforms projected by Lord Mayo were successfully carried out under a Viceroy who lived to consummate the good work which Lord Mayo had begun.

Few of India's chief rulers have ever taken so keen and practical an interest as did Lord Mayo in the due development of her productive wealth. From the first he saw clearly how much of India's progress in wealth and civilization would depend for years to come on her progress in agriculture. To the eyes of a Viceroy who studied the Indian problem by the light of early experiences gained in the working of an Irish farm,[†] the main factor in the future growth of Indian trade was to be found in the improved and extended outturn of old agricultural staples, and the cultivation of new products useful for manufacture or the industrial arts. What has been done of late years with Indian tea, coffee, cotton, jute, oil-seeds, cinchona, might be assayed, he thought, with like success in new directions, if the Government as chief landlord would only point the way to private enterprise, and enable a thrifty, hardworking peasantry to reap some adequate return for all their toil. His earliest wanderings about the country had taught him to discern "an enormous field, not exactly for the reform, but for the investigation of husbandry in India." Further inquiries only deepened his conviction that a special department of Agriculture and Trade was imperatively needed in a country where the State alone can, as a rule, command the knowledge and the capital requisite for educing the full productive powers of the land.[‡]

The great mass of native husbandmen, weighed down by poverty and debt, by the strength of old traditions and the strictness of

---

[*] Hunter.

[†] When he came of age, his father, then Mr. Bourke, rented him one of his farms, out of which young Richard Bourke made enough to pay the cost of attending Parliament for several years—(Hume's "Agricultural Reform in India").

[‡] Hunter.

our land-revenue rules, could do little of themselves for the improvement of their paternal acres. They were too poor even to make full use of the practical knowledge handed down by their forefathers through ages past. They knew all about deep ploughing and the virtue of simple manures, and could tell what kind of crops were best suited to each kind of soil. The right season for sowing, the evils of banks and hedges, the advantage of giving the land rest and of varying one crop with another, were all things of every-day cognizance. They were very careful to weed the growing crops and to gather in their harvests at the right moment. But poverty forced them to use for fuel the dung which should have enriched their fields; and their simple ploughs, which were drawn by weakly underfed cattle, could do little more than scratch the surface of the soil. Many of the peasantry in Western India and Bengal had lately proved their readiness to grow new staples, such as cotton and jute, which promised to enlarge their scanty earnings. But the Government which paid the debts of Maisúr Princes, and helped Oudh Tálukdárs to improve their estates, had done little as yet to aid the peasantry in their lifelong struggle with poverty, debt, hunger, injustice, and sheer despair. Vast numbers of plough-cattle were dying yearly from diseases induced or aggravated by unwholesome or deficient food. Want of manure and other causes had so impoverished the soil, that fourteen bushels an acre was the average outturn of wheat on lands which in Akbar's time had yielded nineteen bushels.*

"Agriculture"—wrote the Viceroy in 1869—"has been almost entirely neglected by the Government." Little good had come of the model farms set up here and there, and managed chiefly by amateurs who had a smattering of science and a short supply of funds. The new Department, as planned at first by Lord Mayo, would have gone far to repair the previous neglect. At its head he would have placed a Director-General, aided by a small staff of experts. A separate Director with a similar staff was to work under him in each province. Model farms and agricultural schools were to adapt the teachings of Western science to the wants and means of the native husbandman. In due time the revenue officers were to encourage the landholders in each district to form agricultural associations and to send their relatives to agricultural schools. The Directors and their Chief were to compile statistics, publish reports and summaries of the crops,

* Hume's "Agricultural Reform in India."

and do their best to develop the production of new commodities for foreign use.

The prime cost of creating such a department was reckoned at nearly a quarter of a million pounds. The same sum represented the net yearly cost of its maintenance. This was not a large price to pay for results so desirable; but in view of the difficulties that confronted him, the Viceroy was driven to modify his scheme of agricultural reform; to content himself with the cheap and modest makeshift implied in a new Secretariat for Revenue, Agriculture, and Commerce. The place of honour in this triad Lord Mayo had designed for Agriculture. But the Jupiter of the India Office willed otherwise. Revenue, wrote the Duke of Argyll, in 1871, was clearly of the first importance; and to Revenue therefore the official title of the new department gave thenceforward the first place. For its first Secretary Lord Mayo chose Mr. Allan Hume, a civil officer of long standing, who had done good service during the Mutiny, had instructed and amused himself for many years past by managing a little farm of his own in the North-West Provinces, and had carefully studied the best English and German works on the theory and practice of agriculture.

To the new Department were transferred many of the duties hitherto discharged or supervised by the Home, Financial, and Military Members of Council. The new Secretary and his staff had to deal with all questions touching the land-revenue and the local taxes on land, the various surveys and explorations, the inland customs and salt manufactures, the collection of statistics, the development of industry, science and art, the protection of emigrants, the improvement of agriculture, and the fostering of trade. The management of forests, fisheries, and municipal finance was also placed under Mr. Hume's control. With his hands thus full of multifarious business, it is not surprising that he found little time to further the special reforms on which Lord Mayo and himself had set their hearts. A Secretary whose office work tied him to his desk for eight or ten hours a day, a Minister for Agriculture who had no experts to advise him, no agents to work for him in different places, no money to lay out on needful experiments, would have small chance of developing any noteworthy change in the habits, aims, and mental appliances of Indian husbandmen.

Much good work, indeed, of various kinds was done by the new Department during the ten years of its brief existence. It published a series of reports and treatises on silk, tobacco, sorghum, the blue gum-tree, on several kinds of grain, fibres, dyes, spices, gums, and so forth. It started a few experimental farms, an inquiry into the causes of opium blight in Bahár, and a number of experiments with Rheea grass, bamboo, Manilla hemp, and other fibres useful for various purposes. It did something to encourage the breeding of sheep in Burmah, of cattle in Maisúr, and of horses in the Panjáb. It made some noteworthy attempts to deal with the deadlier forms of cattle disease, and to improve or extend the production of coffee, cotton, useful trees, and Tasar silk. But for any kind of agricultural progress the practical outcome of Lord Mayo's project and Mr. Hume's labours was exceedingly small. Compared with the good desired, it seemed to the latter like " the scratching of sparrows' feet to deep ploughing."*

" If we are not here for their good,"—the Viceroy once publicly said of the people of India—" we ought not to be here at all." In the spirit of these words, uttered at the opening of the Khámgaon Railway, he developed the large scheme of irrigation works which Lord Lawrence had set on foot in order to protect the people against famine. The progress made in this direction under Lord Mayo was very great. For the first time the Ganges Canal was yielding a clear profit. A canal designed to water the lower part of the Gangetic plain from Fathigarh to Allahábád was begun. Other canals were about to discharge the same office for Rohilkhand and Oudh. The Jamna system of canals was extended to the west and south-east of Delhi. From the Són river a new canal branched off into the thirsty province of Bahár. The irrigation works in Orissa were going steadily forward, and new branches were added to the Godávari system. In every part of India our engineers were engaged in planning or prosecuting similar works, the cost of which was defrayed by loans at the rate of three or four millions a year.†

In order that all such works might prove their usefulness by the amount of revenue they yielded to the State, Lord Mayo desired to levy a compulsory rate on the lands they would help to fertilize. He held it unfair to tax the community at large for the use of water supplied to particular districts. The people for whose benefit a canal was made should provide, at any rate, the yearly interest on the cost of making and maintaining it. Such was the principle adopted in other countries, and he could not see why " works constructed for the exclusive benefit of the Panjáb or the North-

---

* Hume ; Hunter ; Temple.   † Hunter ; Temple.

West should be paid for out of the pockets of the people of Madras and Bombay." Past experience had shown the futility of trusting to voluntary rates. In good seasons the husbandmen would contrive to do without canal-water. It was only in years of drought that a rush was made upon the canals, with results outlasting the momentary gain. A compulsory water-rate would have secured those results from the first. In spite of some grave objections to such a course, the Viceroy passed through his Council an Act for levying a compulsory cess for canals in the Panjáb from all husbandmen and landowners to whose fields the canal-water was brought. The cess was not to be levied until five years after the water had been placed within the husbandman's reach; nor even then if there was no certainty that his net profits, after paying the cess, would be increased by using the canal-water. The Act, however, was disallowed by the Duke of Argyll, who was against compelling the ráyats to pay for a boon of whose surpassing value he himself was not yet convinced.*

To ensure India against famine other things are needed besides tanks and canals, some of which, in dry seasons, may run short of the water they were expected always to supply. Irrigation may counteract a partial, it can never make up for a total, failure of the periodical rains. If one tract or province suffers from dearth, its neighbour is almost sure to rejoice in abundant harvests. If irrigation has not yet proved an unmixed blessing, the want of facilities for bringing food from places where it is cheap and plentiful to places where food happens to be scarce and dear, may be far more harmful than a long drought. India produces food enough from year to year for the maintenance of all her children, if it were so distributed as to reach all. For safeguarding the people against famine, roads and railways are at least as necessary as canals. In the matter of roads, the English rule had already bestowed on India benefits as great and lasting as the Roman rule had once bestowed on Gaul and Britain. Of late years the Local Governments had pushed on the work of road-making with marked success; and even Bengal, under the energetic Sir George Campbell, had begun to emulate the progress made in the Central and Upper Provinces.

With regard to railways, the progress, if far from rapid, was steadily sustained. Under Lord Mayo, a thousand miles were added to the four thousand completed before his time. The opening of the great bridge over the Satlaj in October, 1870, filled up

---

* Hunter ; Temple ; Thornton.

the last gap in the line of railway that linked Lahór with Alláhá-bád and Bombay. On the last day of the same year the Eastern Bengal Railway was completed to Goalanda, in Assam. By the end of 1871 only a link or two were wanting in the iron chain that binds Bombay to Madras. Several hundred miles of new line were in course of making for Oudh and Rohilkhand. In 1870 trains began to cover the whole distance from Lahór to Multán; but some years were yet to elapse before a continuous line of railway supplemented the slower process of river-traffic between Multán and Karáchi. On the guaranteed railways, taken as a whole, the Government had still to pay about two-fifths of the guaranteed interest, although the time was very near when the East Indian and one or two other lines would yield a net revenue of more than five per cent. Of the new State lines, only a few miles had been opened for traffic by the end of 1871; but these were already giving a new impulse to the cotton trade of Berár.*

* Hunter; Statistical Abstract; Indian Railway Report.

NOTE.

Sir Donald Macleod lost his life in 1872, through trying to enter a railway carriage on the Underground Line, just as the train was beginning to move. He missed his footing and got terribly crushed before help could reach him. The good old man lived only a few hours after the sad event which forestalled his appearance at a public meeting he had promised to attend.

CHAPTER IV.

LIKE many of his predecessors, Lord Mayo had a keen appetite for hard work, to the doing of which he brought a stock of bodily health and energy unsurpassed, if ever equalled, by any one of them, from Clive down to Lord Lawrence. His activity was amazing for a man of his large bulk. In the course of three years he had travelled more than twenty thousand miles, many hundreds of which were covered on horseback. His feats of endurance were worthy even of Akbar. One of his morning rides before breakfast would have been for most men in India a good day's work. Now galloping from one frontier post to another, anon inspecting the site for a new hill station or the works for a new railway or canal; one while opening a new line of railway in a cotton district, at another exchanging courtesies with the high-born princes of Rájputána or political talk with the Mahárája of Káshmir; wherever he went, he made all possible use of his own eyes and ears in aid of a quick intelligence and a memory well stored with illustrative facts. His hunger after new knowledge was matched by his insight into the kind of knowledge most suit-able for the public needs. On each of the provinces visited by him, the Viceroy left some impress of his strong but genial vitality, some bright remembrance not only of his care for every local interest, but of the tact, the frankness, the sympathetic charm of his intercourse with lesser men.*

"His public labours and anxieties," says Sir Richard Temple, "never dulled the warm sunshine of his manner towards all with whom he came in contact." His future biographer, Mr. W. Hunter, found it "impossible to work near him without loving him;" and Sir Fitzjames Stephen, who replaced Sir Henry Maine as Law-Member of the Viceroy's Council, has declared that he "never met one to whom he felt disposed to give such heartfelt affection and honour." That ineffable charm of manner which Sir

* Temple; *Allen's Mail.*

Charles Metcalfe alone of former Governor-Generals had possessed in the same degree, won for Lord Mayo a secure place in the hearts of those Native Chiefs and Princes who showed themselves worthy of the friendship offered by him to all alike. Some indeed there were who turned a deaf ear to the Viceroy's counsels, and refused to cultivate the goodwill of a ruler whose interference they resented as troublesome or ill-timed. One of these recalcitrants was the wayward Mahárája of Jodhpur, who had so lately been called to order by Sir John Lawrence. His behaviour at the Darbár which Lord Mayo held in 1870 had drawn upon him a fresh rebuke; but on so hardened a sinner rebukes and warnings were all thrown away. In the following year Lord Mayo held another of his grand Darbárs on the plain before Ajmir. To the assembled Princes and Chiefs of Rájputána the Viceroy, speaking through his interpreter, addressed some words of friendly exhortation touching the duties they owed the British Government in return for the rights and privileges assured to each of them by a Power "which only sought their good."*

Among the princes summoned to that brilliant gathering was the Mahárája of Jodhpur. But his Highness Takht Singh sat, like Achilles, sulking in his tent, while his peers were listening to the Viceroy's address. A question of precedence kept him away. He insisted on claiming the place of honour in any assembly of Rájput Princes, although that question had long since been formally decided in favour of Udaipur. Deaf to the remonstrances of the Political Agent and to the pleadings of his own son, he refused to sit in Darbár below the Rána of Udaipur. His absence on such an occasion was regarded by the Viceroy as a wanton insult to the Paramount Power. Lord Mayo ordered the offender to leave the camp at Ajmir with all his retinue with the first light of the following morning. No guns were fired at his departure, and two guns were afterwards taken from the number of his salute.†

In the affairs of another Rájput State, that of Alwar, Lord Mayo found himself driven to interfere. The young Rajah of Alwar, a small kingdom founded by a successful soldier in the latter half of the eighteenth century, had been going on from bad to worse ever since, in 1863, he took over the reins of power from a Council of Regency. In seven years Seodán Singh had squandered the savings of his minority, plunged the State heavily into debt and wild disorder, and provoked the bulk of his people into

---

* Temple; Hunter. † Malleson; *Allen's Mail.*

open rebellion against the rule of a drunkard, a libertine, a spend-thrift, a robber of public lands and religious endowments, a boon companion of *dakaits*, wrestlers, and low ruffians from the bazaars. He was in the habit of "drinking publicly with low Mohamma-dans, and getting drunk nearly every day." His Thákurs were about to depose him in favour of his infant son, when Lord Mayo decided to avert fresh evils by a timely exercise of his supreme power. A Council of State composed of the leading nobles was placed under the presidency of the British Agent, Major Cadell. To the Rajah himself was assigned a seat in the Council, with a liberal stipend for his personal and public wants. If that "mis-chievous and wily creature," as the Viceroy called him, should still prove incorrigible, he would thus, at any rate, be disabled from doing further harm. Under this arrangement Alwar soon recovered from the effects of past misrule. Peace and order were re-established with the aid of an improved police; the judges re-sumed their seats in the reopened courts; schools sprang up here and there; and the growing revenue sufficed erelong to pay off the public debt. Happily for his country the incorrigible Rajah died in 1874.*

Lord Mayo's impatience of misrule and anarchy in some of the Native States never blinded him to the unwisdom of arbitrary and niggling interference with their internal affairs. He impressed upon his Political Agents the absolute need of tact, forbearance, courtesy, and fixed rules in their intercourse with native princes and chiefs. He was for letting a well-governed state like Bhopál or Jaipur judiciously alone, while keeping a wary hand on those chiefs and princes who stood upon the right divine of kings to govern wrong. Even for the latter he made large allowance, as men whose vicious habits were mainly due to the defective train-ing of their earlier years. Brought up from childhood in the Zanána or the Háram, in the midst of influences hurtful to their moral and mental growth, they had small chance of learning any of the manlier and nobler lessons which help to mould the character of their Western compeers. It was not uncommon even for a prince of rare promise and good disposition to develop into a fierce tyrant or a reckless debauchee. In the hope of raising the stan-dard of life and culture among the princes and nobles of Rájás-thán, Lord Mayo founded at Ajmir a college in which their sons and relatives might receive a special training under English masters in the bodily and mental exercises of the West. Another

* Hunter; Malleson.

of these Indian Etons was opened at Rájkot in Káthiawár, a province ruled by one hundred and eighty-seven chiefs under the wise and fatherly control of Colonel Keatinge. The lads in these schools took kindly to athletic sports, and imbibed something of the manly spirit for which English schoolboys are commonly renowned.*

A school of the same kind had already been opened in one of the palaces at Maisúr for the sons of the nobles and chief officers in that State. Here, at the age of six, the little Rajah of Maisúr began in 1869 the course of instruction that might best prepare him for the task of governing his future kingdom. Under the guardianship of so able and accomplished an officer as Colonel Malleson, the adopted son of the shiftless Krishnaráj learned nearly everything taught in a good English school, or practised in the home of an old English squire. In the same year the youthful Rajah of Kolhápur left his Marátha home to cross the "dark water" on a finishing tour through Europe to the British Islands. But the damp cold of the West struck his vitals, and his death at Florence early in the following year cut short a life full of rare promise. In March of the same year the Rajah Randhir Singh of Kapurthalla, who had fought so bravely on our side during the Mutiny, sailed from Bombay on that visit to England upon which he had so long set his heart. But he had got no further than Aden when it became clear that his life also was very near its end. The disease from which he had long been suffering had taken a mortal turn, and the steamer that bore him home from Aden brought only his dead body back to Bombay.†

It was early in 1870 that Mr. James Fitzjames Stephen took his seat as Law-Member of the Viceroy's Council in the room of Sir Henry Maine. The new Minister's fame as a jurist and a masterly expounder of criminal law had gone before him to Calcutta, and his after services in India did full credit to the name he had already won. His first speech in Council brought out his talent for clear exposition and vigorous debate. His speech in favour of a road-cess for Bengal attested alike his energy in mastering the detailed history of the Perpetual Settlement, his firm grasp of the facts and principles embodied therein, and the strong common sense with which he met and refuted all the objections raised by the Bengal Zamindárs. Several of his speeches on other important measures stand forth as landmarks in the

---

* Hunter ; Temple ; Administration Reports.
† Malleson ; Lepel Griffin; *Allen's Mail.*

history of Indian law-making. That India should be governed on European principles was the first article of his political creed. Legislation he held to be good so far as it tended to enforce those principles on behalf of " peace, order, wealth, and progress in the arts and sciences," under a vigorous and firmly established rule. Only in cases of extreme necessity would he interfere with the social habits and religious opinions of the people ruled. No law should be enacted until the need for it had been clearly perceived and generally felt. But the political and social revolution evoked by our rule might be left to run its course unhindered, provided that we took all due care to guide it into proper channels for the production of good results.*

That the Government had faithfully tried to do its duty in this direction Mr. Stephen readily allowed. Nor did he find it fairly open to the charge of legislating too fast for the public weal. It was impossible, for instance, to refrain from frequent legislation touching questions of revenue and judicial procedure; while the number of new Acts dealing with other points of law and public policy had been surprisingly small. But the need of reducing the written and unwritten law of India to a compact and intelligible form, the need of clearing away a vast amount of surplusage and confusion from the Indian Statute Books, had not become the less urgent for all the progress made since the Mutiny in evolving light and order out of the legal chaos. At this task of condensing, re-moulding, and codifying the law as it then stood, Maine himself, with the aid of his able Secretary, Whitley Stokes, had laboured strenuously for six years past on the lines sketched out by the Law Commission which sat in London. To this task Stephen, in his turn, devoted his splendid energies with a success in some measure due to the helpful influence of Lord Mayo himself.

Of three great measures enacted by Lord Mayo's Government in 1872, two had been originally shaped and brought forward by Sir Henry Maine. One of these, the Act which codified the whole law on the subject of Evidence, was redrawn from beginning to end by Maine's successor with the happiest results. It supplied the civilian judges with a set of plain rules, which no sharp English barrister could thenceforth twist to his own advantage. What the Evidence Act of 1872 did for the law concerning evidence, the Contract Act, as revised by Stephen from the Bill first drafted in 1867, may be said to have done for the great mass of law concerning contracts. Act X. of 1872 embodied a number

* Temple ; Hunter.

of long-desired and carefully-weighed amendments in the Criminal Code. Another Act of the same year was the final outcome of a Bill prepared some years before by Maine, for the purpose of legalizing marriage between persons of a class at that time unknown to the law. The Hindu, the Musalman, the Jain, the Parsi, the Jew, and the Christian, each of these classes had the same legal standing in respect of marriage forms. But outside the circle of these protected creeds were growing up a number of sects and brotherhoods, whose marriages were held to be void' in law. Conspicuous among them was the reformed *Brahma Samaj*, or Church of Brahma, whose pious, learned, and eloquent leader, Kesháb Chandra Sen, had thrown off the last trammels of belief in the Vedic Scriptures, renounced caste ties, and preached a new eclectic Deism, founded on earnest faith in one Divine All-Father, and on grateful reverence for the truths taught by the great thinkers, poets, prophets, and evangelists of every age. In Lord Mayo's time Kesháb's followers already numbered many hundreds of educated men in various parts of India, many of whom had been duly married according to the ritual of the new Church. It was clearly for the public interest that the validity of such marriages should not be called in question. The new Marriage Act, as revised by Fitjzames Stephen, and passed soon after Lord Mayo's death, set that question finally at rest, not only for the Brahmist body, but for all dissentients from any of the older creeds.*

This was the last step in a series of enactments which, dating from 1850, aimed at securing equal rights of property and free action for all classes subject to our rule. In the same spirit of justice and humanity Lord Mayo's Government passed in 1870 an Act for preventing the murder of girl-children in those provinces where social usage still seemed to favour a practice so revolting to English ideas. Another Act, passed in the following year, sought by heavy penalties to restrain eunuchs in Upper India from getting boys into their hands for the purpose of pandering to the most unspeakable of human lusts. In 1870 a special amendment of the Penal Code assimilated the Indian to the English law against sedition. In 1871 was passed an important measure for the registration of criminal tribes in the North-West Provinces and the Panjáb. This Act empowered the police of those provinces to enforce against the Gújars, Mewáttis, and other tribes of hereditary thieves and rogues, the system of preventive control and inspection which the civil officers in the Panjáb had for many

* Hunter; Temple.

years past been working under no other law than the bidding of
the Local Government.

The Panjáb Land Revenue Act of 1871 expressed in clear and
concise terms the points of law which lay buried in a dense tangle
of rules, decrees, and regulations concerning the land revenue of
that province.   Thanks to Fitzjames Stephen's unwearied energy
and the help he received from various quarters, a strange medley
of chaotic principles and incoherent practices was thus for the
first time resolved into one comprehensible and systematic whole.
A Bill of the same purport was prepared under the same auspices
for Bengal. Among measures of little less importance was an
Act which provided fresh safeguards for the well-being of Coolie
emigrants to Ceylon, Mauritius, and other settlements beyond the
sea.   Another Act, inspired by Lord Mayo himself, sought to
relieve the Tálukdárs of Oudh from the financial straits in which
many of their number were still labouring.   It transferred all
heavily encumbered estates into the charge of special Courts
empowered to take steps for clearing off past encumbrances, and
to keep the estates meanwhile under careful nursing for their
owners' good.   Had the Courts been further allowed to sell at
need some slices of these large properties, which often amounted
to thirty, forty, or fifty thousand acres, the experiment might
have proved an untold blessing to the province at large.*

It was in 1860 that Lord Canning's Government had first
accepted as a public duty the task which for seventy years past
had devolved upon volunteer agents of two learned societies, the
Asiatic of Bengal and Bombay and the Literary of Madras.
From the days of Sir William Jones to those of Alexander
Cunningham, a brilliant succession of scholars and archæologists
had pushed their researches to the best of their means and opportunities in this or that field of antiquarian lore.   Immemorial
Cromlechs, Buddhist Topes, Cave Temples, Hindu Pagodas,
monumental pillars, old buildings of all kinds, old coins of every
age and dynasty, the sculptured, painted and written relics of past
centuries, gave up their precious secrets to such men as Cole-
brooke, Colin Mackenzie, Sykes, Horace Wilson, James Prinsep,
James Fergusson, Kitto, Walter Elliot, Alexander Cunningham,
Meadows-Taylor, and other workers in the same rich mine.   To
such as these we owe nearly all our limited knowledge of Indian
history before the Mohammadan Conquests.   But not till after
the Mutiny did the Government itself undertake a systematic

* Hunter ; Irwin.

survey of the field which private enterprise had been left thus casually to explore.

At the head of this Archæological Survey Lord Canning placed James Prinsep's old friend and workfellow General Cunningham, an engineer officer who, as scholar, antiquary, and numismatist, ranked with the best of his day. During the next five years the new Surveyor had carried his researches through nine of the ancient kingdoms of Hindustan; exploring ruined cities and recording old inscriptions from the Panjáb to Central India and Bengal. In 1866 Sir John Lawrence abolished the post of Archæological Surveyor, and Cunningham's labours came to a sudden stop. But they were not to cease altogether. The policy of preserving, describing, and taking casts or copies of all ancient monuments found strong advocates within the India Office; and before the end of 1870 the post of Archæological Surveyor had once more been entrusted to its former occupant, who was soon engaged in summarizing the results of past researches, and in drawing up a scheme of systematic inquiry for the guidance of those who were to work under him. Among the ablest of his future helpmates was Mr. Burgess, head of Sir Jámsatji Jijibhai's school at Bombay.*

In the region of Marine Surveys very little work had been done since the extinction of the old Indian Navy in 1862. Surveys already begun were left unfinished; and of the many new schemes, catalogued in that year by four of the old surveyors, not one had been taken in hand at the end of 1871. Nothing, in short, but a few local surveys of the Chittagong and Orissa coasts were added in those ten years to the good work done in past-times by the servants of the old East India Company.†

Meanwhile the great Trigonometrical Survey, begun by Colonel Lambton in 1800, and continued in turn by Sir George Everest and Sir Andrew Waugh, was steadily nearing completion under Colonel Walker, who succeeded Waugh in 1862. At the end of ten years hardly a gap remained in the network of triangles traced on the chart which recorded the progress made in measuring the height, depth, and breadth, and in fixing the true positions of all the chief mountains, valleys, and plains in the Indian Peninsula. No enterprise of the same kind had ever been conducted on a scale so grand by any Government in the world. Nor could any Government have been better served than was that of India by

* Clements Markham's "Indian Surveys."　　† Clements-Markham.

the picked band of bold surveyors who bore the sextant and the theodolite on from one scientific victory to another, in the face of hardships, obstacles, and dangers of the most thwarting kind. In the cause of science men of the highest culture risked their lives or their health as freely as any leader of a storming party seeking the bubble Reputation in the cannon's mouth. Even among their native assistants volunteers were found for ventures which no European might hope to carry through. One of Walker's ablest subalterns, Captain Montgomerie, undertook the training of a few Hindu and Mohammadan pupils for special survey work in countries adjacent to India, but inaccessible from political causes to white men. In 1865 one of these "Pandits" made his way in the guise of a Buddhist through Káthmandú, along the valley of the Sánpu, to Lhása, the sacred capital of Tibet. In his prayer-wheel he had stowed away some slips of paper, on which he contrived to jot down the results of measurements and observations taken over a course of 1,200 miles. Two years later another Pandit explored the country eastward of the Upper Satlaj as far as the gold-field of Tok-Jálung in Great Tibet. A third travelled in the same fashion to Rudok on the Pangong Lake, and a fourth pushed his way into the lofty uplands behind Mount Everest, the monarch of the Himalayas. A Mohammadan explorer traversed the Pamir Steppe and reached in safety the northern city of Káshgar.[*]

On the Surveyor-General, Colonel Henry Thuillier, devolved one-half of the duties formerly discharged by Waugh alone. Under his able management the work of the Topographical and Revenue Surveys was carried briskly forward over the ground prepared for them by the Great Trigonometrical Survey. While the Revenue Surveys dealt with the fields and villages in districts regularly assessed to the Land Revenue, the Topographical pursued its labours in Native States and in the wilder or more rugged parts of British India; among the forests of the Upper Godávari, the fever-laden hills and valleys of Ganjám, Orissa, and Eastern Bengal, the rocks and sands of Rájputána, the dreary highlands of Ladákh and the Panjáb Frontier. Before the close of 1871, Thuillier's surveyors had in ten years added 300,000 square miles to the area mapped out on the great Indian Atlas.[†]

Before the year 1845 the field of geological research had been left almost wholly to private explorers, civil or military, who found time to use their eyes and brains in the cause of science.

---

[*] Clements-Markham.   [†] Ibid.

From the time when Dr. Voysey examined, in 1819, the rocks of the Dakhan and the petrified shells in the Tápti Valley, to the day when Mr. D. Williams first took charge of the Geological Survey, a succession of unpaid inquirers had pioneered the way for an organized system of geological research. Men like Sleeman, Falconer, Cautley, Durand, Baker, Hutton, Newbold, Sykes, Meadows-Taylor, and the brothers Strachey, had thrown much useful light on the rocks, minerals, and fossil remains in various parts of India.

Williams dying in 1849 was succeeded by Dr. McClelland, who gave place two years later to Dr. Oldham. The new Surveyor began work with a staff consisting of one "peon" or messenger, and one native clerk. Two able assistants, Medlicott and St. George, were presently allowed to share his labours. Lord Canning was the first Governor-General who discovered the true character of the work required from the head of a Geological Survey. He gave Dr. Oldham a larger staff, and enabled him to work upon a regular system within limits carefully defined. Thenceforth the Geological Survey kept making noteworthy progress from year to year under men like Medlicott, Blanford, Lucie Smith, and others, who never spared themselves in their country's service. Before the end of 1871 Oldham and his staff had explored an area about four times as large as Great Britain, and recorded a mass of facts bearing on the physical history of India from the earliest times, and revealing the extent of her mineral resources at the present day.*

In the field of meteorology a host of observers, trained and amateur, had been taking their notes of the wind and weather ever since the days of Warren Hastings. But it was not till the days of Lord Lawrence that a regular system of meteorological reports was set at work in one Indian province after another. The Panjáb led the way in 1866; and next year Mr. Henry Blanford, who had meanwhile done excellent service on the Geological Survey, undertook the post of Meteorologist to the Government of Bengal. His duties included the issuing of daily reports to the newspapers and of storm-warnings to all the stations under his charge. In the course of time Mr. Blanford's control extended over all India, and his yearly reports embodied the results collected during the year from the chief observatories in each province. By means of the work done in his department it

* Clements-Markham.

became possible not only to guard against storms and floods, but to discount the ravages of an impending famine.*

In India the science of the stars had made noteworthy progress at least as far back as the fifth century, when Aryabhata measured the earth's circumference, described the earth as spinning daily round its own axis, and affirmed that planets shone only by the sun's reflected light. In the first half of the eighteenth century the learned Mahárája Jai Singh, one of the keenest astronomers of his day, founded observatories at Delhi, Mathra, Banáras, Ujain, and his own city of Jaipur, and gave up to his favourite study the time which most princes devote to amusements of an earthlier type. About a century later the Rajah of Travankór built at Trivandram, near the Equator, an observatory, the charge of which was conferred in turn on two English astronomers, Caldecott and Brown. In the last years of the eighteenth century Madras itself had been chosen by our countrymen as the great centre of astronomical work, as well as the starting-point for the measurements of the Great Trigonometrical Survey. From the Madras Observatory a succession of astronomers, Goldingham, Taylor, Jacob, and Tennant, explored the mysteries of the southern heavens and strove to fix the exact longitude of Madras. In 1860 Tennant's place was filled by Mr. Norman Pogson, who, with improved appliances, was to achieve in twenty years successes worthy to rank with those recorded in the best observatories of Europe.†

The Flora of India had long been carefully studied by a crowd of zealous explorers, many of whom pushed their researches into every corner of the great Peninsula. The Botanical Gardens of Calcutta are inseparably linked with the names of Roxburgh and Wallich; the Gardens at Sahâranpur with those of Royle, Falconer, and Jameson, the last of whom helped so greatly to ensure the successful culture of tea in Northern India. In the course of his wanderings through many regions, from Assam and Bhotán to Kábul and Khorásán, Dr. Griffith collected thousands of plants with a view to compiling a general history of the Indian Flora. His death in 1845 deferred for many years the execution of a scheme which, in 1872, was officially entrusted to the supervision of Sir Joseph Hooker, whose fame as a botanist and a successful explorer of the Sikhim Himalayas had already passed from India into Europe. The researches of Dr. Wight in Southern India, of Dr. Thomson and Richard Strachey in the North, of Drs. Graham and Birdwood, Dalzell and Gibson in Bombay, call for a word of

---

* Clements-Markham; Temple.   † Clements-Markham.

passing reference. From the writings of Dr. Cleghorn and his successor in the Forest Department, Dr. Brandis, together with those of Dr. Balfour, may be gathered a large body of instructive facts concerning the timber trees and the forest Fauna of India.[*]

The third year of his rule was just over when Lord Mayo, on the 24th of January, 1872, steamed down the Húgbli on a cold-weather tour, the last stages of which he was destined never to accomplish. A large and brilliant party of friends and followers accompanied the Viceroy on his fateful voyage. At Rangoon and Maulmain, the two great ports of British Burmah, he spent some days in busy sightseeing and shrewd inquiry into local affairs. On the 5th of February the *Glasgow* frigate bore him down between the wooded banks of the broad Salwin, on her way to Orissa across the Bay of Bengal. In the middle of the Bay were the Andaman Islands, and the great convict settlement of Port Blair, which some months before had passed under the reforming management of General Donald Stewart, a distinguished officer of the old Company's service. This settlement, founded in 1858, on a group of islands buried in verdure, and peopled by a race of utter savages, who lived only on fish and roots, already contained eight thousand felons of the most dangerous type, kept in order only by a few Englishmen and a handful of Sepoys. For some years life in the colony had been one long struggle against malaria and the wild men of the neighbouring jungles; and the yearly death-rate averaged ten in the hundred. The cost of the convicts, who had to be fed entirely from the mainland, averaged thrice the cost of prisoners in Bengal. In Lord Lawrence's time something was done towards clearing the jungle, reclaiming swamps, raising grain and vegetables, and encouraging the convicts to work at useful trades. In 1870 the death-rate had fallen to one per cent. The savage islanders were also learning to treat their neighbours a little more like possible friends.

But as life became more tolerable for the convicts discipline seems to have grown slack. It was partly with a view to keeping a tighter hand upon the more reckless and refractory classes that Lord Mayo sent Donald Stewart, as superintendent of the Andaman and Nicobar Islands, to Port Blair. And thither he himself was now voyaging at Stewart's own request, to see for himself what had been done already, and how much still remained to do.[†]

On the morning of the 8th of February the *Glasgow* and her

* Clements-Markham ; Temple.   † Hunter.

consort anchored off Hopetown, and in due time the Viceroy went on shore. Accompanied by his staff and many of his guests, he spent some hours in a careful survey of everything he had come to see. The several islands were visited each in its turn. The precautions taken for his personal safety, in view of past warnings and probable dangers, were as complete as every one but himself desired. To a man of his fearless, active nature nothing could have been more irksome than the care with which, for many months past, his every movement had been guarded or controlled by faithful friends and a vigilant police. An hour before sunset found Lord Mayo safe at the Hopetown jetty, and the day's programme fairly worked out. But he insisted on going at once up Mount Harriet, a hill not far off, which might be made to serve as a health-resort for invalids. From the top of the hill he gazed upon the varied beauties of a scene, the loveliest he had ever beheld. It was the last sunset that Lord Mayo was fated to look upon. Before his party regained the shore, the brief twilight of the tropics had faded into darkness, and only the fitful glare of torches helped the tired travellers on their way to the boats.

As they passed along the jetty, Stewart for a moment left the Viceroy's side, to give some last orders about the morrow's plans. The next moment Lord Mayo himself darted forward, ahead of his Private Secretary, to go down the jetty steps; his grey coat and tall figure showing clearly in the torchlight. Only a step or two parted him from his boat. Suddenly his nearest followers heard a rushing noise. One or two of them caught the gleam of a knife in the air; and his own Secretary, Major Burne, looking round saw a man fastened "like a tiger" on the back of his beloved chief. In another moment the murderer was pinned by a dozen strong hands; but his sharp knife and sinewy arm had done their work already. A Pathán highlander, who had been transported three years before for life, on a charge of murder, from Peshāwar, and had since been enlarged on a ticket of leave, had made up his mind to kill some Farangi infidel of high rank. Unseen in the jungles, he had dogged the Viceroy's steps up Mount Harriet and down again to the jetty. At the very moment when all chance of revenge seemed for that day hopeless, his opportunity came. Before help could reach his victim, the unseen foe had sprung upon his back and stabbed him twice between the shoulders—two swift, well-aimed strokes, either of which would alone have served his purpose. " Burne "—gasped the wounded man, as he struggled up to his feet from the shallow

water—" they've hit me." Then, raising his voice, he assured
his friends that he was not much hurt. But half a minute later
he had fainted away ; and before the *Glasgow's* launch had transferred its precious burden to the frigate, where Lady Mayo was
awaiting her husband's return to dinner, the most popular and
not the least able of India's Viceroys had breathed his last.[*]

His murderer was duly tried before General Stewart and
sentenced to the death which his own act had made inevitable.
There was no evidence whatever to connect his crime with the
murder of Chief Justice Norman, or with any plots against the
Government. " God alone "—he said in answer to those who
questioned him—" had any share " in the deed for which he paid
the last penalty on the 11th of March. Meanwhile Lord Mayo's
body had been carried back to Calcutta, and escorted in solemn
pomp from the landing-place to Government House by all the
leading Europeans of the capital. A vast crowd of native spectators lined the two miles of intervening road. In the Council
room, where a month ago Lord Mayo had formed the central
figure, the Burial service was read over his corpse, in the presence
of his widow, his colleagues, his staff, and a few friends. After
lying for several days in State, his coffined remains accompanied
his mourning Countess across the sea to their last resting-place
under the sod of a quiet churchyard in County Mayo.[†]

The news of a death so tragical and so untimely thrilled all
India with horror and genuine grief. People of all classes, creeds,
and races felt the loss of a ruler whose winning manners and
splendid hospitalities deepened the impression wrought by his
mental vigour, his administrative skill, and his large-hearted, yet
thoughtful zeal for the public good. Hindus and Mohammadans
alike came forward to express their loyal sympathy with the
widow of a Viceroy who had quietly lived down the distrust and
obloquy engendered by his earlier fiscal measures, and whose
efforts to redress Mohammadan grievances were already bearing
fruit, when the hand of a young Musalman savage laid him low.
On the princes and nobles of India his death came like a personal
bereavement. " I have made and lost a friend," were the words
in which Sindhia bore sorrowing witness to the kindly tact and
care displayed by Lord Mayo in winning the hearts and moulding
the policy of his native vassals. Nor were such tributes confined
to princes within the border. From his Afghán capital Sher Ali

* Hunter ; Temple ; *Allen's Mail.*
† Hunter ; Temple ; *Allen's Mail ;* London *Times,* &c.

wrote a letter expressing in forcible terms his sorrow for the death of a Viceroy whom, ever since the meeting at Ambála, he had loved and valued as a personal friend. And as such, indeed, Lord Mayo was mourned, not only by prince and noble, but by all who had ever known the charm of personal intercourse with one of the kindliest, frankest, wisest, most genial statesmen of his day.

NOTE.

It was in 1789 that the Bengal Government first utilized the Andaman Islands as a harbour of refuge and a convict settlement. But the deadly climate, the want of provisions, and the incessant raids of the natives, forced them in 1796 to abandon the islands altogether. The atrocities committed by the islanders on ship-wrecked crews and passengers at length drove Dalhousie to set about a revival of the project abandoned more than fifty years before. It was not, however, until 1858 that the new settlement was carried out on its present footing.—(Hunter's "Gazetteer;" Col. Yule's article in "Encyclopædia Britannica.")

CHAPTER V.

LORD NORTHBROOK.

FOR three months after Lord Mayo's death his place at the head of the Government was filled by Lord Napier, the retiring Governor of Madras. The public business went on as regularly as if no sudden tragedy had occurred at Port Blair. Pending Lord Napier's arrival at Calcutta, Sir John Strachey, as senior member of Council, carried on the routine of government for his new Chief. Among other duties it devolved upon him to receive the King of Siam, who had been Lord Mayo's guest in the previous December, and was now resting once more at the capital on his way home. He had also to deal with the later issues of a movement fraught at one time with serious danger to the peace of the Panjáb. During the past year a number of murderous outrages had been inflicted on harmless Mohammadan butchers by Sikh fanatics of the new Kúka sect, whose leader, Rám Singh, aimed at rekindling the stern enthusiasm and reviving the purer practices of the old Sikh faith. Condign punishment overtook the murderers whenever their guilt could be brought home; but to the bolder spirits among the brotherhood this furnished only a strong incentive to acts of violence on a more ambitious scale.

They were soon to learn the folly of defying a powerful Government which made no distinction between vulgar criminals and men who murdered on religious grounds. In the middle of January, 1872, while British troops from many parts of Upper India were massed in the Camp of Exercise near Delhi, one band of Kúka fanatics made a sudden and successful rush into the fort of Malodh, in Sirhind, while another attempted to force their way into the town of Malair Kotla, not far from Nabha, in the same province. Thwarted in their attempt to seize the treasury, and to turn the capital of a small native chiefship into the centre of an organized revolt, the insurgents were speedily hunted down or scattered by the active Deputy-Commissioner, Mr. Cowan, with the help of some local levies and armed police. After a summary trial, fifty prisoners, the last remnant of a band which never mustered 2,000, were blown away from guns by Cowan's orders. For this act of lawless severity, which no pressing need of the moment appeared to justify, the Panjáb Government requited him with a formal censure, and nothing more. Against his error of judgement they weighed his manifest zeal and prompt courage in a trying moment. But Strachey and his colleagues were less merciful, or more alive to the gravity of an offence for which, in their eyes, no real palliation could be found. To their thinking, the outbreak, never very formidable, had utterly collapsed some days before the prisoners underwent their doom. In this view Lord Napier presently concurred, and under orders from Calcutta the offending officer was removed from the public service. A milder punishment, removal from his post, was awarded to the Commissioner, Mr. Douglas Forsyth, for permitting Cowan to deal with his prisoners in the way he might deem best.*

One of the weightiest subjects which Lord Napier had to consider was that of the Budget for the coming year. Lord Mayo had left unsettled the question of renewing the income-tax for another year at the current rate of one per cent. Sir Richard Temple was strongly of opinion that it ought to be renewed. Lord Napier, like his predecessor, was loath to continue an impost which, however workable, would never cease to be unpopular. But as acting Viceroy he had no wish to tie his successor's hands; and the tax was renewed accordingly at the end of March. Temple's Budget foreshadowed a surplus of a quarter of a million, which by the following March had swollen to the sum of a million and three-quarters.†

Early in May, Lord Napier made over the reins of Government to the new Viceroy, Lord Northbrook, who had gone out to India laden with the fruits of a long preliminary training in the India Office, the Admiralty, the War Office, and other departments of State. With these advantages he combined a knowledge of finance worthy of one who belonged to a family of great financiers. As the hot season had set in, Lord Northbrook hastened up to Simla, where, in accordance with recent usage, he and his Council were to pass the summer, not in idleness, but in steady work. His kinsman, Major Evelyn Baring, attended him as Private Secretary. Fitzjames Stephen's place in the Council had just been taken by

* Temple; Strachey; *Allen's Mail.*   † Temple.

Mr. Arthur Hobhouse, a lawyer of good repute, and an intelligent writer on several branches of modern law. About the same time Lord Hobart entered on the government of Madras, while Sir Philip Wodehouse replaced Sir Seymour Fitzgerald in Bombay.

The new Viceroy found India tranquil and generally prosperous. Her foreign trade, recovering from the decline caused by the failures of 1866, had risen to the value of nearly one hundred millions a year. Thanks to Lord Mayo and Sir Richard Temple, her financial prospects were steadily improving, and her public credit stood higher than that of most European countries. The opening of the Suez Canal in 1869 had developed a new and profitable trade between India and the Mediterranean ports. Few signs of popular discontent or suffering cropped up to the surface of affairs. In every province there had been of late a succession of good harvests. The land-revenue was collected with apparent ease; and the civil courts—those barometers of the agricultural market—found no lack of lawsuits on their hands. On the political horizon not a cloud was visible in any quarter within the reach of our arms or our diplomacy.*

One of Lord Northbrook's first acts betokened a laudable desire to walk in the steps of his latest predecessors. The Russian conquerors of Western Turkistán were already preparing to punish the Khán of Khiva, the ancient Khurizm, for the outrages inflicted on Russian subjects by his man-stealing, murder-loving Turkomans. An Envoy from the Khán arrived at Simla to entreat the Viceroy's friendly offices on his master's behalf. To such a request but one answer could rightly be returned, in view not only of practical politics, but of the recent good understanding with the Russian Government. Lord Northbrook therefore dismissed the Envoy with a few courteous phrases, and a message strongly counselling the Khán to offer timely amends for the misdeeds laid to his political charge. Had the advice thus given been honestly followed, in all likelihood the Russian advance to Khiva itself in 1873 would not have taken place; nor would English jealousy have found a pretext for accusing a high-minded Russian Emperor of bad faith, because events had clashed with his avowed intentions, and a Russian garrison got firmly planted on a strip of Khivan ground.†

After a few months spent in useful if unobtrusive work, the new Viceroy set out from Simla in October on a long tour of inspection and sightseeing through nearly all the chief towns of

---

* Trotter; *Allen's Mail.*   † Trotter; Afghán Blue-book.

Northern, Western, and Central India, from Lahór to Bombay and Jabalpur. At several places on his road Darbárs were held, which brought him into friendly contact with a crowd of princes and great nobles north of the Tápti, from Pattiála to Indór. At Multán he received the homage of several chiefs from the neighbouring Deraját. On his way down the Indus he had more than one interview with the Bilúchi Khán of Khalát, whose chronic quarrel with his turbulent chieftains Lord Mayo had for the moment appeased. The two great Marátha feudatories, Holkar and Sindhia, tried to eclipse each other in the splendour of the welcome offered, by the one at Bombay, by the other at Barwai, to their viceregal guest. During those two months of diligent travel Lord Northbrook gathered a full store of useful information and detailed experience on all the leading questions of the day.*

Foremost among these was the question of taxation, a question which had sorely perplexed the minds of successive Viceroys from Canning down to Mayo. How to adjust the evergrowing costs of a well-ordered but foreign Government to the needs, the prejudices, and the fiscal capacity of two hundred million people, mostly poor, was a problem which even Lord Mayo had not gone far towards solving. The murmurs evoked throughout India by the income-tax of 1870 had not been altogether silenced by the subsequent lowering of that unpopular impost. Even the concession of larger powers to the Provincial Governments was regarded by a host of sceptics as an artful blind for new fiscal raids on the tax-paying classes. From the first days of his rule Lord Northbrook set himself to grapple with the salient causes of popular discontent. A careful inquiry pursued by his command into all the taxes, rates, and cesses levied throughout the country issued in the collection of a large body of facts and opinions, which served to guide and strengthen the Viceroy's efforts in this direction. The lessons he had thus been learning emboldened him in the following March to abolish the income-tax altogether as an Imperial impost, to sanction the early enforcement of a road-cess in Bengal, and to warn the Local Governments against any further increase of the local burdens.†

In the forepart of 1873, the excitement lately caused both in India and at home by the progress of Russian arms and influence in Central Asia was partially allayed by the readiness of the Russian Government to accept the new line of frontier laid down by the Gladstone Ministry for Afghánistán, as the limit of English

---

* Temple ; Trotter ; *Allen's Mail.*   † Trotter ; *Allen's Mail.*

influence in the regions beyond the Panjáb. This line included the provinces of Wakhán and Badakshán, over which the Amir of Kábul claimed a sovereignty not always acknowledged by their own rulers. In this concession to the English view of a question which seemed to himself one of mere detail, Prince Gortschakoff discerned "a real guarantee for the maintenance of peace" in Central Asia. It only remained for the Indian Government to try and remove from Sher Ali's mind the mistrust and soreness engendered not only by Russian movements, but by the issues of English arbitration between the Amir and Persia in the matter of Sistán. So strong, indeed, was the Amir's displeasure at the award pronounced by Goldsmid in the previous autumn, that for several months it was very doubtful whether he would bring himself to obey the award. His deep distrust of Russia had shown itself even in his letters to Lord Mayo, who had once at least to impress upon him the need of replying in courteous terms to a courteous and friendly message from the Governor of Russian Turkistán. Lord North-brook, in his turn, had already striven to allay the fears rekindled in Sher Ali's breast by recent letters from General Kauffmann, and by growing rumours of a Russian campaign against Khiva.*

In March, 1873, the Viceroy proposed a friendly interview between Sher Ali and Colonel Richard Pollock, the Commissioner of Peshawar. In compliance, however, with the Amir's request, he agreed to remove the scene of conference from Peshawar to Simla, where he himself would confer with Núr Mohammad Shah, Sher Ali's trusty Minister, on matters of common concern to both parties. Of these the most important, to the Amir's thinking, were the Sistán award and the newly-settled boundaries of Northern Afghánistán. The conference took place in July. The Amir had specially instructed his Envoy to ask what help the Viceroy would give him in the event of a rupture with his great Northern neighbour. By the end of July the Envoy knew exactly how far the Indian Government were prepared to go. The Tzar had already promised to "look upon Afghánistán as completely outside the sphere" of Russian influence, and to keep the Turkomans of Bokhára from wanton trespassing on Afghán ground. Sher Ali therefore, said Lord Northbrook, had no cause to fear attack from any quarter, so long as he followed the Viceroy's counsels and loyally strove to keep the peace within his own borders. In case of actual or threatened aggression the Amir would have, for his own advantage, to "refer

* Afghán Blue-book.

the question to the British Government," who would do their best to settle it by peaceful means. Should these fail the British Government "are prepared to assure the Amir that they will afford him assistance in the shape of arms and money, and will also in case of necessity aid him with troops." The Viceroy further claimed for his own Government the sole power to decide when and in what manner it would interfere on behalf of its Afghán ally.*

These were the only conditions on which a prudent Viceroy, careful to uphold the policy defined by his predecessors, and sanctioned by successive Ministers for India, could honestly have undertaken to defend Sher Ali's dominions from foreign attack. From the standpoint whether of Indian or English interests, no other course was open to a statesman who had studied the chart of Central Asian politics, and knew what pitfalls lurked in the way of a close alliance with any of the border States. To leave the Amir free to demand our help at his own discretion would have served only to encourage him in schemes of adventure dangerous to the public peace. There were those, on the other hand, who would gladly have seen the Viceroy go much further towards limiting the Amir's free action, in manifest breach of agreements made by former Viceroys with Dost Mohammad and Sher Ali himself. But Lord Northbrook held fast to the only arrangement which expediency and good faith alike seemed to warrant; the only arrangement which the Duke of Argyll, as head of the India Office and a member of the Gladstone Cabinet, could have confirmed.

With regard to the Sistán boundary, the Viceroy succeeded in pacifying the Amir by an offer of five lakhs of rupees, as compensation for the losses sustained by those of his subjects who had suffered from the Persian raids. A few weeks later he placed another sum of five lakhs to the Amir's credit, besides presenting him with 15,000 rifled muskets, not of the newest pattern, but quite good enough for Sher Ali's actual needs. At the same time he urged the Amir to spend no money on needless precautions against an unreal foe, and to cease from thinking evil of a Power which had just been promising to look upon Afghánistán as a permanent outpost of British India.†

In reaffirming the pledges given by Lord Mayo at the Ambála Darbár, Lord Northbrook took special care to clear up a misconception which the Amir and his Ministers seemed still to cherish. They professed to believe that the British Government

* Afghán Blue-book.   † Afghán Blue-book.

had undertaken to "comply with any request preferred by the Amir." The Viceroy therefore gave the Envoy distinctly to understand that no such promise had ever been made or thought of. The British Government would maintain at all points the policy pursued by Lord Lawrence and Lord Mayo; but they "reserved to themselves the right of judging as to the propriety of any request preferred by the Amir." Among the questions started at the Conference, but left for further discussion at Kábul, was that of deputing a British officer to "examine the boundaries" of Afghánistán. Lord Northbrook saw clearly enough that the presence of British Politicals at Kábul, Herát, or Kandáhár, however desirable for many reasons, was inexpedient as things stood. But he hoped that the passage of "a judicious officer" through the country might tend to allay the popular mistrust of English strangers, and so pave the way for the permanent planting of British Residents in some of the Afghán cities. Nothing, however, came of a project in which Sher Ali's advisers were pretty sure to espy the old bugbear of foreign interference with Afghán freedom under a new form.*

It is not surprising that the results of the Simla Conference should have failed in some measure to satisfy a sovereign who wanted more than any Viceroy, Lord Mayo included, would have ventured, even had he desired to yield. Lord Northbrook's seeming want of sympathy with the Amir's alarms, grievances, and requests for help on his own terms, undoubtedly vexed Sher Ali's eager spirit and blighted some of his fairest hopes. He felt sore at the difference between the new Viceroy's cold courtesy and that genial warmth of manner which had drawn him towards Lord Mayo as to a personal friend. Whether he had misread the meaning of Lord Mayo's assurances, or had merely been asking for much in order to obtain a little, the Amir's disappointment was anyhow very bitter, and he sulked according to his habit over the fancied wrong. He accepted the proffered rifles, but the lakhs of rupees lay untouched in the Indian Treasury. Whatever his private feelings, he still shaped his public policy on the lines laid down by the Indian Government. In compliance with the Viceroy's counsels he kept his unruly Turkmans from raiding across the border, and procured the release of a Russian officer whom they had caught and held captive with an eye to a goodly ransom. Russia, indeed, had just now a special claim on the Amir's good offices, for among the 30,000 slaves whom the

* Afghán Blue-book.

conquerors of Khiva had lately set free were 400 Afgháns, whom Kauffmann's officers helped forward on their way home.*

After the Simla Conference Sher Ali never attempted to kick against any article of the Sistán award. The letters which at times reached him from the Russian head-quarters at Táshkand were always shown to the Viceroy's Vakíl, who forwarded copies of the same to his own Government. In November, 1873, he proclaimed the child of his mature age, Abdulla Ján, his heir. To his letter announcing the fulfilment of his heart's desire Lord Northbrook returned a courteous answer. When Sher Ali presently refused to let Colonel Baker pass through his dominions on his way from Teherán, the Viceroy politely rebuked him, not for doing what he had a right to do, but for his rude way of refusing an inconvenient request. That there was reason for such a refusal at the moment when Yákub Khán was in arms against his father, Lord Northbrook readily allowed. Nor could he forget the lesson which the Amir had learned from the failure of his attempt to punish the Momand chief, Bahram Khán, by whose hands Major Macdonald had been treacherously murdered in the spring of 1873.

During the same year Mr. Douglas Forsyth had led a second embassy to the Court of our good friend Mohammad Yákub, the Atálik Ghází of Eastern Turkistán. Leaving Yarkand in the last days of November, Forsyth hoped to make his way back to India through Afghánistán. But the Amir declined, this time in courteous language, to let our Envoy pass through a country never safe for English travellers, especially those who came from Persia or Turkistán, and at that moment troubled with the sounds of domestic strife. The Viceroy found nothing unreasonable in Sher Ali's conduct; and Forsyth's party, after exploring the Pamir Steppe, pursued their journey homewards through Káshmir. In return for the hospitable treatment which some members of the Mission had received from the Chief of Wakhán, Lord Northbrook sent a native officer with presents and a letter of thanks to the Chief. But by some mischance the notice which Sher Ali, as Suzerain of Wakhán, ought to have received of this act of courtesy towards his vassal was never forwarded; and the Viceroy's explanations had little effect in allaying the resentment shown by his sensitive ally.†

By the end of 1874 the smouldering irritation had blazed out

---

* Afghán Blue-book ; Central Asian Blue-book.   † Afghán Blue-book.

afresh. The rebellious Yákub Khán had made some overtures towards a reconciliation with his father. The Amir seemed willing to accept them if his son would trust himself to a private interview at Kábul. Under the promise of a safe-conduct, Yákub Khán made his way with a few followers to the Afghán capital. He had no sooner entered his father's presence than Sher Ali reproached him for his late misdeeds, and bade his guards carry him off to prison. At this piece of thoroughly Afghán treachery towards the man who had once brought Sher Ali back in triumph to Kábul, Lord Northbrook could not refrain from expressing his deep displeasure. The Amir in his turn took dire offence at language whose very justice served all the more to inflame the wound inflicted on his pride by this new interference with his domestic concerns. Nor did any good come of such interference to Yúkub himself; for he remained a close prisoner during the next four years.[*]

Forsyth's Mission to Yarkand had not proved quite barren of commercial promise. Its members had received a gracious welcome from their grimly jovial host, who listened approvingly to the terms of a commercial treaty laid before him by the British Envoy. In due time his signature was affixed to a covenant which opened his dominions to European trade, protected by the presence of a British representative at his Court and of commercial agents in certain of his towns. Europeans coming from India were to be furnished with passports from the Indian Government; and all traders from India, of whatever nationality, were to have equal privileges and to pay equal duties, never exceeding two and a half per cent. on the value of their goods. Lord Northbrook entrusted the new agency to Mr. Shaw, who had more than once traversed the dreary solitudes between Ladákh and Yarkand in quest of new markets for Indian teas and English cottons. The new treaty inspired our countrymen with hopes which further experience failed to justify. In 1874 the whole value of our trade with Eastern Turkistán fell short of sixty thousand pounds, nor did it ever rise above that figure during the few years that elapsed before the dominions of the Atálik Ghází once more passed under the Chinese yoke.[†]

During the year 1874 Mr. John Edgar, the Commissioner of Dárjiling, was employed by the Bengal Government in studying the question of promoting trade with Nipál and Tibet. This was

---

[*] Afghán Blue-book ; *Allen's Mail.*   [†] Indian Blue-books.

in effect the same question which Warren Hastings, a century earlier, had attacked with a vigour that merited, if it could not ensure, complete success. To Sir George Campbell and his successor, Sir Richard Temple, it seemed that the time had come for trying to secure that friendly intercourse with the people beyond the Eastern Himalayas for which Hastings' agents, Bogle and Turner, had once gone forth to prepare the way. Chinese jealousy might still seek to frustrate British efforts in this direction, and the road through Nipál to Lhása might remain closed with Jang Bahádur's consent to all traders coming from Bengal. But what if the Tibetans themselves were ready to exchange their goods for ours in defiance of orders from Pekin? Temple believed that the making of a good road through Sikhim would secure for India a profitable trade with the countries beyond Dárjiling. Edgar himself predicted a growing demand for the teas of Dárjiling, if they were allowed to compete on equal terms with the teas exported from China into Tibet. In exchange for English woollens and broadcloths he hoped that Tibet would erelong send across the Himalayas her surplus wealth in cattle, and some portion of the gold and silver that lay untouched in mines extending nearly seven hundred miles from Rudok to Lhása.

Edgar's Report reached the India Office enclosed in a letter from the Indian Government. With famine brooding over Bengal, the Viceroy disliked the notion of spending money on a scheme from which no adequate profit could be expected, even if China were to remove all existing barriers to foreign trade with Tibet. The India Office, on the other hand, took more hopeful views of the question raised in the Viceroy's despatch. Lord Salisbury, who had just succeeded the Duke of Argyll as Minister for India, could see no ground for believing in Chinese antagonism to all attempts at "purely commercial intercourse with Tibet." A fair amount of traffic between the two countries was already worked by Bhotia hill-men, who carried everything on their own backs. The Indian Government, said Lord Salisbury, would therefore do well to undertake a survey in order to ascertain the cost of making a bridle-path through that section of the proposed line which lay within British ground. Temple himself in his summer visits to Dárjiling took up the matter with his wonted eagerness, riding to and fro along the boundary-line "where the two empires of Britain and China meet," amidst the snow-crowned peaks and verdure-teeming slopes of Sikhim. The Viceroy, however, was still sceptical of any good results in this direction, and his treasury could spare no funds for any purpose that might with safety be laid aside.*

A little more fruitful was the treaty which Lord Northbrook concluded in 1874 with the King of Siam concerning the tributary State of Zimmay, which adjoined our own frontier. In this State, as in Burmah, great forests of teak abound, and the trade in that timber was largely engrossed by native merchants from our own province of Tenasserim. But peaceful trade with Zimmay was sadly hampered by difficulties and dangers of many kinds. Protection to life and property there was none. Rival claimants disputed the ownership of forest-lands and the right to fell timber thereon. Bands of robbers plundered or drove away the peaceful traders who had obtained leases from the native Chief. Under the new treaty the King of Siam promised to take efficient means for repressing and punishing robbers and other lawless folk. British subjects trading with Zimmay were to be furnished with passports which would help them in making good their civil claims. Provision was also made for establishing in Zimmay a regular Civil Court on which a British officer would be allowed to sit. Finally, the Siamese Government agreed to take due measures for regulating the action of the forest-owners in the matter of permits to fell and drag timber. Shortly after the conclusion of this treaty the son of the Zimmay Chief paid the Chief Commissioner of British Burmah, Mr. Ashley Eden, a friendly visit, for the purpose of announcing his father's earnest desire to retain the goodwill of the Indian Government.†

Among the new laws lately passed by the Viceroy's Legislative Council the most important were the Revenue and Rent Acts for the North-West Provinces. These two measures, which owed their birth mainly to the reforming energy of Sir William Muir, simplified and amended the existing laws and regulations concerning land and land-revenue in the North-West. Among other improvements on former usage they assured to the occupancy tenant a fixed rent for ten years. Hitherto his rent had been liable to enhancement from year to year, if the landlord chose to enforce his legal rights. Some members of Council were for giving the tenant fixity of rent for twenty or thirty years; but Muir, in apparent justice to the landlord, contended for the shorter term, and the voice of the Lieutenant-Governor was not raised in vain. Under the new law a distinction was made between the landholder's proprietary rights in land and the rights of occupancy

* Indian Blue-book; Temple.　　　† Indian Blue-book.

which the same person might acquire in the fields he cultivated as a tenant. Thenceforth the sale of the former rights for debt would involve no forfeiture of the latter; and thus the erewhile owner of ancestral lands would still be free to cultivate as an occupancy tenant the fields from which he might also have been driven forth a homeless beggar, with wife and children slowly starving by his side.*

* Indian Blue-book.

CHAPTER VI.

THE FAMINE OF 1873–74.

In March, 1873, Temple had to bring out his Budget for the official year beginning from the 1st of April, without an income-tax even of one per cent. In spite of the half million thereby lost to the revenue, his estimates showed a surplus of a quarter of a million, which, but for circumstances then unforeseen, would have grown by the year's end to an amount exceeding the actual surplus of the past year. The yield of revenue from land, opium, salt, stamps, and customs, during 1873 kept rising steadily above the estimates. In the ordinary charges for the same year there was a decrease of more than £800,000. Never since the annexation of the Panjáb had the North-Western Frontier been so tranquil. An agrarian outbreak in the Pabna District of Bengal had ruffled for a time the peace of that province, and threatened mischief to those zamindárs who oppressed their ráyats with forced cesses, fines, rackrents, and other exactions unknown, or seemingly contrary, to the law. But Campbell's sympathy with the aggrieved classes did not allow him to connive at their lawless methods of requiting the wrong-doers. He warned the rioters by proclamation that his Government, however willing to protect the ráyats from force and extortion, would certainly put down all violent and illegal movements on their part. The rioters knew that he would keep his word, and the appeals to violence gave place to the slower but safer process of appealing to the civil courts.

In Orissa also it had lately been discovered that the practice of levying fines and arbitrary cesses from the peasantry was neither new nor uncommon. The practice which still survived in Orissa and Bengal had once flourished in other parts of India. It was akin to the process by which some of our English kings had sometimes sought to refill their treasuries, a process which ended so disastrously for Charles the First. An Indian landlord of the old school, when he wanted money for his father's obsequies, for his children's wedding, or for a feast in honour of his gods, would send his agent round among his villages to collect from each, by one means or another, a certain share of the sum required. Under our rule such practices were declared illegal; but unscrupulous landlords, hard pressed for money, found it easy to defy or evade the law, and the few village Hampdens who took courage to withstand the petty tyrants of their fields were prone to seek redress by means which Hampden would have been loath to sanction. In Orissa, however, where no violence seems to have been employed, Campbell made an example of three zamindárs, against whom the evidence of gross oppression was very clear. He deprived them for a certain period of the management of their estates; and he was planning a new law for the settlement of rent-disputes throughout Bengal, when a matter of far more pressing moment claimed for some months to come his entire attention, and taxed to their utmost the health and strength of all who had to deal with it.[*]

During the past two years the weather in Bengal had been more or less abnormal. In 1871, spite of a heavy rainfall, the crops had been very good. In the following year the rainfall, though light, was evenly distributed, and the crops yielded a fair outturn. In 1873 the little rain that fell was so badly distributed that, while Orissa enjoyed the promise of full harvests, the greater part of Bengal Proper and Bahár was suffering from drought. Over an area of sixty thousand square miles the autumn crops of wheat, rice, and other grains forming the staple food of twenty-five million souls, were withering away for want of the rain which ought to have fallen in August and September. Early in the latter month Campbell gave the Viceroy timely warning of the impending danger, and Lord Northbrook hurried down from his cool retreat at Simla to consult with his Lieutenant on the best means of grappling with a disaster which no human efforts could have forestalled. A message from the Viceroy found Temple on the very point of leaving Ambála on one of his official tours; and the two went down together by train to Calcutta.

There was hope that rain might yet fall in time, if not to save a portion of the doomed crops, at least to prepare the ground for the winter sowings. But this hope was soon dispelled. Some thousands of acres were saved by the timely opening of the Són and Midnapur Canals; but in most places the earth remained hard as iron, and the seed lay lifeless where it fell. In the last days of January, 1874, rain began to fall heavily in the southern districts of Bengal, and during February some showers visited the north also.

[*] Indian Blue-book; *Allen's Mail.*

But in many places the spring crops were ruined beyond recall. There was but little grain in the province remaining over from former years, for the octroi duties levied for municipal purposes had discouraged the *baniyas* from keeping large stocks on hand, while foreign countries were always willing to buy cheaply the surplus produce of Indian fields. It was clear, in short, that the famine foreseen in September would begin to rage in March, and that little food could come to the suffering millions either from Southern Bengal or from the districts adjacent to Bahár, for the drought extended into part of Oudh and the North-West Provinces.*

The Viceroy, however, had not been idle. From the first hour of his arrival in Calcutta he had attacked the formidable problem of bringing food betimes within reach of a hungry province as large and populous as England and Wales. Working in concert with two such men as the Lieutenant-Governor of Bengal and the Finance Minister for India, Lord Northbrook applied the lessons taught by former famines to the shaping out of a grand scheme of famine relief, the like of which no country in the world had ever yet seen. The first step he took in this campaign gave clear earnest of what would follow. In the pages of the *Calcutta Gazette* he announced the coming of a widespread scarcity, in grappling with which the people at large, and especially the trading classes, were called upon to do their best. The Government in its turn would act promptly and powerfully in aid of private helplessness and private enterprise, to the end that none should perish for want of timely succour. Mindful of Lawrence's good example, he held the civil officers in each district accountable for every life that might be lost through want of timely or sufficient care.†

The Viceroy then took counsel with his colleagues touching the question of food supplies for the coming year; the amount of food which private enterprise, spurred on by a great public need and unhampered by trade dues, might be trusted to furnish; and the right moment for offering relief in the shape of wages to persons seeking employment on the public works. In dealing with these and other matters of like importance, Lord Northbrook displayed a statesmanlike breadth of view, a cool judgement, an administrative skill, and a firm grasp of economic facts and methods, such as the ablest financiers and the most enlightened rulers of his day could not have surpassed. He induced the rail-

---

* Indian Blue-book; Temple; *Allen's Mail.*
† Temple; *Government Gazette.*

way companies to lower their rates for the carriage of grain by promising to make their losses good from the public treasury. From the first he took care that work of a useful kind should be found betimes at a moderate wage for all who wanted it, either on canals and railways undertaken by the State, or on roads or tanks designed by the Local Government.

Relief committees were also promptly formed in every district, for the purpose of distributing food, alms, and medicine among those who from age or bodily weakness had no power to help themselves. But all such modes of preventing or relieving distress would have been like drops in the sea of human suffering, but for the measures taken by the Viceroy to ensure the people of Bengal against every foreseeable risk of death from sheer starvation. Public works, relief committees, low railway freights, private enterprise in all its forms, might save many thousands alive for a certain period. There was no lack of funds in the public treasuries. But how long was the drought likely to continue, and what amount of food was absolutely needed for the maintenance of so many million sufferers from drought? In the handling of these great questions Lord Northbrook resolved that nothing should be left to chance. The result of searching inquiries and careful calculations showed that four hundred and fifty thousand tons of grain, chiefly rice, would serve to feed the people in the suffering districts down to the end of 1874. If the monsoon rains in that year fell freely, the famine would cease in the autumn. But this at best was a mere likelihood, which the Viceroy refused to take for a certainty. Choosing rather to err on the side of prudence, he decided to lay in a stock of grain more than sufficient for the probable needs of a whole year.

In British Burmah the rice crop for 1873 proved to be the largest ever known. From this province therefore Lord Northbrook prepared to draw the bulk of his food supplies; and the Chief Commissioner, Ashley Eden, entered heartily into his plans. Skilfully and quietly Eden and his agents set about their task. In due time they succeeded in purchasing nearly three hundred thousand tons of grain without diminishing the regular flow of rice from Burmah to Europe. The supplies thus obtained on behalf of the Government, at rates comparatively cheap, were duly forwarded to Calcutta in the vessels of the British India Steam Company. Smaller supplies from other sources found their way into the Government storehouses in Bengal. The whole quantity thus timely purchased amounted to nearly four hundred and eighty thousand tons, of which only fifty-four thousand three hundred tons had come from countries outside the British border.*

Meanwhile Campbell had issued among his own officers a set of detailed instructions admirably suited to work out the Viceroy's general plan. In almost every point of principle and practice the Viceroy and the Lieutenant-Governor were at one. The main difference between them turned on the question of interference with the free course of trade. Campbell urged upon the Viceroy the need of forbidding the export of grain from British Indian ports to foreign countries so long as the famine might last. Plausible arguments for such a measure were easy enough to find. Many of Campbell's countrymen, and a host of intelligent natives, would have heartily approved of such a step in view of so grave a crisis. But Lord Northbrook had trodden too far and too firmly in the footprints of Cobden, Peel, and Mill, to be led astray by arguments, however specious, based on likelihoods however manifest. He saw that any such departure from ordinary rules would tend only to damage the fair prospects of Indian trade for no countervailing benefit to the people of Bengal. So long as India could be trusted to furnish food enough at need for all her children, there was no excuse for dislocating her foreign trade by compelling her merchants to retain at home the large stocks of surplus grain which their foreign customers had already agreed to buy. Of two evils the Viceroy unhesitatingly chose the less. It was better for India to pay a little more for her immediate needs, than to risk the loss of a large and prosperous trade, the expense of compensating those who would suffer from a sudden stoppage of their regular business, and the likelihood of a large reduction in the acreage sown with food grains.†

After some weeks spent in getting ready for action, Lord Northbrook hastened up the country in order to keep faith with those Native princes and chiefs whom he had long since arranged to receive in public Darbár, some at Agra, others at Lucknow. During his absence Temple took his place as President in Council. It was not long before the Viceroy's versatile deputy was to be engaged on duties more congenial to his active habits. Campbell's health was visibly breaking down under the strain of new anxieties, added to the regular toils and worries of an office in which he never spared himself. The doctors warned him against prolonging his stay in India after the cold weather. He resolved, however, to work on at all hazards for a few months longer. To help

* Temple ; Indian Blue-book ; *Allen's Mail.*   † Temple ; Indian Blue-book.

him in a task which was already outgrowing his strength, Lord Northbrook, on the 21st of January, 1874, deputed Temple to act as head of the Government in Bahár, the Viceroy himself taking charge, meanwhile, of the Imperial finances.

By that time large quantities of the grain already bought for Government in Burmah had been landed at Calcutta, whence the railway carried them forward by hundreds of tons a day to Patna and other spots on the right bank of the Ganges in Northern Bengal. But here the difficulties of the campaign began. · The dry season had already set in, and the streams which flow from the Himalayas into the Ganges were no longer navigable for the boats of the country. Of wheeled carriage for commercial purposes there was a very short supply. All trade in the drought-seared districts north of the Ganges had come to a standstill. Temple, however, was on the spot, full of energy and resourceful zeal. The indigo planters of Bahár had vast numbers of carts and bullocks lying idle, partly on account of the famine. These, in answer to Temple's appeals, they hired out to the Government by tens of thousands; and a staff of picked officers, headed by Colonel Charles Macgregor, of the Quartermaster-General's Department, were at once employed in organizing a transport service equal to the need. Another transport train of bullocks, carts, ponies, and mules, supplied from Northern India, was promptly organized by a civil officer, Mr. Harry Rivett-Carnac. For the same purpose Temple opened a great relief work, in the shape of a railway more than fifty miles long, from the Ganges to Darbhanga in Tirhút. Thousands of able-bodied men were glad to labour at a wage of twopence-farthing a day; and so vigorously were the works pressed forward by Captain Stanton of the Engineers, that in less than two months the line was completed. By such means the great problem of carrying grain into all parts of the suffering districts was solved before the famine could do its worst.*

Temple's next care was to look closely into the physical state of the people placed under his charge. For this purpose he travelled to and fro about the country, often in the burning sun, sparing neither himself nor others in the discharge of duties more trying than any he had yet encountered. In many of the villages through which he passed all the men, women, and children were paraded for his inspection, and no signs of distress or unusual emaciation escaped his eagle glance. At certain places along his road the able-bodied and the infirm were brought together by thousands

* Temple ; *Allen's Mail* ; Indian Blue-book.

at a time, in order that only those who were really unfit for labour on relief works should receive help according to their needs from the relief committees. There remained a large class of probable sufferers, who would rather starve at home than seek help from any public source. Under Temple's auspices a system of regular visiting from house to house in every village was presently set on foot, so that no one, man, woman, or child, should perish, who might, through timely inquiry, have been saved alive. Groups of villages were marked out in each district, and to each group were attached a relief centre and a field hospital.*

Meanwhile the people of England were giving no churlish answer to the cry of distress raised from Far Bengal. The Lord Mayor of London opened at the Mansion House a subscription list, which the Queen herself headed with an offering of a thousand pounds. For several months the stream of private charity kept flowing steadily on through this and other channels. In nearly all the churches and chapels sermons were preached and money collected for the same good object. From the colonies also help came in the shape of alms or food. Nor were our countrymen in India backward in their efforts to relieve or mitigate the growing distress. The merchants of Calcutta, the missionaries and planters of Bengal, subscribed their quotas to the relief fund, or took their part in the work of distributing alms among their poorer neighbours. Many of the native princes and nobles opened their purses freely for the same end, and the zamindárs of Bengal enrolled themselves on the relief committees, found work on their own estates for numbers of the unemployed, and gave largely of their own means towards the maintenance of the sick and helpless.

Invaluable was the help afforded by the East Indian Railway, whose officers and servants, one and all, worked with an energy worthy alike of the occasion and of their race. To their exertions, indeed, it was mainly owing that the Government grain reached its destination in good time. As Commissioner of Bahár, Mr. Steuart Bayley commanded the main army of workers, civil and military, who were to help the Government in warring against famine. In the discharge of his difficult duties he was nobly seconded by Mr. C. T. Metcalfe. Another of Temple's prominent helpmates was Mr. Charles Bernard, who had been Temple's Secretary in the Central Provinces, and was now filling with rare success the critical post of Famine Secretary to the Bengal Government. Among the local officers who bore the burden

* Temple.

and heat of the day, the most conspicuous, in Temple's opinion, were Messrs. C. Macdonnell and F. Magrath.

That all the English army officers sent down to the scene of action by the Viceroy and his Commander-in-Chief would do their work zealously, might almost be taken for granted. In placing a number of picked native officers at Temple's command, Lord Napier of Magdála hit upon a new and effective agency for the distribution of famine relief. Their discipline and training, said Sir Richard, "rendered them extraordinarily apt at this work."[*]

The spirit in which Lord Northbrook had set himself to deal with the coming danger, his strong desire that no one should perish for want of timely succour, we have already seen. But one of his ablest officers, Mr. W. Hunter, the Director-General of Statistics, had lately written a book on famine-warnings, in which he assumed that during a severe drought thousands of the sick and weakly, the " useless gear " as he called them, were sure to die. The shock thus conveyed to the minds of humane Englishmen at home was heightened by the reports of newspaper correspondents, who mistook the normal leanness of an ill-fed peasantry for the signs of actual starvation, and pointed to the low rates of wages paid on relief works as wholly inadequate to the people's needs. Complaints of mismanagement, scant supervision, irregular payments, and fraud on the part of native overseers, found their way to England in the earlier months of this year. Some well-meaning enthusiasts, forgetful of what happened during the Irish famine, went so far as to hold the Viceroy liable to impeachment should a single death occur from starvation.

There was little ground, however, for all the alarms and censures thus hastily spread abroad. It was impossible that a system of relief planned on a scale so gigantic for so vast a population should work from the outset with perfect smoothness and unfailing precision. So far, indeed, were the wages offered from proving insufficient for the average needs of those who earned them, that one gang of labourers in Motihári refused to exchange the lighter tasks at first set them for task-work carrying a higher wage; while another gang struck altogether rather than accept the new conditions. At another place where very light task-work was introduced, the number of coolies fell in one day from 1,300 to 600, although the people in that neighbourhood seemed to be very badly off. The Correspondent of the *Daily News* recanted in April much that he had written in February and March. Among the

---

[*] Temple ; *Allen's Mail ;* London *Times ; Daily News,* &c.

labourers in one district he could find " no symptoms of suffering," their condition indeed being "quite as good as in years of plenty." The wages earned by men, women, and children were enough, he owned, to keep each family alive, if not always on rice, at least on some cheaper food-grain. Experience had already made him wiser, even to the point of frankly avowing his belief that no efforts of any Government in the world could prevent a good many deaths from starvation among a people who would "sit still and starve in their hovels, when a grain store is open at the other end of their village." Yet the feat which he then deemed impossible Lord Northbrook's Government went very near indeed to accomplish.*

In the same month of April Campbell quitted India for the last time, to win for himself erelong a place on the Liberal benches in the House of Commons. In spite of his premature retirement, he left behind him a brilliant record of work accomplished or well begun in many directions. His reforms in the native civil service opened a career to those candidates who possessed a good share of nerve and muscle as well as brains. He found time to spare for details of prison discipline, for the development of central jails, for the promotion of all kinds of public works, including the drainage and improvement of swampy tracts, for looking after the interests of jute-growers in Bengal and tea-planters in Assam. A few weeks before his departure he had launched a well-devised scheme for relieving the pressure of drought in Bengal, by shipping off some thousands of emigrants at the public cost to British Burmah, where most of them were soon employed in cultivating the waste lands. His long-considered scheme of rural municipalities empowered to deal with the sanitary wants of their respective village groups was disallowed by the Viceroy on the score of expense.

A better fortune rewarded his efforts to improve the efficiency of the Covenanted Civil Service in Bengal. Under the old rules for filling up vacancies in that service a civil officer might be transferred from executive to judicial duties, simply because he stood first on the list for promotion to any post carrying a higher salary. A Collector would thus become a Judge, or a Judge be transformed into a Commissioner, without reference to his previous training or his special aptitudes. This led to very frequent changes of district officers, and to less frequent but not less untoward failures of public justice. By readjusting the salaries of district judges Campbell brought the old system into closer

* Temple ; Blair ; *Times ; Daily News ;* Official Papers.

harmony with existing needs. Parallel lines of promotion in
both branches of the service were thus opened out to every officer
of a certain standing, who became free thenceforth to continue in
that line for which his natural gifts or his past training had marked
him out. Thenceforth a Magistrate-Collector might look to retain charge of his district for a reasonable length of time, instead of
being called away to other duties at the end of six or nine months.*

Campbell's successor in the Government of Bengal was Sir
Richard Temple, whom the Viceroy and the public voice had
already named for that post. Before Temple formally entered on
the duties he had for three months been helping to discharge, one
large slice of territory, covering 54,000 square miles and containing more than four million souls, had been formally severed from
the Government of Bengal. This happened in February, when
Colonel Robert Keatinge, fresh from his political labours in
Káthiawár, became Chief Commissioner of Assam, Kachár, and
the hill-tracts on the eastern frontier of Bengal. To this new
province Silhet was added in September of the same year. In
view alike of the relief thus given to the overburdened Government of Bengal, and of the need for bringing the great border
provinces under the Viceroy's direct control, the change thus completed was altogether good.

In April of the same year, Sir John Strachey succeeded Sir
William Muir as Lieutenant-Governor of the North-West Provinces. A few weeks before his retirement Muir had presided at
the opening of the Agra Canal, one of those irrigation works
which help in their degree to fertilize the sunburnt plains of the
great Doáb. By that time, however, the cloud of famine, which
for some months overhung a part of his province, had fairly
passed away ; and the relief works opened in the cold weather
were deserted by all who could find employment in gathering the
spring harvests near their own homes. Of Muir's efforts to shield
the peasantry from the greed of rackrenting landlords and ruthless money-lenders mention has been made already. But no
medicine, however potent for future good, could undo all the mischief arising from an old disease. Both in Western and Northern
India evictions and forced sales of land for debts, swollen by
ruinous interest and fraudulent accounts, had already driven numbers of the old peasantry out of their ancestral homes, or reduced
them to utter bondage under the usurers who had despoiled them
of land and goods. Some of them, in sheer despair or fierce im-

* Temple ; Indian Blue-book.

patience of the wrong-doing allowed by law, broke out in deeds of violent revenge, or took to organized robbery as a means of livelihood. Thus it happened that in 1873 crimes of violence were unusually rife in the North-West. *Dakaiti*, or gang-robbery of the most daring kind, flourished as it had never been known to do since the Mutiny. The *dakaits* no longer worked in secret or with the help of some disguise. Bands of armed men with lighted torches, and the firing of guns, would enter a village, and leisurely proceed to plunder the houses of its wealthiest inmates. It was seldom that the villagers took courage to fight for their property at the risk of their lives.*

The lawless outbreaks in the Dakhan during the same year were followed in the next by agrarian risings among the Marátha peasantry of the Western Gháts. A wild longing to pay off old scores against the village usurers who had grown rich at their expense impelled the rioters to attack the persons or the property of their natural foes. Not a few houses were set on fire in the hope of destroying all legal records of the money-lenders' claims, and several of the money-lending class were slain, or sorely beaten, by unseen assailants. In due time the riots were suppressed. But the evils which provoked them cried aloud for removal or abatement, and Lord Northbrook promptly ordered a Commission of Inquiry into the causes of agrarian discontent. The Report of the Commission disclosed a state of things which explained if it could not justify the previous outrages. The few years of unwonted prosperity which ended in 1866, had enabled the ráyats of Bombay to borrow freely from village bankers on the security of their lands and crops. Untoward seasons and interest at the rate of thirty or forty per cent. placed them at the mercy of creditors not always honest, and seldom loath to exact full payment of their legally-proven dues. As the land law of the province placed no real limit to the creditor's powers of eviction and sale for debt, the results of improvidence on the one hand, of extortion on the other, were easy to conceive. Many thousands of acres were passing into the hands of village usurers, and increasing numbers of once prosperous husbandmen became mere serfs of their fortunate supplanters. The Government of Sir Philip Wòdehouse gave much thought to the question of a remedy for so grave an evil. But some years had yet to elapse before that question received a practical reply.†

* Indian Blue-book; *Allen's Mail.*
† Temple; Indian Blue-book; *Times of India.*

With the month of May, 1874, the full stress of famine set in for Northern Bengal. The spring crops, such as they were, had been already gathered in. For the mass of the people there would be no employment in the fields until the bursting of the next monsoon. The private trade in grain had come to a standstill. The needy and helpless folk in the villages could no longer look to their wealthier neighbours for the help they had hitherto been wont to receive. It was full time for Government to open its stores of hoarded grain, to find employment for famishing multitudes, and to set at work the whole machinery of special relief for all who would otherwise starve at home or perish by the wayside. The sale of Government grain at prices suited to the need accordingly began. Many hundred thousand men, women, and children flocked to the relief works and drew their daily wage in grain. Thousands of paid or volunteer agents of relief committees went from house to house in their respective villages, searching out all cases of real distress, and distributing their daily doles of food and medicine to all whom caste-usage, sickness, or infirmity kept at home. In many a relief camp cooked food was issued at certain hours to those who had no work or little strength for any that came to hand. No effort, in short, was spared to carry out the Viceroy's policy of saving lives at whatever cost.

Week after week the great battle raged with growing intensity. The able-bodied workers grew thinner and weaker by slow degrees. At such a time an outbreak of fever or cholera would have swept away its thousands in the course of a few weeks. Happily, throughout this critical period the health of the people, in spite of their growing weakness, seems to have been remarkably good. The streams in Bahár, however low, still furnished a due supply of pure drinking water; and the medical officers took all care to enforce observance of sanitary rules, so far as their powers extended.[*]

At last, about the middle of June, the monsoon rains began to fall. Thousands of labourers at once left the relief works to look after the tillage of their own fields. Most of these, however, had no means of keeping themselves alive until the next harvest began to come in. They were allowed accordingly to draw on the Government for what grain they needed, on condition of repaying its value by-and-by. Presently a time came when the rains, at first so plenteous, held off, and a second year of famine loomed in sight. But once more the rain fell freely, and all hearts rejoiced

[*] Temple; Famine Commission Report, 1880; *Allen's Mail.*

at the sure prospect of a goodly harvest. Week after week the people employed on relief works kept trooping off to their homes; and by the middle of October all fear of further famine had passed away. The number of deaths directly traceable to want of food was reckoned at twenty-two, so thoroughly had the Viceroy's leading purpose been carried out; and the multitudes whom his humane foresight, aided by Temple's ubiquitous zeal, and the loyal efforts of all his helpmates, had thus kept alive through months of suffering, returned to their ordinary pursuits and labours with health comparatively unbroken, and with a spirit of cheerful self-reliance which their late misfortunes and the moral effects of dependence on public charity had done but little to impair. To their " patient courage, unflinching endurance, self-help in extremity," as well as their eagerness in seeking work for their own hands at the first opportunity, Temple himself has borne admiring witness.*

That only one human being should have died of famine out of every million lives endangered, was an achievement to which Lord Northbrook might well look back in after days with a glow of just pride. Nor was he backward at the time in acknowledging the debt he owed to all who had aided him, from Temple down to the native officers, English planters, and railway servants, in achieving a success so memorable, so contrary indeed to all former experience. How much of that success was owing to the part which he himself bore in planning and carrying out an enterprise which many persons deemed Quixotic, may be inferred from the care he took to count up beforehand the cost of every measure suitable to the end in view, from his skilful management of economic details, and from the steady impulse which his own counsels, orders, and personal presence gave to the full development of his schemes for the common good.

The whole net outlay on famine relief amounted to six millions and a third, of which nearly four millions were charged against the revenue for the year ending in March, 1874. The reserved stocks of grain—some 30,000 tons—had to be sold at a heavy loss, by reason of the low prices consequent on a plenteous harvest. In view of the marked contrast between so large an outlay and the very small total of lives lost, there were some unkind critics who loudly declared their disbelief in the alarming character of the crisis through which Bengal had passed so happily in so short a time. Who ever heard of a widespread famine marked by only a

* Temple ; Indian Blue-book.

score of deaths? These were the kind of people who measure the worth of a military commander by the number of battles he has fought, and the greatness of a victory by the amount of blood poured out on the victor's side. They maintained in effect, as Temple has well put it, that "the danger of famine could not have been extremely urgent because it had been successfully overcome." There were others who murmured at the excessive costliness of the means employed to cope with a danger undoubtedly great. They seemed to question the need of spending so much money for the purpose of saving every soul alive, and they overlooked the fact that Lord Northbrook had to provide against that which fortunately did not happen, the failure of the monsoon in 1874. Against some probable instances of public money misused or wasted may be set Lord Northbrook's crowning achievement, his complete success in applying over a large and populous region, remote from railways and poorly off for roads, the humane principle first proclaimed by John Lawrence, that the Government should spare no effort for the saving of human lives.[*]

This scepticism about the famine did not extend to the natives of Bengal. It was no member of the subject race who broached the curious doctrine that Temple himself had "invented the famine" for his own ambitious ends. From all parts of Bengal the Viceroy and his Lieutenant-Governor received the warmest expressions of heartfelt gratitude for their success in averting a terrible disaster. At every place which Temple visited in his frequent journeys during the famine year and afterwards, he was greeted with addresses which were sure to contain some words of grateful reference to the part which he and his countrymen had borne in the campaign against human suffering. The native gentry of Bahár, in congratulating the Lieutenant-Governor on his late success, reviewed in detail the series of measures by which that success had been made possible. The British Indian Association, speaking for all the Zamindárs of Bengal, set forth in glowing language the gratitude felt by all classes of the people for the help their rulers had brought them in their darkest need. And the native newspapers, one and all, swelled the long chorus of praise and thanksgiving which drowned, if it could not silence, the voice of unfriendly critics judging rather from precedents, theories, or private prejudice, than from ascertainable facts.[†]

---

[*] Temple ; Indian Blue-book ; *Allen's Mail.*
[†] Temple ; Official Papers ; "The Black Pamphlet."

CHAPTER VII.

IN spite of the millions spent on famine relief, the revenue accounts for the year ending in March, 1874, showed a deficit of only £1,807,668. The land-revenue yielded over 21 millions, or only a third of a million less than in 1872–73. Even in Bengal the yield had been nearly equal to the demand; had, indeed, been relatively larger than in Oudh, Madras, and Bombay, where the seasons had been wholly favourable, or incipient drought had been followed by timely rains. In the following year, when Muir had charge of the Imperial Finances, there resulted an actual surplus of £300,000 on an income exceeding 50½ millions, although the balance of famine charges amounted to two millions and a half. By the end of that year the land-revenue had risen to its normal average for the whole of British India, while almost every item of revenue, from salt and opium down to the post-office, forests, and telegraphs, yielded a steady increase on former years. The foreign trade of the country was visibly recovering from the decline that began in 1872. During the same year 12,460 vessels, representing a total burden of nearly 5½ million tons, entered or cleared from British Indian ports.*

The famine gave a new impulse to the extension of roads, railways, and irrigation works. Several hundred miles of new road were made by coolies employed on the relief works in Northern Bengal. In the districts of Sáran, Champáran, and Tirhút, a hundred miles of embankments were finished by the end of 1874. These embankments formed part of a scheme for irrigating Bahár by means of canals drawn from the Gandak. The Són and Midnapur Canals, incomplete as they were, are reckoned to have saved a large breadth of grain crops to the value of £600,000. In another part of Bengal the waters of the Damúda were once more turned into the Kána Nadi, which of late years

* Statistical Abstract; Indian Blue-book.

had shrunken and silted up into a muddy ditch, varied by a chain of stagnant and noisome pools. Of the 600 miles of new railway opened in 1874, more than 400 were made by the Public Works Department alone. Besides the Tirhút Railway, 100 miles were added to the Rájputána lines. The Nizam's Railway, 121 miles long, made with money borrowed from the Nizam's Government, linked Haidarábád with Wadi on the Great Indian Peninsular line. On Holkar's Railway from Indór to a point on the same line 37 miles were opened in the same year ; and work was begun on the line from Indór to Nimachh, towards which Sindhia had undertaken to pay his share.

In 1874 the net earnings of all the railways came little short of four millions sterling, or nearly £800,000 above the total for the previous year. Half of this excess was scored by the East Indian Railway as carrier of all grain sent up from Calcutta to the famine tracts. The Sind, Panjáb, and Delhi Railway also reaped a handsome profit from the grain which left Lahór on the same errand, while the railways of Western India were enriched by the new demand for Indian wheat in the markets of Europe. In the following year, of course, the net receipts fell off by £300,000, but in 1876 they sprang up to four millions and a half, and the time was close at hand when some of the leading railways would earn more than the guaranteed dividend of five per cent.[*]

Meanwhile an important change had taken place in the mode of constructing some of the new State railways. Lord Mayo's Government, as we saw, had adopted the metre-gauge of 3 feet 3 inches as the standard gauge for these lines. On this gauge the works of the Northern Panjáb Railway from Lahór to Pesháwar had since been taken in hand. But both in India and at home a great many competent judges objected strongly to the new arrangement sanctioned by the Duke of Argyll. The narrow gauge might serve perhaps for a time in Rájputána and Central India ; but its application to any great military or commercial line would be a grave and costly mistake. Commercial and military critics alike dwelt on the evils inherent in a break of gauge ; and the latter class, from Lord Napier downwards, further condemned the metre-gauge as unfit for the actual and possible demands of a frontier war. People of many classes looked upon the broad gauge of five feet and a half as clearly the most suitable for the great bulk of Indian produce forwarded by rail.

[*] Statistical Abstract ; Indian Railway Report ; Indian Blue-book.

Experienced engineers and railway managers denied or doubted the relative cheapness of the narrow gauge. In the average cost of construction there was little to choose between the two, save in the matter of bricks and masonry; while the yearly cost of maintenance and working would be found to tell in favour of the broader and safer lines. Much stress was laid on the greater stability of broad-gauge carriages under high rates of speed, and on the danger involved in using carriages and waggons too broad for the rails they would overhang.

For many months, for more than two years, the battle of the gauges went on. A brisk fire of objections and replies passed between Lord Northbrook and the India Office. So long as the Duke of Argyll ruled at Westminster, the friends of the narrow gauge might count on having their own way. But the Duke's successor, the Marquis of Salisbury, having no prejudice either way, gave careful heed to the arguments which Lord Mayo's successor laid before him, and followed with open ears the speeches delivered on both sides in a debate got up by the Institute of Civil Engineers at home. At last, in 1875, the question was settled by a compromise, which enabled Lord Northbrook to adopt the broad gauge for the Northern Panjáb and the Indus Valley lines.*

Among the most notable events of the year 1875 was the public trial of Malhár Rao, the Gaikwár of Baroda, for attempting to poison the British Resident, Colonel Phayre. On the death of his brother, Khandi Rao, in 1870, Malhár Rao had leapt at one bound from a prison to a throne. His past life had ill-prepared him for the sudden change in his fortunes. A childhood of neglect, idleness, and ignorance had been followed by seven years of imprisonment on the charge of attempting his brother's life. From such antecedents little good was likely to come. The 'new Gaikwár soon showed himself a worthless and unteachable ruler. Complaints of his extravagance, folly, and misrule were continually borne to the Viceroy's ears; by none more urgently than by Colonel Phayre, who became Resident at Baroda in March, 1873. In the winter of that year Lord Northbrook ordered a Commission to report upon the actual state of things in Baroda. The Report, as presented in the following February, went far to justify the previous complaints. Lord Northbrook gave the Gaikwár eighteen months for repentance and amendment. If by the end of 1875 his Highness failed to show proof

* Temple; *Allen's Mail;* Report of Institute of Civil Engineers.

of a decided change for the better, he would be " deposed in the
interest of his people, and for the peace and security of the
Empire."

Six months were hardly over when Phayre reported an attempt
to poison him by means of a powder mixed in with his morning
glass of sherbet. Happily he had detected the lurking danger
before swallowing more than one or two mouthfuls of his accustomed draught. The sediment, when examined, appeared to consist of powdered diamond, an ingredient sometimes employed by
powerful and wealthy criminals in Eastern countries. Circumstances strengthened Phayre's first suspicions, and he pointed to
the Gaikwár as in some way privy to the alleged attempt on the
life of a British Resident. Sir Lewis Pelly, who had been
already appointed to replace Phayre, expressed himself to the
same purport. Such an outrage could not be passed over, and
Lord Northbrook ordered Pelly to place Malhár Rao in arrest,
and to take charge of the government pending the issue of a
public inquiry into the whole affair. A special Commission, composed of three English and three native members, was instructed
to hear the evidence and to report to the Indian Government their
verdict on the charges brought against the Gaikwár. At the head
of the Commission was Sir Richard Couch, who had served for
some years as Chief Justice of Bengal; his English colleagues were
Sir Richard Meade, a soldier-political of mark and high standing,
who was destined erelong to replace Charles Saunders at Haidarábád, and Mr. Philip Melvill, Judicial Commissioner for the
Panjáb. The Native Commissioners were the Mahárájas of
Gwáliár and Jaipúr, and Sindhia's crowhile Minister, the wise,
upright, and polished Brahman, Sir Dinkar Rao.*

In thus departing from former usage, and preferring a public
to a private inquiry, the Viceroy showed a generous desire to
leave the accused no ground or pretext for just complaint. For
the first time in Anglo-Indian history a native prince of the first
rank was to be tried in open court by his virtual peers. A leading member of the English Bar, the famous Serjeant Ballantyne,
was allowed to conduct his defence. On the 23rd of February,
1875, Malhár Rao was arraigned before the Commission in his
own capital on four charges, two of which raised the question of
his complicity in the attempt to poison Colonel Phayre. A great
many witnesses were examined on both sides, and the trial was
not over till the last day of March. In due time the Commis-

* Indian Blue-book, 1874-75 ; Malleson ; *Allen's Mail ;* Temple.

sicners presented their report. Sir. R. Couch and his English colleagues-found the Gaikwár guilty of instigating the attempt on Phayre's life. The Mahárája of Jaipúr pronounced him not guilty, while Sindhia and Dinkar Rao held that the charge had not been fully proven.

It remained for the Viceroy in Council, after carefully review-ing the records of this long trial, to pass judgement on the question thus left in virtual suspense. The weight of judicial opinion was clearly on the side of the English Commissioners. No impartial person would have blamed the Viceroy for acting boldly on his own convictions of Malhár Rao's guilt. But was there no way of punishing the Gaikwár without wounding the self-love of Sindhia's party? Lord Salisbury at any rate thought he had found a way, and with his instructions Lord Northbrook hastened to comply. On the 19th of April he issued a proclamation which announced the final decision of his Government on the Gaikwár's fate. Malhár Rao was formally deposed, not on account of the crime for which he had been brought to trial, but because his general conduct had shown him unworthy of the indulgence granted him in the previous year. The Princess Jamna-Bai was to act as Regent, with power to name an heir to the vacant *Gadi*. On the 27th of May she adopted a kinsman, the boy Sayaji Rao, who was duly installed as Gaikwár. During her regency the government was carried on by one of the ablest and most enlight-ened Brahmans in Southern India, Sir Madhavo Rao, who spoke English like his native tongue, and had served with the highest credit as Minister, first to the sovereign of Travankór, afterwards to Túkaji Holkar of Indór. Melvill remained at Baroda as British Resident. With two such men at the helm, the fortunes of the Baroda State were soon on the way to sure recovery from past eclipse.*

Happily the misrule in Baroda formed a rare exception to the general well-doing of the Native States at this period. The re-ports of our political officers from all parts of the country for the year 1875 present on the whole an encouraging picture of the progress made by native rulers in governing their subjects accord-ing to the best European ideas. Many of the Rájput princes and barons were sending their sons and kinsfolk to the Mayo College opened in October, 1875. Gas lamps already lighted the well-built streets and marble palaces of Jaipúr, and the Viceroy him-self opened the Mayo Hospital in that city. Gang-robberies and

* Malleson ; Indian Blue-book ; Parliamentary Papers (Baroda).

violent crimes had greatly diminished throughout Rájásthán. In most of the Native States a new generation was growing up trained in the learning of their own and other lands. English was taught more and more widely in the higher schools and colleges. The people sent their children more and more readily to the public vaccinators. The high-born youths in the Rájkumár College of Káthiawár were learning to ride and play cricket. Túkaji Holkar was busy founding cotton-mills and otherwise developing the resources of Indór, while his eldest son was completing his studies in the collegiate school attached to the Indór Residency. The little State of Kúch Bahár, on the Assam border, could boast of a library richer than any to be found in Bengal outside Calcutta. Several princes vied with the ruler of Jaipúr in spending a liberal share of their revenues on irrigation and other public works. In most of the Rájput States and in Bhartpur, justice was administered as efficiently as in those which had passed for the time under British management or control. One of these States was Kotah, where the Nawáb Faiz Ali Khán, the ablest Mohammadan statesman in India next to Sálar Jang, was governing with marked success in the name of his boy sovereign.*

The attempt to govern according to English methods did not always prove successful. A Council of Regency, controlled or advised by Colonel Herbert, had been appointed to manage the affairs of Udaipur during the minority of its Maharána. In this State, as in many others, the land-revenue was still paid in kind. The Council agreed to fix the assessment on certain districts at a money-rate for a term of ten years. But a heavy rainfall having damaged the crops, the peasantry of a hundred villages set off in a body with all their goods for Málwa, followed by a train of collectors and money-lenders, who earnestly besought them to stay. After a while the fugitives returned to their homes under conditions which left them masters of the field.†

On the part of the Native Princes and Chiefs nothing at this time was more remarkable than the burst of loyal enthusiasm which heralded and accompanied their reception of the Prince of Wales. Before his arrival in Bombay, the question had been mooted by the Governor-General's Agent, whether the Princes and Chiefs of Central India should not waive the custom of offering costly presents to their Royal visitor, who would have to make them some commensurate return. To such a proposal

---

* Indian Blue-book.
† Indian Blue-book; Colonel Herbert's Administration Report.

Holkar, himself the thriftiest of native rulers, would give no ear. "For the first time during your rule"—he said—"India will be visited by her Sovereign ; for in the Shahzáda, the Queen's heir, all will see their Sovereign. We owe it to ourselves to receive the Shahzáda in a becoming manner. I could not meet his Royal Highness without some offering ; and a small one I could not present. Advise the chiefs to offer something of their own ; heirlooms or curios ; and leave the rest to us." Their only wish and care, in short, was to show their loyalty in accordance with their own views of an event which rose above all precedent. The honour of receiving the Shahzáda would for them be a sufficient return. Nor was this spirit confined to one part of India. When the Prince of Wales landed at Calcutta in December, 1875, after a round of visits and sightseeing in Bombay and Madras, many of the leading princes and chiefs from the Panjáb, Rájputána, Central India, and the Doáb were assembled with all their retinues in the Viceroy's capital to do honour to the Viceroy's princely guest. Never had Calcutta beheld so imposing a pageant as that which stirred and coloured the broad Maidan before Chowringhie, when the Prince of Wales held his chapter of the Star of India, in the presence of a numerous array of Knights clad in the varied costumes of the Eastern and Western worlds. Under the same vast canvas roof the Mahárájas of Káshmir and Pattiála, of Jodhpur, Indór, and Gwáliár, were seated in the same line with the great Nipálese Minister, Sir Jang Bahádur, the Begam of Bhopál, and the Mahárája of Travankór. A number of new Knights, English and Indian, received their investiture from the Prince's own hands in the name of their common Queen. Among the English Knights who figured in this splendid gathering was Bombay's former Governor, Sir Bartle Frere, whom the Prince had invited to bear him company during his Indian travels. Lord Northbrook himself had stayed away, in order that no greater official light should outshine that of the Heir-Apparent to the British Crown.*

The Prince's visit to Calcutta was a time of general holiday. On the night after his arrival the whole city was ablaze with illuminations. During his stay at Government House he won all hearts by his gracious bearing, his highbred tact, and his genial readiness to please and be pleased. Those native princes to whom he granted a private audience found their future Sovereign ready to treat them as personal friends. The white citizens feasted

---

* Indian Blue-book ; Temple ; *Allen's Mail ;* Wheeler's "India in 1875-6."

him sumptuously at the Town Hall, and the leading natives entertained him one evening after their own fashion, in one of their own gardens, with all the fairest fruits and appliances of Eastern luxury, taste, and munificence.

At Patna, where he halted for a few hours, on his way up the country, the native chiefs and gentry of Bahár brought out their whole array of elephants, decked in their gayest trappings, to greet the son of their honoured Queen. Those officers, English and native, who had done good service during the famine, were here presented to his Royal Highness by the Lieutenant-Governor of Bengal. His progress everywhere was one long triumph. All those princes who had the pleasure and the good fortune to receive him as a guest in their own capitals vied with each other in the warmth and splendour of their hospitalities. Some of them were able to gratify his love of sport. Holkar received his guest with rare magnificence and with every mark of sincere loyalty. When Sindhia ushered the Prince into his own palace, "There have been Sindhias before me who have won great honour"—he said,—"but no ancestor of mine has been so honoured as I am to-day." At Jammu, in the Káshmir Hills, the loyal son of Guláb Singh entertained his august visitor for several days as royally as if he were Emperor of Hindústan. In Rájputána, Central India, and Bombay, the princes and chiefs of those parts flocked to his receptions, and forgot their petty rivalries and old inherited quarrels in the joy of seeing and conversing with the son of their English Pádishah.

Nor did all this enthusiasm die out with the Prince's departure. The Rao of Kachh, who died soon afterwards, set apart £20,000 for the construction of harbour works at Mándvi in memory of the Prince's visit. A hospital bearing the Prince's name was begun at Kolhapur. Many other native chiefs and gentlemen founded schools, hospitals, or other useful agencies in honour of the same event. In Bombay an equestrian statue of the Prince was set up by the munificent Sir Albert Sassoon. But more important than all these were the memorials which his Royal Highness left behind him in the hearts of men of rank, culture, and social weight, throughout the country. The bluest-blooded of Rájput princes could feel no shame in offering homage to the eldest son of a dynasty little less ancient and far more widely renowned than his own. The least tractable of native rulers succumbed to the spell of friendly intercourse with one who seemed in all respects so worthy of the allegiance due to his mother's son.

To have seen and talked, and exchanged presents with their future Sovereign, to have received him under their own roofs, to have ridden and shot with him over their own domains, were so many pledges of a livelier sympathy, a closer accord between the princes and nobles of India and the British Crown. And to intelligent natives of every class the Prince's visit, so rich in evidences of his unfailing courtesy and thoughtful kindliness towards all who crossed his path, seemed like the dawn of a brighter day for all who had hitherto smarted under the cold condescensions, the rough familiarities, or the insolent rudeness of the average Englishman settled in their midst.*

On the 27th of April, 1875, the untimely death of Lord Hobart deprived Madras of a wise, hardworking Governor, well skilled in economical science, who for three years past had striven with quiet zeal to advance the welfare of his Indian subjects. In those three years the number of primary schools in his province had increased by one-half, and the number of pupils in nearly the same proportion. For the sake of the Mohammadans scattered throughout the Presidency Lord Hobart founded ten primary Urdu schools, besides opening special classes for their instruction in the middle and higher schools. He exhorted the municipal committees to spend more money on the teaching of the masses. To him the model farms at Saidapet owed much of their increasing usefulness as centres of instruction and experiment. In one of these farms he opened a school of agriculture for the scientific training of young men. For the sake of a poor and patient peasantry he fought hard, with partial success, against the Viceroy's scheme for raising the salt-duties in Southern India, as a means of lowering the higher rates paid by the less needy peasants of Bengal and the North-West. The figures and facts he quoted went to prove that the people of Madras already paid for their salt as high a price as most of them could well afford, that the duties bore hard on various industries, especially on the trade in salt fish, that the health of the cattle suffered from a lack of cheap salt, and that any further rise in the duties must tend to check the consumption of an article so necessary to human life.

Lord Hobart's pleadings availed to shelve for a few years longer the question of equalizing the salt-duties throughout India. But in order to prevent smuggling, Lord Northbrook enhanced the duty in certain districts bordering on Southern

---

* Indian Blue-book ; Temple ; *Allen's Mail;* "The Prince of Wales's Tour in India," by W. H. Russell.

Bengal; and an Act was passed empowering the Madras Government to fix the selling price of salt from time to time in each district at a rate proportioned to the amount of duty. In behalf of the fish-curers Lord Hobart, shortly before his death, had decided to set apart certain yards within which they might obtain the needful supplies of salt at a trifle over the cost price. For more than six months after his death the government was carried on by the senior member of his Council, Mr. William Robinson, who was destined some years later to become Sir William Robinson, Governor of Ceylon.[*]

In the latter half of 1875 Lord Northbrook carried through his Council a sweeping measure of reform in the Customs Tariff. Out of fifteen articles on which export duties were still levied at rates varying from three annas a maund to four per cent. of value, he took off the duties from all save rice, indigo, and lac. Cotton goods, wheat, hides, oils, seeds, spices, and lac-dye, were all thenceforth set free. The duty on rice, which yielded half a million a year at the low rate of three annas, or fourpence-half-penny a maund, he could not bring himself to forego. That on indigo, worth only about £40,000 a year, was left untouched for the present, as too light to injure the trade in an article supplied by India alone. Large reductions were also made in the long list of import duties, which yielded a gross revenue of more than four millions. Every article which had hitherto been taxed at 7½ per cent. would thenceforth be charged only 5 per cent. The duty on coffee was taken off; that on spirits and certain wines was somewhat enhanced. One new duty of five per cent. was imposed on the raw long-stapled cotton imported from America for the mills of Western and Central India. This was intended to place Indian mill-owners on an even footing with their rivals in Lancashire, who still kicked against the low duties levied for fiscal purposes on the produce of their mills. But it gave almost equal offence to both parties. The Indian mill-owners resented the new impost as a clog on native enterprise, while the men of Lancashire denounced it as a new pretext for the maintenance of restrictive duties on their own manufactures.[†]

By the end of March, 1876, the revenue accounts for the past year showed a surplus of a million and a third over a total outlay of 49⅝ millions, which included a balance of half a million for famine relief, and nearly a million and a half set down to

---

[*] Indian Blue-book; *Government Gazette; Allen's Mail.*
[†] Indian Blue-book; Statistical Abstract; *Allen's Mail.*

" loss by exchange." The last-named item represented a serious fall in the exchange value of the rupee as applied to the payment of debts incurred in England, where gold is the only standard of value. Owing to various causes, such as the adoption of a gold standard throughout Germany in the place of silver, the excess of silver in the world as compared with gold, and the large sums which the Indian Government had to send home in payment of the Home Council's weekly drafts on Calcutta, the exchange value of the silver rupee had lately fallen from about two shillings to one and ninepence; and it seemed likely to fall yet lower. Every one who wanted to remit money from India to England for whatever purpose had to pay for the accommodation a toll of two and sixpence, if not more, on every pound. In India, however, this fall in the value of silver made no difference to the people at large. The purchasing power of the rupee within the country was in no way diminished, while the low price of silver in Europe served to stimulate India's export trade, and so to benefit all whose industry swelled the volume of that trade.*

In the year 1875-6 India's foreign trade exceeded 102½ millions, more than two-thirds of which represented her dealings with Europe. With Great Britain she exchanged goods and treasure to the value of more than sixty-one millions. A full half of her foreign trade passed through the Suez Canal, of which Italy and Austria had begun to make profitable use. The exports of Indian wheat, chiefly from the North-West Provinces, had quadrupled in one year. Those of tea exceeded twenty-four million pounds' weight, worth 2,183,000 pounds sterling. There was a large increase in the export of oil-seeds, spices, wool, coffee, hides, lac, cotton-twist, and the gunny-bags woven in the jute-mills of Bengal. The rice-trade alone was worth 5½ millions sterling. Of cotton piece-goods somewhat less was exported, but much more was consumed at home. In the matter of imports, which amounted to nearly 42½ millions, Bengal led the way with about 19 millions; while 17 millions' worth was set down to Bombay. For the cotton-mills of the latter province more and more machinery was yearly required from England. The demand for English coal was beginning to slacken in view of larger outputs from the Indian mines. In the imports of the cheaper cotton goods from Manchester there was a marked decline, owing to the successful rivalry of the local mills, of which Bombay alone now possessed

* Temple ; Indian Blue-book.

thirty-three, working more than 900,000 spindles and 8,000 looms.[*]

The collections for the land-revenue of the same year exceeded 21¼ millions, the highest figures as yet recorded under our rule. This amount seems moderate by comparison with the gross yield of 36 to 38 millions, obtained in the time of Aurangzib. In most provinces the sums collected fell little short of the original demand. In spite of heavy floods and an unkindly season, the shortcomings in the Panjáb were less than two per cent. For Madras the difference was somewhat greater, and in Oudh it rose to five per cent., or a little more than the shortcomings from Bengal. A new system of village records was working with marked success in some parts of the North-West Provinces, and promised in due time to furnish the peasantry with accurate registers of their rights. The ráyats of Bengal were still awaiting the measures designed by Temple's Government for the timely settlement of rent disputes. One Act, indeed, was already passed, empowering revenue officers to pronounce summary decrees in cases that specially concerned the public peace. The Bombay Government were pondering the state of things reported by the Commission which inquired into the recent outbreak against the *saukárs* or money-lenders of Púna and Ahmadnagar. Meanwhile they wondered at the preference shown by the peasantry for borrowing from the saukárs at 36 per cent. to paying only 6¼ per cent. for advances offered by the Government. Sometimes no interest at all was asked of them. Owing to the damage done by this year's floods in the district of Ahmadabad, the Government offered the poorer ráyats an advance of ten thousand rupees, free of interest. Not one of the sufferers applied for his share. The danger of losing their old customers had impelled the saukárs to make concessions which the ráyats found it easier to accept than loans involving irksome formalities and gradual repayment within a given date. Few, if any, of the ráyats could afford to offend a banker who charged heavy interest, but in good seasons allowed the debt to run on.[†]

In the Panjáb the value of land had nearly doubled during the past six years. Sales and mortgages of landed property were continually taking place; but the extent of land transferred from its former owners was still comparatively trifling, and much of it passed into the hands of other husbandmen. "No one"—wrote the Financial Commissioner—"who compares the condition of the

---

[*] Indian Blue-book ; Statistical Abstract.   [†] Indian Blue-book.

village proprietors now with what it was twenty-four years ago, can doubt that a large increase of general prosperity has occurred." Blest with light assessments and wise rulers, Dalhousie's model province was still, in many ways, an example to the rest of India. In the Central Provinces, Berár, and British Burmah, more and more waste land was yearly brought under tillage, trade was busy, and the harvests generally good. In Bengal the harvests proved so plentiful that the failure of the winter rice crops in Northern Bahár had little effect in raising the current price of food; and the mischief threatened by a local scarcity was averted by the timely movements of private trade.*

Education was slowly making its way among the people. Out of a million and a half expended on the teaching of 1,700,000 scholars in 50,000 schools and colleges, the Provincial Governments contributed about one-half, the rest being made up from local cesses, municipal grants, fees, endowments, and funds subscribed by the people themselves. In British Burmah one-half, in Bengal, the North-West, and Madras one-fifth of the scholars were taught in schools unaided by the State. In most provinces the great mass of pupils attended either the Government or the aided schools. In the first two years of Temple's rule hundreds of new primary schools gave instruction of the simplest kind to many thousands of new pupils throughout Bengal. A new class of intermediate schools, opened in 1875, served to attract the most promising boys from the village *patshálas* upwards to the middle and higher schools. Temple found the youth of Bengal everywhere eager to learn English as a means of rising in the law or the public service. The study of medicine was fast becoming popular, and the new medical schools at Dákha and Katák were soon filled with attentive students. Even the study of practical mechanics began to commend itself to the Bengáli mind. In memory of the Prince's visit to Bankipur, near Patna, the native chiefs and gentry of Bahár subscribed among them £20,000 for the founding of a local college, in which technical rules and processes should be practically taught. To this undertaking Temple's Government offered a yearly grant-in-aid, equal to the interest on the sum subscribed.

At Lahór a School of Art and Industry was opened in 1875 with a view to training the people in the best means of improving their local manufactures. In Bombay the demand for English teaching grew yearly wider. The new night-schools found special

* Indian Blue-book.

favour with the workpeople in the cotton-mills. Students flocked in ever larger numbers to the Grant Medical College, spite of the heavy fees for a full course; and in the Civil Engineering College at Púna nine out of twelve candidates took their degree. The normal schools in the Central Provinces were beginning to supply good teachers to the several districts. In each of these schools a new industrial class had lately been opened for the training of those who aspired to set up similar classes in the village schools. In Berár the cause of popular instruction had long been unduly neglected in favour of the higher schools and colleges. In respect of primary and indigenous teaching, British Burmah, where every boy might learn his rudiments from the yellow-clad Phúngyi, or village monk, put all our older provinces to shame. Even in Bengal only twelve boys or girls in every thousand of the people were known to be at school, and in some provinces the proportion was still lower.

The number of girls' schools and girl-scholars increased very slowly in most parts of India. In proportion to population Burmah could show the largest total, and next to her at no great distance came Madras, where the noble Rajah of Viziánagram founded or maintained some of the largest schools for girls. In Bengal there were only 18,400 girls at school; but several Zanána Associations, got up by native gentlemen, were employed in teaching many girls of the higher classes at their own homes. To Mrs. Wheeler, the daughter of a Native Christian missionary, the Government assigned the task of inspecting the Zanána classes and the female schools in Bengal. Elsewhere, except in Bombay, the mass of the people still looked coldly at a movement from which they expected more of harm than good. In this direction, as in many others, native prejudice was very hard to overcome. A school for the training of native women as doctors had lately been established in the North-Western Provinces. This school, of which Dr. Corbyn had been the chief promoter, the Government at his own suggestion was now compelled to close, not because the students were slow to learn their duties, but because native prejudices "would hopelessly hamper them at every step."*

* Indian Blue-book; Temple; Statistical Abstract.

CHAPTER VIII.

In the last year of Lord Northbrook's rule, more than 4,000 books of all kinds were registered for publication in various parts of India. More than a third of these were issued in Bengal, and nearly 800 in Bombay, which found a close rival in the Panjáb. About three-fourths of this literature were more or less original, and two-thirds were written in the vernaculars of each province. The steady growth of a vernacular literature is one of the best boons which our rule has conferred on the people of India. As many books—about 500—appeared in English as in all the classical languages of India together. Of the number yearly published nearly a third may be described as school-books, and a half as reprints. As in many other countries, religious works rank first in point of numbers, followed at a long interval by books of poetry, more or less worthy of the name. A few of these were written in English. The taste for fiction and the drama was specially active in Bengal and Bombay. Of the few biographies published in 1875 one was written by a native lady, wife of the Head of the Sanskrit College in Calcutta. Treatises on law and language or grammar employed the pens of many writers. Those on natural science were mostly translations. Some of the ethical and didactic works would have done honour to any nation. Historical works were comparatively few, and books of voyages and travels were almost unknown.*

Some of these books were written in English of which no Englishman need have been ashamed. Anglo-Indians are wont to make merry with the Johnsonese English spoken and written by the average Bábu of Bengal. But many natives all over the country could use our language, whether in speech or writing, with remarkable ease, precision, purity, and grace. As an orator

* Indian Blue-book ; Statistical Abstract.

in English, the Brahmist reformer, Kesháb Chandra Sen, delighted all listeners during his English tour, while his written essays bear a strong resemblance to the style of Emerson and Theodore Parker. Kishari Chand Mittra, the first Native Judge who ever sat on the High Court of Bengal, was a ripe English scholar, who had once edited a newspaper written in English for Native readers, and had since contributed some bright and thoughtful essays to that common mouthpiece of Indian and English culture, the *Calcutta Review*.* Several English journals in Calcutta, Bombay, and elsewhere were written and conducted by Natives of India for the special use of their own countrymen. Sir Madhava Rao, who had raised Travankór from the depths of disorder into a model Native State, had learnéd English thoroughly at the High School of Madras. Among his pupils was the first Prince of Travankór, who afterwards wrote the story of his tutor's life for the *Calcutta Review*, and delivered in English a series of thoughtful lectures on some leading questions of the day.

In 1870 an eminent London firm published a volume of English poetry, which, but for its brief preface, might have been taken, in point of technical merit, for the handiwork of an average English poet.† It contained, in fact, a series of short poems written by different members of one Bengáli family, two of them young ladies of little more than twenty years. Besides the original poems there were many pieces fairly well translated from the German and the French. Four years later another London firm brought out a novel written in English by a Bengáli Christian, Lál Behári Day, to illustrate the distinctive features, the homely joys and trials of village life in his own country.‡ This novel, which had won the prize of fifty pounds offered by the Bábú Jaikishn Mukarji, one of the most liberal and patriotic Zamindárs in Bengal, traced in simple and idyllic prose the fortunes of its peasant-hero from the cradle to the funeral pile, through a chain of incidents true to the facts, surroundings, and social traits of a time still recent.

The native newspapers at this time numbered about 200, with an aggregate sale of more than 100,000 copies. Twenty of the leading journals in Bengal averaged 1,000 copies each. But the actual number of sheets circulated by no means represented the

---

* Mr. Justice Mittra died in 1872. He became a High Court Judge in 1862.

† *The Dutt Family Album.* Longmans and Co., 1870.

‡ "Govinda Sámanta; or, The History of a Bengal Raiyat," by the Rev. Lál Behári Day. Macmillan and Co., 1874.

full amount of influence wielded by the Native Press; for each copy, on a general average, would probably count its readers by the score. Many of these papers were conducted with marked ability, in a spirit of general fairness and even goodwill to the ruling powers. If Native journalists were not very careful about the freshness or the accuracy of their news; if they sometimes dipped their pens in gall and pushed their comments on public men and measures beyond the verge of libel; if they were apt to take offence where none was intended, to put wrong constructions on harmless-seeming, wise, or commendable acts; if some of them launched into wild invectives against English tyranny, greed and selfishness, they might plead in partial excuse the example set and the provocations offered by some of our own countrymen in India; while their worst excesses were matched if not outdone by the tone and language of certain newspapers published in the West. Official persons are commonly thin-skinned; and Englishmen in India are impatient of any criticism which might tend, in their opinion, to lower the ruling in the eyes of the subject race. But those who could rise with Muir and Temple above the prejudices of race or class, were fain to allow that the bulk of Native journalists discharged their functions with fearless honesty, with fair discretion, and with a pleasing show of loyalty towards our rule.[*]

The number of societies formed by Natives for the discussion of social and political questions was increasing year by year. A patriotic Bengáli, Dr. Sarkár, was raising funds among his own countrymen for a Science Association which might furnish students with sound instruction in all branches of scientific lore. To this movement Temple himself gave freely both of his private means and his public countenance. Many of the Native papers in Bombay deplored the loss to science and social culture caused by the death of Dr. John Wilson, the Free Kirk missionary, who had long been furthering in Bombay the good work which Alexander Duff had begun before him in Calcutta. A ripe scholar and an enlightened Christian, he had filled for some years the post of Vice-Chancellor to the Bombay University, in which so many of his former pupils had been doing equal credit to their old teacher and themselves.[†]

In many parts of India the Hindu folk willingly sent their children to the Mission schools, many of which, on account of their excellent teaching in things secular, received grants-in-aid

---

[*] Indian Blue-book; Temple; Hunter.
[†] Routledge's "English Rule in India"; Temple; Indian Blue-book.

from the State. Some of the Native chiefs and gentry even helped to maintain these schools out of their own purses. The new leaven of Western thought and culture was working freely through the mass of Eastern usages and creeds. Native ladies were beginning here and there to exchange the privacy of the Zanána for that free intercourse of men and women which prevails in Europe. Some of the more enlightened Hindus had gone so far as to denounce polygamy, and to educate their daughters in the learning of the West. Eminent Pandits had lately discovered that a Hindu might cross the sea without losing caste, that the eating of flesh was not directly forbidden in the Vedas, and that Hindu widows might marry again without deadly sin. If the number of professed converts to the Christian faith grew very slowly in most parts of India, there was a growing tendency among educated men of all classes to sit loose to the doctrines, while still conforming to the rites and practices, of their ancestral creeds. Having discarded the gods of the Hindu Pantheon, together with a belief in the divine origin of the Shastras, they could not bring themselves to accept the Christian Trinity or the special inspiration of the Christian Bible. It was chiefly among the rude hill-races of Bengal and the Tamil peasants of Southern India, that Christian missionaries won the largest number of converts to this or that form of Western Christianity.*

During Lord Northbrook's rule many of the higher posts in the "uncovenanted" or local civil service had been thrown open to qualified Natives in every province. Native Judges had made their mark in more than one of the High Courts. The Native gentlemen who sat on municipal committees, on the bench of magistrates, and in the Legislative Councils, were seldom found wanting in mental or moral fitness for their work. The Native Judges in most parts of the country were steadily winning the respect and the confidence of their neighbours, white and black. Native students made their way more and more frequently to London in order to obtain degrees in Law and Medicine, or to compete with the pick of our English youth for appointments to the Covenanted Civil Service of India.

In 1874 the peace of Bombay was suddenly broken by a fierce outburst of Mohammadan bigotry, which a very little spark sufficed to set on fire. A Parsi bookseller had published a Gujaráti version of "The Life of Mahomet," by Washington Irving.

* Indian Blue-book ; Trotter ; Temple ; *Allen's Mail.*

Certain passages from this book provoked the wrath of some Mohammadan fanatics, who stirred up their fellow-worshippers to avenge on the Parsi community the insult offered by one of their number to the Prophet of Islám. On the 13th of February a furious mob attacked and gutted a Parsi Temple, plundered and wrecked a number of Parsi houses, insulted or ill-used their frightened inmates, and for some hours rioted unchecked in the Parsi quarter of Bombay. The police, for a time, were powerless or afraid to interfere. The Parsis presently turned upon their assailants, and fighting went on for several days. The great Musalman feast of Moharram was close at hand, when religious frenzy might burn and spread like wildfire. Happily the troops whom Sir Philip Wodehouse had been slow to send for arrived at last, the processions usual at the Moharram were forbidden, and the excitement speedily cooled down.*

During these years the peace of the Panjáb frontier remained unbroken save by a few insignificant raids, for which due reparation was extorted by peaceful means. For some time past a steady improvement had been taking place in our relations with the more troublesome of the frontier tribes. Thanks to a policy of firm repression, tempered by fair and conciliatory measures for encouraging peaceful trade, the border districts—said the Lieutenant-Governor—were now almost as tranquil as any part of the province. Large tracts of once desolate country had been turned into fruitful fields, and rich crops were gathered in the very mouths of the border passes. Along the North-Eastern frontier the Dafla tribes of the Assam border gave the most trouble, raiding into the villages nearest the border, and carrying off a number of peaceful villagers to replace as many of their own dead or disabled slaves. A close blockade of the border passes having failed to enforce the surrender of their prey, a strong body of troops entered the Dafla hills in the cold weather of 1874; and the offending tribes, who had deemed themselves secure in their native jungles, were fain to surrender all of their captives who had survived the hardships of their new lot. In the south-east of Assam the Nága tribes had been growing restless and alarmed at the progress of our survey parties in their native hills. In the beginning of 1875 one party, under Lieutenant Holcombe, was suddenly attacked in the midst of their peaceful labours, and not one was left alive. In the same month of January another party under Captain Butler was attacked twice in one week by bodies

* Routledge ; Indian Blue-book ; *Allen's Mail.*

of Nágas; but on both occasions the assailants were beaten off
with heavy slaughter.*

The Viceroy's relations with the frontier States were as friendly
as circumstances could allow. In Nipál our old ally, Jang Bahádur,
was still as ever our good friend, so long as we forebore from
urging him to throw his country open to our trade. Before the
Prince of Wales left India, the wiry little warrior, who had so
long ruled Nipál in the name of his puppet sovereign, entertained
the Prince's party for several days in the jungles of the Nipál
Tarai, where they enjoyed such sport in shooting tigers and hunting wild elephants as no other part of Asia could have furnished.†

The opening of a fair near Baxa in 1874 for the promotion of
trade with Bhotán marked the renewal of friendly intercourse
with the people who had fought against us ten years before. For
the first time in history the Deb Rajah of Bhotán paid a visit to
the Lieutenant-Governor of Bengal. The meeting took place at
Baxa, where the Rajah assured Sir Richard Temple of his
hearty desire for a closer intercourse and a lasting friendship
between the two countries. In the same year the King of Ava, or
Upper Burmah, proved his goodwill to the Indian Government by
promising a safe passage for the exploring mission which Lord
Northbrook, under orders from the India Office, was about to
send through Burmah overland to Shanghai. Colonel Horace
Browne, accompanied by Dr. Anderson, Sladen's old helpmate,
and Mr. Ney Elias, with a small escort of Sikhs, arrived at Mandalay on the 23rd of December. The King received them in the
friendliest manner. On the 15th of January the party reached
Bhámo, where two days later the brave young Margary joined
them after a long and hazardous journey westward from Hankow.
Passing slowly, not without hindrance from unfriendly Kakhyens,
through the wild hill-country pierced by the upper waters of the
Salwín, the travellers on the 21st of February halted about twelve
miles from Mánwain, where Margary had so lately found a
gracious welcome.

From that day their worst troubles began. Rumours of hostile
movements reached the camp, and Margary rode forward to ascertain the truth, and to prepare the Chinese officials in Mánwain for
the arrival of his comrades. On learning from Margary that the
road was clear, Browne's party moved forward. The next day
their camp was suddenly attacked by overwhelming numbers of

* Indian Blue-book.   † Wheeler's " Visit of the Prince of Wales."

armed Chinese; and in spite of the front shown by their Sikh escort, they had no choice left them but a timely retreat towards Bhámo. It was then they learned that the gallant Margary had been foully murdered, soon after his entrance into Mánwain. The Burmese officers who had accompanied the Mission seem to have stood loyally by their friends in the hour of danger, although the assailants warned them to keep out of the way and leave the "white devils" to their fate. In due time the Chinese Government granted an indemnity to Margary's parents for the cruel and treacherous murder of their son. Some of the murderers were afterwards brought to justice, but the Chinese commander who had planned or prompted the criminal deed suffered only a temporary loss of his command.*

In the border Khánate of Khalát the quarrels between the Khán and his unruly chiefs grew to such a head that in May, 1873, the British Agent, Major Harrison, was withdrawn from the Khán's capital, and the subsidy granted by Lord Mayo had to be suspended. For more than two years of general anarchy and disorder the Bolán Pass remained closed to peaceful traffic, and the Khán himself lacked the power, even if he had the will, to amend a state of things so unpleasant to his civilized neighbours. The Commissioner of Sind, Sir William Merewether, urged the Viceroy to repress these disorders with a strong hand, and to punish the Khán for his supposed share in causing them. But Lord Northbrook shrank from using armed force against an old ally, so long as diplomacy might serve his purpose; and this view found at the time a firm supporter in Lord Salisbury himself, who deprecated any course which might "possibly entail a prolonged occupation" of Khalát. In October, 1875, Captain Sandeman, Deputy Commissioner of Dera Gházi Khán, was therefore ordered to attempt a peaceful settlement of the Khán's disputes with his refractory subjects and vassals, and to devise some plan for re-opening the Bolán Pass to our trade. His earlier efforts among the frontier tribes were so successful that in the spring of 1876 Lord Northbrook placed him at the head of a mission, guarded by a strong escort, to the Khán himself. A few months later he had accomplished all that could be desired.†

Of Lord Northbrook's relations with Sher Ali mention has been made in a former chapter. The Amir's fits of ill-humour never led him to break faith with the Indian Government, or to court the protection of its Northern rival. In November, 1874, he assured

---

* Hunter ; Afghán Blue-book ; *Allen's Mail.*　　† Bilúchistan Papers.

the Viceroy's Vakíl at Kábul that "the friendship between the two Governments was being confirmed and consolidated day by day." Down to the close of Lord Northbrook's rule, and for some months thereafter, he took care to acquaint the Viceroy through his Native Agent with the contents of every letter that passed between himself and General Kauffmann. Lord Northbrook, for his part, had steadily pursued the cautious policy handed down to him by former Viceroys, unmoved alike by the progress of Russian rule in Khokán, by rumours of Russian intrigue on the Oxus, and by the clamour of English alarmists in India or at home. When circumstances drove him to resign his high office, he could still with truth declare that Sher Ali "continued to lean upon the British Government."[*]

Ill-health was the reason formally assigned for Lord Northbrook's departure in the spring of 1876. But the real cause of his retirement from a post which he had filled with so much credit for the last four years was something altogether different. In the beginning of 1875 the Marquis of Salisbury, as head of the India Office, had requested the Viceroy to take measures without loss of time for obtaining Sher Ali's assent to the planting of a British Agency at Herát, as the precursor of a like arrangement for Kandáhár. The Russian movements in Central Asia, and the assumed incompetency of our Native Agents to supply trustworthy intelligence of passing events in Afghánistán and the adjacent countries, were the reasons given for this sudden departure from the policy and the pledges of former years. Lord Salisbury further argued that an Amir who had "more than once expressed his readiness to permit the presence of an Agent at Herát" would make no serious difficulty now, "if his intentions are still loyal."

These instructions, so peremptory, so ill-timed, so strangely opposed to official usage and the spirit of former pledges, came upon the Viceroy and his Council like a thunderbolt in a clear sky. If the Minister for India persisted in his demand, Lord Northbrook knew that he himself must either give way or make room for a more compliant Viceroy. Delay, however, might still avert the dangers he foresaw in a policy which recalled the dark days of Lord Auckland. He telegraphed to England for time to make inquiries and take due counsel with competent advisers on the spot. The request being granted he set to work. Armed with the facts and opinions recorded by Sir Robert Davies, Lieutenant-

[*] Afghán Blue-book.

Governor of the Panjáb, Sir Richard Pollock, his trusty Commissioner for Peshávar, and by other officers of mark employed on the Panjáb frontier, Lord Northbrook in June of the same year sent home a despatch that set forth in calm, weighty, and well-reasoned sentences, the unanimous opinion of his own Council, from Lord Napier down to Muir and Eden, on the questions raised by Lord Salisbury's strange demand.

The despatch of June was one long statesmanlike protest against the policy revealed in the despatch of January. Lord Northbrook argued in effect that the time for planting British Residents in Afghán cities had not yet come ; that Sher Ali himself was in no mood to sanction a step in theory so desirable, and that even if he could be induced to sanction it, no good could ensue therefrom in face of the serious drawbacks involved in Afghán fanaticism. pride, and distrust of those English neighbours who had once spread havoc and slaughter through the land of Dost Mohammad. It was unfair, he hinted, to press upon the Amir a concession still refused by the loyal ruler of Káshmir, a concession which, as things stood, might imperil his own throne, the peace of his country, and the lives of British officers dwelling in Afghán towns. Nor would it be less unfair to make Sher Ali's refusal, if he should refuse, a reason for treating him as no longer our friend, and thus throwing him into the arms of Russia, on whom, according to Sir Richard Pollock, he had come to look with ever-deepening suspicion. With regard to the Amir's own feelings on this matter, the evidence obtained from all authentic sources showed that neither at the Ambála Darbár nor at the Simla conference had he ever expressed a wish to receive an English Resident at Herát or elsewhere. On the latter occasion his Minister, Núr Mohammad, had strongly dissuaded the Viceroy from putting forth a proposal which his master would certainly decline to consider. When Captain Grey reminded the Afghán Envoy by letter of some words he had spoken at Ambála to the contrary effect, Núr Mohammad replied that those words had nearly cost him his life. " It was as much as an order for my death. The matter was laid before the Council, and I was at once pointed out as the abettor of your Government in this design."

On the nature of the information supplied by our Native Vakil at Kábul, the best authorities in India were found to differ widely from Lord Salisbury. Davies and his subalterns on the Panjáb frontier agreed in holding that the half-weekly diaries of our Native Agent, Atta Mohammad, were on the whole as correct, trustworthy, and informing, as circumstances would allow. During the seven years of his residence at Kábul nothing of importance had occurred in Afghánistán of which he had failed to give full and timely information. In the opinion of the Indian Government any attempt to substitute English for Native agency in the present state of Afghán feeling would undo the good already secured by "the policy which was advocated by Lord Canning . . . which was renewed by Lord Lawrence . . . which was ratified by Lord Mayo . . . and which we have since steadily pursued."*

Lord Salisbury, however, with his eyes still bent on Russia and his ears open only to the counsels of such men as Rawlinson and Bartle Frere, gave no heed to the remonstrances of a Viceroy who preferred the path of duty and the teachings of experience to the dreams and schemes of fussy enthusiasts, fierce Russophobes, and strenuous believers in the divinity of might. Replying to Lord Northbrook in November, the Minister for India made light of the Viceroy's strongest arguments, misstated their tenour, reasserted his belief in Sher Ali's shiftiness and Russia's mischievous designs, and finally desired Lord Northbrook, with the least possible delay, to "find some occasion for sending a mission to Kábul, and to press the reception of this Mission very earnestly upon the Amir." The step thus ordered "need not be publicly connected with the establishment of a permanent Mission." There would be "many advantages in ostensibly connecting it with some object of smaller political interest," which it would not be difficult for the Viceroy "to find, or, if need be, to create." If the Amir should offer any hindrance to the measures deemed "necessary for securing his independence," it would be the Envoy's duty "earnestly to press upon" him the risk he ran in so doing. Lord Northbrook was bidden, in short, to use any means, however crooked, in furtherance of a policy not more hateful to the Amir and all his people than false to the covenants made by successive Viceroys with Dost Mohammad and his son.

Lord Northbrook's native honesty revolted from a scheme so redolent of Asiatic cunning. In his letter of the 28th of January, 1876, he declined in effect to embark without further instructions on an enterprise which involved so great a "deviation from the patient and conciliatory policy" hitherto pursued, as well as recourse to false pretences which Sher Ali would be quick to see through, and very sure to resent. If a Mission must after all be despatched to Kábul, its real purpose ought to be announced

* Afghán Blue-book.

"fully and frankly to the Amir," such announcement being duly guarded by the assurance of our desire to make no sensible change in our Afghán policy, and to refrain as carefully as ever from all meddling in the internal affairs of Afghánistán. It was all but certain, however, that the Amir would never yield a hearty consent to the location of British officers in his country; and without his hearty consent such a movement would be not less dangerous than futile. For himself and his Council, therefore, Lord Northbrook still pressed the wisdom of "a patient adherence to the policy adopted by Lord Canning, Lord Lawrence, and Lord Mayo," and earnestly deprecated the fulfilment of Lord Salisbury's orders, "as involving serious danger to the peace of Afghánistán and to the interests of the British Empire in India."*

To all such pleadings, however weightily and calmly urged, the Minister for India remained inexorable. The mouthpiece of a Cabinet ruled by the dreamiest and most astute of English statesmen, he was bent on pursuing a policy condemned by all the coolest and wisest heads in India as well as England. To a statesman of Lord Northbrook's calibre and honest worth the position became intolerable. In February he asked the Home Government to send out another Viceroy in his stead. Before his departure from Calcutta in April, a public meeting, held in the Town Hall, decided to raise a statue in honour of a Viceroy who had laboured quietly and zealously for the public good, had fought successfully against a wide-spread famine, had removed some heavy burdens from Indian trade and industry, and had so carefully husbanded his revenue as to leave behind him a growing surplus after paying off the whole cost of famine relief. In the words of veiled eulogy uttered by a leading native journal, *The Hindu Patriot*, he "could not be considered a brilliant ruler, for he made no war, annexed no territory, committed no plunder; but he gave the land rest."†

* Afghán Blue-book.   † Temple; Routledge; *Allen's Mail.*

BOOK VII.

LORD LYTTON.

1876–1880.

CHAPTER I.

LORD LYTTON AND THE AMIR OF KÁBUL.

As successor to the Earl of Northbrook in India, the Prime Minister of England, Mr. Disraeli, chose Lord Lytton, the son of his old friend and recent colleague, whom the world at large had best known as Lytton-Bulwer, the versatile author of many novels and romances, a few plays, and more than one poem, each of rare merit from a certain point of view. The first Lord Lytton had been ennobled for his party services rather than his genius. His son, the new Viceroy, was chiefly known as a promising poet and a rising diplomatist. Diplomacy is not the best school for an Indian Viceroy, and poets have seldom ripened into successful statesmen. A clever diplomatist, however, need not prove an administrative failure ; and there seemed good grounds for hoping that the statesman who had once selected Lord Mayo for the post of Governor-General would prove no less happy in his present choice.

On the 12th of April, 1876, the new Viceroy took the oaths of office at Government House. In his opening address to the members of his Council he figured as a graceful, fluent speaker, warmed by a fine enthusiasm for the honour of his country and the well-being of the millions entrusted to his charge. His professions of regard for "the just rights of our allies beyond the frontier" sounded like the assurance of his own desire to pursue the settled policy of former Viceroys towards Afghánistán.*

Diplomatists, however, are wont to practise the art of using language to conceal their thoughts. Before leaving England the new Viceroy had been closeted with Lord Salisbury, whose ideas about the just rights of our allies found their latest expression in his despatch of the 28th of February, 1876. In that document the Minister for India instructed the Viceroy to "find an early occasion for sending to Kábul a temporary Mission," empowered to offer the Amir some further benefits on condition of his grant-

* _Allen's Mail._

ing free access to English officers within his frontier. If Sher Ali agreed to such a demand, he might receive some assurance of our material support in terms more definite than those of 1873. If, on the other hand, the Amir's language and demeanour still proved unyielding, he should be "distinctly reminded that he is isolating himself, at his own peril, from the friendship and protection it is his interest to seek and deserve." The penalty for refusal, indeed, was couched in plainer English than the reward for compliance. Something was said about formally acknowledging Abdulla Ján as the Amir's heir, and about a conditional increase of the Amir's subsidy. But the promise of material support against foreign aggressors resolved itself into a mere restatement of the assurances given by Lord Northbrook in 1873. The Government, said Lord Salisbury, "must reserve to themselves entire freedom of judgement as to the character of circumstances involving the obligation of material support to the Amir, and it must be distinctly understood that only in some clear case of unprovoked aggression would such an obligation arise."

Lord Salisbury disclaimed all desire on the part of his Government to "renounce the traditional policy of abstention from all unnecessary interference in the internal affairs of Afghánistán." The disclaimer was itself misleading, for it implied that former Governments had interfered in those affairs, so far as they deemed it necessary; whereas, since the Treaty of 1855, non-interference had always been the rule; and the Russian Government had but lately been informed of our plans for strengthening the Amir's position "without interfering in the internal affairs of his country." Lord Salisbury's lofty sneer at the assurances given to Sher Ali by Lord Northbrook, as "too ambiguous to secure confidence or inspire gratitude," strangely belied the whole tenour of a despatch whose real meaning lay buried in a cloud of ambiguities and fine pretences.

"To invite the confidence of the Amir" was said to be the primary purpose of the Mission which Lord Lytton was to send to Kábul. That confidence was to be secured by proposals which the Amir had always hitherto rejected as dangerous to all concerned, and contrary to the engagements made with him by former Viceroys. These proposals he was now required to accept, on pain of forfeiting the countenance and support of a Power which had repeatedly promised to protect him from external foes, and to abstain from meddling in his internal affairs. In return for concessions thus enforced in the teeth of past assurances, Sher

Ali was to be favoured with promises of support as carefully guarded as those which Lord Northbrook had given him three years before. The only benefits which he could gain from this one-sided bargain were the formal recognition of his younger son as heir, and the hope of occasional gifts in money from the Indian Treasury. In spite of all Lord Salisbury's professions, the word went forth to exchange a settled policy of goodwill and fair dealing towards Afghánistán for a policy of mere intrigue and wanton bullying.* And all this was done at a time when the good understanding between Russia and England was known to be singularly complete.

As a first step in the new direction, Lord Lytton asked the Amir to let Sir Lewis Pelly wait upon him at Kábul, or elsewhere, for the purpose of announcing the Viceroy's accession to office, and the new title which "the great Queen of England" had just assumed as Empress of Hindustán. On the 22nd of May Sher Ali returned a negative answer, wrapped up in a cloud of complimentary phrases. His reasons for refusing were given in a letter written at the time by Atta Mohammad. After what had happened to Major Macdonald he feared for the safety of Englishmen going through Afghánistán. He claimed the right under existing treaties to object to the presence of European officers, whose demands might give rise to unpleasant quarrels. If he were to receive an English Envoy, the Russians might claim to send their Envoy also. If a conference were needed, he would send an agent of his own from Kábul to confer with the Indian Government.

The Viceroy, however, would take no denial. Replying in July through the Commissioner of Peshawar, he declined to receive the Envoy of a ruler who would not receive an Envoy from a Governor-General urged by "a sincere desire to strengthen the bonds of friendship and confidence" between his own Government and that of the Amir. If the latter should persist in "rejecting the hand of friendship now frankly held out" to him, he would certainly place his kingdom in wilful isolation from "the alliance and support of the British Government." In a longer letter addressed to his own Vakíl, the Viceroy renewed his offer to send Sir Lewis Pelly to wait upon the Amir at any place which the latter might appoint, and even proposed to meet the Amir in person next November at Peshawar.†

Still loath to comply with Lord Lytton's main demand, Sher

* Afghán Blue-book.   † Ibid.

Ali in September proposed that Atta Mohammad should cross the frontier to confer with his own Government on the matters in dispute. The meeting between the Viceroy and his Vakíl came off at Simla in October. In reply to Atta Mohammad's statement of Sher Ali's grievances, explanations, and demands, Lord Lytton bade him warn the Amir against the folly of overrating his political importance. It was only the strong arm of the British Government that stood between him and the dangers which beset him on every side. If he still proved refractory, the British Government could " break him as a reed." The help which he seemed so ready to decline might at any moment be transferred to one of his rivals. It was not for his own sake, but for the security of our Indian Frontier that we cared to maintain the independence of Afghánistán. If he incurred our enmity by refusing the free admission of English Agents into Afghán cities, there was nothing to prevent us from combining with Russia to " wipe Afghánistán out of the map altogether." His own son, Yákub, was still so formidable that the Amir on his account could not leave Kábul. With an empty treasury, a discontented people, and conspiracies rife in favour of his son, the Amir's position was "surrounded with difficulties." "And this," said the Viceroy, " is the man who pretends to hold the balance between England and Russia independent of either! His position is rather that of an earthen pipkin between two iron pots."

The Vakíl returned to Kábul furnished with a detailed statement of the conditions on which alone the Viceroy would guarantee the Amir's dominions against foreign attack. These conditions were to form the basis of a conference to be holden presently, if the Amir chose, at Pesháwar, between his own faithful Minister, Núr Mohammad, and the Viceroy's Agent, Sir Lewis Pelly. But no conference was possible unless the Amir admitted the Viceroy's claim to place English officers at Herát and elsewhere on the Afghán frontier.*

While Sher Ali and his Council were pondering the purport of these rude threats and imperious demands, events were happening in Khalát which tended neither to allay their misgivings nor to soothe their ruffled pride. Major Sandeman's careful diplomacy had issued in a peaceful settlement of the long-standing quarrel between the Khán and his chiefs. The reconciled parties had agreed to take steps for re-opening and safeguarding the Bolán Pass. For the better maintenance of peace and order in that un-

* Afghán Blue-book.

quiet country, the British Envoy advised Lord Lytton to retain
for a time at the Khán's Court an experienced English officer, duly
empowered to aid and guide the Khán in the management of
his affairs. Before Sandeman's party crossed the frontier on their
way to Khalát, Lord Northbrook had taken care to acquaint Sher
Ali with the true nature and objects of a Mission escorted by a
thousand men of all arms. Meanwhile, however, Lord Salisbury's
objections to a prolonged occupation of Khalát had been found
compatible with a new-born desire to plant a British garrison
somewhere in that country. Lord Lytton, for his part, was quick
enough to catch at any pretext for securing our troops a permanent foothold in the Khán's dominions. Sandeman's escort being
there already, he found plenty of arguments for keeping it there,
in the interests, not of the Khán alone, nor yet of peace along the
Indian border, but in "the highest and most general interests of
this Empire." The new Imperialism was already washing away
the old landmarks of our frontier policy on that side of India.

The Viceroy sent his Military Secretary, Colonel Colley, to
confer with the Khán and Sandeman about the viceregal plan for
improving the new relations with Khalát. The true purport of
Colley's errand became clear on the 2nd of November, when a
wing of the 4th Sikh Infantry marched into the fortified town of
Kwatta or Shál-kot, the "Fort of Shál," so called from the valley
which it overlooks. In December the Khán of Khalát, with his
leading vassals, came through the Bolán to Jacobabad, where they
found a gracious welcome from Lord Lytton himself. The Viceroy
ratified the new treaty made by Sandeman with the Bilúchi ruler,
and the conversion of Kwatta into a British outpost became
thenceforth an historical fact.*

The Khán himself had cheerfully acquiesced in a move for which
provision had been made in the treaty concluded with his elder
brother, Nasir Khán, in 1854. After many years of futile clamour
and unwilling silence, the advocates of a Forward policy had the
ball at last in their own hands. The old objections to any scheme
for placing a British garrison so far away from its nearest supports
had in 1874 been set forth with renewed emphasis by Lord Lawrence, in his masterly reply to a Minute, penned by Sir Bartle
Frere, in the shape of a letter addressed to Sir John Kaye, the
Political Secretary at the India Office. To Lord Lawrence, with
his cool head, stout heart, and matchless experience in all Indian
affairs, such a course seemed specially unwise, because it would

* Bilúchistán Papers.

"do much to revive and strengthen the old jealousy of the Afgháns," leading them to look upon the advance to Kwatta as a long step forward on the road to Afghánistán. He knew, moreover, that they who called for the occupation of Kwatta were the very men who "contemplated an advance on Kandáhár and Herát." And a little later Lord Salisbury himself declared that translations of English books and newspapers dealing with Indian topics were "carefully studied" by the Amir.*

It was not likely, therefore, that Sher Ali's repugnance to the Viceroy's demands would be weakened by the sight of British troops holding a fort which commanded the road from Sind to Kandáhár and Herát. It was from Kwatta that a British Army had marched forth in his father's days to the conquest of Afghánistán. As things stood, he could hardly help seeing in this new advance to his southern frontier the first step in a new invasion of the country which so many Viceroys had pledged themselves to regard as ground belonging to the Afgháns alone. Nor was the Amir's uneasiness allayed by reports of military movements along the Panjáb frontier, movements seemingly designed for some political purpose which was never afterwards clearly explained. As our relations with Russia were just then becoming somewhat strained, on account of her active sympathy with the Servians in their war against the Turks, these movements appear to have formed part of some unavowed scheme for driving the Russians out of Turkistán.†

At last, however, the bewildered Amir gave way so far as to send his trusty Minister, Núr Mohammad, to meet Sir Lewis Pelly in conference at Pesháwar. Sher Ali still clung with the energy of despair to the hope that his Envoy's pleadings might turn the Viceroy from his settled purpose of placing British officers at Kandáhár and Herát. But Sir Lewis Pelly was hardly the sort of agent whom a friendly Viceroy would have chosen to press an unpalatable demand on a prince already mistrustful of his neighbour's purposes. In his dealings with rude Arab chiefs on the Persian Gulf, Pelly had shown a high-handed vigour well suited for the work required of him. He was known as an officer who would "stand no nonsense," and he had formed strong opinions in favour of a Forward policy on the North-Western frontier. And Lord Lytton had expressly charged him to hold no conference with

---

* "India and Afghánistán" : *Times* Office, 1878 ; Afghán Blue-book.

† *The Allahábád Pioneer* (1878) ; Col. Brackenbury's letter in the *Times* (5th October, 1878).

the Amir's Envoy, unless Sher Ali would accept "the principle that British officers may reside in Afghánistán."

It does not appear that Pelly's bearing towards the Afghán Envoy fell short of the courtesy due to an old acquaintance and the trusted mouthpiece of an acknowledged ally. But the Viceroy's orders were plain and peremptory, and he had to obey them. The Conference opened on the 30th of January, 1877, when Pelly carefully explained the one condition on which his Government would treat with the Amir, or undertake the formal responsibility of aiding him to "defend his country from the attacks of external foes." No room should be left, he added, for future misunderstandings on the cardinal point of the whole business. Only in the settlement of details could room be found for full and free discussion.*

It is curious, by the way, to mark how thoroughly the new policy differed in spirit from the old. Former Viceroys, for instance, had carefully striven to allay Sher Ali's real or pretended fears of Russian encroachment. Lord Mayo had often counselled him to show no distrust of a Power which meant him no harm, and to answer Kauffmann's courteous greetings in a courteous way. Lord Northbrook assured him that he had nothing whatever to fear from a neighbour who had just given the best possible proofs of goodwill to England and England's Afghán ally. The same Viceroy could see no harm in the letters which Kauffmann now and then despatched by a native messenger from Tashkand to Kábul; and he was always ready to put the best construction on Sher Ali's least courteous or friendly acts. But it seemed to be part of Lord Lytton's policy to foster in the Amir's heart every feeling which a prudent Viceroy would have done his best to counteract or keep down. In the autumn of 1876 he discovered danger to the Amir in the complimentary letters which Kauffmann sent to Kábul, copies of which were regularly forwarded to the Indian Government. He incited the Amir to distrust his Russian neighbour as thoroughly as he was learning to distrust his English friends. Other Viceroys had treated Sher Ali with the courtesy due to an independent sovereign; Lord Lytton treated him as a schoolmaster might treat a tiresome or refractory boy. He scolded, threatened, cajoled him by turns, wounding his pride, flouting his prejudices, disbelieving his excuses, and inflaming his worst suspicions. He accused him of stirring up the border tribes against our own people. He even

* Afghán Blue-book.

made it a grievance that Sher Ali took no notice of the letters inviting him to attend the great gathering of Indian princes at Delhi on the first day of 1877, as if the Amir of Kábul were nothing more than a vassal of the Indian Empire.[*]

Lord Lytton's professed desire to relieve the Amir from all anxiety on the score of past agreements received no countenance from the Amir's own Envoy. Again and again during the conference did Núr Mohammad declare that his master had no cause for anxiety in respect of the assurances received from former Viceroys. Dissensions there had been on certain points in Lord Northbrook's time, but "the previous course continued to be observed," and Lord Northbrook on his retirement had "still left the old friendship without change." Such being the case, "what anxiety," he asked, "can there be in the mind of the Amir, that you should now remove it?" Whatever anxiety might now be felt arose entirely, he declared, from the course pursued, "in breach of former agreements," by Lord Lytton himself.

It was this new and persistent demand for the free admission of English officers into Afghán towns which cast into deep shade such minor grievances as the Sistán Award, and the late Viceroy's pleadings on behalf of Yákub Khán. There was nothing which the Afghán Government would not have yielded far more readily than this. "You must not impose upon us a burden which we cannot bear," were the words of entreaty used by Núr Mohammad in a private interview with Pelly's able assistant, Dr. Bellew. What good, he asked, could ever come of placing British officers on the Afghán frontiers, in face of the deep-rooted dislike and dread cherished by the whole Afghán people for a course so fatal, as events had shown, to their independence? And of what avail was any guarantee which the Amir might be forced to give for the due protection of those officers from insult and injury? And, without his cordial support, of what earthly use could those officers be as scouts and news-reporters to their own Government?

These arguments the Envoy from Kábul repeated with telling additions to Pelly himself. Nothing, he declared in tones of simple earnestness, could uproot from the minds of his countrymen their fixed belief that "if Englishmen or other Europeans once set foot in their country, it will sooner or later pass out of their hands." The Amir's acceptance of the Viceroy's conditions could only lead to enmity between two Governments whose

[*] Afghán Blue-book ; Central Asian Papers.

friendship had hitherto remained unbroken; while on Sher Ali and his people would fall "a heavy load of blame and suffering" if any mischief happened to English officers in Afghánistán. Why, then, should the British Government, on whose friendship the Amir had always reckoned, insist on laying so harmful a burden on the shoulders of its sincere friend?[*]

To all his prayers, arguments, remonstrances, the British Envoy could make but one reply. Unless Sher Ali agreed at once to the principle of the Viceroy's demand, the Conference must come to an abrupt close. In that case the Viceroy would be compelled to break off all further negociations, to withhold from the Amir and his dynasty all support "in any troubles, internal or external," and to carry on the work of strengthening his own frontier "without further reference to the Amir." He would hold himself bound, in short, by no engagements save those involved in the treaty of 1855.

These threats were uttered on the 15th of February. In vain did Núr Mohammad four days later appeal from such language to the faith of those engagements which Lord Lytton thus coolly disavowed. From that date the Conference was virtually over, although the British Envoy agreed to await further instructions from his Government on the points raised by Núr Mohammad. In the middle of March the latter received from Sir Lewis Polly a letter embodying the Viceroy's answer to his last appeal. The Afghán Envoy was challenged to give a plain answer to Lord Lytton's demands. But he was then too ill to attend to business, and on the 26th he breathed his last. About that time another Envoy was on his way to Peshúwar, charged with a most conciliatory message from Sher Ali, who had also instructed the Mir Akhor, as Núr Mohammad's temporary substitute, to prolong the Conference by every means in his power. But these signs of tardy submission failed to avert the very issue which Lord Lytton had professed to deprecate. On the 30th of March the Viceroy telegraphed from Simla an order to Sir Lewis Pelly to close the Conference forthwith, on the plea that "there was no basis for negociation," as the Mir Akhor had no authority to act for his late colleague. This order Pelly at once obeyed.[†]

What was the meaning of this abrupt close to negociations which had remained open down to the death of Núr Mohammad? In his subsequent letter to the India Office Lord Lytton owned that, before he stopped the Conference, he had been aware of the instructions which Sher Ali was sending to the Mir Akhor, of the departure of a new Envoy from Kábul, and of Sher Ali's alleged submission to the Viceroy's will. He knew that the "prompt and plain answer" which his Envoy had demanded a fortnight earlier, could not be given by Núr Mohammad's colleague without some further reference to Kábul. If he had ever honestly desired to clear up old misunderstandings, to repair Lord Northbrook's alleged mistakes, to deal fairly as well as frankly with a mistrustful ally, to strengthen the Amir's realm against foreign and domestic foes, why did he suddenly throw up a winning game, and leave the Amir to struggle unaided with the difficulties that beset him? Lord Lytton indeed put forward Sher Ali's seeming lack of "eagerness to deserve and reciprocate" his friendship as a sufficient reason for breaking off a Conference, the prolonging of which "could only lead to embarrassments and entanglements" hurtful to ourselves. But an excuse so hollow was in perfect keeping with the whole spirit of Lord Lytton's frontier policy; and it is but one of many passages in his long and cleverly-composed Despatch of May 10, which must always leave an unpleasant taste in the mouth of every Englishman fairly conversant with the facts discussed, and reared on such plain food as truth, honesty, fair-dealing, and respect for other men's rights.

As a party manifesto, written to justify the new line of policy enforced by the Government at home on its Agent in India, that despatch was a masterpiece of one-sided advocacy. To the student of history it is valuable only for the light it throws on the methods by which that policy of intrigue and provocation was to be carried out. From the first paragraph to the forty-first it is one long perversion of historic facts bearing on our relations with Afghán rulers since the Treaty of 1855. It described that treaty as " the only formal obligation still extant" between the Indian Government and that of Afghánistán. It spoke of the Treaty of 1857 as "limited to the duration of the war" then waging against the Shah of Persia, although one of its provisions did not begin to work until the war was over. It declared that Lumsden's Mission to Kandáhár in 1857 had "met with reasonable success," whereas it had proved a virtual failure, as avowed by Lumsden himself to Lord Lawrence. It treated the written assurances of Lord Mayo and Lord Northbrook as if they had no binding force on the Indian Government. It repeated the old exploded fallacies about the origin and purport of the Simla Conference. It professed to believe that Sher Ali had once shown his readiness to receive

British Agents in some of his Afghán towns. It misrepresented the nature of Kauffmann's correspondence with Sher Ali. It maintained in the teeth of facts that Russia had pledged herself not to annex Khiva, and had afterwards broken that pledge. It carefully magnified Sher Ali's dread of Russia and his rudeness to the late Viceroy; spoke evil of Núr Mohammad in order to damage Lord Northbrook himself; and accused of virtual treachery to his own employers the same Vakíl whom, last October, Lord Lytton had rewarded with praise and presents. And it charged Sher Ali with a number of mischievous and hostile acts, some of which were either harmless or imaginary, while others rested on mere gossip, or, like the attempt to stir up a *Jihád* or holy war, were at worst the outcome not of any deep-laid purpose, but of sheer bewilderment and sudden despair. In the whole of this wonderful State paper there was hardly a paragraph which did not contain some misleading statement, some unfair assumption or reckless innuendo, some trace, in short, of that partisan spirit which delights in making the worse appear the better cause.*

Among the names appended to this Despatch four were those of now Councillors. Lord Napier's place as Commander-in-Chief was now filled by Sir Frederic Haines, a soldier who had fought with honour against the Sikhs under Lord Gough. The Military Member, Sir Henry Norman, had given place to Sir Edwin Johnson. Mr. Whitley Stokes had just succeeded Sir Arthur Hobhouse as head of the Department in which he himself had served so long and ably. Sir John Strachey filled the post of Finance Minister in the room of Sir William Muir. Before Lord Northbrook's retirement Sir Andrew Clarke had already taken his seat as Minister for Public Works, and signed the Despatch in which the late Viceroy had delivered his final protest against the new policy ordained by the India Office. Three of the old Councillors, Norman, Muir, and Hobhouse had strongly dissented from the measures taken by the new Viceroy in the previous July for enforcing the new policy upon the Afghán Amir. From one cause and another the Notes recording the grounds of their dissent had not been turned into regular Minutes before they left India, and the fact of their dissent remained generally unknown in England for the next two years. Except, however, as a record of their own opinions, the written protests of three members in a Council of eight would have had no more power to hinder or even to mould the course of action dictated from England and accepted by Lord

* Afghán Blue-book; the *Times* of June 15, 1877.

Lytton, than the Court of Directors had to fight against the policy which issued in the first Afghán war.*

With the sudden close of the Peshávar Conference ended also our diplomatic relations with the Amir of Afghánistán. The Viceroy's Vakil, Atta Mohammad, who had remained at Peshávar during the Conference, returned no more to Kábul; and the alliance which Lord Lytton had professed himself so anxious to bind yet faster, was virtually disowned. Sher Ali was left, in fact, to stew in his own juice, and to extract what comfort he could from the Viceroy's promise to respect the Treaty of 1855. If, "within a reasonable time," wrote Lord Salisbury in October, the Amir should make friendly advances on the basis of the terms already offered, those advances "should not be rejected." But if he continued to stand aloof, the British Government would hold itself free to adopt such measures for the strengthening of India's North-Western frontier as circumstances might demand, "without regard to the wishes of the Amir Sher Ali, or the interests of his dynasty."†

In plain words, Sher Ali's backwardness in complying with demands urged in the teeth of former engagements had given us a pretext for breaking faith with our ally, and for enlarging our Indian boundaries at the Amir's expense. To Sher Ali himself the closing of the Conference and the withdrawal of our Native Agent seemed very like a summons to yield himself up to our will and pleasure on pain of open war. His cup of bitterness was already full to overflowing. And yet in June of this year the Minister for India had assured his hearers in the House of Lords that our relations with Sher Ali had "undergone no material change since last year," that his feelings were "not in any way more embittered towards the British Government" than heretofore, and that there was "no reason for apprehending any change of policy or any disturbance in our Indian Empire." On the same occasion he declared that no attempt had been made "to force an Envoy upon the Amir at Kábul." Such assurances, which seemed to say one thing while they really meant another, marked the progress of Lord Beaconsfield's ablest convert in a kind of statesmanship new to the countrymen of Peel and Wellington. One of them, at least, strayed very far from the truth, and the rest, if true to the letter, conveyed to most minds a false impression of the facts. If we had not pressed the Amir,

* Causes of the Afghán War: Chatto & Windus, 1879.
† Afghán Blue-book.

for instance, to receive an Envoy at Kábul, we had punished him for objecting to receive one at Kandáhár or Herát. If his feelings were not more embittered than ever by the closing of the Conference and the withdrawal of our Vakíl, they must have been altogether hostile before the end of 1876. And it was clear, at any rate, that our relations with him had undergone a material change in the past twelvemonth.

All this word-juggling, however, served but too well to baulk inquiry and disarm suspicion. It availed to hoodwink statesmen of such experience and calibre as the Duke of Argyll, Lord Lawrence, and Lord Northbrook. The last-named was among the foremost to declare his satisfaction with Lord Salisbury's answer to the Duke of Argyll; and Lord Salisbury listened with a show of assent to the erroneous meaning which political opponents placed upon his words. Lord Lawrence ceased for a time to vex himself with vague forebodings of a change for the worse in our Afghán policy. Every one, in short, who was not behind the scenes fell into the trap thus skilfully laid, and cheerfully took the Ministerial utterance not for waste paper, but for so much sterling gold.*

A few words will suffice to show what sort of change had come over our relations with Sher Ali since the end of 1876. By the close of the following March we had broken off on the hollowest pretexts all intercourse with an old ally. We had withdrawn the pledges given by Lord Mayo and renewed in all good faith by his successor; pledges which Sher Ali had rightly deemed as binding as a formal treaty. We had disowned even the surviving clauses of the Treaty of 1857, and had distinctly warned the Amir that we should take our own way about frontier questions without any regard for his wishes or concerns. We had placed him, in short, helpless and despairing, between the upper and the nether millstone. If his feelings towards us were not embittered by all this unkindly and wrongful usage, Sher Ali must have been the dullest or the most angelic of men.

* The *Times, Daily News,* &c., of June 16, 1877.

CHAPTER II.

THE FAMINE IN SOUTHERN AND WESTERN INDIA.

FROM the heights of his blustering foreign policy Lord Lytton sometimes descended to take part in the ordinary affairs of his great Empire. In the early days of his rule he gratified his theatrical tastes by a noteworthy reform in the fashions of feminine dress. Former Viceroys had been content to open their drawing-rooms to English ladies attired in the customary garments of their day. But the new Viceroy issued a decree that all ladies who wished to attend the State receptions at Government House should wear long trains, after the manner of European Courts. The innovation was generally condemned as costly, needless, and vexatious; but it pleased Lord Lytton to invest his office with all the ceremonial splendour that beseemed the vicegerent of so great a sovereign as the Empress of Hindustán.*

Not long afterwards his apparent zeal for the welfare of his native subjects led the Viceroy into a vehement dispute with the High Court of Allahábád. In the summer of 1876 an Englishman named Fuller was tried by the Magistrate of Agra for slapping the face of a native servant, who died the same day of a ruptured spleen. It appeared in evidence that death was owing not to the blow itself, but to a fall which the servant met with an hour or so later, on his way to seek redress. A fine of thirty rupees was the penalty awarded by the magistrate, in seeming accordance with the rules of the Indian Penal Code. The High Court Judges of that province upheld the magistrate's reading of the law, but allowed that he ought perhaps to have inflicted a heavier fine. All this, however, failed to satisfy the Viceroy that substantial justice had been done in a case of ordinary assault for which some little provocation could fairly be pleaded. On his way out through Egypt he had met the Prince of Wales, who deplored the readiness of his countrymen in India to lift their hands against the natives. In the present instance some of the native newspapers

* *Allen's Mail.*

raised a cry of injustice done to a member of the subject race. The temptation to stand forward as the champion of a popular sentiment proved too great for the Viceroy's self-control. His poetic fancy saw nothing but the blow dealt by an angry, overbearing Englishman, the consequent death of a poor ill-used native, and the crowning default of justice on the part of magistrate and judges alike. With the approval, if not at the instigation, of his Law-Minister, Mr. Arthur Hobhouse, the Viceroy fired off a scolding Minute against all concerned in the Fuller Case. An English magistrate was openly disgraced for doing his apparent duty, and English judges of high standing were loftily rebuked for rejecting the Viceregal version of facts and law. The Lieutenant-Governor himself of a province as populous as the British Islands, was taunted with neglect of duty for not interfering in a matter wherein his interference was not required.[*]

Later in the year Lord Lytton's æsthetic fancies revelled in the congenial task of arranging the details of a ceremonial gathering, the largest and most magnificent that British India had ever seen; a gathering perhaps unmatched by any witnessed in the days of Sháh Jahán or Aurangzíb. In the spring of the year Lord Beaconsfield's Ministry had carried through Parliament a Bill for investing the Queen of England with the formal title of Empress of India. There were many in the House of Commons and elsewhere who questioned the need, or ridiculed the policy, of thus proclaiming the sovereign whose sway over India had been visible to all the world for eighteen years past, and whose Imperial title had been recorded again and again in the official papers that passed between the Viceroy and the Native Governments. But the ingenious author of *Tancred* was the Prime Minister who spoke of England as an Asiatic rather than a European Power; and he appeared to think that the best way of "frightening Russia" was to turn our Queen into an Empress, and to solemnize the process by means of a gorgeous Darbár to be holden at Delhi, the erewhile capital of the Great Moghal. Pomp and pageantry on a grand scale were supposed to captivate the people of India; and the Viceroy's weakness for all kinds of decorative show and glitter made him a ready and useful instrument for carrying out Lord Beaconsfield's designs.[†]

The Imperial assemblage in honour of the new-made Empress of India took place on the New Year's Day of 1877, along the memorable ridge whence, for three months of 1857, our troops

[*] *Friend of India; Allen's Mail.* [†] London *Times*, &c.

had fought so often against many times their number of disciplined mutineers. For a week past nearly all the princes, notables, and chief officers of State in India had been holding high festival and exchanging friendly courtesies with the Viceroy and each other near the spot where the great Darbár Pavilion stood ready for the crowning pageant, whose somewhat tawdry pomp and barbaric splendour Mr. Valentine Prinsep's huge painting has since so faithfully reproduced. At a given hour—half-past twelve—on the first day of the new year, Lord Lytton took the central seat of dignity, on a daïs in front of a resplendent semicircle of princes, grandees, courtiers, standard-bearers, and ladies, seated or standing in due order of rank and precedence, to hear the proclamation of the new title which the Queen of England had deigned to assume. Major Barnes, the tallest officer in the Indian army, decked in the gayest of heraldic blazonry, read out in English the Imperial ordinance with a voice that made itself clearly heard by the assembled throng. Mr. Thornton, the Foreign Secretary, then read an Urdu translation of the same. His last words were caught up and echoed by the sudden thunder of saluting guns, the din of rifle volleys, and the crash of military music from the 15,000 troops paraded outside.

The Viceroy himself then delivered, through his interpreter, a congratulatory address, leading up to a gracious and kindly message from the Queen to her loyal lieges assembled at Delhi. Referring to the hearty welcome which India had lately accorded to her beloved son, Her Majesty trusted that the present occasion would unite her in bonds of yet closer affection with her Indian subjects, and that all, from the highest to the humblest, would feel that "the great principles of liberty, equity, and justice" were secured to them under her rule. In Her Majesty's name the Viceroy further announced a large addition to the Order of the Star of India, and the institution of a new Order—that of the Indian Empire. When the cheers that followed his speech were over, Sindhia and the leading princes sent off a telegram to the Queen, congratulating her on the assumption of her Imperial title. The great assemblage was then formally dissolved, and the native chiefs with their followers rode off on their elephants, a long line of which, decked in gorgeous trappings, towered above the vast crowd of spectators and men-at-arms.*

On the same day, Her Majesty was proclaimed with all due pomp and ceremony at Calcutta, Madras, and Bombay. In

* *Allen's Mail;* Temple.

honour of the new Empress, fifteen thousand prisoners all over India were set free. Darbárs were held at all the chief stations throughout the country, titles and distinctions of various kinds were bestowed on several Englishmen, and a great many natives who had done good service to the State. Sindhia received a Grand Cross of the Bath. He and the Mahárája of Káshmir were gazetted generals in the British Army. Many of the Native Princes besides him of Gwáliár had two guns added to the number of their salute. The Khán of Khalát and his wild-looking Sardárs went home thoroughly satisfied with the welcome they had received at Delhi. Feasting, fireworks, illuminations, races, reviews, and dancing prolonged for a few days the unwonted stir and splendour of the scene enacted on the 1st of January. On the 6th, Lord Lytton himself went off to Pattiála, where he installed the young Mahárája, grandson of the noble Narindar Singh, who had stood by our side so staunchly throughout the troubles of 1857. From thence the Viceroy journeyed to Aligarh, where he laid the first stone of a new Anglo-Mohammadan college, founded by the Moslem gentry at their own cost. Arriving at Calcutta on the 13th, he had to give his mind to business of far more pressing import than the details of an Imperial pageant, or even the coming Conference at Pesháwar.[*]

Among those who took part in the Delhi gathering was the Lieutenant-Governor of Bengal. Temple had but lately returned from visiting the scene of a physical disaster among the hugest and most appalling recorded in history. On the 31st of October, 1876, there had burst upon the northern coasts of the Bay of Bengal one of those cyclones or hurricanes which so often herald the breaking of the monsoon. The whole seaboard of Bengal, from Orissa to Arakan, is one vast delta of sand and mud washed down by the Ganges and the Brahmaputra. These great rivers, flowing through a hundred channels into the sea, find their chief and common outlet through the Meghna, which rolls its turbid waters in deep, broad volume between the districts of Noakháli and Bákarganj; issuing at last in four mouths formed by the islands of Dakhin-Shahbázpur, Hátia, and Sandwíp. In the floods caused by the great cyclone of 1822, nearly 40,000 people and 100,000 head of cattle were drowned. The storm-wave that followed the cyclone of 1867 submerged the whole island of Hátia to a depth of twenty feet. In all such cases the loss of life was attended by the destruction of all the standing crops.

[*] *Times; Gazette of India; Allen's Mail.*

Sometimes the people had timely warning of their danger, and fled to higher ground, or found shelter in the trees that surrounded their homesteads.

On this 31st of October, however, the danger came upon them like a thief in the night. Towards evening the wind freshened, and before midnight, when every one was sleeping, rose into a furious gale. Suddenly, about midnight, in the villages nearest the sea was heard the roar of the tidal wave, followed here and there by a cry, "The water is on us!" The towering storm-wave swept up the Meghna like a moving wall, overwhelming the flat country on either side. A second wave followed presently in the same direction. Then the cyclone, shifting from south to north, blew the great mass of water back again towards the sea. Within three hours the wind and the water had done their ruinous work. Out of 1,000,000 people spread over a surface of nearly 3,000 square miles, more than 100,000 were swallowed up by the storm floods. The women who perished far outnumbered the men. In some villages only a third or a fourth part of the people were left alive. The proportion of deaths was found to be heaviest in the three large islands before-named, especially in Dakhin-Shahbázpur, where nearly half of the people were reported missing. Of all who encountered the full force of the storm-wave very few indeed would have escaped but for the belts of cocoanuts and other trees, up which many a villager contrived to scramble out of the very jaws of death. Where the trees grew thickest the survivors were most numerous. Hardly a bullock or a cow was left alive; but the buffaloes, being excellent swimmers, were nearly all saved.

With daybreak of the 1st of November the waters were fast subsiding, and after mid-day the survivors came down from the trees to find their homesteads utterly wrecked or washed away, their crops destroyed, their tanks mostly filled with brine or choked with corpses. Nearly all the plantain-trees had been stripped of their fruit. But the cocoanuts had mostly weathered the storm; and the contents of their grain-pits would suffice to keep the villagers alive for that present. When Temple and some of his officers had made their way with all possible speed to the scene of disaster, they found the people everywhere busy drying their wet grain in the sun, and sheltering themselves under rude frameworks of broken branches covered with cloth sheets, in the midst of ruined homesteads, gardens "turned into saline swamps," and plains thickly strewn with corpses of men and cattle, that lay "in horrid confusion festering in the sun." No efforts on Temple's part, or on that of his Staff, were wanting to relieve those sufferers who stood most in need, whether of medical or general help. But no amount of medical skill or administrative energy could avert the pestilence which now began to rage in the districts ravaged by the great cyclone. In the course of a few weeks the cholera swept away many thousands of those whom the storm-floods had spared.*

While Temple was yet relieving the distress in Eastern Bengal, a mighty famine had already begun to brood over a large part of Western and Southern India; and more than half a million of poor people were keeping themselves alive on relief works started by the Local Governments. There were many who held that a season of widespread suffering was the very worst time to choose for a great ceremonial gathering of princes and grandees in honour of the Empress of India. But the Imperial assemblage took place, as we have seen, at the time appointed, and among those who had to figure in that showy farce were the Governors of Madras and Bombay. By the end of 1876 it became clear that famine had taken strong hold of the provinces ruled by Sir Philip Wodehouse and the Duke of Buckingham. In Madras alone the area of distress amounted to 80,000 square miles, peopled by nearly eighteen million souls. In Bombay eight million people, covering an area of 54,000 square miles, were suffering more or less from prolonged drought. The province of Maisúr, with an area of 27,000 square miles and a population of five millions, came within the circle of actual or impending danger, which embraced also a part of Haidarábád and the group of small Native States in the Southern Marátha country. A succession of dry seasons and short harvests had ensured the onset of a catastrophe far more wide-reaching than the famine of 1874.†

The Governors of Madras and Bombay had already taken steps to grapple with the growing danger, before duty summoned them to the Delhi Gathering. In the last days of December, 1876, six hundred thousand people were employed on relief works in Southern India, besides a quarter of a million gratuitously fed. The relief works opened in Bombay already kept a quarter of a million souls alive on famine wages. The Duke of Buckingham had begun to purchase for his Government large stocks of grain

---

* Temple's Minute on the Cyclone; *Allen's Mail;* Hunter's "Gazetteer of India."

† Temple; Hunter; India Office Despatch of January 12, 1877; *Allen's Mail.*

as a reserve against future needs. The city and neighbourhood of Madras were thronged with thousands of poor creatures who had wandered thither in quest of food or work. On one day two thousand people were fed by Government on the Madras beach, besides those who found relief elsewhere. In one of the Bombay districts 40,000 persons, with more than 31,000 head of cattle, wandered off to places which the drought had spared. Mr. Charles Saunders and his officers were doing their best to relieve the suffering people of Maisúr. For weeks past the railways had been carrying their heavy loads of grain from all parts of the country towards the drought-stricken provinces, while Burmah and Bengal were shipping off their rice in vast quantities for the people of Madras.*

If the Local Governments rose to the occasion, some of their measures failed to satisfy Lord Lytton's chief advisers. Foremost among these was Sir John Strachey, a shrewd financier, a busy-minded, active, zealous administrator, and a statesman of the hardest grain. If Strachey's influence with Lord Mayo had been great, it was much greater with a Viceroy who had little know-ledge of India's internal affairs, and no great desire to improve that knowledge. It shocked Strachey's economic sense to hear that the Madras Government were buying grain to the extent of 30,000 tons. His financial thriftiness took fright at the liberal scale on which that Government was paying the labourers on the newly-opened works. He had small sympathy with Lord North-brook's humane zeal for saving imperilled lives, at whatever cost to the State. At his suggestion the Viceroy deputed Temple to visit the scene of suffering, to report how things were going on, and to aid the Local Governments with his advice and experience on all points pertaining to famine management and famine relief.

Temple set out early in January, taking with him as secretary the Mr. Bernard who had served under him three years before in Bengal. The instructions furnished for his guidance involved a clear departure from the famine policy of 1874. The saving of lives was no longer to fill the first place in the thoughts of Indian statesmen. "For the future," said Lord Lytton, "the efforts of the Governments to mitigate suffering must be tempered by a strict regard for the severest economy." To save life "irrespec-tive of the cost" was a feat which the Government, in the pre-sent condition of its finances, could never hope to accomplish. On no account would Lord Lytton "attempt the task of preventing

* *Allen's Mail, Times,* &c.

all suffering, and of giving general relief to the poorer classes of the community." Famine relief, in short, must be administered as cheaply as possible, on the narrowest possible scale. How to "provide efficient assistance without incurring disastrous expenditure" was the problem which Lord Lytton set his officers to solve as they best could. Applicants for State help were to undergo a strict labour test. The rate of wages on relief works should suffice only for a bare subsistence. Gratuitous relief was to be supplied only in cases of extreme necessity, and then chiefly in the shape of cooked food. Instead of small local works, good enough at the outset of a seeming scarcity, large works, on which large gangs of labourers could be employed under close supervision, should be opened in places where food was plentiful, and access easy from the suffering districts. And such works should always be of a permanently useful and remunerative kind. For weaklier persons employment could be found in poorhouses or on roads and other easy tasks.

In the same spirit of stern economy Lord Lytton's Government declared that every province ought to bear the chief cost of relieving its own famines. The due enforcement of such a principle would establish "a powerful and most useful check upon extravagance" on the part of Local Governments and local officers. The praise bestowed on the Bombay Government for not interfering with the action of private trade was followed by a virtual censure on that of Madras, for having laid in a large stock of rice which private traders might have imported more cheaply on their own account. At the same time it was admitted that, for certain places distant from railways and large markets, the purchase of grain by Government from the nearest depôt might tend to stimulate rather than discourage trade.*

Before Temple's departure from Bengal it was arranged that in the May following he should succeed Sir Philip Wodehouse in the Government of Bombay. Meanwhile Mr. Ashley Eden was called from Burmah to become Lieutenant-Governor of Bengal in the room of the new Famine Commissioner. In the middle of January the latter reached the banks of the Tumbadra, where it divides the Nizam's country from the Presidency of Madras. In ten days he had sped by rail and road from Delhi through the famine tracts of the Dakhan, stopping here and there in his cheerless course to inspect relief works, to make inquiries, and to prepare reports of what he had seen or heard. He found little if

* Temple ; *Allen's Mail* ; Official Papers.

any fault with the rules of action laid down by the Bombay Government, or with the way in which the local officers applied those rules. The principle of granting relief only to those who absolutely needed it was enforced on the whole with gratifying success. The rate of wages on relief works had not been pitched too high, nor was the task-work made too easy for the labourers' strength. On one point, however, Wodehouse seemed still prone to err on the side of prodigality. Suspensions of land-revenue were perhaps inevitable ; but remissions of land-revenue, such as Wodehouse favoured, could be reckoned only as a dead loss to the State. At Temple's request the Viceroy desired the Governor of Bombay to grant no more remissions save in the utmost need.[*]

Crossing the Tumbadra near Adoni, Temple passed through a wide tract of country almost bare alike of trees, herbage, and crops. For miles on miles stretched the plains of black soil, strewn here and there with patches of withered grain and dotted at wide intervals with clumps of trees. In the districts of Karnúl, Belláry, and Kadapa, still known as the Bálághát or Land above the Gháts, the crops had been utterly ruined, and nearly a million people—about one in every four of the whole number—were already thronging the relief works ; while many thousands were living on public alms. There was no real dearth of food in these parts, for the railway that linked Bombay with Madras ran right through them, and the grain it brought down by hundreds of tons a day was pouring steadily into all the adjacent markets, along good roads furnished with a full supply of wheeled carriage. But prices had risen fourfold, and the mass of the people, living usually from hand to mouth, and already driven by weeks or months of forced idleness to the end of their small savings, would very soon have starved in the midst of plenty, but for the wages offered them on the Government works. It was a famine not so much of food as of money. Even those who could still maintain their own families were no longer able to relieve the wants of that large class of infirm and needy folk which in India is commonly kept alive by private charity.

Disease was already preying upon the people who most needed help. Cholera, dysentery, and small-pox were becoming more and more rife as the water in the wells and tanks grew scantier and more impure. An outbreak of cholera would send the gangs of labourers flying from the relief works, while the want of food speedily brought them back again. In the city and suburbs of

[*] Temple ; *Allen's Mail* ; *Times.*

Madras Temple found in full flood the misery caused by want and disease. Refugees from the surrounding country and from the lands of neighbouring chiefs had flocked thither by thousands in quest of the help which to many of them must come too late. In spite of hospitals and relief-camps and the best of medical supervision, numbers of starving wretches died of exhaustion or disease.

From Madras the Famine Commissioner hastened northwards to Nellór, where thousands of coolies were at work on the broad canal destined to connect Madras with the Kistna. Returning thence by way of Arkot and Vellór, he journeyed southwards through the districts of Salem, Trichinopoly, Koimbatór, Madura, and Tinnivalli, all suffering more or less keenly from the drought. His next visit was to Maisúr, where the Chief Commissioner and his small staff of English officers were doing their best to relieve the misery caused by three successive years of drought or un-seasonable weather. Reservoirs and other important works employed many thousands of people around Bangalór, while more than thirty thousand were kept alive by public and private charity. Thus far the distress in that province, though sharp, was still manageable, and Temple found that relief was administered " with humane care, though with due regard to economy." But there, as elsewhere, the worst of the crisis was yet to come.*

At the time of Temple's first visit to Madras the rate of relief wages in Southern India was higher than the rate pro-scribed in the Western Presidency. Seeing no good reason for the difference, Temple urged the Duke of Buckingham to adopt the Bombay scale. The question was referred to the Sanitary Officers of Madras, who declared that the rate could not be lowered with-out serious harm to the labourers' health and strength. As the Sanitary Commissioner for Bengal took the opposite view, the rate of wages in Madras was lowered accordingly. But the new arrangement seems to have proved less successful than it ought in theory to have done. A pound of grain a day, with half an anna or three farthings besides, had been found to afford a bare subsistence to every adult labourer on the Bombay works. For women and children the wage was a trifle less. Temple argued that the same rate of wages would suffice for labourers on the Madras side also. But whether the latter were less able to bear the strain upon their vital powers, or depended more entirely on their daily wage, or suffered more from the mistakes of careless or

* Temple ; *Allen's Mail ;* Indian Blue-book for 1877-78.

the tricks of fraudulent overseers, the result in their case was disappointing. After some weeks' trial of the new scale the Sanitary Commissioner, Dr. Cornish, protested strongly against its further enforcement. The people, he declared, were now dying at the rate of 930 per thousand in the year, mainly from diseases due to wasted tissues and the wearing away of the membrane that lines the lower bowel. Pregnant women were becoming rare in the suffering districts, the birth-rate was steadily falling, and the children born of famishing mothers were nothing but skin and bone.

On these points a lively controversy ensued between Dr. Cornish and the Famine Delegate. The Sanitary Commissioner appealed from the Temple of 1877 to the Temple of 1874, and showed that in some places "one anna would not purchase even a pound of grain," while the coolies often, from various causes, got less than their nominal wage of an anna and a half. In two months the numbers employed on relief works had fallen, he said, by one third, while the numbers receiving cooked food in relief houses had been trebled in the month of March alone. He insisted, in short, that the Indian labourer could not live and work on less than a pound and a half of grain daily. Temple, on his part, appealed to the teachings of late experience in Bombay, and expressed the conviction, to which careful enquiry had led him, that in ordinary times the village labourer could "hardly get more than a pound of grain a day." At last the question was decided in favour of Dr. Cornish, and in May the old wage of two annas a day was once more issued to the labourers in Southern India.*

In spite of the rain that fell during March and April, the distress in Southern and Western India began slowly to increase. The cattle were dying off in great numbers. Of human beings not very many had died as yet of sheer starvation; but cholera and other diseases were slaying their thousands week by week. After another round of inspections in the Southern Presidency, Temple set off in April on a tour through Western India. By that time the Local Governments, especially that of Madras, had been strongly reinforced by batches of officers, civil and military, borrowed from Bengal and the Upper Provinces for famine work. In Bombay Temple found the labourers distributed, for the most part, among large relief works, well planned and closely supervised by officers of the Public Works Department, acting under the

---

* *Allen's Mail;* Indian Blue-book.

orders of General Kennedy, the Chief Engineer. The making of a railway from Dhond to Manmar alone employed more than 18,000 labourers, who earned their daily wage by a fair, if necessarily low average, of useful work. The high prices ensured a continuous flow of grain from the more favoured provinces, and the railway officers were often at their wits' end for the means of accommodating the vast traffic which events had thrown into their hands.*

On the 1st of May Temple formally took over the Government of Bombay from Wodehouse, whose management of the famine he had always commended. At that time the distress was slowly tightening, and the number of persons daily fed by the State was rising steadily in Bombay as well as Madras. In the course of June the monsoon rains set in with cheering persistence, and numbers of people left the relief works to seek employment on the land. But in July the rainfall slackened, and in some districts altogether ceased. Even in large tracts of Northern India the crops began to suffer from untimely drought. By the end of July nearly two million people in the Madras Presidency were employed on relief works, or received charitable relief in their own villages, or relief in local camps from the State. About two hundred thousand, two-thirds of whom were gratuitously fed, underwent the like treatment in Maisúr, and more than twice that number in Bombay.

The month of August brought no change for the better. The rain still held off in most places. Rice was selling at seven or eight pounds to the rupee. Vast multitudes of transport cattle were dead or dying in the very districts which depended most upon them for their food supplies. Hunger, and the diseases engendered or stimulated by scanty or unwholesome food, foul air, and such-like causes, were doing their deadly work in all directions. In many villages the people had no shelter from sun or rain, for the thatch of their cabins had gone to feed the cattle, and the rafters they had sold to buy food. In Maisúr the distress became well-nigh unmanageable. The country around Bangalór, said an eye-witness, was like a vast desert. A special service had been organized to keep the streets of that city clear of the dead and dying; but outside might be seen the worst horrors incident to a prolonged famine; bodies lying frequently by the wayside, starving women and children poking into the dung-heaps for stray

---

* *Allen's Mail;* Indian Blue-book.

grains of undigested corn, and even at times some low-caste sweeper prowling with cannibal intent among the dead.*

So dark was the prospect for Southern India at the end of July that the Duke of Buckingham, as mouthpiece of a large meeting held in his own capital, made a formal appeal for help, not only to the public in India, but to the Lord Mayor of London and the various Chambers of Commerce in this country. By that time the Viceroy himself was hastening down from Simla to see with his own eyes what was doing for the relief of distress, and to confer with the Governor of Madras about further measures for the same end. His interview with Temple at Púna resulted in the transfer of General Kennedy from Bombay to Southern India, where his marvellous skill, energy, and management were especially needed to cope with a calamity more disastrous than any which India had known for a century past. For the sad truth grew daily clearer that the famine, at least in Maisúr and Madras, would last far into its second year.†

Happily for Western India the September rains saved the bulk of the standing crops from utter ruin. Numbers of labourers left the relief works for employment in the fields during the month of October, and before the end of November the works were all closed. But the chills and damps of a wet autumn told with deadly force on a people already weakened by hunger and bodily suffering; so that many thousands of those whom the Government had kept alive during the worst of the famine were now dying off from epidemic fevers.

In Madras, on the other hand, the September rains were too partial to bring much relief to the districts which most required it. During that month the numbers dependent on State-help averaged two millions and a quarter weekly, of whom more than a million and a half were gratuitously fed. The current prices of ' rice and coarse food-grains had risen to four and five times their ordinary value. A change for the better began in the middle of October, when the whole number of persons receiving State-help fell below two millions. By the end of that month it had fallen to thirteen hundred thousand, and in two months more to half a million. The north-east monsoon of November had rained new life upon the barren fields, and filled with new hope the hearts of hungry, naked, and destitute millions.

There was still cause, however, for prolonged anxiety. In the beginning of 1878 a fresh rise in prices checked the decline in the

---

* *Allen's Mail;* Indian Blue-book; Temple. † *Allen's Mail;* Temple.

number of persons relieved by the State. New relief works had to be opened in Bellâry and North Árkot. Swarms of locusts were eating up every green thing in Tinnivalli. Still, by the end of March, the numbers on relief had fallen to a quarter of a million, and they kept on falling until June, when the dearth of employment in the fields and the holding off of the south-west monsoon sent the poorer husbandmen once more flocking to the public works. Happily the monsoon burst freely a fortnight after time, and the people streamed back again to their roofless homes and their accustomed labours on the land. By that time, also, the relief committees in each district were zealously discharging the important task which private charity had committed to their hands. The Duke of Buckingham's appeal to his countrymen and the natives of India had not been made in vain. In the course of a twelvemonth, more than £800,000, collected from all parts of the world, passed into the hands of the local committees, who applied the money to a number of purposes outside the special sphere of State agency. They found for their self-chosen labours an ample field in the provision of clothing, shelter, agricultural tools, seed-grain, and plough-cattle for those who had lost every-thing but their lives; in the support of helpless orphans and destitute widows; and in the dispensing of alms and medicine to all who would else have died for want of timely succour.*

It was not till the end of this year—1878—that all need for working the machinery of State-relief finally disappeared. In Maisúr, where the distress had been prolonged and terrible, the relief works were closed a few weeks earlier. Towards the end of the same year a few of the Bombay districts came once more within the circle of distress. Vast swarms of rats and locusts preyed upon the growing crops of Gujarát and the South Dakhan; and the old machinery of famine relief had to be kept going down to the autumn of 1879. During the height of the Madras famine a like calamity threatened more than one province in Northern India. For a time there was partial suffering in the Panjáb. But the pinch of drought and high prices was felt more sharply for a longer period in the North-West Provinces and Oudh, both of which had lately been united under one Lieutenant-Governor, Sir George Couper. Towards the close of 1877 crowds of hungry people began flocking to the relief works opened in Oudh and Rohilkhand. In the following year the distress grew sharper and the cry for relief more general. The Government doubled the

* Indian Blue-book; *Allen's Mail;* Hunter.

private subscriptions, and suspended a large fraction of the land-revenue demand. But the Viceroy and Sir John Strachey found grave fault with Sir George Couper's humane proceedings, taken at a time when so much revenue was being sunk elsewhere for a like purpose. After some vain remonstrances, Couper made up his mind to carry out the Viceroy's orders, happen what might. In the course of 1878, nearly all the arrears of revenue were recovered by his unwilling Collectors from an impoverished peasantry. The relief works were closed with untoward haste, and before the year's end a million and a quarter of human beings had died from causes more or less due to want of nourishment.*

In Southern India, during the famine, two million acres of land were thrown for the time out of cultivation. The loss of land-revenue in those two years exceeded two millions and a quarter, only a sixth of which was afterwards recovered. In Bombay the loss was only £400,000. The loss of life, directly or indirectly, caused by famine in Southern and Western India was reckoned at five and a quarter million men, women, and children, of whom 1,250,000 perished in Maisúr, and three millions in Madras. Nearly half a million died of cholera alone. In Bellary and North Arkot one-fourth of the population perished of hunger or disease. In the city of Madras the death-rate for 1887 was reckoned at 116 per thousand, and in one relief-camp in Salem District 746 persons died during May out of 7,000 there collected. Of the Bombay districts Sholápur and Kaládgi were the heaviest losers. During the period of distress, numbers of the peasantry kept themselves alive by the sale of their silver ornaments and hoarded coins. The value of the bullion which thus, in two years, passed into the Bombay Mint amounted to $2\frac{1}{4}$ millions sterling, against only £4,000 in the previous year.

To the havoc wrought by death may be added the loss involved in a large reduction of the yearly birth-rate. During the two years of suffering the number of births in Southern India fell short of the average by one-third; and even in 1879, it was only a little higher than in 1877. The State outlay on famine relief all over India, apart from the loss of land-revenue, has been reckoned at eleven millions sterling; against which may be set the permanent value of such works as the Dhond-Manmar and the South Indian Railways and the "Buckingham" Canal, as well as the partial saving to the Government from the abnormal traffic on the guaranteed lines of railway. The cost of famine relief in Maisúr

* *Allen's Mail;* Official Papers; Famine Commission Report, 1880.

swallowed up the savings of many years—nearly half a million—and plunged the State in debt to the Indian Government to the amount of half a million more. But for the railways that brought food in plenty to each famishing province, the total loss of life would have been far greater. In view of the help thus given, of the sums expended on famine relief, of the zeal and energy displayed by the Local Governments and all who worked with them for the saving of human lives, "it is saddening to reflect how great a multitude died from causes avowedly traceable to want of food." "The fact remains"—said Temple himself—" that despite all measures of relief, many succumbed to famine alone." Actual starvation coming suddenly with a rush "slew its thousands," said Dr. William Hunter, for "no administrative capacity and no philanthropic zeal could cope with a distress so intense, and extending over so wide an area."

In 1874 the circle of distress had been comparatively small, and the task of supervision comparatively light. There was no epidemic disease; the labour wage was liberal, and the famine lasted only for one year. In Southern and Western India, on the other hand, the area of real suffering was far wider; the people on the whole were more scattered, more prone to wander in hard times, less strong to withstand the pressure of high prices on their scanty means; while the civil districts, especially in Madras, were very large, and the English who administered them too few to cope efficiently with any sudden or extraordinary need. Many of their native assistants proved unequal to the strain which a great public danger placed on their honesty, helpfulness, and active zeal; and at no time was the staff of competent overseers, English or native, numerous enough for the work they had to do. In this case, moreover, the famine held its course with few and brief pauses for two whole years.[*]

In spite of the vast sums expended on famine relief, and of the experience gained from dealing with former famines, it is to be feared that many lives were sacrificed to that dread of incurring " disastrous expenditure," which Lord Lytton's code of instructions seemed especially to enforce. If Lord Northbrook's more generous policy involved some waste of public money, the new demand for strict economy would naturally tend to counteract the old motives to benevolent spending. Low rates of wages on relief works and strict labour tests must often have increased the suffering they were meant to mitigate. The fear of spending too much

[*] Famine Commission Report; Temple; Hunter.

money withheld timely aid from many who must have sorely needed it in their own homes. For lack of timely or adequate supervision thousands of weakly and starving people were allowed to roam away from their own villages, and swell the numbers of sick and dying in or near the larger towns. If Lord Lytton's Government spent less in proportion than Lord Northbrook's on famine relief, it was certainly, after all deductions and allowances, far less successful in saving human lives.

CHAPTER III.

DOMESTIC AFFAIRS AND LEGISLATION.

WHILE the famine was yet raging, Lord Lytton's Government prepared a noteworthy scheme for ensuring India against future visitations of the same kind, by means of a special fund to which husbandmen, traders, and artisans should contribute yearly in fair proportion from their taxable wealth. The scheme itself, as propounded by Strachey before the close of 1877, aimed at enforcing the principle enounced three years before by Lord Northbrook, that it behoved the Government to provide somehow from its yearly revenues against a calamity which, having of late years recurred so often, might be expected to recur from time to time in the future. As the last and the present famine between them had cost the State more than fifteen millions, Strachey proposed to raise by a licence-tax on all trades and a moderate cess upon the land, something like a million and a half a year. This sum was to be expended only in payment of famine debts or on public works, whether canals or railways, of a purely "protective" kind. "We have pledged ourselves"—said the Viceroy in laying this scheme before his Legislative Council—"not to spend one rupee of the special resources thus created upon works of a different character."

In the spring of 1878 the new scheme passed into law. A licence-tax on all trades and industries, the profits of which exceeded Rs. 200 a year was imposed in every province at rates which varied according to the taxpayer's ostensible means from one rupee to five hundred rupees. The remainder of the sum required for famine insurance was made up by means of a special cess upon the land in every province save Madras and Bombay. For these, however, the Government had prepared their own burden in the shape of a marked addition to the salt-duties. As a first step in the process of equalizing those duties all over India, the decree went forth to raise them in Bombay and Madras from one rupee thirteen annas to two rupees and a half, or five shillings the maund of 82 pounds. In the course of 1878 the duty in Bengal was reduced to two rupees fourteen annas, and in Upper India to two rupees eight annas the maund. The people of Southern and Western India had to pay somewhat dearly for the boon thus granted to the more numerous and thriving peoples in the North.*

The sad tales of suffering which reached England weekly, sometimes even daily, during the great famine, drove numbers of thoughtful Englishmen to ponder the likeliest safeguards against so cruel a scourge. Those who gave special heed to the virtues of irrigation, as shown in some of the districts which had escaped the common disaster, cried aloud for more canals and waterworks. Others, who had noticed the good work done by railways in bringing food to the suffering millions, were urgent in demanding a swift and wide expansion of the railway system. Emigration, poor laws, improvements in the working of land-revenue systems, were panaceas which found no lack of eager advocates. The rival claims of canals and railways were pressed on the one side by Sir Arthur Cotton and Mr. John Bright, on the other by Mr. Juland Danvers, Government Director for Indian Railways, by Lord Salisbury himself, and by Sir Andrew Clarke, Lord Lytton's Minister for Public Works. There was one argument which told strongly on the side of railways. To ensure India against famine by an efficient network of canals properly filled with water would demand—said Sir Andrew Clarke—"an outlay of at least some three hundred millions sterling." But an outlay even of two hundred millions would entail a yearly charge of eight millions for interest alone on account of works which would yield at best a partial and precarious profit. For seventy or eighty millions, on the other hand, we could build ten thousand miles of new railway, which would give India "an insurance, not against famines, but certainly against extreme scarcity, distress, and death from want."

To the making of railways, therefore, the Indian Government continued to apply the larger share of its available resources. Irrigation, however, was not to be neglected. Writing to the Viceroy in January, 1878, Lord Salisbury dwelt upon the need of sanctioning only such projects as might serve to protect the people against famine, "in a degree at all corresponding to their cost." The list of canals which the Government could undertake without loss could not in his opinion be largely extended. While freely acknowledging the usefulness of canals in time of drought,

* Indian Blue-book ; *Allen's Mail.*

wherever they could be made without excessive cost and fed with a full and peimanent flow of water, he contended that in Southern India the same lack of rain which parched the fields would also neutralize the benefits of irrigation works, by emptying the tanks and lessening the volume of the rivers which fed the canals. In view of the demands lately put forth by "persons of authority" for the construction of new works on a vast scale in Madras, he warned the Viceroy against lightly sanctioning any scheme which close and careful inquiry might fail to justify as a great public good.*

One good result of Lord Salisbury's ponderings was the appointment of a Special Commission, headed by General Richard Strachey, which proceeded in the latter part of 1878 to explore the famine districts, gathering as they went a mass of fruitful information as to the causes of past famines in India, and the likeliest means of preventing or allaying such calamities in the future. A prominent member of the Commission was Mr. James Caird, a noted authority on all agricultural questions at home. Mr. H. S. Cunningham had a wide experience in matters of Indian revenue and finance, and the rest of Strachey's colleagues were men of weight and marked capacity in the Indian services. The fruits of their researches were afterwards embodied in a long and masterly Report, brimfull of lessons evolved from a diligent study of all the facts revealed or dimly shown in the accumulated records of Indian famines. For the Commissioners had done their work with a thoroughness that knew no rest or limit, pushing their researches into every corner of a field as wide as the economic history of all India, and storing up a rich treasury of instructive facts, inferences, and counsels for the use of their countrymen in after times.

In an Indian province the general amount of crime against person or property varies regularly from year to year with the ruling prices of food-grains. Cheap food means fewer cases of housebreaking, robbery, theft, fraud, and violence of various kinds. High prices swell the list of criminals even among the patient peasantry of Southern India, whose quiet endurance of inevitable ills matched their readiness to forego State-help at the very first glimpse of any useful labour to which they could set their hands. In 1877–78 grain-riots and robberies of grain were specially frequent in the Panjáb and the North-West Provinces. Many women in the latter jumped down wells with children in their

* *Allen's Mail; Times; Official Papers.*

arms rather than face the approach of death from slow starvation. In Mairwára scarcity and high prices drove many of the less civilized Mairs back into the lawless habits of former days. Madras had its high tide of crime in 1877, when the number of known offences more than doubled that of 1875, and cases of *dakaiti* or gang-robbery increased more than sevenfold. In Maisúr during the same year the tide rose still higher, and strong measures had to be taken against a new phase of Thaggi—robbery by means of stupefying drugs. The same epidemic of lawlessness which swept over the Bombay Dakhan in 1877 passed on with the following year through Sind and Gujarát. Many cases of child-murder by starving mothers were reported during the famine in Southern India; and other forms of murder were unusually rife. Cattle-stealing also became a common offence in many of the districts where distress made itself most widely felt. In some places girls were kidnapped with the connivance of their own kins-folk. At such times even the spread of sickness would drive men to violent deeds. In the Chattisgarh Division of the Central Provinces a sharp burst of cholera led to an outburst of popular fury against a number of harmless women, who were done to death or cruelly treated as witches guilty of producing or spreading the disease.*

About the end of 1878, while the traces of past suffering were still fresh in parts of Western India, a startling outbreak of Dakaiti was reported from the highlands of the Western Gháts. For several months the peace of the Dakhan from Khándesh to Satára and Sholapur was disturbed by the raids of robber bands, who sallied out from their hill retreats against the neighbouring villages, and carried off much plunder, not always won without bloodshed. The leader of some of these bands was Wásudeo Balwant Phádki, a Marátha Brahman who had come to cherish a fierce hatred of the Government in whose service he had but lately been employed. In his band of freebooters he saw the germs of a popular rising against British rule. A proclamation issued in his name called upon the people to treat the apparent bandits as their real friends, who sought to deliver them from the yoke of their common oppressors. The police alone were unable to cope with these gentry, who, with the help or the connivance of their friends and fellow castemen, infested even the high roads about Púna, and caused a vague disquietude among our countrymen at Bombay.

* Indian Blue-book.

The year 1879 was a time of political ferment in India. We had gone to war with Sher Ali, and our troops had lately marched beyond the passes into the heart of Afghánistán. Temple knew that Dakaiti in Maharashtra had often been the prelude to a concerted outbreak among the countrymen of the daring Sivaji. Of the Brahmans who still formed the ruling class in the Dakhan, he believed that many were ambitious, discontented, ripe for any movement which promised to bring back the good old days of the Bájis and the Bálajis; while the Marátha peasantry, after so many seasons of prolonged suffering, were no doubt the more inclined to follow any leader who appealed to their patriotism through their empty pockets, their growing debts, and their natural longing for relief from present ills. Two regiments of Sepoy Foot and one of Horse were accordingly sent to aid Major Daniell's police in hunting down the Dakaits, and bringing their leaders to a stern reckoning. Soldiers and police did their work so thoroughly under Daniell's guidance, that within three months the robber bands were all broken up, and their leaders either slain or lodged in prison. Wásudeo himself, after a vain attempt to enlist fresh recruits from among the Rohillas of Haidarábád, was tracked and caught by the Púna police in a temple on the British side of the Nizam's border. Convicted of treason by a Púna jury, he was condemned to transportation for life.*

Meanwhile an incident occurred at Púna which seemed to lend new significance to the outbreak in the Western Ghâts. The fine old palace of the Marátha Peshwas, built mainly of teakwood, and adorned with wood carvings of rare excellence, had of late years been used by the Bombay Government as a kind of Record Office for the departments of justice and education. One day this beautiful relic of Marátha greatness and art was set on fire by the hand of an incendiary, and in a few hours burnt to the ground. The records and the carved work were alike destroyed. The actual doers of the deed were caught, convicted on their own confession, and punished according to law; but those who had prompted them to this act of wanton mischief were never discovered.†

With the return of better seasons the revenues of the country began rising even above their wonted level. For the year ending with March, 1879, almost every source of income yielded an excess on any former year. The land revenue amounted to $22\frac{1}{3}$ millions;

---

* Indian Blue-book ; Temple ; *Allen's Mail.*
† Temple ; Indian Blue-book.

opium brought in more than 9⅓ millions, the salt-tax nearly 7 millions, and stamps more than 3 millions. The receipts from excise, the post-office and telegraphs were also larger than ever. The receipts from customs showed a decline, due chiefly to the contraction of India's import trade during the famine. On the other hand, the unwonted impulse which the Delhi Assemblage and the famine had given to the railway traffic in 1877 died off in the following year, and the net earnings of Indian railways fell from six to five millions sterling. At the end of two more years, however, they had nearly recovered all their lost ground, while nearly 1,900 miles of new railway had been added in three years to the mileage opened in 1877.

The completed accounts for the financial year 1878-79 showed a surplus of more than two millions, in spite of nearly three millions lost to India through the low rate of exchange for the rupee, which had fallen in value to about 1s. 7¼d. of English money. Under the new form of accounts adopted in 1876, the whole of the Indian revenues, Imperial and Provincial, were brought together under one head, which included also the profits derived from railways and other public works. In the year aforesaid, this total exceeded sixty-five millions, of which less than forty millions were drawn as taxes from the people of British India. In this and the following year the receipts from customs were sensibly reduced by the repeal of import duties on certain classes of cotton and linen goods, on wood furniture, candles, fruits, and vegetables, cordage, hides, lace, pitch, railway-plant, soap, and a few other items of less account. In spite of hard times, India's foreign trade, which in 1877 had risen to the value of 124 millions, still amounted to 108½ millions, or nearly six millions above the total for 1875.*

For some time past the Bombay Government had been carefully pondering the best means of redressing the grievances set forth by the Special Commission to which the agrarian riots of 1873 had given birth. Sir Philip Wodehouse had shrunk from applying a new legal remedy to evils which our laws and revenue systems had certainly helped to foster. But Sir Richard Temple and his colleagues had a livelier faith in the power of legislation to make good its own shortcomings; and with their concurrence an Act was passed through the Viceroy's Council in 1879, which, if it failed at first to do all that Temple wanted, still gave the peasantry of the South a liberal measure of relief from present burdens, and

---

* Indian Blue-book ; Statistical Abstract.

full security for the future from the worst consequences, whether of their own foolishness or of other men's greed.

The Southern India Agriculturists' Relief Act may be said to have restored, as between the husbandman and the money-lender, that fair balance of rights and chances which, for many years past, had unduly inclined against the former. It virtually took away the money-lender's power of selling up a ráyat's holding in payment of his debts; and it enabled the insolvent debtor to get quit of all past liabilities on certain conditions at the end of a given term of years. In the case of a debtor to the amount of fifty rupees, the Court may order him to pay as much of his debt as he can, and may then grant him a discharge for the remainder. For the relief of debtors to a larger amount the Act provided that no ráyat's holding should be attached or sold in execution of any decree, unless it had been expressly mortgaged for the debt named in such decree. Even in the latter case the Court may order the debtor's holding, a part of which shall have been reserved for his own support, to be cultivated on behalf of the creditor for seven years at the outside, after which the debtor shall be discharged. If the debtor himself seeks relief as a bankrupt under certain clauses of this Act, his immovable property shall be treated according to the same rule. Arrest or imprisonment of ráyats in execution of decrees for money was thenceforth done away. Nor could a creditor thereafter bring his claim against a ráyat before the District Court, until he had first tried the method of arbitration prescribed by the new law. If the village "conciliators" appointed for this end, failed to arbitrate between rúyat and money-lender, they might grant the latter a certificate to that effect. But without such certificate the creditor was debarred from carrying his suit into any Civil Court.*

In Bengal, on the other hand, a large class of the peasantry were crying out for protection, not against the village bankers, but against the Zamindárs, who still contrived to enhance at pleasure the rents of all those ráyats for whom no special safeguard had been provided by the Rent Law of 1859. The experience of twenty years had impressed the Government with the need of enlarging the scope and amending the practical defects of that law. In 1879 Sir Ashley Eden appointed a Special Commission to inquire into the whole matter, and to propound such measures of reform as the evidence before them seemed to justify. About a year later the Commissioners sent in their Report, and a Bill

* Temple ; Hunter.

embodying their proposals was circulated among the members of the Legislative Council. The leading feature of this scheme was the bestowal of certain tenant rights on a large class of husbandmen hitherto unprotected, or but partially protected, by the Rent Law of 1859. For the two classes of ráyats who already held their lands at fixed rents no special provision was required. In the case of the third class, who, having a twelve years' right of occupancy, could have their rents raised only by a decree of Court, the Commissioners proposed to make their rights transferable by sale, gift, or inheritance, and to secure them an equal share with the landlord in the "unearned increment" of the land and its produce. Next in their scheme appeared the most numerous class of all, the class of tenants who had held their lands for three years. In view of the growing competition for land, and of the misery thence certain to arise under present conditions for the great mass of a purely agricultural people, this class also were to be endowed with rights almost amounting to fixity of tenure. If a three years' tenant refused to pay an increased rent, he was not to be turned out of his holding until the landlord gave him substantial compensation both for disturbance and for improvements. As the former would be reckoned at one year's increased rent and the latter would probably have all been made by the tenant himself, few landlords would care to purchase a prospective gain at a cost so inconveniently heavy.

A scheme which involved issues so wide-reaching, so unpalatable to the landed gentry and merchants of Bengal, so sure to be assailed by the champions of vested rights, class privilege, freedom of contract, and things as they are, was likely to wait long before it became law. For several years the Bengal Tenancy Bill crawled through its various stages in the Viceroy's Council; nor had it become law when Lord Lytton's successor resigned his post in the latter part of 1884.*

The last year of Lord Lytton's Government saw a marked impulse given in a new direction to the policy first proclaimed in the days of Lord William Bentinck. The Charter Act of 1833 had decreed that no Native of British India should "by reason only of his religion, place of birth, descent, colour, or any of them, be disqualified from holding any place, office, or employment" under the East India Company. To the principle thus tardily affirmed

---

* Hunter; Draft of Bengal Tenancy Bill; Report of Committee of Legislative Council. An Amended Bill was passed a few months later by Lord Dufferin's Government.

by the British Parliament the Court of Directors gave full support in words of the clearest and broadest meaning :—" That there shall be no governing caste in British India ; that, whatever other tests of qualification may be adopted, distinction of race or religion shall not be of the number ; that no subject of the King, whether of Indian, or British, or mixed descent, shall be excluded either from the posts usually conferred on uncovenanted servants in India, or from the Covenanted Service itself, provided he be otherwise eligible ; " such was the interpretation placed by the India House on the Act aforesaid.

During the next five-and-twenty years Native Indians of pure or mixed blood gradually made their way into certain offices formerly reserved for white men alone. Under the rules of open competition, as first applied in 1853, all persons of a certain age became free in theory to seek admission into the Covenanted Civil Service of India, in which no Native had hitherto found a place. The policy announced in 1833 was formally reaffirmed in the Royal Proclamation of 1858. In point of fact, however, even the cleverest and most ambitious youths of Bengal or Bombay might seek in vain to enter the public service through the door of examinations holden in London only. The expense and the loss of caste involved in a voyage to England deterred many a good scholar from a competition so full of hazard even for English youths. Hence it happened that in the year 1878 only nine Native Indians held posts in the Covenanted Civil Service of their own land.

Ten years earlier Lord Lawrence had tried to smooth the way for Native candidates by founding a number of scholarships worth £200 a year each, tenable in Great Britain for three years. The scheme found favour with Sir Stafford Northcote ; but his successor at the India Office, the Duke of Argyll, brought the working of it to an early and unforeseen close. Not that he sought in any way to annul the Great Concession of 1833. He himself in 1870 carried through Parliament a Bill empowering the authorities in India to appoint Native Indians, under such rules as the Governor-General, with the sanction of the India Office, might from time to time prescribe, to posts hitherto held by Covenanted Civilians alone. But, looking to the need of maintaining before all things our rule in India, the Duke held that a large proportion of the higher offices must always be reserved for his own countrymen. Natives, he wrote, should be selected chiefly for judicial, seldom if ever for executive duties.

He would prefer the principle of selection in India to that of open competition at home, which afforded no true test of administrative vigour or capacity for rule. The system of scholarships was therefore laid aside, and the Indian Government were bidden to find some better way of reconciling the just claims of Native ambition with the due safeguarding of British supremacy.

Five years had to pass before a set of rules drawn up by the Indian Government in accordance with the Act of 1870 were finally sanctioned by the new Secretary for India, Lord Salisbury. In the following year one or two Natives received appointments under these rules. Meanwhile in England the age of candidates for the Civil Service was lowered to a point which placed Native Indians virtually outside the pale of free competition. What had been barely possible for an Indian youth of nineteen, became in effect impossible for one of seventeen. If the rulers of India meant to keep faith with their Native subjects, it was high time to consider the best way of lessening the gulf that still yawned between the promises and the practice of more than forty years past. The duty and the advantage of employing Native Indians as largely as possible in the Government of their own country were fully acknowledged by statesmen of all parties. On the other hand the Indian Government had to reckon with the prescriptive rights enjoyed or claimed by the old Covenanted Service, and with the seeming danger of appointing Natives to high office in places more or less frequented by Europeans impatient or distrustful of Native control.

At length, in 1878, Lord Lytton's Government put forth a well-considered scheme for carving the Covenanted Service into two parts, the one recruited as heretofore from England, the other reserved under due conditions for Native aspirants alone. The posts required for this new class of civil officers were to be taken partly from the Covenanted, partly from the Uncovenanted Service. The members of the new Service were to be selected as far as possible from men of rank and birth, who would draw lower salaries than their English rivals, but would stand in other respects on an equal footing with the latter.

To the leading principle of this scheme, the admission of Natives to some of the higher offices hitherto reserved for competitioners from England, Lord Cranbrook, the new Minister for India, gave ungrudging support. But the formation of a close Service for Natives only, and the formal exclusion of Natives from the field of open competition, seemed to him a difficult and dangerous method of securing the end in view. No application to Parliament for the purpose of repealing a clause in the Act of 1833 would have any prospect of success, nor would he himself undertake so profitless a venture. He pointed out a way, however, in which Lord Lytton's purpose could best be accomplished within the four corners of the existing law; and the rules which the Viceroy framed in accordance with these directions received Lord Cranbrook's final endorsement in the summer of 1879. Thenceforth a certain number of appointments in the Covenanted Service were to be allotted yearly to Native probationers duly selected by the Local Governments. At the end of two years these probationers, if they had passed all needful tests of fitness for further service, would finally enter the new class of Statutory Civilians, on two-thirds of the salary payable to English Civil Servants of corresponding rank. As several branches of the Uncovenanted Service had meanwhile been reserved for Natives only, Lord Lytton's amended scheme went nearly as far, perhaps, towards fulfilling the pledges of 1833 as the claims of expediency would have allowed.*

Among the measures which had already passed Lord Lytton's Council was an "Act for the better control of Publications in the Oriental Languages." In one day of March, 1878, the Viceroy, armed with the previous assent of the India Office, carried through all its stages a law which virtually abolished, while professing only to regulate, the freedom of the Indian Vernacular Press—that freedom which Metcalfe had bestowed upon it forty-three years before. It was enacted that the publisher of any article which the District Collector deemed libellous or seditious should bind himself under a penalty fixed by the Collector, with the sanction of the Local Government, to refrain from repeating his offence. If he declined to give this pledge for his good behaviour, he would have to lay the proof-sheets of each number of his journal before a Censor appointed by the Government. A second offence of the same kind would involve the suppression of his journal and the payment of a heavy fine. The Native journalist was placed, in short, under the arbitrary control of a District Officer, who might sometimes be sorely tempted to mistake his private grudges for public zeal.

In defence of a measure which could hardly have been justified even by the stress of another Indian Mutiny, its advocates pleaded the proneness of Native journalists to indulge in libellous

* Papers relating to the admission of Natives to the Civil Service of India, 1879.

attacks on our own countrymen, or on Native officials and gentlemen of rank, and in highly seditious language against India's
rulers. There was no other means, they said, of checking the
mischief thus engendered; for the punishments provided by the
Penal Code were too severe for any but the worst offenders, while
both the Government and private persons were loth, for different
reasons, to bring these offences before a Court of Justice. It
seemed to be forgotten that the Judges who might have to try
such cases were not bound to inflict the highest penalties set forth
in the Code, and that no unwillingness to make use of the existing
law against libel and sedition could justify its supersession by a
law founded on race distinctions, and involving a needless insult
to the whole Native community. One member of Council read
out a number of choice passages from vernacular prints, the
wildest of which were moderation itself compared with many an
outburst of party rancour and race or class antipathies nearer
home. One journal, for instance, charged the Government with
hypocrisy and deceit. Another described it as a monster that
destroyed its own children. A third declared that England had
reduced all India to poverty and the ráyats to despair. A fourth
complained of our countrymen as mostly " selfish, rough-tempered,
mean-spirited, and hostile to Natives." England, said another,
was losing all her old influence in the politics of Europe, and the
valour of her sons was steadily declining. Another journal
ascribed the growth of intemperance in India to the working of
the Abkári or liquor-duties. Another exhorted the people to bear
present calamities with a hopeful heart, for " the shortlived
kings of the present time can have no stability." An Indór paper
spoke of the Nána Sahib as about to invade India with a Russian
army for the purpose of restoring the empire of the Marátha
Peshwas.

Such was the kind of " objectionable matter " which the Viceroy and his colleagues sought to purge out of Native journals by
means of a remedy worse than the disease. Such were the
grounds on which Lord Lytton justified the new scheme for
" preventing ignorant, foolish, and irresponsible persons from
recklessly destroying the noble edifice which still generously
shelters even its vile detractors." The extravagant rhetoric of a
few silly journalists was supposed to endanger the existence of an
Empire which, at the close of Lord Northbrook's rule, had stood
to all appearance firmer even than before. In his eagerness to
curb the licence of the Native press, Lord Lytton gave no heed to

the danger of driving the political disease inwards, or to the folly of heaping fresh fuel on the flame of popular discontent. The nuisance he complained of was buried out of sight ; but what poison it contained was left to work more fatally than ever underground. Sedition could still circulate freely through the post, or by other channels yet safer from official scrutiny.*

* *Allen's Mail; Times;* Act IX. of 1878.

CHAPTER IV.

THE SECOND AFGHÁN WAR.

IN the course of this year (1878) things were happening which ended by involving India in her second war with Afghánistán. The spring of the year witnessed the march of a victorious Russian army on Constantinople, and the despatch of a picked Indian force, eight thousand strong, by way of Egypt to Malta. The latter move was another stroke of the policy which had aimed at frightening Russia by proclaiming the Queen of England Empress of Hindustán. Lord Beaconsfield appeared to think that the unwonted spectacle of a few thousand Indian troops in the Mediterranean would in some way deter Russia from pushing too far her late successes against the Turks. The Russian answer to this curious challenge came from Samarkhand, whence General Kauffmann presently sent off an embassy under Colonel Stoletoff to Kábul, with the hope of winning the Amir's support in the event of a hostile movement on our part against Russian Turkistán.

In the early part of June, a month before peace between Russia and Turkey was ratified at Berlin, Stoletoff led his embassy towards the Oxus. Sher Ali was sadly puzzled what course to take in this conjuncture. The earthen pipkin found itself drifting hopelessly between the two iron pots. "A plague on both your houses" would be a fair translation of his feelings towards the rival Powers on either side of Afghánistán. He desired only to be let alone. An Envoy from the Grand Turk had vainly pressed him to raise a religious war against the white infidels in Central Asia. Thus far he had given the Viceroy of India no pretext for an open quarrel. He tried, however vainly, to delay the advance of Stoletoff's Mission across the Oxus. But Kauffmann had clearly hinted at the danger of provoking Russia's enmity to a prince for whose throne there was at least one formidable candidate near at hand; and so Sher Ali ceased struggling against his fate.*

* *Times* ; Afghán Blue-book ; Central Asian Papers.

Before the Russian Envoy reached Kábul the Treaty of Berlin had been already signed. The knowledge of this fact erelong relieved Sher Ali of his worst anxieties and deprived the Mission of its political sting. Stoletoff's intercourse with his Afghán host speedily toned down into a mere exchange of compliments and courtesies, at which no prudent Viceroy should have taken offence. But Lord Lytton had not shown himself a prudent Viceroy. In the hospitalities at Kábul he saw only a fresh proof of Sher Ali's readiness to plot mischief against his old ally. The mere reception of a Russian Embassy in the face of Sher Ali's previous refusals to receive an English Resident, seemed to him cause sufficient for insisting at all hazards on swift compliance with his former demands. On the 14th of August he despatched from Simla a Native officer, charged with a letter which informed Sher Ali of the Viceroy's intention to depute Sir Neville Chamberlain on a Special Embassy to his Court. For this end the Amir was requested to make all needful arrangements without delay.

On hearing the contents of this letter the Amir was "much displeased." It seemed, he said, as if the Mission was to "come by force," without his consent being so much as asked. He had received the Russian Mission because he could not help himself, and he would gladly in good time receive an English Mission also, in the hope of clearing up old misunderstandings. Grief for the death of his favourite son, Abdulla Jún, had given him "no time to think over the matter." There was sickness among the Russians then at Kábul; but as soon as he could decently dismiss these guests, he would arrange for the safe-conduct of Chamberlain's Mission from Peshawar. Appealing to the friendship which had so long existed between the two Powers, he warned the Viceroy against subjecting it to a strain which it could not safely bear.

Lord Lytton's own Agent, Gholám Husain Khán, saw the danger of forcing on Sher Ali the pill, which, if time were given him and due deference paid to his wishes, he might come to swallow of his own accord. The Mission, he wrote to the Commissioner of Peshawar, should not cross the frontier without the Amir's consent; for "otherwise harm would occur." The Russian Envoy would soon be leaving Kábul, and then, no doubt, the Amir would send for the British Mission. But the Viceroy would hear no reasons for delay; while the Amir, wrapt up in his private sorrows, and annoyed by the messages, more harsh than conciliatory, which reached him from Peshawar, allowed things to take their course. For several weeks of August and September he shut himself up in his palace, half-crazed with grief for the loss of his darling Benjamin. A formal letter of condolence was the only act of courtesy with which Lord Lytton tempered the rudeness of his language towards a neighbour, whose silence he imputed to ill-will alone. With a full knowledge of what would happen if he sent Chamberlain forward without the Amir's consent, he ordered the Mission to start on the 19th of September.

On the 21st Chamberlain encamped at Jamrúd, close to the mouth of the Khaibar Pass. The Afridis of the Khaibar, who owed the Amir a nominal allegiance, had already been bribed to let the Mission go forward in peace. On the same day Major Cavagnari rode on with a small escort to the hill-fort of Ali Masjid, guarding the road through the Pass. The officer in command of this Afghán outpost declared in courteous language that he had no orders to let the Mission advance. In reply to Cavagnari's questions he warned him of his intention to resist the advance of the Mission by force; "and you may take it"—he added—"as kindness, and because I remember friendship, that I do not fire upon you for what you have done already." The Englishman and the Afghán then shook hands; and as the former turned his horse's head homewards, the Sardár said with a smile of frank courtesy, " You have had a straight answer."*

Another officer, Colonel Jenkins, had been present during this parley, and both he and Cavagnari were "very favourably impressed" by the perfect courtesy with which they had been turned back. A few days later, however, all England was startled to hear, through a brief official telegram, that an English Envoy had been "forcibly repulsed" from an Afghán outpost on his way to Kábul. Every one was led to suppose that a gross outrage had been inflicted by Sher Ali's orders on the representative of an Indian Viceroy. Ignorant of what had happened before, and misled by the wrongly-worded statement of a disagreeable fact, the people of England raised a general outcry for strong measures against the ruler who had thus wantonly provoked the wrath of the British Lion. Almost alone among his countrymen Lord Lawrence, old and in feeble health, strove to allay the rising storm. In his letter of September 27, addressed to the *Times*, he pleaded earnestly for all due forbearance towards an old ally, whose alleged discourtesies had been provoked by our own shortcomings.

* Afghán Blue-book.

We had no right, he argued, to force the Mission upon Sher Ali in the teeth of all former pledges and of every moral consideration which justified his resistance to so dangerous a demand. Our own aggressiveness had provoked the consequent rebuff ; and it clearly behoved us, as the wrongdoers, to open out to Sher Ali some way of escape from a war whose end no one could foresee, a war not more ruinous to India's finances than fatal to the growth of a strong and friendly Afghán Power. "There will be no real dishonour "—he concluded—" in coming to terms with him ; whereas, by pressing on him our own policy, we may incur most serious difficulties and even disasters."*

Such were the words of age that still glowed with the fire of youth. Lord Lawrence allowed, indeed, that " no force of Afgháns could stand against our troops when properly brought to bear against them." But he saw more clearly than most men that our real difficulties would begin only when the war was over ; and to those difficulties he could forecast no speedy or desirable end.

In subsequent letters to the same journal he continued his brave appeal to the good sense of his countrymen against the folly of their rulers. Again and again he showed that no good whatever could be gained by another Afghán war, especially a war based on grounds of obvious injustice ; that our Indian frontier, remarkably strong by nature, could be yet further strengthened at a moderate cost ; and that any advance beyond that frontier would only weaken our present means of defence against foreign assailants. The Afgháns, he declared, " will never cease to resist as long as they have a hope of success, and when beaten down, have that kind of elasticity which will ever lead them to renew the struggle whenever opportunity of so doing may recur." We wanted them, in short, " as friends and not as enemies." As for our quarrel with Sher Ali, he held that to wage war upon him for refusing to receive our Mission, or for the rectification of our frontier, or for any other colourable purpose, would be " a gross injustice and a grave stigma on the character of the English nation."†

The position at this moment bore a striking resemblance to that of Lord Auckland's Government in 1838, when the Persian army withdrew from the siege of Herát. Had Lord Auckland then listened to the voice of prudence and common justice, the war with Dost Mohammad would never have broken out, and one dark chapter of Indian history would have remained unwritten.

* Afghán Blue-book ; *Times*, 1878.   † *Times.*

And so, too, when the Treaty of Berlin had once been ratified, there remained no valid pretext for the high-handed policy which led up to a fresh invasion, followed by a fresh retreat from Afghánistán. Had Sher Ali's prayer for delay been granted, our fancied "prestige" in Asia would have suffered no loss, and the people of England would have had time to judge for themselves how far the Amir's behaviour and that of his officers justified the Viceroy's insistence on a policy which events already called upon him to forego.

But the force of circumstances was still for a time to overrule the counsels of prudence, honesty, and fair-play. While men's minds were yet simmering over the insult offered by one of Russia's jackals to the British flag, another telegram in the latter part of October informed the world that Sher Ali's reply, when at last it came, to the Viceroy's first demand was a flat refusal, couched in phrases of insolent defiance. This was far from an accurate description of a letter which neither refused nor accepted anything save the decree of Fate, and which contained nothing more insolent than complaints of the rude and harsh language used by the Commissioner of Pesháwar, nothing more defiant than a disavowal of enmity to the Indian Government and a quiet appeal to Allah for help in the hour of trial. But the mis-statement served to keep alive the popular belief in Sher Ali's wickedness, until the blow designed by the Viceroy and Lord Beaconsfield had been struck beyond recall.*

Lord Lytton was eager to strike that blow at once. Troops were already massing on the frontier for a forward march into Afghánistán. But the Home Government had not lost all regard for decency in their desire to rectify a "haphazard and un-scientific frontier;" and some of their political opponents were beginning to suspect them of foul play. Lord Cranbrook, who had lately taken Lord Salisbury's place at the India Office, bade the impatient Viceroy stay his hand until the 20th of November, in order that Sher Ali might have time for repentance. Meanwhile the leaders of the Liberal party in England were growing more and more uneasy at the prospect of another campaign against the Montenegrins of Central Asia. Lord Lawrence had not sounded the alarm entirely in vain. In November, Lord Northbrook delivered at Winchester a powerful protest against the policy which Lord Lytton seemed bent on pursuing to the bitter end. There was not a rag of evidence, he declared, to

* Afghán Blue-book ; *Times.*

show that, after the arrival of Stoletoff's Mission, the Amir had entered into any agreement hostile to the British power. In the course of the same month a number of gentlemen, including several officers who had served and suffered in the first Afghán War, formed themselves into an Afghán Committee for the purpose of preventing a struggle which Lord Lytton and the Indian Services were manifestly longing to begin.*

In spite of his failing health, Lord Lawrence consented to act as Chairman. On the 16th of November he asked the Prime Minister by letter to receive a deputation from his Committee, in the hope of persuading him to leave the question of peace or war in the hands of Parliament, which was so soon to meet. Lord Beaconsfield's answer was a refusal, expressed in language that read like one continuous sneer. Before the end of November those papers for which Lawrence had vainly asked in 1877, and which the Government had agreed to publish in July, were given to the world, too late to avert an unjust and impolitic war, but not too late to open men's eyes to the tricks and wiles which had made that war possible. Before Parliament met in December, all chance of a peaceful settlement had passed away, and our troops were marching as enemies through the country of our old ally.†

It was only on the 31st of October that Lord Lytton spoke his last word—through the Post-office—to the Amir. Besides demanding a full and suitable apology for past transgressions, he bade Sher Ali "consent to receive a permanent British Mission within his territory." Unless his acceptance of these and other conditions were made known to the Viceroy by the 20th of November, the Amir would be "treated as a declared enemy of the British Government." A statesman honestly desirous of a peaceful issue would have granted a longer term of grace, and forborne from irritating so obstinate a sore as the question of a permanent Mission. But the Afghán winter was fast approaching, and time was precious to a Viceroy already chafing under prolonged delays.

On the 20th of November, no answer had arrived from Kábul to the ultimatum posted in the letter-box at Jamrúd. On the following day Lord Lytton declared war in a manifesto which accused the Amir of requiting the steady friendship and unvarying kindness of the British Government with nothing but open discourtesy and active ill-will. Besides all the offences laid more

---

* *British Quarterly Review; Daily News,* &c.
† Afghán Blue-book ; *Times; Daily News.*

or less unfairly to his account in former years, he was shown to have forfeited all claim to our forbearance by his late reception of a Russian Embassy despatched in open disregard of Russian pledges, by the forcible repulse of an English Envoy from an Afghán outpost, and, finally, by refusing to accept "a last opportunity of escaping the punishment merited by his acts."*

Even the last-named charge turned out to be as far from the truth as nearly all the rest. Sher Ali had sent off an answer to the Viceroy's ultimatum; but the messenger who bore it had been delayed by some mischance on the road. The Amir had expressed his willingness to receive a British Mission of the same dimensions as that which Stoletoff had led to Kábul. But before his letter reached Peshâwar hostilities had begun. One column of our troops, under the veteran Sir Samuel Browne, had already mastered the fort of Ali Masjid and was marching on through the Khaibar to Jalálabád, while another, pushing on from Thal through the Kuram Valley, under the dashing Frederic Roberts, had driven the enemy with loss from the high ridge that crowned the Paiwúr Pass. A third column, starting from Kwatta, marched, under the able Sir Donald Stewart, up the Pishín Valley to Kandáhár. Before the winter had set in, General Sam Browne's force was firmly planted in Jalálabád, and Roberts's brigade guarded the further side of the Kuram Valley, while Kandáhár was safe in Stewart's keeping. On the 13th of December the ill-starred Amir, accompanied by the Russian Mission, fled from Kábul towards Afghán Turkistán, leaving his son Yákub free to make what terms he could with his own countrymen and his father's foes. On the 21st of February, 1879, Sher Ali himself died of grief and disease at Mazar-i-Sharif. Yákub Khán had meanwhile been acknowledged as Amir by his own people. A little later our troops advanced to Gandámak, near the chain of mountain passes which had beheld the slaughters of 1842, and the march of Pollock's avenging army on Kábul. Here they awaited the result of negotiations opened with the new Amir. For some weeks messengers went to and fro between Kábul and Gandámak. At last, in the month of May, when the preliminaries had all been settled, Yákub came into the British camp, prepared to sign the treaty which circumstances had forced him to accept.

Thus far the Viceroy's plans had prospered to his heart's contentment. The treaty which presently bore Yákub's signature bound him to receive and protect an English Resident at his

* Afghán Blue-book.

Court, to place his foreign relations under our entire control, and to make over to our keeping a long slice of his southern frontier, comprising the districts of Thal-Chotiáli, Sibi, and Pishín. This was the new scientific frontier of which Lord Beaconsfield had lately spoken as superior to the line of rugged mountains that guarded the Indus Valley from Kotri to Peshawar. In plain truth its only superiority lay in the command it gave us for aggressive purposes over the roads to Kandáhár, Herát, Ghazní, and Kábul. From Kwatta to the Khaibar our line of outposts now threatened the very existence of that Afghán Kingdom which former Viceroys had been so careful to maintain and strengthen. Under the new treaty the Amir had even been constrained to give up all claim to the allegiance of those border tribes who guarded the way to Kábul through the Kuram Valley and the Khaibar Pass.*

All this had been done as a countermove to the alleged designs of a Power which had given us no real cause of offence, or even of lasting anxiety, when it despatched to Kábul a Russian Mission by way of answer to certain unfriendly movements on our own part. The Treaty of Berlin once signed, no harm could anyhow have befallen us from an exchange of compliments between Kauffmann's Envoy and the Amir, who, spite of our past unkindness, had done nothing worthy of grave-reproach. Lord Lytton's unseemly haste had brought on the collision which policy and justice alike forbade. The courteous stoppage of Chamberlain's Mission was made the pretext for a raid, whose real object was to give India a frontier so "rectified" as only to weaken her defensive strength. Sher Ali lost his kingdom and his life because, in circumstances of cruel provocation he had delayed in sending an answer to the Viceroy's final demands. The Treaty of Gandámak seemed for the moment to secure everything for the attaining of which Lord Lytton's Government had cast aside the settled policy of former Viceroys, and disowned the faith of old treaties and of written promises not less binding than treaties. The new policy had thus far proved so successful that few people in England cared to remember the prophetic warnings of Lord Lawrence, the weighty remonstrances of the Earl of Northbrook, or the slashing eloquence of the Duke of Argyll.

There were some few, however, who saw clearly that, when the first fighting was over, our real difficulties would begin. In July, 1879, Sir Louis Cavagnari—for he had just been knighted—took

* *Times; Allen's Mail;* Hunter; Temple.

up his abode as British Resident at Kábul, where the new Amir received him with every mark of courtesy and goodwill. For a few weeks all went merry as a marriage bell, and the new Resident saw no reason for fearing evil. Lawrence himself had lived to hear that the war was over, and that our troops were slowly retiring within the new frontier. But he did not live to hear of the storm that was so soon to follow that delusive calm. On the 3rd of September the very disaster which he had predicted came to pass. A crowd of armed men and Afghán rabble attacked the Residency, which Cavagnari and his small escort of Guides defended with all the courage of mingled hope and despair. But no help reached them from the powerless Amir, and in a few hours not one of the small garrison was left alive.[*]

No time was lost in avenging the murder thus successfully accomplished under Yákub's eyes, if not, as many believed, with his connivance. Donald Stewart once more set out for Kandáhár. Early in October General Roberts led his troops up the Kuram Valley and marched with all haste on to Kábul. A sharp fight with the Afgháns on the heights before the city left Roberts master of the field and of the city itself. The Bála Hissár was partially dismantled, and our troops took up their winter quarters in a fortified cantonment outside the city. Yákub Khán, whose spirit seemed to have been broken by his long imprisonment, and who feared the English less than his own subjects, threw himself on the victor's mercy, and was sent off a State prisoner to Peshawar. For several months anarchy reigned in most parts of Afghánistán. Large bodies of armed Afgháns hovered around Kábul, and once in December our troops suffered a serious check at the hands of a brave and wily, if ill-disciplined foe. Roberts, however, was enabled erelong to turn the tables upon his assailants, and his stern enforcement of martial law kept the people quiet for miles around Kábul. In the city and province of Kandáhár Stewart maintained order through the agency of a Native Governor lately appointed by Yákub Khán.

Yákub's abdication had left his people as sheep without a shepherd. The need for installing a new Amir in his place grew more and more urgent as time went on, and India's resources in men, animals, and money to meet the expenses of holding a conquered country and overawing a hostile population ran lower and more low. The special surplus of a million and a half which Lord Lytton had set aside for famine insurance had been swallowed up

---

[*] *British Quarterly Review*, January, 1879 ; Bosworth-Smith ; *Allen's Mail.*

in the deficit already caused by war. In March, 1879, the Viceroy had calmly declared that the famine-fund had " virtually ceased to exist." Recruits for the frontier were now coming in but slowly, and the Panjáb and Sind were almost drained of their wealth in camels and ponies. Yákub's brother, Ayub Khán, held Herát as his brother's rightful heir, while other Afghán chiefs in the Eastern Provinces proclaimed their loyalty to Yákub's infant son. Lord Lytton's Government turned their thoughts to Sher Ali's exiled nephew, Abdurrahman Khán, as the prince best qualified to fill the vacant throne. In the spring of 1880 Stewart led the bulk of his troops out of Kandáhár for a march to Kábul by way of Ghazni. His hard-won victory at Ahmad Khél over a large Afghán force, strengthened by several thousand Ghází fanatics, quelled one formidable rising and opened the road to Kábul, where his able lieutenant, Roberts, had so long held an iron sway. On the 22nd of July, Abdurrahman was formally acknowledged as Amir on condition of keeping faith with his future ally and pro-tector. In the following month the troops which had so long garrisoned Kábul began their homeward march.

By that time, however, a new Viceroy had gone out to India in Lord Lytton's stead. The general election which took place in the spring had brought into power a Liberal Government pledged to undo, as far as possible, the aggressive policy pursued every-where by that of Lord Beaconsfield. In April, 1880, Lord Lytton resigned the post from which he might else have shortly been recalled. If his rule in India had been fraught with little good to the people at large, if he was unfortunate in having to deal with a prolonged and widespread famine, the evil he had done was yet to live after him. More lives and more money were yet to be wasted on account of the mischief he had set rolling in Afghánistán. In June, 1880, Ayub Khán set out from Herát in hopes of becoming master of Kandáhár. As he neared the Helmand his force was strengthened by the very troops which the Wali or Governor of Kandáhár had sent out to intercept him. The rout of a British brigade at Maiwand in July placed Kandáhár itself for a time in serious danger.

Happily Stewart and Roberts were both at Kábul, and they resolved between them to lose no time in relieving the weakened garrison of Kandáhár. Placing the best of his own troops under Roberts's command, Stewart sent him off in August, with a com-pact force nearly ten thousand strong, to make the quickest of his way to the scene of danger. In twenty days Roberts marched the whole distance of three hundred and ten miles. This feat of energy was crowned on the 1st of September by the brilliant victory which Roberts gained near Kandáhár over an army well posted for defence. Ayub fled with a handful of followers back to Herát, and Kandáhár was safe from further attack.[*]

In the following year Lord Ripon's Government withdrew the British garrisons from Kandáhár and Pishín. The Treaty of Gandámak became in most respects a dead letter. No attempt has since been made to force a British Resident on the Afghán Amir. We have done our best to heal the wounds of our inflicting. We have once more owned the folly of breaking up a stable kingdom ruled by a fairly faithful ally, and of turning against us the hearts of a manly, fierce, and stubbornly independent people, in order to deal a blow at the shadow cast by Russia's ripening greatness in Turkistán. Unhappily the lesson had to be learned at no small sacrifice of our national honour, and at a cruel cost to the Indian taxpayer, who was saddled with the payment of fifteen out of the twenty millions expended on a war waged for objects in which the people of India had no substantial concern.

[*] *Allen's Mail; Calcutta Review; Times.*

EPILOGUE.

UNDER the just, humane, enlightened rule of the Marquis of Ripon, who, as Lord de Grey, had once for a few months served as Secretary for India, that country enjoyed four years and a half of peaceful prosperity and steady progress in the field of social and political reform. The Native press once more became free. The municipal committees throughout India were remodelled on a basis of popular election, which aimed at training the people in the due management of their local affairs. A careful inquiry into the whole system of State education resulted in measures for limiting the outlay on higher education in order to improve and extend the system of primary and middle schools. Railways, canals, and other public works showed a yearly increasing balance on the credit side. A series of good seasons favoured the growth of trade, and enabled the Government to fill its treasuries without recourse to new taxes. A general lowering of the salt-duties entailed no marked or permanent loss to the revenues. The foreign trade of the country rose to about £140,000,000 a year. In his foreign policy Lord Ripon followed the old lines off which his predecessor had so widely strayed. His zeal for justice and his honest sympathy with Native efforts and aspirations brought him, like one or two former Viceroys, into untoward conflict with the mass of his countrymen in India, touching the right of Natives in the Covenanted Service to wield equal powers of punishment with their English peers over all criminals, white or black. The Ilbert Bill, as it was called after the Law Member of his Council, aroused against him a storm of obloquy fiercer than that which had once raged around Drinkwater Bethune. But the storm was finally allayed by a compromise which left Lord Ripon master of more than half the field; and the rancour of his opponents endeared him all the more strongly to the hearts of his Native subjects. The demonstrations of loving sympathy which everywhere greeted him on his last journey through Upper India far surpassed in extent and heartiness all similar outbursts of popular feeling evoked in favour of any former Viceroy. If Lord Ripon's successors take the lesson to heart, there will be little cause to fear for the prolonged continuance of British rule in India.

INDEX.

—o—

B.

Babádur Sháh, King of Delhi (*q. v.*), 315, 316 ; he and his wife in prison, ii. 32 ; his trial (Jan. 1858), ii. 33 ; his sentence ; transported (Dec.), ii. 34

Babár, campaign against Kúnwar Singh in (1858), ii. 66 ; signs of coming famine (*q. v.*) in, and in Bengal (1873-74), ii. 313

Babrampur, Sepoy mutiny at (Feb. 1857), 356

Báji Ráo, adoptive father of Nána Sahib (*q. v.*) dies Jan. 1853, 313

Bakhar occupied by British (1838), 38

Bandras kept in order by its civil officers during May 1857, 411 ; Neill's arrival at (June 3) ; arrangements for disarming the Sepoys (June 4), 412 ; resistance and rout of the mutineers ; Surat Singh saves the Treasury, 413 ; order maintained in, with severity, 414

Banks, Major, killed in Lucknow (1857), 447, 450

Bardwán, Rájah of, his relief of distress (1845), 156

Baróli, murderous outbreak of mutiny at (May 1857), 391 ; fighting at and capture of (1858), ii. 63

Barnard, Sir Henry, Commander-in-Chief during the Mutiny (*q. v.*), 390 ; his death at Delhi (July 1857), 475

Barnes, George, his services and death (1861), ii. 136

Baroda, Outram's zeal against *Khatpat* at, 249 ; Malhár Ráo (*q. v.*), Gaik-wár of (1873), ii. 328 ; is deposed (1875), ii. 330 ; the Regency and new Gaikwár, ii. 330

Barrackpur, disbanding of Sepoys at (March 1857), 357 ; murderous outbreak of Mangal Pandi, 358

Bashiratganj, Havelock's victories at, July, Aug., 1857, 451, 452

Bassein, brilliant capture of (1852), 292, 293

Batson, Dr., his adventures in flight from Delhi to Karnál (1857), 373

Bazótis on Panjáb frontier, campaign against (1868), ii. 218

Beaconsfield, Lord, his plan for frightening Russia, ii. 367

Beadon, Mr. Cecil, Governor of Bengal (1862), ii. 147 ; his conduct as to the Orissa famine (1865-66), ii. 182, 186 ; his retirement from Bengal (1867), ii. 193

Beatson, Capt., his death (July 1857), 439

Bemarú, success and defeat of British troops at (1841), 59

Bengal, East India Company become masters of (1765), 6 ; revival of Dakaity in, 259, 260 ; office of Lieutenant-Governor created (1853), 327 ; first complete census of (1872), ii. 275 ; road-cess in (1873), ii. 303 ; famine (*q. v.*) in (1873-74), ii. 313 ; great cyclone in Lower Bengal (Nov. 1864), ii. 175 ; and in Eastern Bengal (Oct. 1876), ii. 370 ; consequent cholera, ii. 371 ; Assam, Kachár, and the hill-tracts separated from (1874), ii. 321

Bengal Army, mutiny in (1844), 102

Beni Madhu, decisive defeat of (Nov. 1858), ii. 85 ; is killed (Nov. 1859), ii. 88

Bentinck, Lord William, his rule in India (1828-35), 9, 14, 15

Berár ceded to the Company (1853), 311, 312

Bethune, Mr. Drinkwater, his Act respecting criminal Europeans (1849), 262 ; his middle-class girls' school, 263

Bháwalpur, the Nawáb's loyal aid against the outbreak at Multán (*q. v.*), 174 ; rewarded for his loyalty, 226 ; British officer acts as Regent at (1866), ii. 228

Bhíls in Gujarát, fighting against (1868), ii. 217

Bhopál, disturbances in (1846), 109 ; loyal conduct of the Begam during the Mutiny, ii. 11

Woodfall & Kinder, Printers, Milford Lane, Strand, London, W.C.